Contesting Catholics

Series information:
RELIGION IN TRANSFORMING AFRICA
ISSN 2398-8673

Series Editors
Barbara Bompani, Joseph Hellweg, Ousmane Kane and Emma Wild-Wood

Editorial Reading Panel
Robert Baum (Dartmouth College)
Dianna Bell (University of Cape Town)
Ezra Chitando (University of Zimbabwe)
Martha Frederiks (Utrecht University)
Paul Gifford (SOAS – School of Oriental and African Studies)
David M. Gordon (Bowdoin College)
Jörg Haustein (University of Cambridge)
Paul Lubeck (Johns Hopkins University SAIS – School of Advanced International Studies)
Philomena Mwaura (Kenyatta University, Nairobi)
Hassan Ndzovu (Moi University, Eldoret)
Ebenezer Obadare (University of Kansas)
Abdulkader I. Tayob (University of Cape Town)
M. Sani Umar (Northwestern University)
Stephen Wooten (University of Oregon)

Series Description
The series is open to submissions that examine local or regional realities on the complexities of religion and spirituality in Africa. Religion in Transforming Africa will showcase cutting-edge research into continent-wide issues on Christianity, Islam and other religions of Africa; Traditional beliefs and witchcraft; Religion, culture & society; History of religion, politics and power; Global networks and new missions; Religion in conflict and peace-building processes; Religion and development; Religious rituals and texts and their role in shaping religious ideologies and theologies. Innovative, and challenging current perspectives, the series provides an indispensable resource on this key area of African Studies for academics, students, international policy-makers and development practitioners.

Please contact the Series Editors with an outline or download the proposal form at www.jamescurrey.com.

Dr Barbara Bompani, Reader in Africa and International Development, University of Edinburgh: b.bompani@ed.ac.uk
Dr Joseph Hellweg, Associate Professor of Religion, Department of Religion, Florida State University: jhellweg@fsu.edu
Professor Ousmane Kane, Prince Alwaleed Bin Talal Professor of Contemporary Islamic Religion & Society, Harvard Divinity School: okane@hds.harvard.edu
Dr Emma Wild-Wood, Senior Lecturer, African Christianity and African Indigenous Religions, University of Edinburgh: emma.wildwood@ed.ac.uk

Previously published titles in the series are listed at the back of this volume.

Contesting Catholics

Benedicto Kiwanuka and the Birth of Postcolonial Uganda

JONATHON L. EARLE AND J. J. CARNEY

James Currey
is an imprint of
Boydell & Brewer Ltd
PO Box 9, Woodbridge
Suffolk IP12 3DF (GB)
www.jamescurrey.com
and of
Boydell & Brewer Inc.
668 Mt Hope Avenue
Rochester, NY 14620–2731 (US)
www.boydellandbrewer.com

© Jonathon L. Earle and J. J. Carney, 2021
First published in hardback 2021
Paperback edition 2023

First published in Uganda in 2021 by Fountain Publishers Ltd
P.O. Box 488 Kampala, Uganda
E-mail: sales@fountainpublishers.co.ug; publishing@fountainpublishers.co.ug
Website: www.fountainpublishers.co.ug

The right of Jonathon L. Earle and J. J. Carney to be identified as
the authors of this work has been asserted in accordance with
sections 77 and 78 of the Copyright, Designs and Patents Act 1988

All Rights Reserved. Except as permitted under current legislation
no part of this work may be photocopied, stored in a retrieval system,
published, performed in public, adapted, broadcast, transmitted,
recorded or reproduced in any form or by any means, without the
prior permission of the copyright owner

The publisher has no responsibility for the continued existence or accuracy of
URLs for external or third-party internet websites referred to in this book, and
does not guarantee that any content on such websites is, or will remain, accurate
or appropriate

British Library Cataloguing in Publication Data
A catalogue record for this book is available from the British Library

ISBN 978-1-84701-240-1 (James Currey hardback)
ISBN 978-1-84701-365-1 (James Currey paperback)
ISBN 978-9970-19-605-0 (Fountain Publishers paperback)

In a context in which thinking about current politics and the history of politics in Uganda fall into well-worn, fundamentally unproductive habits of thought, the authors prove that basic assumptions about religion in Ugandan politics are deeply flawed. No one has written authoritatively on this topic for half a century. [...] a superb book, meticulously evidenced and insightfully contextualised.

Holly Hanson, Mount Holyoke College

For a few short months Benedicto Kiwanuka wielded power as Uganda's first prime minister. Most of his political career, however, was spent in the opposition; and at the end he was martyred by President Idi Amin. In this insightful biography, Earle and Carney draw from Kiwanuka's private library and illuminate the logic of his politics. Here we see Uganda's history as Kiwanuka saw it: as a drama that demanded both principled clarity and pragmatic flexibility. This book gives religious history an exciting new vocation, and greatly expands the scope and scale of political biography.

Derek R. Peterson, University of Michigan

Earle and Carney's work sheds radically new understanding on the dramatic history of Uganda. It is centred on the Democratic Party and its staunch Catholic leader Ben Kiwanuka, who led the country to independence before being jailed by Obote and murdered by Idi Amin. Roman Catholics, the largest religious group in Uganda, have been politically discriminated against since the 1890s. This book challenges brilliantly Uganda's biased historical narrative and puts back 'Contesting Catholics' where they belong, at the centre of the country's nation building.

Henri Médard, Institut des Mondes Africains (IMAf)

By drawing on hitherto unused sources, and paying careful attention to regional complexities, Jay Carney and Jonathon Earle tell a new story of how religion inflected politics in twentieth-century Uganda. *Contesting Catholics* is not merely about Catholic politics in the home of Africa's first canonised martyrs, rather it reframes our understanding of Ugandan history in the late colonial and postcolonial periods writ large. Moreover, the book delivers compelling insights about how to conceptualise the place of religion in politics in Africa and beyond.

Elizabeth A. Foster, Tufts University

The authors of this book have mined personal papers, especially of their major subject, Benedicto Kiwanuka, and of other decolonisation political actors in Uganda. They interviewed key witnesses of the late colonial and early postcolonial period, mastered local languages, including Luganda and Ateso, in order to read the literature first-hand. They also utilised archives in Uganda, Britain and the United States in order to write an outstanding book on one of the leading Ugandan nationalists, Benedicto Kiwanuka, a leader of the Democratic Party who sought to build a united Uganda. I highly recommend this book for any student or researcher wishing to understand Uganda's religious and political history.

Samwiri Lwanga Lunyiigo, Makerere University

Covers the religious milieu of the 1950s and 1960s, and the era's complicated politics, connecting Kiwanuka and Catholicism to party formation, ethnicity, and the making of a new Uganda and new Ugandan political elite and set of practices. [...] a well-researched, careful exploration of a complex, understudied, fascinating time.

Carol Summers, University of Richmond

This study throws a powerful searchlight on a critical population in Uganda struggling for political and social freedoms in the country immediately before and after independence from Britain.

Michael Twaddle, Institute of Commonwealth Studies

This carefully researched and elegantly written story of admirable twentieth-century Ugandan Catholic layman Benedicto Kiwanuka shows how the political party he led was thwarted in Uganda's early years after independence. Regional and ethnic differences stretched its pursuit of Catholic values while seeking national unity and blocked its electoral hopes. Carney and Earle demonstrate the oversimplification of earlier accounts of how religiously inflected politics tragically undermined Uganda's first few postcolonial decades.

Paul Kollman, CSC, University of Notre Dame

To Maurice Kagimu Kiwanuka and Emmanuel Katongole, in gratitude for their steadfast support over many years.

In Memory of Benedicto Kiwanuka, who gave his life in the pursuit of truth and justice.

Contents

List of Illustrations	xi
Acknowledgements	xiii
Abbreviations	xv
Glossary	xviii
Maps	xxi
Introduction	1
1 Benedicto Kiwanuka, Catholic Uganda, and the Gospel of Democracy	23
2 Republicanism and Secession in Tesoland and Rwenzururu	59
3 Catholic Violence and Political Revolution in Bunyoro and Kigezi	81
4 Acholi Alliances and Party Insurrection in Ankole	109
5 Catholic Patronage and Royalist Alternatives in Buganda	139
6 'I offer today my body and blood': Violence, Resistance, and Martyrdom	167
Conclusion	195
Bibliography	207
Index	229

Illustrations

Maps

1	Provincial boundaries of colonial Uganda	xxi
2	Ethnic polities and districts of colonial Uganda	xxii

Figures

I.1	Benedicto Kiwanuka's newspapers, c. 1964	17
1.1	Archbishop Joseph Kiwanuka, c. 1964, the first African Catholic bishop in modern times	35
1.2	Benedicto Kiwanuka with his Catholic missal, c. 1962	37
1.3	Maxencia Zalwango Kiwanuka and family, 1960	40
1.4	Party emblem of the Democratic Party, c. July 1959	56
1.5	Benedicto Kiwanuka after his electoral victory, 1961	57
2.1	Milton Obote, Leader of the Opposition, and Cuthbert J. Obwangor, a member of the Legislative Council for Teso, at the Uganda Constitutional Conference, Lancaster House, September 1961	66
2.2	*Omukama* Rukirabasaija Sir George David Matthew Kamurasi Rukidi III, with British governor, Sir Frederick Crawford, c. 1960	73
3.1	Ganda patriots protesting Bunyoro's reacquisition of the 'Lost Counties', 1962	92
4.1	Benedicto Kiwanuka with recently elected Ugandan Catholic leaders Hon J. H. Obonyo and Hon E. B. Bwambale, and John F. Kennedy, White House, Washington, DC, 17 October 1961	127
4.2	J. H. Obonyo and Acholi celebrate Kiwanuka's premiership, Lugogo Stadium, 1 March 1962	130
5.1	'Semakula Mulumba speaking in Trafalgar Square at a demonstration against the collective punishment and indiscriminate killing of Africans by white settlers in Kenya', 23 August 1953	150

5.2	Ministers of the kingdom of Buganda at the Uganda Independence Conference, Marlborough House, June 1962	157
6.1	DP activist Gilbert Mulindwa poses with the party's closed fist following an attack on his property, April 1962	174
6.2	Paul Ssemogerere, DP publicity secretary, with Benedicto Kiwanuka, c. mid-1960s	184
6.3	Kiwanuka's newspaper clipping from the *Uganda Argus*, 21 August 1971, showing how Amin had begun to use the press to portray Catholics as Asian sympathisers	191
C.1	Banners in Namugongo, on Uganda Martyrs' Day, June 2010, advocating for Julius Nyerere's canonisation	202
C.2	Chief Justice Kiwanuka's bust outside the High Court building in Kampala, 2018	204

Acknowledgements

In the process of writing this volume, we have benefited from the time, support, and insights of numerous friends and colleagues. This project would not have been possible without the unrelenting support of the children of Benedicto Kiwanuka. We are especially grateful to Imelda Kiwanuka, Josephine Kiwanuka, and Ambassador Maurice Kiwanuka, who gave generously of their time to encourage our work along the way. Without Ambassador Kiwanuka's vision, we would not have had access to the private collections that animated this project. To him we dedicate this book.

Much of the early inspiration of this project emerged out of conversations with a number of the founders of the Democratic Party, whose insights quickly showed that the party was far more complicated than is often described in the existing literature. We are especially grateful for our interviews with Aloysius D. Lubowa, William S. Kajubi, Simon Mwebe, Samwiri Lwanga Lunyiigo, Brother Anatoli Wasswa, Fr Benedict Ssettuuma, and L. Mathias Tyaba. George Lutwama Mpanga provided essential contributions to the completion of this work, including translations.

The manuscript was enriched by the critical suggestions of two anonymous reviewers. Jaqueline Mitchell and the Editorial Board of the Series have been incredibly encouraging and insightful along the way. We are also grateful to David Livingstone Ilakut, Christopher Muhoozi, and Patrick Otim, who provided political insights and critical commentary on ideas and sections in the book. The maps were produced by Miles Irving, while the book was expertly indexed by Ed Emery. We wish to thank Waveland Press, Inc., who kindly granted permission to use an extended citation from Okot p'Bitek's *Song of Lawino Song of Ocol* in Chapter 4. Any omissions remain exclusively our own.

Jon Earle wishes to thank the Faculty Development Fund Committee of Centre College, which graciously provided a research leave for the completion of the manuscript. The outstanding History Program of Centre College was equally supportive. I am grateful for Jay Carney, who decided to commit to this project. This has been a deeply rewarding journey together. Additional encouragement was provided by Apollo Makubuya, Valentine Mujuzi, Nakanyike Musisi, *Omulangira* Kassim Nakibinge, Jake Davis, Jennifer Goetz,

Katherine Bruce-Lockhart, Lindsay Ehrisman, Sam Foster, Sarah Holloway, David Kunze, Parker Lawson, John Lonsdale, Sara Loy, Derek Peterson, Laurie Pierce, Matthew Pierce, Richard Reid, Ethan Sanders, Katie Solomon, Madison Stuart, Edgar Taylor, and Gray Whitsett. Over the course of writing, my partner and dearest friend, Jennifer, battled Leukemia. Her bravery, and the resiliency and courage of our children, Kiah, Jacob, and Karis, continue to inspire me in ways that are indescribable. That I was able to continue writing during the past two years is a testament to their love, and the support of our family and friends at Centre College and Trinity Episcopal Church.

Jay Carney first wishes to thank Jon Earle for the invitation to participate in this joint venture – it has been a true pleasure to collaborate on this book. Creighton University's Kripke Center for the Study of Religion and Society, the George F. Haddix Faculty Research Fund, and the College of Arts and Sciences' Summer Faculty Research Fellowship provided grants that supported field research over the past five years. The U.S. Fulbright Program provided a generous nine-month grant that enabled me to complete field research in Uganda; I am so grateful to my wife Becky and my children, RJ, Annabelle, Samuel, and Adelaide, for sharing this formative year together. I thank the interlocutors who provided important feedback at public lectures and conference papers that shaped my early thinking on Benedicto Kiwanuka: 'Le missioni in Africa: la sfida dell'inculturazione Conference', the Fondazione Ambrosiana Paolo VI, Milan, Italy, September 2015; the African Studies Association annual meeting, San Diego, CA, November 2015; and Penn State University's African Studies Program, January 2018. During 2018/19, my colleagues at Uganda Martyrs University were rich dialogue partners. I offer a special word of thanks to Professor Jimmy Spire Ssentongo for organising two public lectures on Benedicto Kiwanuka, and I am grateful to all the students, faculty, and community members, especially Hon Paul Kawanga Ssemogerere, who provided important feedback to me at these gatherings. I also thank the anonymous peer reviewers who provided critical comments on my article, 'Benedicto Kiwanuka and Catholic Democracy in Uganda', *Journal of Religious History* 44.2 (2020): 212–29. Finally, I dedicate this book to Professor Emmanuel Katongole of the University of Notre Dame. It was Fr Emmanuel who first introduced me to the intersection of theology and politics in Great Lakes Africa. For nearly twenty years, he has been my intellectual inspiration, sounding board, and trusted mentor. *Webale nnyo, Ssebo! Neyanzizza.*

Abbreviations

ARP	Audrey Richards Papers
BKMKP	Benedicto Kagimu Mugumba Kiwanuka Papers
BNA CO	British National Archives, Colonial Office
CMS	Church Missionary Society
DP	Democratic Party
ICS	Institute of Commonwealth Studies Archives
JFKOF	John F. Kennedy Presidential Archives
KANU	Kenya African National Union
KY	*Kabaka Yekka* Party (King Only Party)
Legco	Legislative Council of Uganda
MAfr	Missionaries of Africa (White Fathers/Pères Blancs)
MUA	Makerere University Africana Archives
NARA II	National Archives at College Park
OAU	Organisation of African Unity
RDA	Rubaga Diocesan Archives
TANU	Tanganyika African National Union
SDA	Soroti District Archives
UM	Uganda Museum
UNA	Uganda National Archives
UNC	Uganda National Congress
UPC	Uganda People's Congress
UPU	Uganda People's Union

Glossary

Abairu	Cultivators, sometimes used to describe ordinary political subjects
Amazima n'obwenkanya	Truth and justice, the motto of the Democratic Party
Bajenjeeka	Timid or wandering communities, those held loosely
Banakazadde Begwanga	Mothers of the Nation, political organisation during the 1950s
Basajjansolo	Literally, 'animal-men', associated with *misambwa*, spirits that appear in the form of an animal, especially a leopard
Bulange	Building in Mmengo housing Buganda's parliament
Burungi bwansi (pulani)	Acts committed for the good of the nation
Cuius regio, eius religio	Latin term meaning 'Whose realm, his religion'; used to describe the religious partition of colonial Buganda
Dini ya Papa	'Religion of the Pope', a pejorative Swahili phrase used by political opponents to describe the Democratic Party
Ebitongole	Peripheral land holdings acquired by Buganda, mostly through war
Eishengero	Parliament of the kingdom of Ankole
Enganzi	Prime minister of Ankole
Enkola Enkatolike	Catholic Action, a Catholic lay organisation in colonial Uganda
Ggombolola	Sub-county administrative territory
Imurok	Witchdoctors in Tesoland
Kabaka	King of Buganda

Kabaka atta nabbe	'The Kabaka kills the red ant, or the one who destroys the termite mound.' A Luganda proverb commonly used by Ganda royalists to call for the annihilation of the Democratic Party
Kabaka Yekka	King Only, the most consequential royalist party in late colonial Uganda
Kkanzu	Long robe, worn by men, especially during political and ceremonial events
Katikiiro	Prime minister of Buganda, customarily Protestant; only under the regnum of *Kabaka* Mutebi II (r. 1993–present) have Catholics been selected
Kutoria	Term used in 1850s Acholiland to describe Arab traders
Lokekerep	Term in Ateso used to describe a lunatic
Lukiiko	Parliament of Buganda
Mailo	Private land holdings
Matalisi	A messenger, the name of a notable Luganda newspaper during the 1950s
Mmengo	Capital of Buganda
Muganda (Baganda pl.)	Ganda person (people)
Muluka	Parish administrative territory
Munno	Earliest meaning of the term is disputed, but it is commonly translated, 'your friend'; name of Uganda's oldest newspaper, a Catholic periodical founded in 1911
Nnamasole	The Queen Mother of Buganda
Nnamunswa	Queen Aunt, a title of the king of Buganda
Okutiisatiisa	To intimidate
Omufalansa	White Father missionary
Omugabe	King of Ankole
Omugabe Wenka	King Only, the Ankole iteration of *Kabaka Yekka*
Omukama	The term used for either the king of Toro, or the king of Bunyoro-Kitara

Omukatuliki	Onomatopoeia used in Buganda to describe a Catholic convert
Omukungu	Appointed chief, or high-ranking official in Buganda
Omulamuzi	Chief Justice in Buganda, customarily held by a Catholic
Omumackai	Earliest term used in Uganda to describe a Protestant convert, so named after Ganda converts who were politically loyal to the Anglican missionary Alexander Mackay
Omumapera	Earliest term used in Uganda to describe Catholic converts, so named after Ganda converts who were politically loyal to the Catholic missionary Siméon Lourdel
Omukopi	Commoner, a term used in Buganda to describe a subject of no particular role in high politics
Omungereza	A person from Europe, especially the United Kingdom
Omupolotesitante	Onomatopoeia used in Buganda to describe a Protestant convert
Omusoma	Christian catechumen
Omutaka	Hereditary clan head in Buganda
Omuwanika	Treasurer, customarily Protestant
Parti du Mouvement de l'Emancipation Hutu (Parmehutu)	Leading political party of the Hutu social revolution in Rwanda, late 1950s and 1960s; associated with the Democratic Party in Kigezi, Uganda
Persona Christi	Latin term meaning 'Person of Christ'; associated with Eucharistic theology and martyrdom in Roman Catholicism
Rubanga	Term used in Acholiland to describe God; the name of a precolonial spirit
Rukurato	The term used for the parliaments of the kingdom of Toro, and Bunyoro-Kitara
Rwot	Title of a chief in Acholiland

Ssaza	Administrative county in Buganda
Tornade	French term for 'Tornado'; used by Catholic missionaries in Rwanda to describe the mass conversions of Rwandans during the interwar period
Uganda Eyogera	Uganda Speaks, a pre-eminent Luganda newspaper in late colonial Uganda
Vox populi, vox Dei	Latin term meaning 'Voice of the people is the voice of God'

Map 1 Provincial boundaries of colonial Uganda

Map 2 Ethnic polities and districts of colonial Uganda

Introduction

> If we want democracy in Uganda we have got to work for it. We should be prepared even for death itself. [...] 'D.P.' as we are called through the country, is an organisation of serious-minded men and women whose sole intention is to do good to all in Uganda and in the world. We shall not rest until our principles have been firmly established both in Buganda and in Uganda.
>
> ~Benedicto Kiwanuka, 1962[1]

Benedicto Kagimu Mugumba Kiwanuka was Uganda's most controversial and disruptive politician of the 1950s and early 1960s, and the most important Catholic politician in twentieth-century Uganda. He was the country's first elected prime minister (1961–62), before he and his party were outflanked by opposition political alliances. Shortly after being released from prison for allegedly backing the assassination attempt of President Milton Obote, he served as the country's first Ugandan Chief Justice between 1971 and 1972,[2] when members of Idi Amin's security apparatus murdered him.

Kiwanuka provided the most original, far-sighted political thinking in late colonial Uganda. The resuscitation of his career demonstrates the extent to which Ugandans have a heritage of politics that is more than people 'eating' power or the state, what Jean-François Bayart described as *la politique du ventre*.[3] Kiwanuka's activism and intellectual history helps us understand in new ways how arguments about pluralism and democracy unfolded in late colonial Uganda. Ideas about 'truth' and 'justice' were foundational political and

---

[1] RDA 904.4 Benedicto Kiwanuka, 'Uganda Elections–1962', p. 44.
[2] Uganda's first three postcolonial chief justices consisted of two Britons, K. G. Bennet and Dermot J. Sheridan (the latter of whom was born in Kenya), and the Nigerian barrister Egbert U. Udoma.
[3] Jean-François Bayart, *The State in Africa: The Politics of the Belly*, trans. by Mary Harper, Christopher Harrison, and Elizabeth Harrison (London: Longman, 1993).

theological ideals that evoked regional ruptures and solidarities. Activists and organisers, operating in various regions of the country, intentionally underscored different aspects of these ideals to imagine representative possibilities in the postcolony. Cosmopolitan claims and local interests animated competing historical claims and charismatic competition that eventually led, not simply to the failure of the Democratic Party (DP), but to extrajudicial killing and civil war.

This book seeks to recover the power, possibilities, and pitfalls of Benedicto Kiwanuka's and DP's Catholic, liberal democratic nationalism in independence-era Uganda. Our project demonstrates the complicated ways in which ethnic, religious, and regional identities overlapped, co-existed, and collided, while also reinforcing the importance of local politics in DP's and Kiwanuka's struggle to 'conceive the nation'. Shaped by his own Ganda Catholic roots as well as international Christian democracy, Kiwanuka helped to mould DP into a viable nationalist alternative to the Uganda People's Congress (UPC) in the late 1950s and early 1960s. Although deeply grounded in Uganda's Catholic community, DP was never simply a sectarian 'Catholic party', contrary to what both its critics at the time and later scholars have often assumed. In fact, although DP remained a primary vehicle for the mobilisation of Catholic voters, its political appeal rested in part in how its vision stretched beyond defending sectarian religious interests. Namely, Kiwanuka and DP sought to create a nationalist movement that would expand political participation, advocate for social justice, and challenge Uganda's entrenched sociopolitical hierarchies.

Despite its national aspirations, Kiwanuka's and DP's project was constrained by the regional politics of the era. In ways that were enriched by local variety and change, Catholics across party boundaries asked for fairness, openness, inclusion, and self-sacrifice. But what this all *meant* looked drastically different across time and space. Our study analyses the complicated and often conflicting ways in which Catholic and political identities intersected in Buganda, Tesoland, Toro, Kigezi, Ankole, Acholiland, and West Nile.

In much of Uganda's political history, DP is cast as a Catholic political party that sought to upend political Protestantism in the kingdom of Buganda. Catholic politics, though, constituted a dynamic moral economy of competing regional historiographies and disputations.[4] By pushing the

---

[4] The language of moral economy borrows from John Lonsdale, 'Moral Ethnicity and Political Tribalism', in *Inventions and Boundaries: Historical and Anthropological Approaches to the Study of Ethnicity and Nationalism*, ed. by Preben Kaarsholm and Jan Hultin (Roskilde: International Development Studies, Roskilde University, 1994), pp. 131–50.

boundaries of DP beyond Buganda and beyond a singular conception of anti-royalist, political Catholicism, we recover the various political possibilities with which Uganda's Catholic activists imagined a postcolonial future.

The Colonial Roots of Uganda's Religious Conflicts

Writings on Uganda's colonial political history have built upon the legacies of Buganda's late-nineteenth-century religious revolution. It is not our goal to recount these histories in detail, which have attracted a large body of literature following the pioneering work of John Rowe, Semakula Kiwanuka, and Michael Twaddle.[5] It is sufficient to note that in a highly competitive public arena, Ganda courtiers and chiefs established various allegiances with Muslim, Protestant, and Catholic traders and missionaries. Competing alliances culminated in a series of religious civil wars during the late 1880s and early 1890s, out of which Protestant chiefs secured control of the state with the military backing of the Imperial British East Africa Company (IBEAC). These conflicts were also bound up with conflicting succession claims made by three separate kings, Mwanga, Kiweewa, and Kalema, each of whom ruled Buganda on different occasions between 1888 and 1889.[6]

The solidification of Christian power in Buganda followed a series of state executions, which religious communities recast as martyrdoms. Like his father, Muteesa I (r. 1856–84), *Kabaka* (King) Mwanga was apprehensive about the erasure of royal authority in the kingdom's capital. The historian Samwiri Lwanga Lunyiigo suggests that Mwanga was able to command the allegiance of no more than sixty-five out of his six thousand pages.[7] In an effort to reinforce monarchical authority, Mwanga ordered the construction of a massive artificial lake in the capital. As Holly Hanson summarises, 'a royal

---

[5] John A. Rowe, 'The Purge of Christians at Mwanga's Court: A Reassessment of This Episode in Buganda History', *Journal of African History*, 5 (1963), 55–72; Semakula Kiwanuka, 'Kabaka Mwanga and His Political Parties', *Uganda Journal*, 33 (1969), 1–16; John A. Rowe, 'The Baganda Revolutionaries', *Tarikh*, 3 (1970), 34–46; Michael Twaddle, 'The Emergence of Politico-Religious Groupings in Late Nineteenth-Century Buganda', *The Journal of African History*, 29 (1988), 81–92; John A. Rowe, 'Eyewitness Accounts of Buganda History: The Memoirs of Ham Mukasa and His Generation', *Ethnohistory*, 36 (1989), 61–71.

[6] The best overview of this transition remains: John M. Gray, 'The Year of the Three Kings of Buganda', *Uganda Journal*, 14 (1949), 15–52. See also, Apolo Kaggwa, *The Reign of Mwanga II (A Later Addition to Ekitabo Kya Basekabaka Be Buganda)*, trans. by Simon Musoke (Kampala: Typescript found in the University of Cambridge Library, 1953).

[7] Samwiri Lwanga Lunyiigo, *Mwanga II: Resistance to Imposition of British Colonial Rule in Buganda, 1884–1899* (Kampala: Wavah Books, Ltd., 2011), pp. 73–74.

drum "everybody must come with soil" was beaten calling people to work on the lake at three o'clock in the morning'.[8] But Christian converts were elusive; and for their obstinacy Mwanga ordered the execution of over one hundred converts between 1885 and 1887, forty-five of whom were eventually canonised. Twenty-three of Uganda's Martyrs were Anglican, twenty-two Catholic. Earlier, *Kabaka* Muteesa I had no fewer than seventy Muslims killed over circumcision rites, with an additional 1,000 persecuted or forced into exile.[9]

For Mwanga, Christians' refusal to work signified competing political alliances. The early etymologies of Christian identities created the political terms upon which Uganda's late colonial parties eventually developed. The Luganda[10] terms for *Protestant* (*omu/abapolotesitante* – sing./pl.) and Catholic (*omu/abakatuliki*) were onomatopoeic. Converts – or readers (*abasoma*) – were associated with their religio-political solidarities. Buganda's Protestants were largely seen – by themselves and their political opponents – as having allied with British explorers and missionaries (*abangereza*); and late nineteenth-century Catholics with the French White Fathers (*abafalansa*). Nineteenth-century converts were identified by their allegiances to specific missionaries. For example, because of their solidarity with the White Father Siméon Lourdel – or Mapera (My Father) – early Catholics were designated as *abamapera*, or the 'people of Mapera'. For their close association with the Scottish missionary Alexander Mackay, who worked with the Church Missionary Society, Protestants were called *abamackai*.[11] Religious conversion seldom signified theological abstraction – it embodied shifting personal loyalties and emerging political factions in the kingdom.

Mwanga was ultimately removed from power by a broad-based Christian coalition, whose respective Protestant and Catholic factions violently turned on each other after the coup. By 1894, Protestant chiefs with the support of the IBEAC controlled the capital. *Kabaka* Daudi Chwa II was appointed monarch in 1897 – at the age of one – with the backing of the Native Anglican Church.[12] Until his maturation, he was placed under the Christian regency of

---

[8] Holly E. Hanson, *Landed Obligation: The Practice of Power in Buganda* (Portsmouth, NH: Heinemann, 2003), p. 103.

[9] Ahmed Katumba and Fred B. Welbourn, 'Muslim Martyrs of Buganda', *Uganda Journal*, 28 (1964), 151–63. See also, Michael Twaddle, 'The Muslim Revolution in Buganda', *African Affairs*, 71 (1972), 54–72.

[10] Luganda is the language spoken by the Baganda people.

[11] An elderly Catholic interlocutor at Kasubi Nabulagala raised this point to Earle in June 2013. The claim was then corroborated at the Nateete Martyrs Church, which commemorates the missionary career of Alexander Mackay.

[12] For further insights on the early history of the Church in Buganda see Adrian Hastings, 'From Mission to Church in Buganda', *Zeitschrift Für Missionswisenschaft*

Buganda's prime minister (*katikkiro*), Apolo Kaggwa, chief justice (*omulamuzi*), Stanislaus Mugwanya, and treasurer (*omuwanika*), Zakariya Kisingiri. He was succeeded by *Kabaka* Edward Muteesa II in 1939. Muteesa II governed Buganda until 1966, when he was removed in a coup.

The central legacy of the religious revolution was that political organisation now followed religious loyalties in the kingdom.[13] After the religious wars, land holdings and chieftaincies were distributed according to denominational allegiances. Buganda's political order was restructured around sectarian parties and boundaries.[14] These discrepancies and Buganda's resulting Protestant order were principal sources of grievance and dissent for Catholic and Muslim activists throughout the colonial period. By the early 1900s, Catholics constituted the largest of Buganda's confessional communities. Be that as it may, Buganda's Protestant chiefs and the British Government distributed only 37.4 per cent of public land holdings to Catholics, while Protestant chiefs were apportioned 61.6 per cent.[15] Private land holdings (*mailo*) were distributed similarly. Where Protestant chiefs received 60.6 per cent of Buganda's *mailo* lands, Catholics were allocated only 25.5 per cent, less than half the total of their Protestant counterparts.

A chief's religious loyalties determined – both by the parliament of Buganda (*Lukiiko*) and the colonial government in Entebbe – whether an area was administratively considered Catholic, Muslim, or Protestant (echoing the early modern European principle *cuius regio, eius religio*, 'whose realm, his religion'). Eleven of Buganda's twenty counties were placed under the authority of Protestant chiefs; eight would be governed by Catholics. The remaining smaller sections of land were distributed to Muslim chiefs. To prevent a possible Muslim uprising, the principal Muslim county of Butambala was placed between the Protestant county of Ggomba and the Catholic county of Mawakota.[16]

Und Religionswissenschaft, 53 (1969), 206–28; John V. Taylor, *The Growth of the Church in Buganda: An Attempt at Understanding* (London: SCM Press, 1958); Louise Pirouet, *Black Evangelists: The Spread of Christianity in Uganda, 1891–1914* (London: Rex Collings, 1978); John Mary Waliggo, 'The Catholic Church in the Buddu Province of Buganda, 1879–1925', PhD thesis, University of Cambridge, 1976 (published Kampala: Angel Agencies, 2011).

[13] Henri Médard, *Le royaume du Buganda au XIXe siècle: Mutations politiques et religieuses d'un ancien état d'Afrique de l'Est* (Paris: Karthala, 2007), pp. 446–7.

[14] Holger Bernt Hansen, *Mission, Church, and State in the Colonial Setting: Uganda 1890–1925* (New York: St. Martin's Press, 1984), pp. 110–15.

[15] Henry W. West, *The Mailo System in Buganda: A Preliminary Case Study in African Land Tenure* (Entebbe: Government Printer, 1965), p. 173.

[16] County borders were not only the work of abstraction; they demanded physical

Administrative posts and government salaries also favoured members of the Native Anglican Church. The *Lukiiko* was comprised of forty-nine Protestant chiefs, thirty-five Catholics, and five Muslims.[17] These early distributions remained consistent throughout the colonial period. A 1934 survey showed that while Catholic populations exceeded Protestants in Buganda by 14 per cent, they occupied 22 per cent fewer chieftaincies. In consequence, Protestant administrative earnings were higher by 35 per cent.[18] Uganda's late colonial political parties capitalised upon these long-standing grievances.

Silencing Sectarian Violence in Uganda's Nationalist Historiography

Politics of the 1950s and 1960s drew on particular narratives of the country's religious past. These histories emphasised kingship and conquest, expropriation and dissent, and people's search for religious knowledge, patrons, and cosmopolitan opportunities. For most Ganda writers, interpreting Uganda's late colonial moment, the Ugandan state and the kingdom of Buganda did not unravel until 1966. This is not how Benedicto Kiwanuka viewed Uganda's political history. For Kiwanuka and his party colleagues, Uganda was a de facto Protestant state that existed at the expense of Catholics and Muslims. Uganda's moment of independence, far from being an occasion for pan-African optimism, was the culmination of decades of violence and religious discrimination.

How is Uganda's national story typically told? According to most accounts, Uganda's three principal parties were divided according to strict sectarian boundaries.[19] In these standard accounts, the Democratic Party was estab-

---

perimeters that were particularly well constructed between Protestant and Catholic counties. See Jonathon L. Earle, *Colonial Buganda and the End of Empire: Political Thought and Historical Imagination in Late Colonial Buganda* (Cambridge: Cambridge University Press, 2017), pp. 187–90. The sectarian redrawing of Buganda's counties resulted in cartography that provided a topographical logic for the kingdom's new order: BNA MP K122 'Map of Uganda Protectorate Showing Distribution of Chieftainships among Adherents of Different Religions in the Kingdom of Uganda' [early 1900s].

[17] Hansen, *Mission, Church, and State in the Colonial Setting*, p. 111.
[18] Rubaga Diocesan Archives (RDA) 31.6 'Synopsis of Comparative List of Catholic and Protestant Chiefs in Buganda', 1934.
[19] Donald A. Low, *Political Parties in Uganda, 1949–1962* (London: University of London Athlone Press, 1962) p. 47; Audrey I. Richards, 'Epilogue', in *The King's Men: Leadership and Status in Buganda on the Eve of Independence*, ed. by Lloyd A. Fallers (London: published on behalf of the East African Institute of Social Research by Oxford University Press, 1964), pp. 357–95 (p. 375); Fred B. Welbourn, *Religion and Politics in Uganda* (Nairobi: East Africa

lished in 1954 as a Catholic party. It participated in Uganda's 1961 election. Meanwhile, the government of Buganda boycotted the election for fear that national independence would challenge their kingdom's regional autonomy. In consequence, DP secured control of the federal government, which they maintained only until 1962. A separate, second party, UPC was founded in 1960. Its membership was ostensibly Protestant. It was comprised of members of Uganda's first nationalist political party, the Uganda National Congress, and members of the predominantly Busoga-based movement, the Uganda People's Union. The UPC powerbase resided mostly outside of Buganda. *Kabaka Yekka* (KY – King Only), the third party, emerged in 1961 to publicly advocate for the supremacy of kingship in Buganda and, more sweepingly, to advocate for a federal arrangement that guaranteed the political integrity of Uganda's precolonial kingdoms: Ankole, Buganda, Bunyoro, Busoga, and Toro. Their principal ambition was to dislodge from power the Democratic Party, which had subjugated a Protestant king to the government of a Catholic commoner, Benedicto Kiwanuka.

Most historical accounts underscore that UPC and KY entered into an electoral arrangement in 1961 to ensure that Kiwanuka and DP did not maintain power after the 1961 elections. To oblige the terms of the coalition, UPC guaranteed that the question of the 'Lost Counties' (Chapter 3) was tabled until DP was removed from power and independence was secured.[20] The government of Buganda would also maintain constitutional powers to directly appoint its members to the Legislative Assembly. The terms of agreement also guaranteed that the *Lukiiko* would retract its bid for secession and commit to UPC's independence timeline.[21]

Publishing House, 1965), p. 15; Mahmood Mamdani, *Politics and Class Formation in Uganda* (London: Heinemann Educational, 1976), p. 218; Jan Jelmert Jørgensen, *Uganda: A Modern History* (New York: St. Martin's Press, 1981), p. 198; A. B. K. Kasozi, *The Social Origins of Violence in Uganda, 1964–1985* (Montreal: McGill-Queen's University Press, 1994), pp. 63–8. One important exception to this general trend is Michael Twaddle, 'Was the Democratic Party of Uganda a Purely Confessional Party?' in Christianity in Independent Africa, ed. by Edward Fasholé-Luke (Bloomington: Indiana University Press, 1978), pp. 255–66.

[20] The terms were met at the second Constitutional Conference at Marlborough House in June 1962.

[21] Until late 1961, political parties in Uganda maintained different timelines for independence. See, for instance, 'D.P. aim – independence by 1962' *Uganda Argus*, 13 September 1961; 'October 9 is the Day: Self-rule to come in March, then General Elections', *Uganda Argus*, 10 October 1961; 'Independence speed-up urged: Earlier Solution to Problems – UPC', *Uganda Argus*, 11 October 1962.

In the parliamentary election of April 1962, the UPC and KY coalition secured control of the government.[22] The arrangement was electorally partitioned: UPC stood for all of the seats outside of Buganda; KY for those exclusively in Buganda. Benedicto Kiwanuka and DP vacated their short-lived tenure following electoral defeat. Uganda's government would be controlled by a coalition government between UPC, led by the northern, republican statesman Milton Obote, and KY, whose membership backed the southern, monarchical presidency of Sir Edward Muteesa II, the king of Buganda and first president of Uganda. The UPC/KY alliance was short-lived; it disbanded by August 1964.[23]

Feeling that it was no longer essential to comply with the government of Buganda – and in immediate response to the *Lukiiko*'s declaration that it no longer recognised the federal government's authority on Ganda soil – Prime Minister Obote ordered the Ugandan army, under the command of Colonel Idi Amin, to apprehend the *kabaka* in May 1966. Obote formally charged Muteesa with abrogating the constitution. During the attack, Muteesa II escaped from the palace compound by discreetly scaling the north-western wall. He briefly took refuge at the Catholic rectory at Rubaga Cathedral (Chapter 6). He then travelled via western Uganda into Burundi before flying to London, where he died in ambiguous circumstances in 1969.[24] In late 1967, Uganda's hereditary kingdoms were constitutionally abolished, and Buganda was electorally remapped. Buganda was not mentioned in Uganda's 1967 Constitution. A presumably unified kingdom simply became the 'Districts of East and West Mengo'.[25] Obote's 1966 and 1967 initiatives

---

[22] For a detailed review of the results of the 1962 Election, see 'Report of the Uganda Independence Conference, 1962' (London: Her Majesty's Stationery Office, 1962); Welbourn, *Religion and Politics in Uganda*, Tables 1–3.

[23] According to KY activists, the coalition failed because UPC began opening party branches in Buganda and criticised the *kabaka*, both of which caused the 'decision to dissolve the alliance' (MUA KY 1 'Statement issued by *Kabaka Yekka* Executive Committee in conjunction with *Kabaka Yekka* members of the National Assembly', 25 August 1964). For Milton Obote, on the other hand, KY and Mmengo (seat of the Buganda Government) were problematically unwilling to support the constitutional referendum to return the 'Lost Counties' to Bunyoro (A. Milton Obote, *Myths and Realities: Letter to a London Friend* (Kampala: Consolidated Printers, 16 November 1968), pp. 5–6).

[24] The best account of Muteesa's escape from Kampala is A. B. K. Kasozi, *The Bitter Bread of Exile: The Financial Problems of Sir Edward Muteesa II during his Final Exile, 1966–1969* (Kampala: Progressive Publishing House, 2013), pp. 73–79.

[25] NARA II RG 59/Central Foreign Policy Files/POL 15-5 'The Constitution of the Republic of Uganda', 1967, pp. 95, 101.

were oracular – ominous signs of the political instabilities that would characterise state and society between the early 1970s and late 1980s.

In the conventional historiography, the year 1966 is the keystone that holds Uganda's postcolonial history writing intact. The historian Phares Mutibwa argues that the 'crisis of 1966 can be viewed as a definite watershed in the history of post-independence Uganda [...]; some may see it as the beginning of the agonies of Uganda, when things started to fall apart'.[26] Mutibwa's language is insightful. He draws from Chinua Achebe,[27] but unlike Achebe does not associate the state's 'falling apart' with the beginning of colonial rule. For Mutibwa, social order falls apart in 1966. For Professor A. B. K. Kasozi, similarly, the 1966 crisis 'ended five hundred years of Bugandan and African history'.[28] It signified, as he entitled his work on the topic, 'the social origins of violence in Uganda'. By contrast, if 1966 constituted a moment when Uganda's social order became unhinged, Uganda in the late 1950s was supposedly characterised by 'manners and courtesy', as David Apter would have it, a time when 'politeness covers up the ambitions of men'.[29]

These standard historical summaries, though, in addition to overlooking political perspectives beyond central Uganda, disregard the experiences of violence that frequented anti-DP politics during the 1950s and 1960s. They also fail to account for the force of royalist Catholic politics in Buganda and the numerous Catholic political alternatives that circulated throughout the country. Kiwanuka's Uganda was not a place of manners and hidden aspirations; it was a fierce field of immense contestation and public duress. The state did not 'fall apart' in 1966. For Kiwanuka, such notions were mythological, royalist fabrications that disregarded the perspectives of Catholic communities for whom the state – for seven decades – was largely a facade over political realities that were far less pleasant.

What did Kiwanuka's Uganda look like, if it did not fall apart in 1966? By 1962, just as Apter was reflecting on the ubiquity of political nicety in Uganda, Benedicto Kiwanuka was filing complaints and reports to the Criminal Investigation Department of the Uganda Police Headquarters. His reports concerned the practice of government-led violence and intimidation.[30] Between 1 January and 20 December 1962, there were no fewer than

---

[26] Phares Mutibwa, *Uganda since Independence: A Story of Unfulfilled Hopes* (Trenton, NJ: Africa World Press, 1992), p. 23.

[27] Chinua Achebe, *Things Fall Apart: A Novel* (New York: Anchor, 1994 [1959]).

[28] Kasozi, *The Social Origins of Violence in Uganda*, p. 87.

[29] David E. Apter, *The Political Kingdom in Uganda: A Study of Bureaucratic Nationalism*, 2nd edn (Princeton, NJ: Princeton University Press, 1967), p. 15.

[30] BKMKP/Confidential 2/Benedicto Kiwanuka to M. Macoun, Inspector-General of Uganda Police, 12 December 1962.

639 offences committed against DP supporters, 498 of which were prosecuted and 306 convicted.[31] One DP report noted that in Katera, like other areas throughout Buganda, '[c]hiefs used to pass between the lines of voters and threaten them that if they voted they would be removing their Kabaka from the throne, and they would be killed and their bodies exhumed along with those of DP members'.[32] The KY chiefs' words were not idle, Kiwanuka maintained. The kingdom's royalists, whom Kiwanuka dubbed 'barbarians', were fulfilling strategies 'to kill our followers and to rape our women supporters'.[33] When Audrey Richards penned an epilogue for Lloyd Fallers' *The King's Men* in 1964, she built upon her correspondence with S. B. K. Musoke, the editor of the Catholic press *Munno*, to argue that Benedicto Kiwanuka's rise to power solidified 'the distress and fury of the Buganda Government, which saw for the first time in history a Muganda [Kiwanuka] holding a higher post of authority in the country than the *Kabaka*'.[34]

Outside of Buganda, scholars have been more willing to acknowledge the histories of anti-DP and anti-Catholic violence in late colonial Uganda. Dan Mudoola, following A. G. G. Gingyera-Pincycwa,[35] argues that Uganda's late colonial moment included the widespread harassment of members of DP. Mudoola concludes: 'Independence found a sour and alienated Catholic community as evidenced by subsequent utterances and developments.'[36] S. R. Karugire suggested that the entire police force of the Uganda Protectorate 'could not have prevented crop slashing, house burning, livestock maiming and various acts of arson which were normally perpetrated at night against those adjudged to be "disloyal" to the *Kabaka* – i.e. [...] mostly DP supporters'.[37] As Buganda's king recalled, members of DP 'were seen as traitors to

---

[31] BKMKP/Confidential 2/G.A. Anderson, Inspector General of Police, to Benedicto Kiwanuka, 20 December 1962. At the time of the letter, 30 cases were awaiting trial.

[32] Kiwanuka, 'Uganda Elections–1962', p. 54.

[33] Ibid., p. 43.

[34] Audrey I. Richards, 'Epilogue', in *The King's Men: Leadership and Status in Buganda on the Eve of Independence*, ed. by Lloyd A. Fallers (London: published on behalf of the East African Institute of Social Research by Oxford University Press, 1964), pp. 357–95 (p. 374).

[35] A. G. G. Gingyera-Pincycwa, *Issues in Pre-Independence Politics in Uganda: A Case-Study on the Contribution of Religion to Political Debate in Uganda in the Decade 1952–62* (Kampala: East African Literature Bureau, 1976).

[36] Dan M. Mudoola, *Religion, Ethnicity and Politics in Uganda*, 2nd edn (Kampala: Fountain, 1996), p. 29.

[37] S. R. Karugire, *A Political History of Uganda* (London: Heinemann Educational Books, 1980), p. 179.

Buganda[;] [they] became and remained the most insulting of swear words'.[38] For Kiwanuka, Uganda's independence was not a cause of celebration. In contrast, it compelled him to reflect extensively on the 'desolation' of the state.[39] Neither Uganda nor Buganda fell apart in 1966; they were never fully put together in the first place. Such an association challenges scholars and political activists to reorient the origins of violence in the colonial and postcolonial state, and the development of democratic ideals.

Contesting Catholics: Decentring the Church in African Catholic Studies

Political violence and Catholic activism varied significantly throughout different areas of Uganda. The Democratic Party's motto was 'Truth and Justice'. But communities developed different ways of thinking about the motto and implementing its variegated political lessons. There was not a universal political Catholicism or singular political ideology around which DP could unify to overcome its political opponents, however strongly the central committee of the party wished to impose a common agenda. We have titled our book *Contesting Catholics* to capture the contentious history of Catholic agendas in Uganda. The histories, claims, and competing agendas of the country's Catholic communities remained too varied to unify into a sectarian or sustainable nationalist project. The political work of Uganda's Catholics was not confined by the church and ecclesiastical hierarchies. Kiwanuka and Catholic activists contested the kingdom of Buganda, they contested each other, and they contested an emerging vision of the state. Theirs was a national contest over what a political Catholicism might look like in the public square. By paying close attention to how Catholic politics operated in overlapping and conflicting ways throughout Uganda, we are able to expand the horizons of current approaches in African Catholic studies.

Following the emergence of social and cultural history writing during the 1980s, a number of excellent studies have been authored on Catholicism in colonial Africa. Consistent with studies that have prioritised local adaptations of international religions,[40] scholars have worked to understand the different

---

[38] *Kabaka* Edward Muteesa II, *Desecration of my Kingdom* (London: Constable, 1967), p. 158.
[39] Kiwanuka, 'Uganda Elections–1962', p. 43.
[40] See, for example, Adrian Hastings, *The Construction of Nationhood: Ethnicity, Religion and Nationalism* (Cambridge: Cambridge University Press, 1997), pp. 1–34; 148–66; J. D. Y. Peel, *Religious Encounter and the Making of the Yoruba* (Bloomington: Indiana University Press, 2000); Frederick Cooper, *Africa Since 1940: The Past of the Present* (Cambridge: Cambridge University Press, 2002), pp. 27–30; 58–62; Derek R. Peterson, *Ethnic Patriotism and the East African*

ways in which Catholic missions and the colonial state intersected. Reuben Loffman's recent work on Catholicism in south-eastern Congo shows how local Catholic political authority developed around the frontier mission station of Kongolo, where White Father founder Charles Lavigerie hoped to create a 'Christian kingdom in Central Africa'.[41] The ambiguities of the colonial state and, in time, anticolonial liberation movements, created competing infrastructures of political organisation.[42] In late colonial Mozambique, for instance, as Eric Morier-Genoud argues, varying missionary orders were engaged in highly contested debates among themselves and their catechists about strategies of activism, resignation, and censorship.[43]

While Catholicism developed in the absence of colonial authority in south-eastern Congo, in Zimbabwe missionaries worked closely with the Rhodesian colonial project. Jesuit missionaries, whose disciplinary ethos had attracted the admiration of Cecil Rhodes, acquired over 180,000 acres of mission land to farm.[44] It was only after the Second World War – following the proliferation

---

Revival: A History of Dissent, c. 1935–1972 (Cambridge: Cambridge University Press, 2012); Cheikh Anta Babou, *Fighting the Greater Jihad: Amadu Bamba and the Founding of the Muridiyya of Senegal, 1853–1913* (Athens: Ohio University Press, 2007); Joel Cabrita, *Text and Authority in the South African Nazaretha Church* (Cambridge: Cambridge University Press, 2014); Elizabeth A. Foster, *African Catholic: Decolonization and the Transformation of the Church* (Cambridge, MA: Harvard University Press, 2019).

[41] Reuben A. Loffman, *Church, State and Colonialism in Southeastern Congo, 1890–1962* (New York: Palgrave Macmillan, 2019), p. 4.

[42] Likewise, Catholicism in early colonial Nyasaland (later Malawi) remained largely a peripheral religion, entrenched by the White Fathers' relationships with Portuguese traders. In the words of Ian and Jane Linden: 'As a result of Portuguese patronage the missionaries had found themselves astraddle the main trade routes for ivory and slaves' (Ian Linden and Jane Linden, *Catholics, Peasants, and Chewa Resistance in Nyasaland, 1899–1939* (Berkeley: University of California Press, 1974), p. 34). Elizabeth Foster's work on colonial Senegal also shows how Catholic missions failed to secure state sanction in French West Africa. Despite religious workers' best efforts, 'the colonial administration kept Catholic missionaries at arm's length and refused to endorse their vision of a civilizing mission' (Elizabeth A. Foster, *Faith in Empire: Religion, Politics, and Colonial Rule in French Senegal, 1880–1940* (Stanford, CA: Stanford University Press, 2013), p. 179).

[43] Eric Morier-Genoud, *Catholicism and the Making of Politics in Central Mozambique, 1940–1986* (Rochester, NY: University of Rochester Press, 2019).

[44] Ian Linden, *The Catholic Church and the Struggle for Zimbabwe* (London: Longman, 1980), p. 17. See also Aquinata Agonga, 'Soror nostra es: Jesuits, Protestants, and Political Elites in Southern Africa among the Shona and the Ndebele, 1889–1900', in *Encounters between Jesuits and Protestants in Africa*, eds. Robert A. Maryks and Festo Mkenda (Leiden: Brill, 2017), pp. 132–49. Agonga shows how

of religious orders – that Catholicism and anticolonial politics became more compatible, typified most clearly in the politics of the Catholic schoolteacher Robert Mugabe.[45]

In colonial Rwanda, state power was also connected to the Catholic Church. In the 1930s and 1940s, during the mass conversion of Tutsi elites, described by missionaries as *la tornade*, Rwanda's political hierarchy became formally Catholic, as did its monarchy.[46] The White Fathers had been committed to creating a state that was uniquely Catholic, in part because they saw how religious competition had created political violence in late nineteenth-century Buganda. By the late 1950s, the intersectionality of Rwanda's political order and Catholic social teaching inadvertently offered aspiring Bahutu the theological authority to imagine a violent republican revolution. Acts of political intimidation against Tutsi elites were not propelled by anti-Catholic sentiments; the Catholic faith crossed the boundaries of ethnicity and class. But that did not make Catholic social vision any less salient. Hutu revolutionaries readily recalled a time in the early 1900s when the church was 'closely connected to the liberation of the poor masses and the establishment of a more egalitarian Rwandan society marked by social justice, democracy, and economic equality'.[47]

Beyond church-state relations, Elizabeth Foster has worked to draw out the complexities and polemics of Catholic political discourse in late colonial West Africa. Foster argues that throughout the post-war period, French missionaries and African Catholic elites were engaged in a fierce intellectual struggle over the legacies of French colonialism and the European 'civilising mission' in Africa, the relationship of Catholicism to colonisation, and the emerging character of the African indigenisation of the Catholic Church.[48] Ultimately the Vatican under Pope John XXIII supported African elites in calling for the 'de–Occidentalizing' of the Catholic Church in Africa, influencing the Second Vatican Council's (1962–65) decision to embrace the ideal of a universal church that would serve as a 'force to liberate the world's subjugated and exploited populations'.[49]

---

the close collaboration between Jesuits and British colonial officials resulted in the military subjugation of Ndebele leadership in the 1890s.

[45] Linden and Linden, *Catholic Church and the Struggle for Zimbabwe*, pp. 32–4, 60.
[46] J. J. Carney, *Rwanda Before the Genocide: Catholic Politics and Ethnic Discourse in the Late Colonial Era* (New York: Oxford University Press, 2014), pp. 36–43.
[47] Ibid., p. 3.
[48] Elizabeth A. Foster, *African Catholic: Decolonization and the Transformation of the Church* (Cambridge, MA: Harvard University Press, 2019), pp. 4–7.
[49] Ibid., p. 258.

Our book parts ways from this trajectory in the scholarship by de-centring church-state relations or the internal ecclesial politics of the Catholic Church. Nor do clergy, missionaries, or bishops play central roles in our narrative. Rather, we turn to the lay politicians and community leaders who drove Catholic political activism in the late colonial period. Our interest in this book is to illustrate how Catholic political discourse and activism operated differently throughout late colonial Uganda. While there was a general sense among Catholics throughout Uganda that their communities had been systematically disenfranchised, in reality, activists had varied relationships to the state and early colonial violence. Communities – whose allegiances did not easily operate within sectarian boundaries – bolstered and reworked associations, common points of historical reference, and political and religious ideologies. Benedicto Kiwanuka's challenge was to implement a sufficiently liberal political project that attracted competing Catholic agendas and traditions throughout the country, while simultaneously including Protestants and Muslims who championed democratic liberalism. Catholic politics in Uganda was not homogeneous. As Kiwanuka and DP activists navigated the clashing currents of independence and public life in the postcolony, they did so in ways that confound any simple sectarian narrative.

Catholic Alternatives and the Birth of Postcolonial Uganda: Sources and Chapters

Despite the significance and controversy of DP and Kiwanuka, his career has resulted in few studies. To date, three partisan histories have been written about Kiwanuka and DP. In 1984, DP activists produced two accounts – one in Luganda and one in English – both of which were published with the Foundation for African Development in Rome for the purpose of legitimising DP and the presidential campaigns of Paul Ssemogerere during the 1980s.[50] Over ten years later, the Ugandan historian Albert Bade published a sympathetic biography of Kiwanuka, during which he presented the DP leader as a righteous and uncompromising figure who 'rejected the marriages of convenience and [...] resisted the temptation to join those who controlled power and the resources'.[51] Other scholars have largely ignored Kiwanuka and his legacy in modern Ugandan politics. David Apter offered only one passing

---

[50] Samwiri Lwanga Lunyiigo, *A Short History of the Democratic Party*; Simon Mwebe and Anthony Sserubiri, *Ebyafaayo bya DP: 1954–1984* (Rome: Foundation for African Development, 1984).

[51] Albert Bade, *Benedicto Kiwanuka: The Man and His Politics* (Kampala: Fountain, 1996), p. i.

statement about Kiwanuka, whom he simply described as a 'well known Kampala lawyer'.[52] Donald A. Low's subsequent reading of Kiwanuka was schematic; it suggested that Kiwanuka's electoral victory in 1961 signified the party's transition out of its clear-cut Catholic phase into one that was generally democratic.[53]

Our book draws substantially from the private papers of Benedicto Kiwanuka to re-examine his political career and the history of DP. Earle unearthed his private papers in 2009 during the course of his doctoral research. The collection was concealed in a discreet, secure location in a suburb of Kampala immediately after the Amin government assassinated Kiwanuka. Benedicto Kiwanuka's son, Ambassador Maurice Kagimu Kiwanuka, implemented the necessary precautions to ensure that the collection was protected from rain, rodents, and ruin. Without his foresight – and the larger support of the Kiwanuka family – the collection would have likely fallen into disrepair. As it remains, though, the collection is preserved in Kiwanuka's original file folders, and his library has been mostly conserved. The collection is comprised of approximately 4,900 pieces of textual evidence, filed in eighty-three folders. The tin trunk in which the collection is kept also contains 900 pages of loose-leaf material. The larger collection consists of several dozen books, some of which include marginalia, annotated newspapers in English, Luganda and Swahili, and course notepads that Kiwanuka used in law school during the mid-1950s. Earle used the collection as the basis of the chapter on Kiwanuka in his previous monograph,[54] which did not fully exhaust this historical treasure trove. The collection includes political pamphlets, campaign agendas, finance reports, Catholic prayers, national correspondences between DP membership and Kiwanuka, complaints and threats, family memos, private notes, photographs, international letters, and more. These sources enabled us to think about Kiwanuka and Catholic politics in ways previously unattainable – to move beyond the Kiwanuka of the Catholic and state archives. As opposed to showing how the politics of DP was structured around the career of a single biography, Kiwanuka's papers allowed us to see a much larger arena of competing regional ambitions and contested authority.

Second, we examine Kiwanuka's private papers alongside the *Uganda Argus*, Uganda's national newspaper in the late colonial and early postcolonial periods. While we use the Luganda press to understand internal debates that were unfolding in Buganda, in the course of this project it became apparent

---

[52] Apter, *The Political Kingdom in Uganda*, p. 342.
[53] Donald A. Low, *Buganda in Modern History* (Berkeley: University of California Press, 1971), 184.
[54] Earle, *Colonial Buganda and the End of Empire*, Chapter 5.

that the English-language *Uganda Argus* constituted a vital imaginary space within which the origins and future of the state were envisioned and questioned for many public activists across Uganda. Like Emma Hunter and Derek Peterson, we see the press as an arena of management, standardisation, and public disputation.[55] By 1958, there were 8,200 copies of the partly European-owned *Argus* in daily circulation.[56] The paper was Uganda's only daily national press. Throughout the 1960s, party activists were anxious about the political co-optation of the *Argus*, which compelled nationalists to inundate its pages with editorials, press releases, and party iconography.[57]

Anxieties about managing the national press helped foster a public space where Ugandans standardised, catalogued, and accessed various chronologies and regional and national histories. Kiwanuka's annotated copies of the *Argus* and his private correspondence show that he used that newspaper extensively to gauge and participate in national politics. He thought deeply about the political function of a national press. Kiwanuka's files show that he maintained a running list of newspaper quotations, mostly from the *Uganda Argus*, which he then reworked into party press releases and political letters throughout the 1960s (Figure I.1).[58] By the end of the decade, Kiwanuka believed that the national press had become the socialist mouthpiece of UPC, especially after the republican revolution of 1966. In response to the February 1966 suspension of the 1962 Constitution, Kiwanuka forwarded a three-page diatribe to Milton Obote, which included concerns about the *Argus*: 'I am giving this letter wide publicity because I know that our local English newspaper, the *Uganda Argus*, will not dare show a fourth of it for reasons well known to you.'[59] In an effort to challenge what Kiwanuka saw as the socialist take-over of the *Argus*, he solicited Catholic colleagues in West Germany to begin a new press in Uganda.[60] It did not materialise.

---

[55] Derek R. Peterson and Emma Hunter, 'Print Culture in Colonial Africa', in *African Print Cultures: Newspapers and Their Publics in the Twentieth Century*, ed. by Derek R. Peterson, Emma Hunter, and Stephanie Newell (Ann Arbor: University of Michigan Press, 2016), pp. 1–45.

[56] Apter, *The Political Kingdom in Uganda*, p. 274.

[57] '"Argus is biased against D.P." – Youth Wing', *Uganda Argus*, 5 February 1962; 'Attack on Argus must be condemned', *Uganda Argus*, 8 February 1962.

[58] BKMKP/Not Marked 6.

[59] BKMKP/Confidential 2/Benedicto Kiwanuka to Milton Obote, 3 March 1966.

[60] In an undated, partially preserved petition to a Catholic associate, Kiwanuka emphasised 'the fact that the Uganda Argus – the only English newspaper in the country – was not able to show more than ¼ of my statement' (BKMKP/Not Marked 6/Benedicto Kiwanuka to Undesignated Recipient in West Germany, n.d.). With conviction and passion, he asked: 'Is there no good Catholic of sufficient means who can help us in the name of God?' He continued: 'If East Germany can give about 4 times the help I need to those who go there, why not West

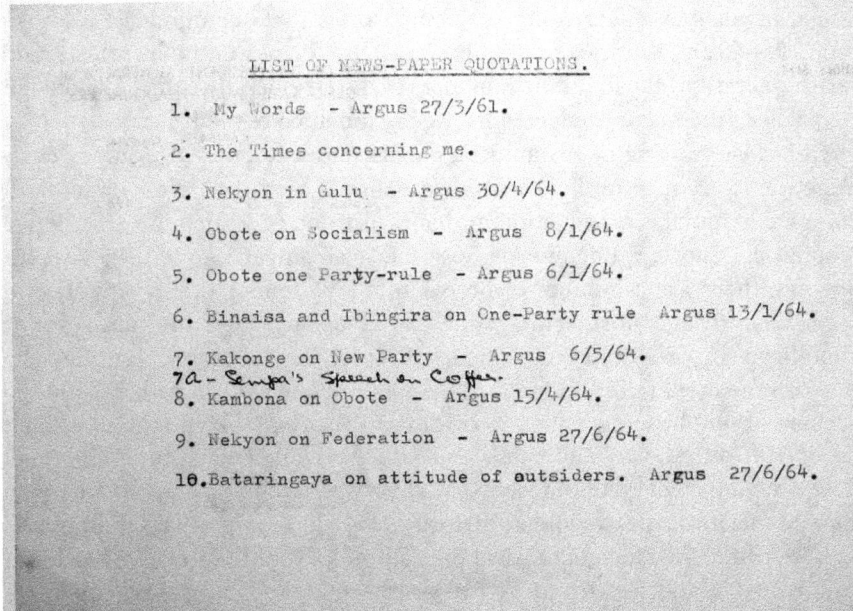

Figure I.1 Benedicto Kiwanuka maintained a running list of newspaper quotations, which he reworked into his speeches and writings, c. 1964. *Benedicto Kiwanuka Papers*.

Third, we supplement our reading of Kiwanuka's private papers and the national press with material that we have identified in institutional archives on three continents. To think carefully about the interiority of Catholic political hierarchies and social production, we draw from the Rubaga Diocesan Archives at the Archdiocese of Kampala, District Archives, the Africana collection (Makerere University), the British National Archives, and the Institute of Commonwealth Studies. Each houses a broad range of textual and material sources that illuminate the 1960s, as do Audrey Richards' papers (London School of Economics) and the Classified General Records of the Foreign Service Posts of the United States Department of State, which are housed in College Park, Maryland.[61]

Last, our work draws from the insights of interviews, conversations, and intermittent fieldwork in eastern Africa over the past two decades. We have

---

Germany which is richer and of better intentions? Is the expansion of communism of more importance to the human race than the preservation of Christian principles?'

[61] BKMKP/Democrat II Dem-Cor-1/M.M. Barlow, Assistant Librarian, Africana, to Secretary General, Democratic Party, 17 March 1969.

gained invaluable insights into the complexities that surrounded Kiwanuka and DP – from Kiwanuka's family, local historians, Catholic priests and parishioners, and the founding members of the Democratic Party. As noted in the pages of the Acknowledgements, we are indebted to many.

Our close reading of Kiwanuka's papers and available DP sources challenged us to reimagine how Uganda's political history is often organised. Colonial mapmakers and ethnographers divided Uganda into distinctive geopolitical zones.[62] Buganda is described as central Uganda. In western Uganda, there are a number of precolonial kingdoms, notably Ankole and Toro. Eastern and northern Uganda are associated with the non-state or republican societies of Acholi, Lango, and Teso. The kingdom of Bunyoro sits between the monarchical regions of the western and central regions, and the northern republican societies. According to this logic, kingdoms are often clumped together, while northern and eastern Uganda constitutes a parallel construct: a paradigm of difference.[63] There are in some instances a logic to these associations due to longer histories of trading, migration, and linguistic borrowing. Yet Benedicto Kiwanuka's project could not be confined into such neat boundaries. He looked to northern Ugandans to back his position against Ankole delegates in western Uganda. He drew from the ideas of missionaries in Acholiland to develop party iconography on the streets of Kampala. He saw republican and secessionist politics in far eastern, western, and southern Uganda as overarching spaces of ideological circulation and party mobility. It is for these reasons that we decided to break with the conventional method of structuring Uganda's political story according to well-worn regional tropes. In doing so, we hope to contribute to a larger conversation about decolonising Uganda's cartography and the political rubrics that have animated it.[64]

---

[62] Both Ganda administrators and British ethnographers advocated for Uganda's regional cartography. See Hamu Mukasa, *Journey to Bukedi by the Saza Chief, 1917–1918* (manuscript housed in Kwata Mpola House, Mukono); and John Roscoe, *The Northern Bantu: An Account of Some Central African Tribes of the Uganda Protectorate* (Cambridge: Cambridge University Press, 1915). For secondary review, Michael Twaddle, *Kakungulu & the Creation of Uganda, 1868–1928* (London: James Currey, 1993). To review how the legacies of colonial administrative divisions have shaped Uganda's secondary curriculum see Byamugisha Bweebare C., *A Geography of Uganda: An 'A' Level Geography Approach with Field Work*, Revised edition (Kampala: Simplified & Low Priced Textbook Centre, 1994).

[63] Our language borrows from V. Y. Mudimbe, *The Idea of Africa* (London: James Currey, 1994).

[64] The legacies of regional compartmentalism remain evident in the Uganda Studies

Chapter 1 introduces Benedicto Kiwanuka's early biography and the Catholic and political contexts that shaped his emerging sensibilities. Kiwanuka's religious convictions and conception of liberal democracy emerged out of his identification with each of Uganda's three Catholic missions, whose leaders were French, English, Dutch, Italian, and Ugandan. His burgeoning political interests were also impacted by military service during the Second World War, Catholic education in southern Africa, and legal training in London. The Democratic Party emerged in Uganda during a time when the Catholic Church was reorienting its ecclesiastical and theological priorities in response to postwar populisms and anticolonial protest. Members of DP argued that liberal reform must prioritise the political and economic interests of Catholics, whose communities had been the subject of systematic marginalisation by the kingdom's government and colonial state.

In Chapter 2, we move Kiwanuka and DP beyond the conventional historiographies of southern Uganda. The history of Catholic politics and DP in Tesoland problematises normative sectarian associations. Tesoland was predominantly a Catholic region in eastern Uganda. But Kiwanuka's associations with Ganda sub-imperialism in the area compelled Catholics to strategise their interests through UPC. The foremost Catholic activist of the period in Tesoland was Cuthbert Obwangor. He served as an executive of UPC for nearly one decade, during which he drew from older Teso ideas about republicanism and the egalitarian traditions of the Mill Hill Mission to advocate for the economic rights of Teso farmers. Obwangor's story shows that UPC was hardly an Anglican stronghold in eastern Uganda. The history of party politics in Toro, western Uganda, also shows the extent to which UPC was a pro-royalist party in national public life prior to the mid-1960s. At the same time, DP's solidarity with the Rwenzururu secessionist kingdom shows how Kiwanuka embraced royalist alternatives to secure regional support in an area where Catholic conversion was long associated with Toro dissent. Party associations with royalist and republican boundaries, like religious associations, varied tremendously throughout Uganda. They were far more fragmentary than has been typically argued.

Kiwanuka, though, did not view all secessions similarly. He argued strongly against Buganda's bid for independence in the early 1960s. He was also an outspoken proponent of the return of Bunyoro's 'Lost Counties', which radicalised Ganda patriots against him and DP. We show in Chapter 3 how the 'Lost Counties' controversy emerged out of a time when Buganda's Catholic chiefs and converts of the late nineteenth-century used violence to 'eat' the

---

Association, where a scholar's work tends to be confined to a specific region: northern Uganda, eastern Uganda, western Uganda, or a particular kingdom.

southern counties of Bunyoro. In an effort to build Catholic solidarities across the Buganda-Bunyoro border, Kiwanuka was obliged to support the return of the counties, a choice that drew inspiration from a Nyoro historical research society and his Nyoro family connections. Kiwanuka hoped that by supporting the return of Mubende to Bunyoro, he would both unify Catholics and bolster DP's vision for national unification. While DP was associated with returning land to the kingdom of Bunyoro, the party was affiliated in Kigezi with the cause of Bakiga farmers, Bahutu migrants, and a republican revolution that was unfolding across the border in Rwanda. In contrast, UPC worked to empower older forms of royalist authority that were associated with elite Protestants and Bahororo state-building in Kigezi.

Where Chapters 2 and 3 show how religious, royalist, and republican politics worked differently in Tesoland, Toro, Bunyoro, and Kigezi, the following two chapters focus largely on intra-Catholic political competition. In Chapter 4, we rethink the genealogies of Ugandan nationalism by exploring sectarian politics in the northern Ugandan regions of Acholiland and West Nile. As Richard Reid has recently argued, northern Uganda's late colonial intellectuals were at the forefront of imagining postcolonial society.[65] We show how these visions were rooted in long-standing Protestant and Catholic competition. Two of Acholiland's foremost Protestant activists were Okot p'Bitek and Daudi Ocheng. The former, who backed UPC, used his novels and poetry to pen blistering critiques of economic opportunities in colonial Buganda, the Catholic Church, and DP. Daudi Ocheng, by contrast, was one of Uganda's foremost defenders of royalism and, as one of *Kabaka* Muteesa's closest advisors, a proponent of Buganda's special status. Whatever Ocheng's and p'Bitek's influence, Acholiland was in fact a Catholic stronghold in Uganda. DP activists in Acholiland helped initially secure the premiership of Kiwanuka. But Catholic alliances could not be taken for granted: the highest concentration of Catholics in Uganda lived in West Nile, where DP lost their parliamentary election. In Ankole, Catholic activists in DP backed the cause of the Ankole monarchy, resulting in the appointment of a Catholic *enganzi* (prime minister) there in 1961. The power of DP leadership in Ankole resulted in an alliance that sought to upend Kiwanuka's hold on power. To maintain his grip on the leadership of the party, Kiwanuka returned to Acholiland, whose delegates ensured that Kiwanuka would continue to lead the party beyond independence.

In Buganda, Catholic allegiances were hardly straightforward. Chapter 5 explores two of the more consequential Catholic alternatives in 1950s Buganda and the politics of patrimony and patriarchal authority. We begin by exploring

---

[65] Richard J. Reid, *A History of Modern Uganda* (Cambridge: Cambridge University Press, 2017), pp. 185–9.

the politics of the Catholic radical Semakula Mulumba. The fraught relationship of Mulumba and Kiwanuka raises insight into larger struggles over patronage, masculine politics, and priestly authority. In his quest to reimagine priestly authority in Ganda public life, Mulumba backed the career of Matia Kigaanira Ssewannyana, a Catholic layperson who became a priest for Kibuuka, the Ganda god of war, during a moment of national crisis. His career emerged during the exile and return of *Kabaka* Muteesa II (1953–55). Riding on the coattail of royalist populism, the Catholic activist Aloysius Darlington Lubowa ensured that Buganda's Catholic chiefs and parishioners resisted Benedicto Kiwanuka and DP. Lubowa's campaign compelled the vast majority of Catholics in Buganda to join or support the royalist movement, *Kabaka Yekka* (KY). In ways that have often been blurred in Uganda's nationalist historiography, we show that it was not Catholics – in the broad sense of the term – who were targeted and attacked by patriots in early 1960s Buganda. Rather, targeted violence was directed against Catholics who joined DP. There was also considerable intra-Catholic violence. The triumph of political royalism in Buganda divided the kingdom's Catholics, which compelled Archbishop Joseph Kiwanuka to intervene with a series of publications. Far from calming the situation, though, his circulars instigated additional violence. A close examination of the activism of Benedicto Kiwanuka, Archbishop Kiwanuka, and Lubowa highlights an intra-Catholic dispute within the operation of KY that has been overlooked. KY was not simply a party for royalist Protestants; it was a platform upon which Catholic royalists aimed to prove their worth.

As we show in Chapter 6, Ugandan politics during the late 1950s and 1960s was not an exercise in unmitigated optimism during an allegedly golden age of African nationalism; it was an emotional parade of fits and starts, shaped by reflections and debates about death and political and religious martyrdom. Like the Uganda Martyrs, Kiwanuka believed that he was the leader of a persecuted movement. As party members were murdered and threatened with decapitation, Kiwanuka worked to inspire a party whose leaders were increasingly deserting. With growing concerns about his life, Kiwanuka increased his life insurance policies, purchased a pistol, and had protective fencing placed around his home. He also argued for the importance of what he described as 'prophetic resistance' in the expectation of God's deliverance. To this end, Kiwanuka was an outspoken critic of Obote. After being associated with a failed assassination attempt on Obote's life in 1969, Kiwanuka was arrested. In 1971, Idi Amin released Kiwanuka from prison. Kiwanuka believed that God had sent Idi Amin to deliver him and Uganda from the dictatorship of Milton Obote. But after appointing Kiwanuka as the country's first Ugandan Supreme Court Justice, Amin orchestrated his murder in September 1972. Kiwanuka's violent death ushered him into the pantheon of Uganda's political and religious martyrs, the memory of which we explore in the Conclusion.

The culminating result of these chapters is a new way of thinking about the birth of postcolonial Uganda. By describing the emergence of postcolonial Uganda as a process of birthing, we are not eliciting the sort of arguments made by Rhoda Ann Kanaaneh, Lisa Forman Cody, or Rhiannon Stephens, whose convincing works show in different ways how reproductive politics and ideologies of motherhood extended beyond patrilineal and linguistic boundaries.[66] Rather, we are arguing that Uganda experienced a profound political crisis at the inception of the state that revolved around Benedicto Kiwanuka and the Democratic Party. In eastern Africa's historiography, it has been argued that Uganda did not experience a late colonial crisis that served as a cause for national unification,[67] in contrast to Kenya's Mau Mau, Rwanda's political revolution, or even Tanzania's formation around a unified language and the integration of Zanzibar with Tanganyika. We wish, by contrast, to suggest that the politics of Benedicto Kiwanuka and DP were far more consequential in propelling Uganda's nationalist politics than has been previously understood, as both a party that struggled to streamline regional interests and as a party that was condemned on religious grounds across the country. Like birthing, the politics of late colonial Uganda was loosely predictable, bloody, hopeful, and excruciating. Its independence was not a foredrawn conclusion. But what this 'birthing' meant for those who experienced its anxieties most intently is the aim of this book.

---

[66] Rhoda Ann Kanaaneh, *Birthing the Nation: Strategies of Palestinian Women in Israel* (Berkeley: University of California Press, 2002); Lisa Forman Cody, *Birthing the Nation: Sex, Science, and the Conception of Eighteenth-Century Britons* (Oxford: Oxford University Press, 2005); Rhiannon Stephens, *A History of African Motherhood: The Case of Uganda, 700–1900* (Cambridge: Cambridge University Press, 2013).

[67] Many would name the 1953–55 *kabaka* crisis, but the post-crisis trajectory was toward national division rather than unity. In turn, Cherry Gertzel has argued that the development of a unitary state in Uganda was precipitously fabricated by Sir Andrew Cohen following the *kabaka* crisis. See, 'Kingdoms, Districts, and the Unitary State: Uganda, 1945–1962', in *History of East Africa*, ed. by D. A. Low and Alison Smith (Oxford: Clarendon Press, 1976), III, 65–106 (p. 70). Richard Reid has recently argued for a much longer history of national integration in Uganda's political history (*A History of Modern Uganda*).

CHAPTER 1

Benedicto Kiwanuka, Catholic Uganda, and the Gospel of Democracy

> Our foes have chosen, out of complete jealousy, to denigrate
> our name by calling us a religious organization. There is noth-
> ing farther from the truth. We are a band of well-intentioned
> men and women out to do good. If this is not enough let me,
> Sir, extend an open invitation to all your African readers to join
> our camp. Come ye all. Come ye Muslims, Protestants, pagans,
> Catholics. Come to our camp. Join in this great struggle to
> bring light to the people of this country.
>
> ~Benedicto K. M. Kiwanuka, 1958[1]

In the midst of an August 1967 speech on democracy to the Makerere University student guild, Benedicto Kiwanuka made a remarkable claim. Following the lead of Tanzanian President Julius Nyerere among others, President Milton Obote and his Uganda People's Congress (UPC) had justified Uganda's continuing drift toward a one-party system by labelling it a uniquely 'African' form of democracy. Kiwanuka scoffed at this claim. Uganda's political system was not the embodiment of some kind of uniquely inculturated, 'African' democracy. Rather than a praiseworthy example of political inculturation, Uganda's political system was an oligarchy 'where a few people govern for their own interests, unconcerned about the views of the majority Democracy'.[2] Kiwanuka went on to assert that political systems like democracy or socialism

> cannot be known in terms of continents. Africa is a Continent and not a race
> or government [...] Our behaviour varies from region to region, or probably,
> from tribe to tribe. A Fulani in Nigeria is as different in behavior in ordinary

---

[1] 'D.P. Leader's Appeal', *Uganda Argus*, 30 September 1958.
[2] ICS PP.UG.DP.10 Benedicto Kiwanuka, 'What is Democracy', 2 August 1967, p. 5.

life from a Muluhia in Kenya as a Somali is from a Greek [...] apart from our colour Africa has nothing to make us Black men one.'[3]

To say that such comments cut against the grain of 1960s pan-Africanism would be an understatement. When Kiwanuka gave this speech in 1967, the Organisation of African Unity (OAU) was four years old. Tanzania hosted anti-apartheid freedom fighters from South Africa, and Congolese President Joseph Mobutu was about to launch his *authenticité* campaign in the soon-to-be-renamed Zaire. In the world of religion, the Kenyan scholar John Mbiti was publishing his groundbreaking work theorising *African Religions and Philosophy*,[4] and even Pope Paul VI would stand in Kampala exactly two years later and proclaim to a continent, 'You can, and you must, have an African Christianity.'[5] Yet here was Benedicto Kiwanuka, Uganda's first prime minister, boldly rejecting such pan-Africanist discourse for casting an ideological veil over the brutal reality of postcolonial Ugandan political life.

People are detained and thrown into gaol at the caprice of a single person [...] You yourself do not know whether you will ever come out alive or die there. The Courts are outside your reach, and your future is as black as that of the devils in Hell. In these countries a country's Constitution can be thrown away by a single person as easily as throwing a dirty handkerchief in a bedroom basket.[6]

For Kiwanuka, it was not African *authenticité* but rather authentic democracy that promised Uganda a brighter postcolonial future. He argued that democratic principles looked the same all over the world: freedom from arbitrary arrest; the right to elect representatives in open elections at regular intervals; the right to assemble; the right to free speech within the general limits of slander and libel; the right to join a political party; the right to property and banning of 'expropriation without compensation'; freedom of worship; and an individual's right to enjoy political privilege 'without regard to his origin or religious belief'.[7] Ultimately, for Kiwanuka, democracy is a 'form of Government where supreme power resides and PERPETUALLY REMAINS in the people, i.e. the masses' and where leaders 'are not masters, but servants of the people'.[8] Five years removed from political office, now the leader

---

[3] Ibid., p. 8.
[4] John Mbiti, *African Religions and Philosophy* (Oxford: Heinemann, 1967).
[5] Agbonkhianmeghe E. Orobator, *Theology Brewed in an African Pot* (Maryknoll, NY: Orbis, 2008), pp. 130–31. This speech, part of the historic first papal visit to sub-Saharan Africa, was delivered on 2 August 1969.
[6] Kiwanuka, 'What is Democracy', p. 5.
[7] Ibid., p. 4.
[8] Ibid., p. 9. Emphasis original.

of a dwindling opposition party, Kiwanuka lamented what he saw as Uganda's authoritarian turn under President Obote and the Uganda People's Congress.

In this chapter we explore the early biography of Benedicto Kiwanuka and his fervent commitment to both Catholicism and the sorts of liberal democracies that emerged after the Second World War. Here we offer a detailed overview of the Ganda Catholic contexts in which he was raised and the controversial origins of the Democratic Party (DP) in post-war Buganda. In doing so, we trace how Kiwanuka's vision of democratisation intersected with Catholic historical experiences in Buganda/Uganda (henceforth B/Uganda) as well as international Catholic political movements such as Christian Democracy. Although DP was founded to give a political voice to Ganda Catholics, Kiwanuka's political vision did not support either Ganda ethnic patriotism or Catholic religious tribalism. Rather, he furthered DP's transformation into a nationalist party that espoused religious non-sectarianism, the empowerment of peasants and other small farmers, land reform, and pan-ethnic nation-building. Ultimately, Kiwanuka's deep Catholic religious convictions were transposed politically into an ardent faith in the 'gospel' of democracy.

Kiwanuka's Early Life and Catholic Origins in Uganda

Benedicto Kagimu Mugumba Kiwanuka was born on 8 May 1922 in Kisabwa village of Masaka District in Buddu province, the heartland of Ganda Catholicism in south-western Buganda.[9] As a toddler, he was taken to his maternal grandfather's home in the village of Kitanda and later moved to Kawoko at the age of five. Three years later, he returned to his father's home near Masaka. His father, Fulgensio Daniel Musoke, was a low-ranking village chief at Ssabagabo who struggled with alcoholism. Kiwanuka's home life has been described as 'harsh and chaotic'.[10] Like the many *abasoma* or Christian 'readers' in early colonial Buganda, Kiwanuka found solace and channelled his ambitions in the Catholic mission. In 1929 he enrolled in a local Catholic school where he was exposed to English literacy and Catholic catechesis. After several years moving in and out of school, Kiwanuka in 1934 convinced his reticent father to give him five shillings so he could study at the Catholic primary school at

---

[9] Early biographical information here is drawn from Benedicto KM Kiwanuka Papers (BKMKP)/Confidential 2/'Benedicto Kiwanuka Biography', undated; 'Bendicto [sic] Kagimu Mugumba Kiwanuka: A Martyr of Truth and Justice', Proposal to open process for beatification, Archdiocese of Kampala (Kampala: N.P., 2014), pp. 1–3; Albert Bade, *Benedicto Kiwanuka: The Man and His Politics* (Kampala: Fountain, 1996), pp. 1–5.

[10] 'Bendicto Kagimu Mugumba Kiwanuka', p. 1.

Villa Maria in Masaka. Associated with the primatial church in Buddu province, Villa Maria Primary School was one of the first schools started by the Missionaries of Africa or White Fathers, Uganda's first Catholic evangelists. Kiwanuka's mentor at Villa Maria was Fr Benedicto Nsubuga, one of the first indigenous Ugandans to be ordained as a Catholic priest. Kiwanuka went on to pursue secondary school studies at St Peter's Nsambya, a prominent Kampala junior secondary school run by the British Mill Hill Missionaries. Even in his own schooling, then, Kiwanuka was shaped by three key Catholic currents in colonial Uganda: the White Father missionaries, the Mill Hill Missionaries, and African priests from the Buddu/Masaka region, the first Catholic territory in sub-Saharan Africa to be turned over completely to indigenous clergy. Early in his career, he would also engage the Verona Fathers of northern Uganda, better known as the 'Combonis'. Let us turn now to a deeper analysis of these Catholic foundations.

French Missionaries of Africa, better known as the 'White Fathers', initiated Catholic evangelisation efforts in the region. Landing on the shores of Entebbe in February 1879, they followed representatives of the British Protestant Church Missionary Society (CMS). Its first missionaries had arrived in Buganda in 1877 in response to an invitation from Buganda's king, *Kabaka* Muteesa I, passed through the hands of the British-American explorer Henry Morton Stanley.[11] Although his ties to Islam went back to the 1860s,[12] Muteesa appeared to decide that Stanley and Christian missionaries could facilitate trade relations with Great Britain or France, an appealing prospect in the face of Sudanese encroachment from the north. The arrival of Fr Siméon 'Mapera' Lourdel and his French White Father confreres initiated a bitter intra-Christian struggle to win the allegiances of Muteesa, a monarch who seemed alternately intrigued and perplexed by the two missions' theological disputes.[13] The

---

[11] Samwiri R. Karugire, *A Political History of Uganda* (Nairobi: Heinemann, 1980), p. 52. The initial CMS party withdrew quickly. A more lasting CMS presence arrived under the leadership of the Scottish Calvinist Alexander Mackay in November 1878 (Adrian Hastings, *The Church in Africa 1450–1950* (Oxford: Clarendon, 1994), p. 372).

[12] Muslim traders first arrived in Buganda in 1844, and Muteesa began observing Ramadan in 1867. Given the taboo surrounding the mutilation of a Ganda king, Muteesa refused circumcision. Foreshadowing his son's attitude toward Christian pages a decade later, Muteesa fell out with some zealous Muslim pages in 1875–76 and killed over one hundred of them. As Henri Médard notes, this massacre likely followed Stanley's visit, rather than coming before (Henri Médard, *Le royaume du Buganda au XIX siècle* (Paris: Karthala, 2007), pp. 370, 375, 392, 453).

[13] 'Mapera' was a Luganda derivative of the French *'mon père'* ('my father'). This was Lourdel's most common local name.

Church Missionary Society and the White Fathers competed for the loyalties and affections of the king, but they also refused to compromise on several key matters. For example, both missions criticised Muteesa's polygamy, and both refused to facilitate the firearms trade and military alliances that Muteesa coveted since they saw their work as purely 'religious' in nature.[14] Whatever his ambivalence, Muteesa tolerated the competing missions, playing them off each other and keeping both under a watchful eye near his court. Frustrated at their failure to convert the *kabaka* and their low number of converts, the White Fathers in 1882 withdrew to Bukumbi on the south side of Lake Victoria.[15]

The Catholic mission grew more quickly under local leadership during the missionary exile period of 1882–85. Most early Catholics and Anglicans were young teenage pages serving at the *kabaka*'s court, attracted by Christianity's new technology, modern cosmopolitanism, and the spiritual hope of resurrection.[16] In the meantime, Muteesa died in 1884 and was succeeded by his eighteen-year-old son Mwanga. Although Mwanga had frequented the Catholic missions in the early 1880s, he became increasingly suspicious of missionaries' foreign connections and his Christian pages' moral obstinacy, especially their refusal of his sexual advances.

In late 1885, Mwanga initiated a persecution that would have lasting impact on Christian identity in Buganda. In October, he ordered the killing of incoming Anglican Bishop James Hannington in neighbouring Bukedi. Fearing that Christians were a 'fifth column' for European invaders,[17] he executed Joseph Mukasa Balikuddembe, a Catholic leader among the court pages, in November 1885. Six months later in May and June 1886, he executed several dozen more Anglican and Catholic pages. Ultimately, twenty-three Anglicans and twenty-two Catholics would be lifted up as the Buganda, later Uganda, Martyrs. The legacy of the 'B/Uganda Martyrs' became a central dimension of Christian and especially Catholic self-identity in Buganda, and it also facilitated broader international notoriety. Introducing their cause for beatification in 1912, White Father Bishop Henri Streicher captured this sense of Buganda and its martyrs as Catholic exemplars: 'When the Europeans read

---

[14] Samwiri R. Karugire, 'The Arrival of the European Missionaries: The first fifteen or so years', in *A Century of Christianity in Uganda, 1877–1977*, ed. by Tom Tuma and Phares Mutibwa (Nairobi: Uzima, 1978), pp. 1–15.

[15] For John Mary Waliggo, Muteesa never 'expelled' the White Father missionaries. Rather, White Father superior Léon Livinhac was discouraged by Muteesa's religious ambivalence and the social structure of polygamy in Ganda society. It was Livinhac who made the decision to withdraw over the opposition of Lourdel (J. M. Waliggo, *Catholic Church in the Buddu Province*, pp. 26–27).

[16] Médard, *Le royaume du Buganda*, pp. 395–96, 401–03.

[17] Ibid., 440.

about it, they were amazed to hear that there is a nation of black people which has produced heroes, although religion had just been brought there. This was never heard of, apart from the generations that followed the disciples.'[18]

In addition to propagating the cult of devotion to the Buganda Martyrs, the White Fathers also prided themselves on their commitment to a transnational and pan-ethnic church, an ethos that Benedicto Kiwanuka would embrace decades later. For example, although he recruited primarily from France and Belgium, White Father founder Charles Lavigerie (1825–92) exhorted his missionaries to remember their primary identity as 'Christian' and 'apostle' rather than 'Frenchman' or 'European'.[19] Within Uganda, the White Fathers and a fleet of Ganda lay catechists evangelised well beyond Buganda kingdom, including the western regions of Toro, Ankole, and Bunyoro, the home of Kiwanuka's future wife, Maxencia.[20] And even if the White Fathers and many of their early Ganda Catholics were commonly classified as '*wafaransa*', or the 'French-speakers',[21] Catholic-Protestant relations were by no means uniformly hostile in the 1880s. Catechumens frequented both missions, and even European missionaries co-existed and at times enjoyed 'courteous' relations.[22]

Under political pressure, however, such ecumenical aspirations collapsed in the early 1890s. In the aftermath of the 1886 persecutions, the political authority of Christian chiefs expanded; their internal rivalries also grew fiercer. After forcing *Kabaka* Mwanga into exile in September 1888 and briefly uniting to topple his successor, the Muslim *Kabaka* Kalema, in late 1889, Protestant and Catholic chiefs fell out over which 'politico-religious' faction

---

[18] Henri Streicher quoted in J. L. Ddiba, *Eddini Mu Uganda*, Vol. 2 (Masaka, 1967), p. 183. For Streicher, the beatifications of the Martyrs would also demonstrate that the Catholic Church 'does not discriminate among its followers on the grounds of race, to say that is black, this is white'. Rather, the Church 'looks for commitment. Where there is commitment, it is where it [the faith] spreads among the whole group of people' (183).

[19] Charles Martial Allemand Lavigerie and Xavier de Montclos. *Lavigerie: la mission universelle de l'église*. Foi vivante 280 (Paris: Cerf, 1991), p. 94.

[20] Deogratias M. Byabazaire, *The Contribution of the Christian Churches to the Development of Western Uganda 1894–1974* (Frankfurt: Peter Lang, 1979), pp. 46–54.

[21] Darius Magunda, 'The Role and Impact of the Missionaries of Africa in Planting the Church in Western Uganda 1879–1969', unpublished ThD thesis, Pontifical University Sancta Crucis, Rome, 2006, p. 283.

[22] See Yves Tourigny, *So Abundant a Harvest: The Catholic Church in Uganda, 1879–1979* (London: Darton, Longman and Todd, 1979), p. 24; John Mary Waliggo, 'The Catholic Church in the Buddu Province of Buganda, 1879–1925' (unpublished PhD thesis, University of Cambridge, 1976), p. 22; Médard, *Le royaume du Buganda*, p. 458.

would ultimately triumph.²³ These tensions were exacerbated by the May 1890 death of Fr Lourdel, who had been a moderating influence, as well as increasing Protestant concern that *Kabaka* Mwanga would become a Catholic.²⁴ After Mwanga showed up at Rubaga Catholic mission on New Year's Day 1892 with 10,000 followers, Protestant leaders took action. Several radical Protestants burned the nearly constructed Rubaga Cathedral to the ground.²⁵ At the end of January, Frederick Lugard, representative of the Imperial British East Africa Company (IBEAC), distributed weapons to the Protestants including a semi-automatic maxim gun, enabling the Protestants to triumph over the Catholics in several pitched battles in early 1892.²⁶ Over the next fifteen months, 15,000–20,000 Catholics migrated to the western *ssaza* (county) of Buddu under the leadership of the Catholic chief Alikisi Ssebowa.²⁷ As we show in the following chapters, the military victory of southern Protestants adversely impacted ecumenical relations throughout Uganda, especially as the British looked to 'consolidate the Protestant party'.²⁸ In turn, Ganda Catholicism developed in the 1890s an anticolonial edge. It was in Kiwanuka's home region of Buddu that *Kabaka* Mwanga found the most support for his 1897–99 revolt against the British, aided by Catholic chiefs such as Gabriel Kintu. As Médard has argued, Catholics strategically converted those who opposed the dominant Protestant power.²⁹

In the aftermath of the Protestant military victory of 1892 as well as the British decision in 1894 to establish a protectorate over Buganda,³⁰ the White Fathers decided to give up their monopoly on Catholic evangelisation. With

---

23 Michael Twaddle, 'The Emergence of Politico-Religious Groupings in Late Nineteenth-Century Buganda', *The Journal of African History,* 29 (1988), 81–92. For Twaddle these divisions became much harder during the 1889–92 conflicts; prior to this 'Ganda Christians behaved in a decidedly interdenominational manner toward one another' (p. 84).
24 Mwanga had long since reconciled with the Catholic party; the White Fathers gave him refuge in Bukombi (modern-day Tanzania) during part of his 1888–89 exile (Hastings, *Church in Africa 1450–1950,* p. 381).
25 Médard, *Le royaume du Buganda,* p. 483.
26 Ibid., pp. 488–91.
27 Waliggo, 'Catholic Church in the Buddu Province', p. 55.
28 Holger B. Hansen, *Mission, Church and State in a Colonial Setting: Uganda 1890–1925* (London: Heinemann, 1984), p. 28.
29 Médard, *Le royaume du Buganda,* pp. 558–59. On Kintu's important role in Mwanga's revolt – and his fallout with European Catholic missionaries who supported the British – see Médard, *Le royaume du Buganda,* pp. 515–25.
30 See David E. Apter, *The Political Kingdom in Uganda: A Study in Bureaucratic Nationalism,* 2nd edn (Princeton, NJ: Princeton University Press, 1967), pp. 76–80.

the support of the British Government, they lobbied Pope Leo XIII and the Holy See to invite the English-speaking St Joseph's Foreign Missionary Society – better known by their London location as the 'Mill Hill Missionaries' – to come to Uganda. Arriving in September 1895, the Mill Hill Fathers settled on Nsambya hill in Kampala and other areas east of the kingdom's capital. From the start, their mission was marked by an emphasis on the transnational nature of Catholicism – an emphasis that veered toward the apologetic in light of the widespread association of Catholicism with the French-speaking White Fathers. In the words of Mill Hill Bishop Henry Hanlon's opening address to *Kabaka* Mwanga in September 1895:

> By nationality we were completely identified with the [British] resident working in Uganda, and in religious matters we were completely identified with the White Fathers labouring in his dominions; that our religion was Catholic and therefore not confined to any particular country: that difficulties said to arise from nationality were now at an end as far as the Catholic religion was concerned.[31]

Whatever his rhetoric, Bishop Hanlon's own relations with British colonial officials never came close to the church-state partnership enjoyed by the Anglican CMS.[32] And although Hanlon's relations with CMS were better than those between White Father Bishop Jean-Joseph Hirth and Anglican Bishop Alfred Tucker, internal tensions between Mill Hill's Dutch and British missionaries remained problematic.[33] Although their actual evangelical successes were somewhat modest – on the eve of the First World War, Mill Hill counted 26,000 Catholics in Upper Nile Vicariate versus over 150,000 baptised Catholics in the western Ugandan areas overseen by the White Fathers[34] – they did succeed in establishing what H. P. Gale described as 'a kind of

---

[31] Hanlon quoted in H. P. Gale, *Uganda and the Mill Hill Fathers* (London: Macmillan, 1959), p. 111.

[32] On CMS relations with the British protectorate, see Hansen, *Mission, Church and State*. As Hansen notes, even Anglican missionaries never wanted a formal 'state church' but rather state favouritism. For their part, colonial officials aimed to 'limit the independence of the mission in order to minimize its chances of becoming an independent centre of power' (468).

[33] Paul Kollman and Cynthia Toms Smedley, *Understanding World Christianity: Eastern Africa* (Minneapolis: Fortress Press, 2018), p. 40; Médard, *Le royaume du Buganda*, p. 499; Robert O'Neil, *Mission to the Upper Nile* (London: Mission Book Service, 1999), p. 120. Throughout the colonial period, Mill Hill rotated its superiors between British and Dutch missionaries to placate each faction.

[34] Waliggo, *Catholic Church in the Buddu Province*, p. 184; Gale, *Uganda and the Mill Hill Fathers*, p. 306.

spiritual buffer state between the Anglican Mission and that of the White Fathers'.³⁵ Like the White Fathers, Mill Hill was known for its primary and secondary schools, especially Namilyango College and St Peter's Secondary School on Nsambya hill where Kiwanuka studied in the late 1930s. In eastern Uganda, Mill Hill Christianity extended to its converts a particular egalitarianism that was not always as clearly evident in southern and western Uganda. In regions like Teso and Bukedi dominated by Anglican chiefs, Mill Hill prided itself as the congregation that 'doesn't eat chieftaincies',³⁶ a grassroots focus that Kiwanuka and DP would imitate in the east and elsewhere in the 1950s (Chapter 2).

The third and final major Catholic male missionary community to evangelise Uganda was the Verona Fathers of the Sacred Heart of Jesus, later known as the 'Combonis' after their founder, the Italian Daniel Comboni.³⁷ Comboni had first come to Sudan in the late 1850s, and his 1864 'plan for the regeneration of Africa' had tremendous influence on late nineteenth-century Catholic missiology, especially in its emphases on medical mission and 'saving Africa through Africa' by evangelising through local agents.³⁸ Italian Combonis arrived in northern Uganda in 1910 and spearheaded Catholic dominance in the regions of Arua, Acholiland, and Lango. The Combonis were by no means anticolonial agitators; Comboni historians in the 1950s described the early British governor Samuel Baker as a Moses figure delivering the Acholi people from pagan darkness to civilised light.³⁹ Yet their Italian Catholic identity also made their situation tenuous in a British Anglican colony, leading to their internment and forced relocation during the First and Second World Wars. Several dozen more Combonis were expelled by the Obote and Amin regimes between 1967 and 1975 for their sociopolitical activism. The most notable Comboni social activist was Fr Tarcisio Agostoni, who

---

35 Gale, *Uganda and the Mill Hill Fathers*, p. 311.
36 O'Neil, *Mission to the Upper Nile*, p. 22.
37 On Comboni origins in Northern Uganda, see Mario Cisternino, *Passion for Africa: Missionary and Imperial Papers on the Evangelisation of Uganda and Sudan, 1848–1923* (Kampala: Fountain, 2004), pp. 340–490; Kathryn Pinkman, *A Centenary of Faith: Planting the Seed in Northern Uganda* (Kampala: Comboni Missionaries of the Heart of Jesus, 2010). On Daniel Comboni, see Aldo Gilli, *Daniel Comboni: The Man and his Message* (Bologna: Editrice Missionaria Italiana, 1980); Fidel Gonzales Fernandez de Aller, *La Idea Misionera de Daniel Comboni, Primer Vicario Apostolico del Africa Central, en al Contexto Socio-Eclesial del Siglo XIX*. (ThD Diss., Universidad Pontificia de Salamanca, 1979).
38 On Comboni's wider Catholic influence in nineteenth-century Europe and Africa, see Hastings, *Church in Africa 1450–1950*, pp. 253–54.
39 Todd D. Whitmore, *Imitating Christ in Magwi: An Anthropological Theology* (London: T&T Clark, 2019), pp. 64–67.

pioneered Catholic social teaching in Uganda. Agostoni was also a confidant of Benedicto Kiwanuka, as we will discuss at the end of this chapter.[40]

The Ugandan Catholic tradition that formed and educated Kiwanuka was by no means exclusively dominated by European missionaries, however.[41] Led by Catholic chiefs after the post-war religious settlement of the 1890s, Buddu province became the spiritual nerve centre of the Ganda Catholic Church. The largest Catholic populations grew up in Buddu, and Buddu catechists in turn spread the Catholic faith – and Ganda sub-imperialism – much further afield to regions such as Busoga, Ankole, Toro, Bunyoro, Kooki, Bweera, Mawogola, Kigezi, and even Rwanda.[42] As Waliggo has argued, Buddu Catholicism was notable for its strongly Marian and sacramental spirituality with a heavy emphasis on moral discipline and heroic witness.[43] These Catholic emphases would have no small impact on the young Kiwanuka, both of which influenced his emerging sociability. When Kiwanuka instructed his brother to 'always

---

[40] On Agostoni's vision of Catholic social teaching in the public sphere, see his *Every Citizen's Handbook: Building a Peaceful Society* (Nairobi: Paulines Publications Africa, 1962, revised edition 1997).

[41] Nor was Catholic evangelisation exclusively male, although these male groups appeared to have more influence on Ben Kiwanuka. Prominent Catholic women's missionary groups included Franciscan sisters from Mill Hill Abbey in London, led by the famous Mother Kevin Kearney who initiated one of Uganda's first Catholic hospitals at Nsambya. The White Sisters and the Verona Sisters also operated in western Uganda and northern Uganda, respectively. Even more important were indigenous women's congregations, including the Bannabikira Sisters (or Daughters of Mary), founded in Buddu/Masaka in 1910, as well as the Little Sisters of St Francis-Nkokonjeru in Lugazi. (See Therese Tinkasiimire, 'Women's Contributions to Religious Institutions in Uganda (1962–2011)', in Aili Mari Tripp and Joy C. Kwesiga, *The Women's Movement in Uganda: History, Challenges, and Prospects* (Kampala: Fountain, 2002), pp. 138–45). On Ugandan sisters' influential role in social development in Buganda, see China Scherz, *'Having People, Having Heart': Charity, Sustainable Development, and Problems of Dependence in Central Uganda* (Chicago: University of Chicago Press, 2014).

[42] M. Louise Pirouet, *Black Evangelists: The Spread of Christianity in Uganda 1891–1914* (London: Collings, 1978), pp. 7–13; Waliggo, *Catholic Church in the Buddu Province*, p. 74; Ian Linden and Jane Linden, *Church and Revolution in Rwanda* (Manchester: University of Manchester Press, 1977), pp. 32–42; Hastings, *Church in Africa 1450–1950*, p. 471. Native catechist missionaries played similarly central roles in Anglican evangelisation (see Emma Wild-Wood, *The Mission of Apolo Kivebulaya: Religious Encounter and Social Change in the Great Lakes c. 1865–1935* (Oxford: James Currey, 2020).

[43] Waliggo, *Catholic Church in the Buddu Province*, p. 75. See also Frederick Tusingire, *The Evangelisation of Uganda: Challenges and Strategies* (Kisubi: Marianum, 2003), pp. 90–96.

blend your studies with the devotion of the rosary',[44] he was speaking in the idiom of Buddu Catholic spirituality. Buddu was also a heartland for political resistance, from the time of *Kabaka* Mwanga's and *Omukama* Kabalega's 1897–99 rebellion against British rule, to the late 1940s *Bataka* (clan head) revolts that drew disproportionate support in the region and adapted Catholic organisational principles.[45]

In addition, Buddu became the first African Catholic territory fully entrusted to local clergy. Despite their vows of celibacy, Ganda priests were viewed as prestigious assets to local Ganda families, helping to ensure a steady flow of seminarians. Critically, Fr Lourdel's successor, Bishop Henri Streicher, prioritised the indigenisation of Catholic clergy.[46] Between 1913 and his retirement in 1933, Streicher oversaw the ordination of forty-six local priests and the consecration of 260 Ugandan Catholic sisters. As early as 1921, Ganda priests were administering parishes without missionary supervision, and in 1934 all parishes in Buddu, Mawogola, and Kabula counties were turned over to indigenous clergy.[47] In 1939, Rome established the Diocese of Masaka in the former territory of Buddu, led by Ganda Catholic Bishop Joseph Kiwanuka.[48] Established in the heart rather than the periphery of the Ugandan Catholic Church, Masaka became a demonstration plot for the Catholic Church in Africa.[49] Pope Pius XII is said to have whispered at Joseph

---

[44] Benedicto Kiwanuka quoted in Bade, *Benedicto Kiwanuka*, pp. 3–4.

[45] Carol A. Summers, 'Catholic Action and Ugandan Radicalism: Political Activism in Buganda, 1930–1950', *Journal of Religion in Africa*, 39 (2009), 60–90 (pp. 82–5).

[46] Streicher arrived in Buganda in January 1891 after the death of Fr Lourdel in May 1890. He initially worked at Villa Maria mission before serving as superior of the White Father missions in Uganda from 1897 until 1933. Streicher once claimed that 'to get one indigenous priest is to me more important than to convert ten thousand people' (quoted in Waliggo, *Catholic Church in the Buddu Province*, p. 100). On Streicher's pastoral vision, see Aylward Shorter, *Cross and Flag in Africa: The White Fathers during the Colonial Scramble (1892–1914)* (Maryknoll, NY: Orbis, 2006), pp. 49–50, 56–58.

[47] Kollman and Toms Smedley, *Understanding World Christianity*, p. 117; Hastings, *Church in Africa 1450–1950*, p. 571.

[48] Adrian Hastings, 'Ganda Catholic Spirituality', *Journal of Religion in Africa*, 8 (1976), 87; Waliggo, *Catholic Church in Buddu Province*, p. 102; Hastings, *Church in Africa*, p. 565.

[49] Uganda was decades ahead of other Catholic territories in Africa. As late as 1952, there were only seventy African priests in all of French West Africa and thirty-five in the region of French Equatorial Africa (Elizabeth Foster, *African Catholic: Decolonization and the Transformation of the Church* (Cambridge, MA: Harvard University Press, 2019), p. 156).

Kiwanuka's 1939 consecration in Rome: 'If you do well other African Bishops will follow. If you don't, you will be the first and the last.'[50]

As the first Ugandan White Father priest, one of the first two Africans to earn a doctorate in canon law in Rome, and now the first black African bishop in modern times, Joseph Kiwanuka was the most important Catholic leader in colonial Uganda (Figure 1.1). Pastorally, Bishop Kiwanuka was memorably firm; he once required an excommunicated penitent to walk eight miles per day for six months to attend 6 a.m. daily Mass before readmitting him to the Eucharistic table.[51] At the same time, the 'Bishop of Buddu' could be justly described as a proto nation-builder.[52] He served on the Hancock Commission in 1954–55 that helped negotiate *Kabaka* Edward Muteesa II's return from exile in Britain (Chapter 5).[53] Describing his political role in 1947 as 'educator of the nation', Bishop Kiwanuka posited that 'I have discovered that the leadership people want me to exercise in the country is not political as such, but rather leadership of offering good and wise education, which will help our nation and put it on the right track. In such responsibility I can be a leader without necessarily annoying the political rulers'.[54] In addition to starting Bwavumpologoma Cooperative Union in Masaka that later became the foundation for the influential Centenary Bank, Bishop Kiwanuka also challenged cultural taboos against the education of young women and sought scholarships for Muslims and Anglicans alike.[55] All of this helped him develop a reputation as an ecumenical nationalist rather than a Catholic tribalist, although he did

---

[50] Charles M. Kimbowa, 'Archbishop Joseph Kiwanuka as I Knew Him', 21st Archbishop Joseph Kiwanuka Memorial Lecture, 20 June 2013, Kampala, Uganda, p. 6. Even if these comments were apocryphal, Propaganda Fide's formal instructions echoed these sentiments. 'The success of your Vicariate will be considered success for the entire continent of Africa and will be followed by the creation of numerous local churches led by African bishops. While your failure will mean delay in the advancement of the Church in Africa' (quoted in John Mary Waliggo, 'The Life and Legacy of Archbishop Joseph Kiwanuka', 4 June 1989, in John Mary Waliggo, *The Man of Vision: Archbishop J. Kiwanuka* (Kisubi: Marianum, 1991), p. 16).

[51] Kimbowa, 'Archbishop Joseph Kiwanuka as I knew him', p. 11.

[52] Summers, 'Catholic Action and Ugandan Radicalism', p. 66.

[53] D. A. Low, *Buganda in Modern History* (Berkeley: University of California Press, 1971), p. 123. Low in particular credits Bishop Kiwanuka for helping to convince the British to not integrate Buganda into a broader East African federation in the mid-1950s, recognising Buganda's status as a separate 'political nation'.

[54] Quoted in Waliggo, 'Life and Legacy of Archbishop Joseph Kiwanuka', p. 24.

[55] Freddie Ssekitto, *Uganda Martyrs Canonisation: 50 Years After, 1964–2014* (Kisubi: Marianum Press, 2015), p. 14. Margaret Zziwa, 'Archbishop Kiwanuka and the Empowerment of the Girl-Child', 23rd Annual Archbishop Kiwanuka Lecture, Kampala, Uganda, 25 June 2015. This event was attended by Carney.

Figure 1.1 Archbishop Joseph Kiwanuka was the first African Catholic bishop in modern times and one of Benedicto Kiwanuka's mentors. *Benedicto Kiwanuka Papers*.

not hesitate to voice Catholic grievances, especially in the 1956–61 period.[56] The eponymous but unrelated Benedicto Kiwanuka would share a close friendship with the bishop, as well as many of his Catholic and nationalist instincts.

These then were some of the Ganda and missionary Catholic traditions that formed Benedicto Kiwanuka. Born in Buddu, educated by the White Fathers and Mill Hill Missionaries, guided by Uganda's first generation of indigenous priests, and befriended by Comboni missionaries, Kiwanuka reflected the diverse foundations of Catholic experience in Uganda, a diversity that would play out in strikingly divergent political options in the 1950s and 1960s. He brought a devout Catholic commitment into adulthood where he would attend daily Mass and carry around his daily breviary (Figure 1.2).[57] In turn, he shared what Paul Gifford has described as 'the [Ugandan] Catholics' chronic sense of grievance in political matters',[58] an ethos that originated in Buddu and broadened into a national issue as Catholic political representation did not keep up with its demographic growth in colonial Uganda.[59] In the early 1940s, however, new opportunities took Kiwanuka well beyond Buddu and Uganda, vastly altering the life trajectory and cosmopolitan horizons of this *mukopi* commoner.

---

[56] In 1956, Joseph Kiwanuka spoke out against anti-Catholic discrimination, assuring Catholic loyalty to the *kabaka* yet also issuing a veiled threat if Catholic interests were not protected: 'To keep such a number calm was not a minor job. If they decided to become rebels, the entire country would have been disturbed' (Kiwanuka, quoted in Kevin Ward, 'African Nationalism, Christian Democracy and "Communism": The Rise of Sectarian Confessional Politics in Uganda 1952–1962', in *Changing Relations between Churches in Europe and Africa: The Internationalization of Christianity and Politics in the 20th Century*, ed. by Katherina Kunter and Jens Holger Schjorring (Wiesbaden, Germany: Harrassowitz Verlag, 2008), p. 81). We will discuss Kiwanuka's 1961 defence of DP Catholics in Chapter 5.

[57] Ambassador Maurice Kiwanuka, interview with Carney, Kampala, Uganda, 6 July 2017. Breviaries include the morning, evening, and night prayers of the Catholic Liturgy of the Hours. Priests and religious are expected to pray the breviary, but this was a rare devotion for Catholic laity in Kiwanuka's era.

[58] Paul Gifford, *African Christianity: Its Public Role* (Bloomington: Indiana University Press, 1998), p. 117.

[59] By 1949, the colonial annual report recorded that there were 418,457 Protestants and 545,696 Catholics in Buganda ('Annual Reports on the Kingdom of Buganda[,] Eastern Province[,] Western Province[,] [and] Northern Province for the Year ended 31st December, 1949' (Entebbe: Government Printer, 1950), p. 20). Ten years later, the Archdiocese of Rubaga estimated the local Catholic population at 44 per cent and the Protestant population at 33 per cent (RDA 'Rapports Annuel, 1959–60', Missionaries of Africa, Archdiocese of Rubaga, p. 122).

Figure 1.2 Benedicto Kiwanuka with his Catholic missal, c. 1962. *Benedicto Kiwanuka Papers.*

Kiwanuka in Diaspora: The Emergence of a Ganda Catholic Nationalist, 1942–56

After completing three years at St Peter's Nsambya, Benedicto Kiwanuka's secondary education came to a premature end when he ran out of school fees following the death of his father in 1940.[60] Financial insecurity was a constant challenge during his youth, especially in light of his father's spendthrift ways, and worries about money would remain throughout his life.[61] Shortly after leaving St Peter's in 1941, he enlisted in the King's African Rifles, the British colonial regiment based in eastern Africa. Over the next four years, he trained in Kenya and then served in Egypt and Palestine, working first as a warrant officer and clerk before rising to the rank of sergeant major.[62] Like many young African men of his generation, this experience in the war broadened his cultural and intellectual horizons.[63] For example, Kiwanuka's observations of modernised Arab dress in Egypt led him to publicly call for the banning of traditional *kkanzu* dress in Buganda, as he was distraught to find that the *kkanzu* was worn with greater consistency in Buganda than throughout Arab societies, from whence it originated.[64]

Kiwanuka continued to seek ways to expand his education during the war. In particular, he explored correspondence courses in commerce and accounting with the ultimate goal of training as a bookkeeper. He enquired of related institutes in South Africa and Jerusalem before settling on a course in bookkeeping and accounting with the Cairo-based British Institute of Engineering and Technology Near East and the British Institute of Commerce and Accounting. He ultimately earned a diploma in bookkeeping at the end of the war. During his final year in military service, he also

---

[60] This section draws on Jonathon L. Earle, *Colonial Buganda and the End of Empire: Political Thought and Historical Imagination in Africa* (Cambridge: Cambridge University Press, 2017), pp. 198–200.

[61] Kiwanuka's private papers include numerous reports and letters concerning personal debt, which was common among eastern Africa's aspiring public activists. For additional insights into colonial banking practices, see Gareth Austin and Chibuike Ugochukwu Uche, 'Collusion and Competition in Colonial Economies: Banking in British West Africa', *Business History Review*, 81 (2007), 1–26.

[62] BKMKP/Villa Maria O.B. Association/'Appendix B to Gen Order 1100 of 1944', 29 August 1945; 'Bendicto Kagimu Mugumba Kiwanuka: A Martyr of Truth and Justice', p. 2.

[63] For further discussion, see Timothy Parsons, *The African Rank-and-File: Social Implications of Colonial Military Service in the King's African Rifles, 1902–1964* (Portsmouth, NH: Heinemann, 1999).

[64] BKMKP/In Memoriam/B. K. M. Kiwanuka to the Editor of Matalisi Newspaper, 14 May 1944.

enrolled in an additional course in economics while continuing to acquire texts in English and political economy.[65]

After returning to Uganda in 1946, Kiwanuka leveraged his wartime experience and education to secure a job as a clerk and interpreter with the High Court of Uganda in Kampala.[66] Here Kiwanuka revealed what would become a trademark penchant for protesting what he perceived to be unfair financial terms, complaining of the delay in his eligibility for a raise.[67] Whatever his frustrations with his salary, Kiwanuka continued to serve as a clerk with the Uganda High Court until 1950.

In the meantime, he also married. After returning from the war, Kiwanuka relentlessly courted Maxencia Zalwango, a devout Catholic and Munyoro whom he met in Villa Maria. After months of ambivalence, Zalwango agreed to marry him in February 1947, foregoing her own interest in becoming a Catholic nun. Zalwango's Catholic devotion mattered more to Kiwanuka than her Nyoro ethnic identity, and the marriage proceeded despite substantial family opposition to this inter-ethnic union, especially from Kiwanuka's mother.[68] The first of their ten children would be born within a year (Figure 1.3).[69] We will return to the politics of Kiwanuka's marriage in Chapter 5.

His experience on the Uganda High Court furthered Kiwanuka's interest in law. In 1949 he applied for a pre-law liberal arts degree course with the Metropolitan College of Law at St Alban's College in England.[70] He was not

---

[65] A wide array of correspondence on this topic is included in Kiwanuka's personal papers. See BKMKP/Miscellaneous/British Institute of Commerce and Accounting to Kiwanuka, 13 October 1943; Benedicto Kiwanuka to Berlitz School Jerusalem, 23 October 1943; Benedicto Kiwanuka to Director of Studies, Union College South Africa, 6 December 1943; British Institute of Engineering Technology to Benedicto Kiwanuka, 10 April 1944; Benedicto Kiwanuka to British Institute of Engineering and Technology, 20 November 1945.

[66] BKMKP/Miscellaneous/Greenwood to Benedicto Kiwanuka, 22 August 1947.

[67] BKMKP/Miscellaneous/Benedicto Kiwanuka to Chief Secretary Entebbe, 27 November 1947.

[68] Bade, *Benedicto Kiwanuka*, pp. 9–10, 15; Regina Kiwanuka, interview with Carney, Kampala, Uganda, 8 May 2019.

[69] Their children included: Fulgensio Musoke, b. November 1947; Emmanuel Mugumba Kiwanuka, 21 December 1948 – 31 May 2014; Imelda Sylvia Namukundi, b. 23 May 1950; Mary Josephine Nalwoga, b. 18 January 1953; Benedicto Musajjakawa, 19 March 1954 – August 1968; Stephen Mukasa Kakadde, 31 October 1957 – 16 June 1987; Regina Mauricia Nampewo, b. 24 April 1960; Maurice Kagimu Muwanguzi Victor Mwamiakolerwa, b. 22 September 1961; Peter Maximiano Kiwanuka, 24 February 1964 – 24 February 1964; Maxencia Nabizizi, b. April 1967.

[70] BKMKP/Miscellaneous/Benedicto Kiwanuka to Metropolitan College of Law, 31 October 1949.

Figure 1.3 Maxencia Zalwango Kiwanuka; Flugensio Musoke (*kneeling*); Stephen Mukasa (*holding hand*); Imelda (*between Maxencia and Benedicto*); Benedicto Kiwanuka; Josephine (*looking up at Benedicto*), 1960. Maxencia and Benedicto had ten children together. *Benedicto Kiwanuka Papers.*

able to secure a scholarship, however, perhaps due to his Catholic identity.[71] In 1950 Kiwanuka gained enrolment in a pre-law Bachelor of Arts matriculation course at Pius XII Catholic University in Basutoland (modern-day Lesotho).[72] He raised his tuition fees through Catholic networks in and around Masaka. Kiwanuka spent the next two years in southern Africa. In addition to his pre-law liberal studies, he joined an American-based Catholic literary foundation and studied Swahili, even ordering a Swahili version of the Gospel of John.[73] Kiwanuka excelled in his coursework, earning the accolades of Catholic staff in the process. Commending Kiwanuka's plans to pursue a law degree at the University of London, one Pius XII priest framed Kiwanuka's future work in terms of a Catholic vocation to public service: 'But keep on! Africa needs men who shall give her a social and political organisation thoroughly inspired by the message of Our Lord as interpreted by His Vicar on earth, Our Holy Father the Pope'.[74] With such exhortations ringing in his ears, and after receiving generous funding from Catholic prelates such as Archbishop Kiwanuka and Louis J. Cabana, Archbishop of Rubaga, Kiwanuka and his family arrived at the University of London in the fall of 1952 for his long-awaited course in law.

Benedicto Kiwanuka spent the next four years, 1952–56, as a law student in the United Kingdom. He immersed himself in London's standard law curriculum, passing exams in Roman Law, Constitutional Law, Contracts, and the English Legal System.[75] He was also active outside of the classroom. He became secretary of the Uganda Students Association in 1953 and collaborated with the association to staunchly oppose the British Colonial Office's suggestion of a potential East African Federation of Uganda, Kenya, and Tanganyika.[76] He engaged broader anticolonial movements in London, for example by attending the Congress of People Against Imperialism's 'Africa

---

[71] The *katikkiro* overseeing scholarships at the time was Paul Kavuma, a Protestant. This claim of religious bias is made in Risdel Kasasira, 'Ben Kiwanuka: The Chief Justice who died for justice', *Uganda Heroes* 1.1 July 2006 (consulted in 'Bendicto Kagimu Mugumba Kiwanuka', Appendix 31).

[72] BKMKP/Hon the Chief Justice – Ranch Scheme/J.A.N. Kibue Pius XII Catholic University to Kiwanuka, 15 February 1950.

[73] BKMKP/Hon the Chief Justice – Ranch Scheme/Benedicto Kiwanuka to C.M.S. Bookshop Nairobi, 28 March 1951; BKMKP/Confidential 2/Catholic Literary Foundation to Benedicto Kiwanuka, 30 January 1951.

[74] BKMKP/Hon the Chief Justice – Ranch Scheme/Pius XII College Rector to Benedicto Kiwanuka, 5 April 1952. Underscore is Kiwanuka's.

[75] BKMKP/University of London, University of London Special Intermediate Examination in the Faculty of Laws: Roman Law; Constitutional Law; Elements of the Laws of Contract; English Legal System, June 1953.

[76] Bade, *Benedicto Kiwanuka*, p. 22; Samwiri Lwanga Lunyiigo, *A Short History of the Democratic Party 1954–1984* (Rome: Foundation for African Development,

Must Be Free' conference in September 1953.[77] Kiwanuka also became close with *Kabaka* Edward Muteesa II during the latter's exile in London between 1953 and 1955, serving as a 'house helper' and accompanying the *kabaka* on holiday to Spain.[78] Ironically in light of his later anti-monarchical reputation, Kiwanuka fervently supported the *kabaka*'s return to Buganda, once penning a 1954 editorial to the London-based *Catholic Herald* in which he protested a British female settler's opposition to independence for Buganda. Arguing that white settlers were foreigners in Buganda, he questioned this settler's right to insert her voice in Buganda's political debates. Drawing directly on the Gospel of Mark, Kiwanuka angrily wrote, 'She should understand [that] she has less title to such rights than that of the devils who cried out in rage in Carpharnaum [sic] of Galilee'.[79] Rumours of Kiwanuka's political activism rose to such a fever pitch that Ganda Catholic seminarians were banned from exchanging correspondence with him and other allegedly 'communist' Ugandan students in London.[80]

This debate over Kiwanuka's purported 'communist' sympathies offers a revealing insight into how he reconciled his identities as both a devout Catholic and a Ugandan nationalist. In a blistering August 1953 letter that he also copied to Bishop Kiwanuka and Archbishop Cabana, Kiwanuka rhetorically asked his interlocutor, the rector of St Thomas seminary in Katigondo, if he was a 'missionary come to Africa to preach the Gospel of the Lord – the Brotherhood of Man? – or a political agent to suppress nationalism'?[81] Kiwanuka went on to demand that Catholic missionaries should distinguish between nationalism and communism, arguing that a young African could remain a loyal Catholic while opposing European colonialism.[82]

1984), p. 31. This volume was initially published under the pseudonym Richard Muscat and later republished under Lwanga Lunyiigo's name in 2015.

[77] BKMKP/Loose Papers/Congress of Peoples Against Imperialism British Centre, 'Africa Must be Free Conference', 26–27 September 1953.

[78] 'Bendicto Kagimu Mugumba Kiwanuka: A Martyr of Truth and Justice', p. 4.

[79] BKMKP/Villa Maria O.B. Association/Benedicto Kiwanuka to Editor of *Catholic Herald*, 27 February 1954. The language here draws on Mark 1:23–27 where Jesus expelled demons from a man with an unclean spirit in a Capernaum synagogue.

[80] BKMKP/Govt House Copies of Minutes/Benedicto Kiwanuka to Archbishop Cabana, 4 October 1953.

[81] BKMKP/Govt House Copies of Minutes/Benedicto Kiwanuka to Rector of St Thomas Aquinas National Seminary Katigondo, 17 August 1953.

[82] Catholic African nationalists faced similar tensions in other parts of the continent. For example, in Senegal, Léopold Senghor offered very similar critiques of French missionaries for failing to distinguish between their colonial and Catholic loyalties and falsely invoking anti-communist discourse to keep Africans in their place (Foster, *African Catholic*, p. 22).

If I say I do not like Europeans, am I not as an individual entitled to hold this opinion just because I am a Catholic? And does that in fact make me a Communist? Was it so ordained by Our Lord that we, the Africans, shall be under foreign domination forever? [...] What has the European done to the African in South Africa? What has he done to him in Southern Rhodesia? What in Kenya?[83]

When the rector failed to respond to Kiwanuka, Kiwanuka wrote an even angrier diatribe to Cabana, a White Father himself. Here he lamented that 'this loose, idle and irresponsible talk about Africans (in general) now endemic among ministers of religion (of European origin) will do irreparable damage to our religion in Africa if not checked in time', demanding that the Archbishop remove the rector from his position and allow the 'inmates of Katigondo' to receive mail from expatriate Ugandan students.[84] Kiwanuka even threatened to leave the Catholic Church over the dispute: 'I shall choose to be so excommunicated rather than to remain in the Church if the view of the Rev. Father Superior of Katigondo in this matter are a part of what constitutes the Catholic faith'.[85] Kiwanuka also reflected here his growing sense of cosmopolitan identity, arguing that Ganda students should not be kept home in Buganda for fear that they would lose their faith in diaspora.

Unlike his Ganda contemporary Semakula Mulumba, erstwhile former Catholic brother turned anti-clerical political activist in London (Chapter 5), Kiwanuka did not leave the Catholic Church.[86] In fact, while at the University of London, Kiwanuka ordered a Miraculous Medal and connected with the Legion of Mary and the Catholic Newman Society.[87] He spent the summer of 1953 reading *Apologia Pro Vita Sua*, the intellectual and religious autobiography of the nineteenth-century English Catholic convert John Henry

---

[83] BKMKP/Govt House Copies of Minutes/Benedicto Kiwanuka to Rector of St Thomas Aquinas National Seminary Katigondo, 17 August 1953.

[84] BKMKP/Govt House Copies of Minutes/Benedicto Kiwanuka to Archbishop Cabana, 4 October 1953.

[85] Ibid.

[86] On the reverberations of Mulumba's decision to leave the Church within 1950s Catholic circles, see Ward, 'African Nationalism, Christian Democracy and 'Communism', p. 76. We discuss Mulumba's views in detail in Chapter 5.

[87] BKMKP/Villa Maria O.B. Association/Barclays Bank to Benedicto Kiwanuka, 26 June 1953; BKMKP/University of London, Legion of Mary & Catholic International Club, 16 May 1953; BKMKP/University of London, Newman Association International Committee, 7 November 1953. A common twentieth-century Catholic devotional practice, miraculous medal traditions originated with alleged revelations of the Virgin Mary to the French sister St Catherine Labouré in 1830.

Newman.[88] For Kiwanuka, Newman was most helpful as a prophetic Catholic voice of truth within an Anglican-dominated British state – a persona that fit Kiwanuka's own personality and would embody his public reputation by the late 1950s. Dated to June 1953, Kiwanuka's annotated notes on Newman's *Apologia Pro Vita* are quite revealing in this regard. Here Kiwanuka showed particular interest in Newman's understanding of papal infallibility and the way in which Newman connected infallibility with the 'power of excommunication' and the 'responsibility to confront great social evil'.[89] Kiwanuka was especially struck with Newman's reflections on 'lying and equivocation', writing 'I agree' next to Newman's claim that 'the first of virtues is to tell the truth and shame the devil,' and that 'silence is also absolutely forbidden to a Catholic, as a mortal sin [...] when it is a duty to make a profession of faith'.[90] For Kiwanuka, as for Newman, 'veracity is for the sake of society'. Earlier in the document Kiwanuka also underlined a similar passage emphasising the importance of conviction over compromise:

> I wished men to agree with me, and I walked with them step by step, as far as they would go; this I did sincerely; but if they would stop, I did not much care about it, but walked on, with some satisfaction that I had brought them so far.[91]

For Kiwanuka, speaking truth to power was the pearl of great price; compromising one's convictions for the sake of a political deal was morally reprehensible. For better and for worse, he would carry such unbending convictions into the fervent debates that marked Uganda's transition into independence between 1958 and 1962.

---

[88] Newman had been a prominent member of the Anglican Oxford Movement in the 1830s–40s that looked to reconnect the Anglican church with older patristic and medieval currents of the Christian tradition. He ultimately chose to convert to Roman Catholicism in 1844 and was later named a bishop and cardinal. Suspicious of ultramontane arguments for absolute papal authority, Newman was a reluctant supporter of the First Vatican Council's (1869–70) formal definition of papal infallibility. His embracing of the 'development of doctrine' has been cited as an important precursor of the Second Vatican Council's (1962–65) acceptance of modern innovations like religious freedom.

[89] BKMKP/Library/Newman, *Apologia Pro Vita Sua*, p. 168, annotation.

[90] Ibid., p. 225, annotation.

[91] Ibid., p. 29, annotation. This passage approximates Kiwanuka's attitude at the 1961 London conference in which he refused to compromise on the principle of direct elections for Buganda, sealing the KY/UPC alliance that would prove his political undoing.

The Birth of Uganda's Democratic Party in Global Catholic Context

As Kiwanuka's London studies and accompanying political activism came to a close, Catholics were also mobilising back home in Uganda. The Democratic Party (DP) was founded in October 1954 in part to serve as a vehicle for representing the interests of Buganda's politically marginalised Catholics. Catholics were not well represented in the leadership circles of Uganda's first national political party, the Uganda National Congress (UNC), founded in 1952. For example, in 1956 only one member of UNC's central organising committee was a Roman Catholic.[92] The need for a political movement that would represent Catholics was brought home by the closely contested 1955 *katikkiro* (prime minister) election, in which the Mmengo establishment refused to countenance the appointment of Matayo Mugwanya, the former *omulamuzi* (chief justice) of Buganda.[93] In a narrow *Lukiiko* (Buganda Parliament) vote, the Anglican Mikaeri Kintu was chosen instead.

In the telling words of the Protestant newspaper *Uganda Post*, 'God helped the public because there might have been throwing of stones had Mr. Kavuma or Mr. Mugwanya been elected Katikiro.'[94] For Catholic DP activists, this decision echoed the sidelining of Mugwanya's grandfather, Stanislaus Mugwanya, in 1920.[95] Elected to represent Mawokoto county in the *Lukiiko* in July 1956, Matayo Mugwanya's election was not confirmed by *Kabaka* Edward Muteesa II or the Mmengo government. Shortly thereafter, Mugwanya was banned from serving in the *Lukiiko* on the nebulous grounds that he had accepted a position with the Transport Advisory Council of the East African High Commission. Despite public protests and the support of a rival political party and the editors

---

[92] 'Faith & Party', *Uganda Argus*, 12 October 1956.
[93] On this controversial election and its galvanising effect on Catholic political mobilisation, see T. V. Sathyamurthy, *The Political Development of Uganda: 1900–1986* (Brookfield, VT: Gower, 1986), p. 371; Ward, 'African Nationalism, Christian Democracy and 'Communism', pp. 80–81; Fred B. Welbourn, *Religion and Politics in Uganda 1952–1962* (Nairobi: East Africa Publishing House, 1965), p. 18.
[94] Uganda Information Department, Summary of the Local Press No. 1019, *Uganda Post*, 26 August 1955. A Catholic, Joseph Kavuma was the first president of DP from 1954 to 1956.
[95] Stanislaus Mugwanya had served as Catholic *katikkiro* alongside the Protestant *katikkiro*, Apolo Kaggwa, from 1893 until the 1900 Buganda Agreement made Kaggwa sole *katikkiro*. Mugwanya continued to serve as *omulamuzi* (chief justice) until he resigned in 1920 to protest what he perceived as Kaggwa's nepotism in a judicial case. This trajectory of discrimination from 'Mugwanya to Mugwanya' is a central historical theme in Benedicto Kiwanuka's own analysis of Ganda political history (RDA 904.4, Benedicto Kiwanuka, 'Uganda Elections – 1962', pp. 2–3).

of *Uganda Argus*, Mugwanya was not allowed to take his seat.[96] He filed a court motion in early 1957 in which he was represented by none other than Benedicto Kiwanuka. Arguing before the High Court, Kiwanuka framed the Mugwanya case as emblematic of a broader struggle between democracy and monarchy. 'Before a man has even been duly elected, no man in this country has any power to refuse him to be appointed a member of the Lukiko, not even the Kabaka.'[97] Although Mugwanya was awarded damages in this case, the *Lukiiko* did not relent throughout 1957, and Mugwanya never assumed his seat.[98]

Convinced that they would never get a fair hearing in the Protestant-dominated Mmengo establishment, Catholic elites looked to form their own movement to represent their own political interests in Buganda and across the Uganda Protectorate. Mugwanya was elected DP president-general in August 1956. In his opening speech as leader, Mugwanya explicitly framed DP as a national, non-sectarian party, denying it was a 'Catholic party', positing that DP stood for 'equal human and political rights for all sections of the community of the Protectorate', and claiming that it had '10,000 members of all tribes and creeds'.[99] Mugwanya's rhetoric demonstrates that the 'religious party' language was more often lobbed against DP than invoked by its own members. Writing in the *Uganda Argus* shortly after DP's public launch, editors and readers, including I. K. Musazi, castigated the 'move to create religious political parties', the 'formation of parties based on tribe and religion', and, in Musazi's words, 'their attempts to build little States within our State'.[100] In contrast, Catholic writers protested that DP was not a 'Catholic party', while also defending the role of religion in public life.[101] There was also something of a double standard at work here. Even though UNC, Uganda's first

---

[96] On the Mugwanya *Lukiiko* dispute, see 'Katikiro's Statement on barred member: Electors will lose', *Uganda Argus*, 19 December 1956; 'Progressives attack action of Lukiko', *Uganda Argus*, 25 December 1956; 'Democratic' Editorial, *Uganda Argus*, 29 December 1956; 'Broadcast by Katikiro – Do not attend meeting of Democratic Party', *Uganda Argus*, 29 December 1956; 'Party Man Attacks action of Lukiko', *Uganda Argus*, 31 December 1956.

[97] 'Court Action against Katikiro in Kampala', *Uganda Argus*, 15 February 1957. The court ultimately awarded Mugwanya damages in this case.

[98] 'Lukiko's Rejection of Mugwanya attacked by Democratic Party', *Uganda Argus*, 6 May 1957.

[99] 'New Political Party Formed in Uganda', *Uganda Argus*, 21 August 1956. For background on DP's founding, see Lwanga Lunyiigo, *A Short History of the Democratic Party*, pp. 24–26.

[100] See *Uganda Argus*: 'Religion and Politics', 8 October 1956; 'Religion and Politics', 11 October 1956; 'Faith and Party' (UA Editorial), 12 October 1956; 'Mr Musazi on politics and religion', 23 November 1956.

[101] See the letters to the editor from H. L. Acanga and J. Kasule (first DP president),

political party, was dominated by Protestants, it was rarely if ever tagged as a 'Protestant party'. In turn, for DP activists, the discourse of political secularism masked continuing Protestant hegemony and deep-seated opposition to the empowerment of Catholics in Uganda's public space. For example, supposedly non-sectarian moves such as *Kabaka* Muteesa's 1957 proposal to stop using religious identity as a basis for the appointment of chiefs masked the continued disenfranchisement of Catholics for political leadership and educational scholarships.[102]

Nor did the Catholic angle exhaust DP's political platform. Described in British intelligence reports as a 'moderate political party', DP goals also included imminent self-government, fighting against both the East African Federation and Communist ideology, preserving Ugandan cultural and royal traditions, and, in a line straight out of Thomistic natural law theory, respecting the 'Universal Natural Code'.[103] It should be noted that DP leaders made early overtures to Anglican leaders about forming a 'joint Christian party', but Anglican Archbishop Leslie Brown resisted this idea on the grounds that 'the Church should not support any political party'.[104]

In envisioning a joint Christian party, DP fit squarely within the rise of Christian Democracy political movements in post-war Europe and beyond. European Christian Democracy parties were generally centre-right in their politics, pro-capitalist if not libertarian, anti-communist, and committed to 'promote Christian principles in politics'.[105] The 1950s were a veritable gold mine for Christian Democracy in Western Europe. Prominent Catholic leaders such as West Germany's Konrad Adenauer, France's Robert Schumann, and Italy's

---

respectively (*Uganda Argus*: 'Religion and Politics', 11 October 1956; 'Religion and Politics', 29 October 1956).

[102] 'Buddu protest on Kabaka's address', *Uganda Argus*, 11 December 1957. Three hundred Catholics showed up at this public gathering to oppose *Kabaka* Muteesa's announcement that religious identity would no longer be considered in the appointment of chiefs.

[103] BNA CO 822–858, 'Extracts from Uganda Monthly Intelligence Appreciation', 29 February 1956. The anti-communist angle remained a redeeming feature of DP's Catholic identity among British colonial officials, whatever their personal distaste for Kiwanuka: 'Mr. Kiwanuka, as leader of a predominantly Catholic party, is not thinking of help from behind the Iron Curtain' (Sir Leslie Monson, quoted in Gardner Thompson, *African Democracy: Its Origins and Development in Uganda, Kenya, and Tanzania* (Kampala: Fountain, 2015), p. 132).

[104] Kathleen Lockard, 'Religion and Political Development in Uganda, 1962–72', unpublished PhD thesis, University of Wisconsin-Madison, 1974, p. 39; Welbourn, *Religion and Politics in Uganda*, p. 18.

[105] Owen Chadwick, *The Christian Church in the Cold War* (London: Penguin, 1992), p. 10.

Alcide De Gasperi stood at the forefront of post-war European reconstruction; the relationship between Schumann and Adenauer was critical to the political reconciliation embodied in the early vision for the European Community.[106] These movements also reflected broader European Catholic efforts to imagine new transnational possibilities for post-war European union.[107] Nor were such movements confined to Europe. In Chile, Eduardo Frei's Christian Democracy party came to power in 1964,[108] seeming to herald a 'new Christendom' where Catholic actors could shape the common good through implicit Christian principles rather than through the earlier twentieth-century 'Catholic party' approach of serving as the political wing of the institutional church.[109]

Uganda's DP shared this approach as a broadly nationalist party dominated by Catholics but resistant to adopting any explicitly 'Catholic' label. Kiwanuka would also cultivate relationships with Christian Democracy movements in Europe, for example by seeking logistical support and political endorsement from West Germany's Christian Democratic Union (CDU) party and the Netherlands' *Katholieke Volkspartij* (Catholic People's Party).[110] But if

---

[106] Ian Linden, *Global Catholicism: Towards a Networked Church* (London: Hurst, 2012), p. 29.

[107] As an emerging body of scholarship has begun to show, the idea of a unified Christendom in post-war Europe evoked extensive debates about the connections between 'Western' and 'spiritual' discourse and the formation of the European Economic Community, whose treaty was negotiated in Rome in 1957 (Philip Coupland, 'Western Union, "Spiritual Union," and European Integration, 1948–1964', *Journal of British Studies*, 43 (2004), 366–94; Wolfram Kaiser, *Christian Democracy and the Origins of the European Union* (Cambridge: Cambridge University Press, 2007); Mark Royce, *The Political Theology of European Integration: Comparing the Influence of Religious Histories on European Politics* (Basingstoke: Palgrave Macmillian, 2017).

[108] William T. Cavanaugh, *Torture and Eucharist: Theology, Politics, and the Body of Christ* (Oxford: Blackwell, 1998), p. 197. See also Jeffrey Klaiber, *The Church, Dictatorships, and Democracy in Latin America* (Maryknoll, NY: Orbis, 1998), pp. 17–18.

[109] On the Catholic political precursors to Christian Democracy, see Tom Buchanan and Martin Conway, eds, *Political Catholicism in Europe, 1918–1965* (Oxford: Clarendon, 1996); Wolfram Kaiser and Helmut Wohnout, eds, *Political Catholicism in Europe 1918–45* (New York: Routledge, 2004); Gerd-Rainer Horn, *Western European Liberation Theology: The First Wave (1924–1959)* (Oxford: Oxford University Press, 2008); Carolyn M. Warner, *Confessions of an Interest Group: The Catholic Church and Political Parties in Europe* (Princeton, NJ: Princeton University Press, 2000).

[110] BNA CO 822-2119 1960 Kiwanuka DP, 'From Bonn to (British) Foreign Office', 2 November 1960; 'From (British) Foreign Office to Bonn', 3 November 1960; BKMKP/Personal Correspondence/G. Gielen, Foreign Section, *Katholieke Volkspartu* to B. K. M. Kiwanuka, 21 May 1960.

Kiwanuka was not looking to institute a theocracy or Catholic state constitution, he saw in Catholicism the possibility of envisioning political solidarity during a moment of social rupture. As we will see, Kiwanuka's catholicity also extended to him an analytic framework within which he could begin to conceptualise the integration of varying communities with competing pasts and political interests.

The Democratic Party also originated at the apogee of the influence of Catholic Action in global Catholicism. Started by Pope Pius XI in the early 1920s to help counter reactionary neo-fascist movements like *Action Française*, Catholic Action was committed to establishing the 'social reign of Christ' in the modern world through a 'see-judge-act' methodology that emphasised both social analysis and lay activism.[111] After the collapse of the 'Catholic Party' movements of the early twentieth century and interwar periods, Catholic Action embraced an apolitical but 'social' Catholicism that, in the words of William T. Cavanaugh, aimed to 'resist the privatization of religion in bourgeois societies and to disentangle the church from its dysfunctional relationships with party politics'.[112] Movements such as the Belgian priest Joseph Cardijn's *Jeunesse Ouvrière Chrétienne* (JOC) developed strong corollaries in African colonies like Rwanda and the Belgian Congo.[113]

Already in the early 1930s, Catholic Action was established across Uganda. In Buganda, Catholic Action began as *Ekitebe kyaBakaiso*, or the Uganda Martyrs Guild, and was later called *Enkola Enkatolike*.[114] By the 1950s Buganda boasted of multiple Catholic Action movements such as Young Christian Workers, Young Christian Students, and Young Christian Farmers. As Carol Summers and Alison Fitchett Climenhaga have argued, Ganda branches initially steered clear of sociopolitical questions, emphasising rather issues surrounding marriage, family, sacramental participation, and education.[115] During the same years that DP was initially organising, however, Catholic Action's focus also shifted toward defending Catholic interests in society and

---

[111] Linden, *Global Catholicism*, p. 21.

[112] Cavanaugh, *Torture and Eucharist*, p. 138.

[113] J. J. Carney, *Rwanda Before the Genocide: Catholic Politics and Ethnic Discourse in the Late Colonial Era* (New York: Oxford University Press, 2014), p. 54.

[114] Alison Fitchett Climenhaga, '"I want to be a convinced and influential Catholic": Catholic Action and Church-society relations in Uganda, 1930–1990', pp. 1, 3. Unpublished paper, American Catholic Historical Association conference, New York, NY, January 2020; Summers, 'Catholic Action and Ugandan Radicalism', p. 63.

[115] Summers, 'Catholic Action and Ugandan Radicalism', p. 74; Fitchett Climenhaga, 'I want to be a convinced and influential Catholic', p. 5. Summers notes that Catholic dissidents involved in the *Bataka* movement of 1945–49 borrowed from both Catholic Action's structure and principles (pp. 83–84).

later to nation-building itself, encouraging Catholics to 'spread Catholic influence on non-Catholics in the workplace, to seek Catholic influence in the civic and political sphere'.[116] The Canadian White Father Yves Tourigny was especially involved in mobilising lay movements in 1950s Buganda. He initiated the establishment of the Uganda Social Training Center at Rubaga, organised a Lay Apostolate Council in every diocese, and oversaw the All-Africa Leaders' Meeting of the Lay Apostolate (1953) and the follow-up All-Uganda Lay Leaders Meeting (1957), both hosted at Kisubi Seminary near Entebbe. These gatherings preceded Vatican II's 'turn to the laity' by a decade, focusing on issues ranging from education, women, and family to labour rights and rural development.[117] It should be noted that Benedicto Kiwanuka was involved in this lay empowerment movement and served in lay leadership in the Archdiocese of Rubaga (later Kampala) before he became prime minister in 1961.[118] Catholic Action groups were even more extensive in northern Uganda where future UPC stalwart Felix Onama briefly led the movement.[119] It was also in northern Uganda that Comboni Father Agostoni started the magazine *Leadership* to circulate the core ideas of Catholic Action, planting seeds that the DP movement would build on by the late 1950s.

The Gospel of Democracy

After finishing his law degree in 1956, Kiwanuka returned to a Buganda that had only five attorneys in private practice.[120] He set up Kiwanuka and Company Associates in downtown Kampala and spent the next two years in private practice. The lure of politics was never far away, however, and in 1958 Kiwanuka formally joined DP, claiming later that it was the only party that any 'decent man' could support in the late 1950s.[121] The Democratic Party was beginning to make inroads in Buganda, securing the largest number of delegates in *Lukiiko* elections after refusing *Kabaka* Muteesa's call for a boycott.[122]

---

[116] Diocese of Masaka, 1953 Bakaiso Report, quoted in Fitchett Climenhaga, 'I want to be a convinced and influential Catholic', p. 8.

[117] Tourigny, *So Abundant a Harvest*, pp. 161–2; Kollman and Toms Smedley, *Understanding World Christianity*, p. 71.

[118] Samwiri Lwanga Lunyiigo, interview with Carney, Kisubi, Uganda, 29 September 2018.

[119] Lockard, 'Religion and Political Development', p. 280.

[120] L. A. Fallers, 'The Modernization of Social Stratification', in *The King's Men: Leadership and Status in Buganda on the Eve of Independence*, ed. L. A. Fallers (London: Oxford University Press, 1964), pp. 117–57 (p. 140).

[121] RDA 904.4 Benedicto Kiwanuka, 'Uganda Elections – 1962', p. 4.

[122] Sathyamurthy, *Political Development*, p. 374. Kiwanuka himself was elected to

Yet the party was restless for new leadership. The DP founder and president Matayo Mugwanya hailed from an older generation, and he had never been allowed to take a seat in the *Lukiiko* after winning a 1956 by-election from Mawokota county.[123] In balloting for new leadership at the DP annual conference in August 1958, Kiwanuka was elected secretary-general, or president, of the party with over 100 votes, outpolling his nearest challenger by forty-five votes.[124] Kiwanuka's tenure as DP president got off to a rocky start as his party was significantly outpolled by the Uganda National Congress (UNC) in Uganda's first Legislative Council (Legco) elections in October 1958.[125] Despite this setback, he began to place his stamp upon the party by countering its reputation as a sectarian Catholic group and reframing DP as an anticolonial nationalist party committed to the uplift of the common peasants (*bakopi*) under the guiding principles of truth and justice.

First, moving away from its 'moderate' mid-1950s roots, DP embraced a more antagonistic, anticolonial nationalism after Kiwanuka came to power. This began with the expulsion of Mugwanya from his leadership position in the party after he had joined the Legco as a colonial government backbencher in 1958.[126] Shortly thereafter, DP refused to participate in ceremonies associated with the British Queen Mother's 1959 visit to Uganda, and expressed its support for the Asian trade boycott in Buganda. Along with DP's repeated demands for the Africanisation of the civil service, Kiwanuka opposed special representatives for Asians and Europeans on the Legislative Council as well as the appointment of the Indian Amar Maini as government minister for commerce and industry. In Kiwanuka's words, 'we will not in future take part in any Government in which there is an Asian as a minister. Seeds must be sown now which will make Uganda a purely African state, that is to say politically

---

the *Lukiiko* to represent Buddu county in 1959 ('Bendicto Kagimu Mugumba Kiwanuka: A Martyr of Truth and Justice,' p. 4). Unlike Mugwanya, he was allowed to take his seat.

[123] Lwanga Lunyiigo, *Short History*, pp. 24–25.

[124] BKMKP/Misc Confidential/Democratic Party General Meeting Minutes, August 1958.

[125] The 1958 elections were the first direct elections for African members of the Legco. UNC won five of the ten contested seats, independents took four seats, and DP won a single seat in West Nile. DP lost narrowly to UNC in Kigezi, Bukedi and Acholiland ('National Congress Success at Polls', *Uganda Argus*, 27 October 1958).

[126] BKMKP/Confidential 2/Benedicto Kiwanuka Press Release Statement, 21 November 1958; BKMKP/Om A. Sebaggala e Gulama/'DP Officials Turning Backbenchers', Democratic Party Branch Eastern Headquarters to Benedicto Kiwanuka, 16 November 1959.

African'.[127] The Democratic Party also came out against voting rights for Asian and European residents, arguing that 'it was impossible to fight imperialists with imperialists in your ranks'.[128] Not surprisingly, Kiwanuka's political rhetoric took on an increasingly revolutionary tone, as expressed in DP's April 1960 election manifesto, 'Forward to Freedom'.

> For the last 70 years or so we have been subjected to so much oppression, suppression, exploitation, and indignities of all kinds that our capacity for taking more has been exhausted [...] Let us, therefore, join in this great struggle for freedom. Divided we shall lose; but together, like the 13 American Colonies and the People of France, we shall win without a doubt.[129]

Second, the DP anticolonial nationalism in Buganda entailed an intentional downplaying of any explicitly Catholic identity, countering Protestant stereotypes of DP as *'Dini Ya Papa'*, as noted, Swahili for 'Religion of the Pope'.[130] Toward this end, Kiwanuka reached out to the Protestant-dominated Progressive Party in late 1958 and early 1959, acceding to influential Anglican minister and political commentator Fred Welbourn's entreaties that a merger would restore the intra-Christian unity of the 1880s martyrs and 'save Buganda from mere tribalism [and] make possible independence for Uganda as a whole'.[131] He also expanded DP leadership in 1958–59 to include both Muslims and Protestants.[132] This included recruiting two notable Protestants: William S. Kajubi, then an instructor at King's College, Budo, and Enoch E. K. Mulira, the brother of the prominent Protestant intellectual

---

[127] BKMKP/Cuttings 1972/Democratic Party Statement, 11 February 1959.

[128] 'Democratic Party to build HQ in Kampala', *Uganda Argus*, 6 November 1959. Despite this rhetoric, Kiwanuka and DP continued to assure non-Africans that their civil rights would be protected in an independent Uganda ('Barrister to help Uganda to self-rule', *Uganda Argus*, 11 August 1959).

[129] ICS PP.UG.DP.39 'Forward to Freedom: Being the Manifesto of the Democratic Party', 11 April 1960, pp. 1–2.

[130] Welbourn, *Religion and Politics in Uganda*, p. 1.

[131] BKMKP/Loose Papers/F. B. Welbourn to Benedicto Kiwanuka, 9 February 1959; BKMKP/Confidential 2/BKM Kiwanuka, 'Statement', 21 November 1958.

[132] Michael Twaddle, 'Was the Democratic Party of Uganda a purely confessional party?' in *Christianity in Independent Africa*, ed. by Edward Fasholé-Luke, Richard Gray, Adrian Hastings, Godwin Tasie (London: Rex Collins, 1978), pp. 255–66. Even before the founding of DP, Kiwanuka in 1953 had encouraged organisers to 'get as many pagan, Muslim and Christian supporters together as possible' (Lwanga Lunyiigo, *Short History*, p. 19). He also publicly highlighted the presence of a Muslim on DP's central executive committee ('Democratic party 'not religious body'", *Uganda Argus*, 3 October 1959).

Eridadi M. K. Mulira.[133] Furthermore, DP ran over twice as many Protestant candidates in 1961 legislative elections as UPC did Catholic candidates, and, during DP's brief year in power, four of the nine government portfolios were held by non-Catholics.[134] Kiwanuka also continued DP's growth into a truly national party whose electoral base extended far beyond its Buganda roots. As the next three chapters explore in greater detail, the party developed strong branches in Teso, Toro, Bunyoro, Kigezi, Acholiland, and Ankole, helping it to compete nationwide.

Finally, far from emphasising 'political denominationalism' or an identity politics of empowering Catholics *qua* Catholics,[135] Kiwanuka called for the broader empowerment of the common people according to DP principles of truth, justice, democratisation, and human rights. Kiwanuka confessed that he was an 'ardent' Catholic, but 'I am not a bigot. I cherish Christian principles because I am convinced that they are the best for human society [...] Let us suffice to say that our principles in the Democratic Party are based on the idea of tolerance and fair play.'[136] Kiwanuka continued to pray at the 1959 DP annual conference that 'our Blessed Lord give us His guidance in our deliberations', but Christ's guidance was now sought to support DP's own version of the four freedoms: 'freedom of worship, freedom of movement, freedom of speech, and above all freedom of thought'.[137] In turn, DP's primary policy goals focused on universal aspirations – especially for rural *bakopi* – rather than interests unique to Catholics. These included free primary education, industrialisation, agricultural development, the raising of coffee prices, road and infrastructural development, more private sector loans, and respect for private property rights.[138] While the patriarchal priorities of the 1950s often dominated party

---

[133] William S. Kajubi, interviews with Earle, Kampala, 2 December 2009, 17 February 2010.

[134] Lockard, 'Religion and Political Development in Uganda', p. 41; Lwanga Lunyiigo, *Short History*, p. 40. In the 1961 elections, fifty-nine DP candidates were Catholic and thirteen were Protestant. In contrast, only five Catholic candidates stood for UPC, which had formed in March 1960 from the anti-Baganda Uganda People's Union (UPU) and Obote's non-Baganda wing of the Uganda National Congress (UNC) (Giovanni Carbone, *No-Party Democracy? Ugandan Politics in Comparative Perspective* (Boulder, CO: Lynne Rienner, 2008), p. 13).

[135] The phrase is taken from Thompson, *African Democracy*, p. 96.

[136] RDA 904.4 Benedicto Kiwanuka, 'Uganda Elections – 1962', p. 42.

[137] BKMKP/Uganda Versus/Benedicto Kiwanuka, 'DP Presidential Address 1959', 7 August 1959. Here Kiwanuka referenced the famous 'four freedoms' speech of Franklin D. Roosevelt in his 1941 State of the Union address.

[138] BKMKP/Not Marked 5/'Democratic Party 13-point Programme of Priorities from Our Manifesto', 1 December 1960. For further detail, see ICS PP.UG.DP.39 'Democratic Party Manifesto: Forward to Freedom', 11 April 1960.

politics (Chapter 5), DP's manifesto included women's empowerment, including female voting rights, property inheritance, and expanded higher education, sparking criticisms that the party was encouraging a disruptive gender egalitarianism in both the public and private spheres.[139] In sum, for Kiwanuka,

> A Party cannot survive on one religion alone in a country such as ours; and besides, it is not good to base one's political thought on one's religion because, once this is done, the person concerned will not stop there but will cultivate a tendency to religious intolerance. The Party's motto was 'Truth and Justice' and religious intolerance was incompatible with our principles.[140]

If anything, Kiwanuka's and DP's evangelical zeal was transposed from propagating the Catholic faith to advocating for democratisation. For Kiwanuka, all major political decisions should be subject to direct voting, whether federal versus unitary government, the composition of the head of state, or, most controversially, elections for Buganda's representatives to the National Legislature.[141] Commitment to direct elections was a 'cardinal principle in a democracy', equivalent for Kiwanuka to a theological dogma such as Christ's divinity, as he expressed in a series of letters with Anglican Archbishop of Canterbury Geoffrey Fisher in October 1961 (Chapter 6).[142] Kiwanuka's commitment to genuine democratisation was also one of the primary reasons that he continued to reject communism and financial support from the USSR and China.[143] In turn, he feared for the future of democracy 'if after the next General Election another Party which is not this one got into power here'.[144] If Ghana's Kwame Nkrumah famously encouraged his followers to 'seek ye first the political kingdom',[145] Kiwanuka's political

---

[139] Man'gwe Akwacha 'You cannot have two masters in one home', *Uganda Argus*, 27 December 1961.

[140] RDA 904.4 Benedicto Kiwanuka, 'Uganda Elections – 1962', p. 4.

[141] Kiwanuka lays out his views on the debate between a federal and unitary state in BKMKP/Unmarked 5/'Views on Forms of Government and Head of State', 11 April 1960.

[142] BKMKP/Federal Status/Benedicto Kiwanuka to Archbishop Fisher, 2–10 October 1961. Kiwanuka kept several copies of this correspondence in his personal records, likely reflecting his deep-seated fears of an international Anglican conspiracy. Publicly, he pinpointed Fisher's intervention as a key turning point in the London negotiations (see RDA 904.4 Benedicto Kiwanuka, 'Uganda Elections – 1962', pp. 9–18).

[143] BKMKP/Uganda Versus/Benedicto Kiwanuka, 'DP Presidential Address 1959', 7 August 1959.

[144] BKMKP/Confidential 1/Benedicto Kiwanuka, 'Presidential Address', 20 August 1960.

[145] Quoted in Adrian Hastings, *A History of African Christianity 1950–1975* (Cambridge: Cambridge University Press, 1979), p. 86.

theology ultimately revolved around the 'sacred' ideals of popular sovereignty and national self-determination. Drawing from the Sermon on the Mount (Matthew 5:1–12), the DP manifesto 'Forward to Freedom' captured this transposed religious-cum-political discourse: 'BLESSED ARE THEY WHO STRUGGLE AND TOIL FOR THE SAKE OF SELF-GOVERNMENT FOR THEY WILL HAVE EVERLASTING SELF-SATISFACTION IN A SELF-GOVERNING UGANDA.'[146]

Such language reminds us that while Kiwanuka and DP marketed themselves as non-sectarian, religious symbolism was deeply interwoven within their ostensibly secular gospel of democracy. One sees this intermixing most prominently in the party's symbol. In 1959, the Comboni missionary, Fr Tarcisio Agostoni, convinced Kiwanuka to use the iconography of the Catholic Missal to develop the party symbols of DP. Agostoni envisioned the DP symbol as a sun with rays shining across Uganda, emblazoned over the initials T and J for 'Truth' and 'Justice' (Figure 1.4). Again echoing the Sermon on the Mount – this time Matthew 5:45 – Agostoni argued that the symbol of the sun reflected the egalitarian ethos of DP: 'The sun is equal for all; it rises for all and sets down for all.'[147] Likewise, the sun is the key to the growth of crops and the blooming of life itself. In this vein, for Agostoni, DP would herald the new birth of an independent Uganda: 'So the D.P. will be the life for the country, the heat (the love); will provide for economics and industry; is the one to awaken people from the sleep and to open their eyes as the sun in the morning.'[148]

The Democratic Party had a brief chance to implement Agostoni's hopes. Between March 1961 and April 1962, Kiwanuka and DP held power in Uganda.[149] They expended much of their political energy on issues such as Africanising the civil service, providing foreign scholarships to Ugandan students, raising coffee prices and the overall minimum wage, and determining if and how Uganda could embrace a federal system after independence. Although the British continued to control foreign policy and defence, Kiwanuka's period in office coincided with major steps toward further devolution of political power. Most significantly for Kiwanuka, he was named Chief Minister on 1 July 1961 and Prime Minister on 1 March 1962. Democratic Party supporters celebrated the former by carrying him on their shoulders after his plane landed at Entebbe Airport (Figure 1.5). The party's and his political apotheosis

[146] ICS PP.UG.DP.39 'Forward to Freedom: Being the Manifesto of the Democratic Party', 11 April 1960, p. 12 (emphasis in text).
[147] BKMKP/Chief Minister's Office, 1949–72/Chief Minister's Personal Correspondence/Tarcisio Agostoni to Benedicto Kiwanuka, 8 July 1959.
[148] Ibid. For Agostoni, where the colours, rays, light, and patterns of DP symbolised God's blessing on Kiwanuka and his party, the UPC's black symbols pointed to spiritual and social darkness.
[149] We explore the political background to these elections in Chapters 4, 5, and 6.

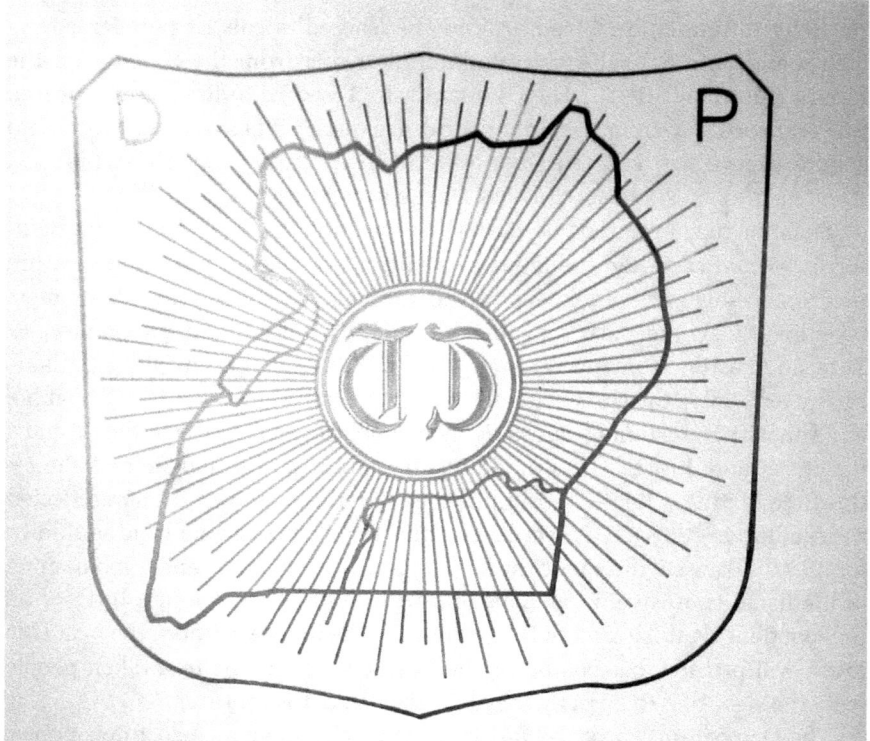

Figure 1.4 Party emblem of the Democratic Party, which repurposed the Christ monstrance of the Catholic missal, c. July 1959. *Benedicto Kiwanuka Papers.*

would be short-lived, however. As we will see in subsequent chapters, the vagaries of national politics proved difficult to navigate for Kiwanuka and his fellow DP evangelists.

Conclusion

In this chapter we have offered a detailed overview of the early life, career, and intellectual thought of Benedicto K. M. Kiwanuka, the central figure in our study of Catholic politics in Uganda in the late colonial period. Here we have highlighted the influence of Buddu Catholicism, a rigorous and disciplined tradition shaped equally by the White Fathers and a cohort of Uganda's first indigenous clergy. Yet Kiwanuka's Catholic identity was not simply parochial. Educated by the Mill Hill Missionaries, he also had extensive contacts with Combonis such as Tarcisio Agostoni. Kiwanuka's service in the Middle East during the Second World War and his international education in Lesotho and the UK exposed him further to cosmopolitan political currents, enabling him

Figure 1.5 Benedicto Kiwanuka is elevated by party supporters following the electoral victory of the DP, 1961. *Benedicto Kiwanuka Papers.*

to synthesise his Catholic identity with anticolonial and nationalist currents circulating internationally in the 1950s.

This chapter has also introduced the Democratic Party, Uganda's primary Catholic political movement in the late colonial period. We have argued that DP fits squarely within the rise of the global Christian Democracy movement, signifying a post-war shift in Catholic politics from defending the institutional interests of the Church toward a more pluralistic service of liberal democracy and the common good. It was by no means a 'Catholic party', as Kiwanuka insisted on many occasions. The party shared much of the anticolonial, nationalist discourse of its rivals and strove to incorporate Protestants and Muslims into its ranks (with admittedly limited success).[150] Echoing the early modern 'migration of the holy' from the church to the state and from the religious to the political,[151] DP transferred Catholic evangelical zeal toward the propagation

---

[150] As Kiwanuka's biographer Albert Bade notes, 'despite Kiwanuka's efforts to build a secular national party, DP continued to be a predominantly Catholic-based party both in leadership and membership' (Bade, *Benedicto Kiwanuka*, p. 37).

[151] William T. Cavanaugh, *The Myth of Religious Violence* (New York: Oxford University Press, 2009), pp. 175–6; Ernst Kantorowicz, *The King's Two Bodies: A*

of liberal democracy in the postcolony. Rhetorically, theological and religious language remained integral to this ostensibly secular and political mission, as demonstrated in DP's 'Forward to Freedom' manifesto and Kiwanuka's own debates with Archbishop Fisher.

But throughout the 1950s, Catholic political priorities varied throughout Uganda. Part of DP's strategic challenge was finding a way to develop national consensus. Religious loyalties and sectarian boundaries worked differently throughout the country. There was not one Catholic expression or set of political ideologies around which all Catholics could rally. The party's campaign to develop national networks also raised questions surrounding the translatability of political liberalism and Christian democracy within Uganda'a distinctively regional politics. As we see in the following chapter, UPC in Tesoland was organised by Catholic elites, including Cuthbert Obwangor, whose political republicanism reworked the egalitarian values of the Mill Hill Mission with older ideas about social mobility. In Toro, dissenting Catholics and DP backed the secessionist project of Rwenzururu. It is to their stories that we now turn.

Study in Mediaeval Political Theology (Princeton, NJ: Princeton University Press, 2016).

CHAPTER 2

Republicanism and Secession in Tesoland and Rwenzururu

> During your visit to Soroti before you left for the London Conference [...] [the] Teso who came at the airport to welcome you, complained bitterly, because the speech was in Luganda and they could not [grasp] what was going on.
>
> ~President DP, Teso Branch, to Benedicto Kiwanuka, 25 October 1961[1]

In the last chapter, we showed how Benedicto Kiwanuka developed a political philosophy – a 'gospel' of democracy – that was consistent with international Catholic democratisation movements that emerged following the Second World War. In theory, Kiwanuka envisioned a non-sectarian political world characterised by pan-ethnic nation-building. Part of the appeal of DP throughout the 1950s and 1960s was its attempt to argue that democratisation entailed the accommodation of regional polities and interests. Rather than simply offer defensive, oppositional politics, DP provided creative, integrative approaches to imagining a postcolonial state. On the ground, though, it proved very difficult to move beyond regional, sectarian interests. Benedicto Kiwanuka struggled to navigate Uganda's peripheral cosmopolitanisms, whose competing political traditions were difficult to unify into a coherent national project. For Kiwanuka and his UPC rivals, Tesoland in eastern Uganda, and the Rwenzururu-Toro question in western Uganda, constituted two of the more contentious arenas of political competition on the eve of independence. By securing the electoral control of these regions, activists in DP saw themselves as both stimulating and regulating Uganda's nationalist pulse. Kiwanuka saw these areas as 'curtain raisers' for what was to come.[2] The DP publicity secretary, Paul Ssemogerere, maintained that electoral

---

[1] BKMKP/Democrat II Dem-Cor 1/President DP, Teso Branch, to Benedicto Kiwanuka, 25 October 1961.
[2] 'DP Man Romps Home in S. Teso', *Uganda Argus*, 27 January 1962.

victory in Uganda's far eastern and western districts was 'indicative of the firm allegiance which his party enjoyed in different parts of the country'.[3]

In this chapter, we show how DP activists in eastern and western Uganda sought to rework many of the lofty ideals that Kiwanuka had developed internationally and in Buganda, especially his commitment to republicanism and the political priorities of rural *bakopi*. In Uganda's Eastern Province, party activists in Tesoland, whose republican societies were largely decentralised, confronted a political world that was increasingly consolidated from the early 1900s onward. Political centralisation compelled communities to think about family authority, colonial chiefs, and the ordering of public space in ways that complemented and challenged older notions of republicanism. Tesoland was also predominantly a Catholic region, but it was nevertheless a UPC stronghold. The case for national unity among UPC Catholics extended the possibility of moving Uganda beyond its religious fault lines, and in ways that echoed the earlier work of the Mill Hill Fathers. The foremost UPC intellectual in Tesoland, Cuthbert Obwangor, was a Catholic, not a Protestant. His career and the history of UPC in Tesoland more broadly challenge many of the popular correlations that have been made between DP and the Catholic Church on the one hand, and UPC and the Anglican Church of Uganda on the other. In Tesoland, UPC was primarily developed and led by Catholic activists. The supposed sectarian alliances that have framed Uganda's nationalist historiographies do not hold in eastern Uganda (Introduction). Democratic Party strategists could not rely upon Catholic solidarities to marshal party support among Iteso (the people of Tesoland). To attract supporters, they rotated the assembly points of their party in ways that were designed to underscore the region's older histories of mobility and heterarchical authority. Their strategy failed.

In western Uganda, by contrast, concepts about national unity emerged during a period when the area's monarchies were unravelling. In western Uganda, debates about party allegiance were scripted in religious discourses that dated to the early twentieth century. Until now, the history of dissent in Toro has been understood in the context of Protestant revivalism or the indigenisation of local Christianity.[4] But in no area of Uganda was Catholic

---

[3] Ibid.
[4] Where Derek Peterson shows how revivalists publicly accosted Catholic priests alongside the roadside in southern Uganda, Jason Bruner's more recent monograph argues that revivalists were jailed in Kigezi for singing rude songs outside of Catholic churches. Both say little to nothing about Catholic politics in Toro. Derek R. Peterson, *Ethnic Patriotism and the East African Revival: A History of Dissent, c. 1935–1972* (Cambridge: Cambridge University Press, 2012), p. 68; Jason Bruner, *Living Salvation in the East African Revival in Uganda* (Rochester, NY: University of Rochester Press, 2017), p. 142.

conversion more associated with the critique of royal power than it was in colonial Toro. In the kingdom of Toro, whose communities were predominantly Catholic, DP activists were ardent critics of the Toro monarchy and its Protestant trappings. By the 1960s, mobilisers in both UPC and DP worked diligently to associate secessionist violence in the region with the opposing political party. Toro royalists rallied around UPC, where Rwenzururu separatists politically allied with DP. Although this electoral alignment initially favoured DP, UPC ultimately triumphed after independence. By thinking closely about Catholic activism in eastern and western Uganda, we see how communities developed different strategies for decentralising regional authority.

Colonial Administration in Eastern Uganda

It was the Ganda military general Semei Kakungulu who incorporated eastern Uganda into the Protectorate of Uganda during the early twentieth century. The name that Ganda elites and colonial administrators used first to describe eastern Uganda was *Bukedi,* a pejorative term that described 'the land of the naked people'.[5] As one colonial administrator summarised, Bukedi encapsulated 'the unsubdued and unclad tribesmen who lived on the east side of the Nile opposite'.[6] Ron Atkinson has also shown how 'accentuating differences between the Baganda and others and representing such differences as inherently "tribal" served to justify the unequal distribution of capital and infrastructure development that marked the "special" relationship between the British and the Baganda'.[7]

Michael Twaddle's research on the biography of Semei Kakungulu convincingly demonstrates that Buganda's military administrators struggled to effectively govern the communities that inhabited Bukedi, which encompassed the Iteso, Uganda's second largest ethnic community.[8] Kakungulu undermined age-set ceremonies, in particular, which Iteso had used in the past to regulate generational authority and organise migration and military campaigns.[9]

---

[5] Michael Twaddle, *Kakungulu & the Creation of Uganda, 1868–1928* (London: James Currey, 1993), p. 139.
[6] J. C. D. Lawrance, *The Iteso: Fifty Years of Change in a Nilo-Hamitic Tribe of Uganda* (London: Oxford University Press, 1957), p. 3.
[7] Ronald R. Atkinson, *The Roots of Ethnicity: The Origins of the Acholi of Uganda Before 1800* (Philadelphia: University of Pennsylvania Press, 1994), p. 4.
[8] Twaddle, *Kakungulu & the Creation of Uganda.*
[9] In addition to Twaddle's excellent study, see: G. Emwanu, 'The Reception of Alien Rule in Teso: 1896–1927', *Uganda Journal,* 31 (1967), 171–82; John M. Gray, 'Kakungulu in Bukedi', *Uganda Journal,* 27 (1963), 31–59; Joan Vincent, *Teso in Transformation: The Political Economy of Peasant and Class in Eastern Africa*

Louise Pirouet's work on the history of Ganda evangelists also shows that Protestant missionary work in the area was equally fraught. Protestant church work accompanied the introduction of cotton and the hut tax.[10] Anglican Ganda catechists also failed to learn Ateso, which only reinforced the scepticism and ire of Teso chiefs, many of whom resisted Protestant forms of Christianity.[11]

The difficulty with which Ganda chiefs governed in eastern Uganda compelled the Protestant chief Hamu Mukasa and colonial officials to conduct an investigation in the region. Mukasa argued that careful attention was required to understand the customs of Buganda's eastern neighbours. With the extension of the railway line from Jinja northwards to Namasagali in 1912, he worried that his Ganda colleagues, including Apolo Kaggwa, were increasingly substituting the care that political incorporation and management demanded with the conveniences of speedy travel. Mukasa noted in his unpublished Luganda manuscript, *Journey to Bukedi by the Saza Chiefs*, that Kaggwa used the train often to move throughout Busoga and the southern end of Lake Kyoga. Mukasa worried that Kaggwa's quick-paced travels prevented him from adequately understanding the areas where Buganda had growing economic and political interests. On one occasion, Mukasa questioned Kaggwa, who, in his hurry to catch the train, failed to see and experience the food of Bukedi during a well-publicised trip in eastern Uganda between late 1917 and early 1918.[12]

The attempt to create centralised nodes of power in Tesoland instigated considerable debate throughout the colonial period. Many Iteso viewed the region's colonial chiefs as wielding authority that their positions did not afford in the past. Regional apprehensions were particularly seen in debates surrounding sexual practices. Chiefs that used their privilege to demand sexual services were *imurok* (s. *emuron*), a term used to describe 'witch doctors' or 'night dancers'. In November 1948, Iteso in the village of Kanyumu, Kumi, petitioned the District Officer to 'come immediately and save us' from the work of the sub-county chief (*etem*). The chief was accused of being 'very much after the women of the peasants', which 'is a disgraceful thing in the whole of our Etem [sub-county] for a man who sleeps with a woman in the bush is according

---

(Berkeley: University of California Press, 1982); J. B. Webster, 'Pioneers of Teso', *Tarikh*, 3 (1970), 47–58; F. Lukyn Williams, 'Teso Clans', *Uganda Journal*, 4 (1936), 174–6.

[10] M. Louise Pirouet, *Black Evangelists: The Spread of Christianity in Uganda, 1891–1914* (London: Collings, 1978), p. 186.

[11] Ibid., pp. 180–89.

[12] Hamu Mukasa's manuscript is housed in the library of the Kwata Mpola House in Mukono.

to our native customs regarded as a [witchdoctor]'.¹³ Following their opening critique, the writers of the letter articulated three additional concerns:

> He [the sub-county chief] has misled the Kanyum Etem Court in getting bribes and for this reason cases are not cut justly – he has a tendency of awarding too much compensation and less fines. He uses prisoners to cultivate his own shambas and does keep them in his lock-up for more than a month.
>
> He uses compulsion in getting oxens [sic] and ploughs of the peasants for cultivation of his shambas. A woman [accused] of adultery he takes her and makes her to become his wife for a week or so. [For example] there is one woman whom he [is affectionate with] [...] and the case is now in Kumi Ebuku Court. This woman [who] is in question belongs to a prisoner serving a two year sentence.
>
> He shouts too much in the court as if [he] is mad – Sir [...] get him examined medically at Ngora, for this man might also run mad and we Kanyum people will be held responsible.

The writers concluded by criticising the appointment of chiefs, who were selected 'without our knowledge and are transferred without saying a word of good-bye to us'.

The letter from Kanyumu described a political order characterised by judicial obstruction, forced labour, sexual impropriety, and mental instability. The 'madman' of Teso, *lokekerep*, a term that Catholic communities in Teso also used to describe an incessantly boisterous person,¹⁴ lacked sociability, the necessary skills to depart with grace. Soroti's District Archive contains numerous colonial reports that show how local communities leveraged accusations of witchcraft to delegitimise appointed chiefs.¹⁵ At one level, Teso writers sought to capitalise on the fears and spiritual paranoia of Protestant administrators, who had by 1918 introduced Witchcraft Ordinances to undermine older constructions of public authority.¹⁶ In Teso's moral economy, though, such associations also help explain why Protestantism failed to become Tesoland's

---

[13] Soroti District Archives (SDA) Minute Papers Miscellaneous 12/4 People of Kanyum, Kumi, to District Officer, Teso, 8 November 1948. Subsequent quotations are taken from this same letter.

[14] Rev Father J. Kiggen, *Ateso-English Dictionary* (London: St. Joseph's Society for Foreign Missions, 1953), p. 165.

[15] See, for instance: SDA Minute Paper 135/35 Office of the Assistant Superintendent of Police, Soroti, to District Commissioner, Soroti, 10 October 1933.

[16] Peter Rigby, 'Prophets, Diviners, and Prophetism: The Recent History of Kiganda Religion', *Journal of Anthropological Research* 31 (1975), 116–48.

predominate form of colonial Christianity. It was too closely associated with the high-handed behaviour of colonial chiefs and Ganda administrators.[17]

Missionaries with St Joseph's Society (the Mill Hill Fathers) began working in eastern Uganda by the early 1900s (Chapter 1). The development of Mill Hill schools in the region helps us understand the extent to which the mission's influence expanded. The congregation operated ten primary schools for boys and girls in eastern Buganda and the Eastern Province by 1905. In terms of national representation, the numbers were relatively small when compared to the Church Missionary Society's 442 schools and the White Fathers' thirty.[18] Weddings were comparatively small for the Mill Hill Mission, whose priests conducted approximately 146 ceremonies each year between 1909 and 1913.[19] During this same period, the White Fathers conducted around 1,103 annually and the Church Missionary Society 504. Education grants remained significantly smaller for the Mill Hill Mission, which received £300 per year by the end of the First World War, whereas the Church Missionary Society was apportioned £1,900 and the White Fathers £950.[20] Be that as it may, by the end of 1920, there were 20,188 students enrolled in Mill Hill secondary schools, numbers that were only marginally less than rates for the Church Missionary Society and White Fathers throughout the entire country.[21]

Mill Hill Christianity was largely successful in Tesoland, insofar as a plurality of communities in the region self-identified as Catholic. Uganda's 1959 census showed that by the end of the colonial period, approximately 32 per cent of the population of Bukedi described themselves as Catholic, and 28 per cent identified as Protestant.[22] In Teso, the disparity was more noticeable. Catholics constituted 33.3 per cent of the population, nearly 11 per cent more than Protestants. As we will now show, one of the reasons why

---

[17] Robert O'Neil, *Mission to the Upper Nile* (London: Mission Book Service, 1999), pp. 22–4.

[18] 'Colonial Reports – Annual Report for 1904–5' (London: Printed for His Majesty's Stationery Office, Darling & Son Ltd., 1905), pp. 18–19.

[19] 'Colonial Reports – Annual Report for 1913–14' (London: Printed under the Authority of His Majesty's Stationery Offices by Barclay and Fry, Ltd., 1915), p. 20.

[20] 'Colonial Reports – Annual Report for 1920 (April to December)' (London: His Majesty's Stationery Office, 1922), p. 13.

[21] Ibid., p. 14. CMS reports placed their secondary education enrolments at 26,799; and the White Fathers counted 20,701 students in secondary schools.

[22] The findings of the census are reproduced in Fred B. Welbourn, *Religion and Politics in Uganda: 1952–1962* (Nairobi: East African Publishing House, 1965), Table 3.

the Mill Hill project expanded in Tesoland was that converts interpreted the mission's political objective in ways that reverberated with older ideas about egalitarianism in the region.

The Catholic Republicanism of Cuthbert J. Obwangor

Cuthbert Joseph Obwangor was one of the most important Catholic intellectuals to emerge out of Uganda's Mill Hill community. He was born in 1920 in the northern Teso region of Katakwi.[23] After studying in a Mill Hill primary school in Ngora, Obwangor enrolled at Namilyango College, which was founded by the Mill Hill Fathers in 1902. According to Obwangor, he was sent to England for one year during his studies to become fully fluent in English, which would enable him to translate a Mill Hill book into Ateso.[24] After completing Namilyango, Obwangor worked for the Kenya and Uganda Railways and Harbours in Nairobi, before studying accountancy at the London School of Economics. He returned to Tesoland by the early 1950s, after which he became involved in farmer union politics and, in time, the establishment of UPC in Tesoland. He was appointed Minister of Justice by the ruling party (UPC) in 1964 (Figure 2.1).[25] By the mid-1960s, he was the Minister of Commerce and Industry in the Uganda Government, and treasurer of UPC.[26] After independence, when Prime Minister Milton Obote abrogated Uganda's constitution in 1967, Obwangor joined DP, with which he was associated during his arrest in 1969 following the failed assassination of Milton Obote.[27] For Obwangor, UPC had overextended its reach by the late 1960s, a point to which we will return. After the 1970s, Yoweri Museveni and the National Resistance Movement (NRM) often claimed Obwangor as one of their own to bolster the Movement's fledgling support in Tesoland following the Luwero conflict and

---

[23] Obwangor recounted his biography to the *Observer* newspaper in 2007, which was republished online following his death in 2012: www.observer.ug/features-sp-2084439083/57-feature/18873-feature-the-life-and-times-of-cuthbert-obwangor, accessed 15 June 2018.

[24] Unfortunately, Obwangor does not specify the book in the available transcription.

[25] BKMKP/Not Marked 3/C. J. Obwangor to Clerk of National Assembly, 18 August 1964.

[26] NARA II RG 0084/P74/5/POL 15/Department of State Declassified Report, Kampala Embassy, 24 June 1966.

[27] For further discussion on Obwangor's influence in DP, see: Samwiri Lwanga Lunyiigo, *Short History of the Democratic Party* (Rome: Foundation for African Development, 1984), p. 83; Simon Mwebe and Anthony Sserubiri, *Ebyafaayo Bya D.P., 1954–1984* (Kampala: Foundation for African Development, 1984), p. 70.

Figure 2.1 Milton Obote, Leader of the Opposition, and Cuthbert J. Obwangor, a member of the Legislative Council for Teso and leading Catholic activist. Uganda Constitutional Conference, Lancaster House, September 1961. *Royal Commonwealth Society COI/A/599. Reproduced by kind permission of the Syndics of Cambridge University Library.*

Mukura Massacre (1989).[28] The Teso activist's arguments for multi-partyism created evident tensions within the NRM,[29] a point that Museveni openly acknowledged after Obwangor's death in 2012.[30]

---

[28] The community's political report on the massacre was circulated in a booklet: Lino Owor Ogora, 'Justice and Reconciliation Project: The Mukura Massacre of 1989' (JRP Field Note XII, Gulu, March 2011). For additional conversation on the history of insurgency in Teso, see Ben Jones, *Beyond the State in Rural Uganda* (Edinburgh: Edinburgh University Press, 2009).

[29] Obwangor's formal recommendations for multi-partyism are noted in two works, both of which are housed in the Africana archive at Makerere University: C. J. Obwangor, *Ideological Conflict in Uganda since Independence 1962–1989 (Position Paper on Uganda Constitutional Issues)* (Kampala: Uganda Constitutional Commission, 1989); C. J. Obwangor, *Political Parties (Position Paper on Uganda Constitutional Issues)* (Kampala: Uganda Constitutional Commission, 1990).

[30] The audio recording of Museveni's interview is published online by the Uganda Radio Network: https://ugandaradionetwork.com/story/museveni-mourns-former-minister-obwangor, accessed 27 April 2020.

Obwangor's political biography developed during a time when Tesoland was generating large amounts of capital on account of its cattle and the production of colonial cotton. As an indication of its wealth, J. Lawrence, who served as Teso's District Commissioner for five years following the Second World War, noted that Teso was the largest cigarette-consuming district in colonial eastern Africa.[31] As in other areas in Uganda, the Indian management of land and ginneries raised considerable consternation throughout Tesoland. The colonial archives contain numerous reports and letters of complaint submitted by Teso farmers against Indian traders. Indians were criticised for circulating gossip about Teso elders and for their inabilities to herd cattle, which, when not corralled properly, trampled local crops.[32] By the mid-1950s, public criticism focused extensively on the Indian monopolisation of land, especially in Teso's urban trading centres.[33] Colonial officials worried that grievances and the expansion of trade unions in Tesoland would translate into 'interracial friction' with eastern Uganda's Indian communities, who possessed 'predominance [...] in the retail trade'.[34]

To undermine the domination of Indian economies, trade unions expanded rapidly in post-war Tesoland. The Ganda organisers Ignatius Musazi and Erieza Bwete, who had established Uganda's first trade unions, were active campaigners in eastern Uganda.[35] Throughout both Tesoland and central Uganda, Musazi and Bwete underscored the seizure of land in Kenya by settlers to compel Ugandans to organise local unions. To Teso farmers, they argued, 'since the Mau Mau are succeeding in driving white men out of the Kenya Highlands the Europeans are preparing to seize land in Uganda'.[36] The argument gained extensive traction. As one colonial official worryingly noted: 'The story has wide currency and I have heard it as much as 60 miles from [Soroti's (?)] centre of activity.' Trade unions facilitated political solidarity between

---

[31] Lawrance, *The Iteso*, p. vii.
[32] SDA Minute Papers Miscellaneous 12/4 Shariff Abdulrahman El-Awal, Is-Hakia (Uganda) Association to District Commissioner, Teso, 27 August 1948; SDA Minute Papers Miscellaneous 12/4 District Commissioner, Teso, to Ishakia Community, 11 September 1948; SDA Minute Papers Miscellaneous 12/4 E. Ogwangi, Eitela Chief, Ngora, to District Commissioner, Teso, 18 October 1948.
[33] SDA District Commissioner Files Schools: Mohammedan (Muslim)/African Education/17 Education Officer, Teso, to District Commissioner, Teso, 7 March 1956.
[34] SDA District Commissioner Files/5 Extract from the Minutes of the PC's Conference, 23–24, November 1951.
[35] SDA District Commissioner Files District Commissioner's Office, Mbale, to Registrar of Co-Operative Societies, Entebbe, 21 August 1951; SDA District Commissioner Files/28 M.I. Cooper, Co-operative Officer, Teso District, to Commissioner for Co-operative Development, 7 March 1957.
[36] SDA District Commissioner Files/22 Cooperative Officer, Teso, to Commissioner for Cooperative Development, 23 July 1953.

activists in Teso and communities throughout Uganda, and through unionist doors passed most of Teso's first generation of national officials, including the founding members of UPC in eastern Uganda and Cuthbert Obwangor, who throughout the 1950s and 1960s drafted Teso's orders of business and cooperative complaints in Entebbe and Kampala.[37]

But Obwangor did not advocate for a strong, centralised government, at least in ways that were developed by UPC following Milton Obote's socialist 'Move to the Left' in the late 1960s. Nor did he share Musazi's and Bwete's Protestant convictions.[38] Obwangor's electoral success was due in large part to his ability to identify with older ideas about mobility and flattened hierarchies. Generally speaking, Teso activists throughout the twentieth century rallied against hierarchical politics and the centralisation of social authority. Unlike the Catholicism of the White Fathers or CMS, the Mill Hill Mission was not particularly interested in 'eating chieftaincies'.[39] As we showed in the previous chapter, the Mill Hill Mission itself was invited to work in Uganda precisely because it was hoped that its English-speaking missionaries would mediate tensions between Francophone Catholics and British Protestants. Their task was to attenuate competing political hierarchies in the state, not reify them.[40] For Teso converts, ideas about egalitarianism were reworked according to local political priorities, first, and then used to make larger claims about how authority and economies ought to work in the state more broadly.

When Obwangor began writing in the national press in the late 1950s and early 1960s, he advocated for an inclusive, populist state. One editorial is especially insightful. In November 1960, he argued that 'all power exercised over a nation must come from the political community', and 'power which is assumed is usurpation'.[41] For Obwangor, the constitution 'becomes a political Bible of the state' to the extent that it enables people to 'decide freely', while

[37] SDA District Commissioner Files Usuku Co-Operative Council to District Commissioner, Teso, 26 August 1965.
[38] Jonathon L. Earle, *Colonial Buganda and the End of Empire: Political Thought and Historical Imagination in Africa* (Cambridge: Cambridge University Press, 2017), pp. 39–76.
[39] O'Neil, *Mission to the Upper Nile*, p. 22.
[40] Lofty expressions about reconciliation were more complex. Carol Summers argues that there were ongoing controversies between British colonial officials in the region and the missionaries of the Mill Hill Mission, the latter of whom used questionable forms of discipline and whipping to bolster conversion and church attendance (Carol Summers, 'Force and Colonial Development in Eastern Uganda', in *East Africa in Transition: Communities, Cultures, and Change*, ed. by J. M. Bahemuka and J. L. Brockington (Nairobi: Acton Publishers, 2002), pp. 181–207 (pp. 193–9).
[41] C. Obwangor, Letter to the Editor, *Uganda Argus*, 18 November 1960.

also weakening the tendency of governments to regulate their citizens' affairs. Obwangor's argument was not libertarian; he was in fact building upon much older discourses circulating in Tesoland about distributive power. The argument was, in turn, well-received. As one northern Teso supporter ingratiatingly commented: 'Mr C. J. Obwangor is the best representative Teso has ever had, in that he has proved himself before the Teso intelligentsia, and above all the peasants, by consistence, common sense, and leadership.'[42]

Obgwangor's egalitarian ethos set the political terms within which DP activists competed. In numerous contexts, party organisers in the area employed strategies that sought to demonstrate inclusivity and political mobility. In Soroti town, extensive efforts were made to rotate party meetings to attract followers and to demonstrate that they were not attempting to use their party to monopolise landholdings, which was an accusation levied against Indian merchants and the African Muslim Association.[43] More broadly, the strategy of inclusive mobility built on the local historiographies of regional migration. Teso communities had begun settling in eastern Uganda following a series of migrations from the seventeenth century onward. The word -*teso* was derived from the older gloss *ates*, or child, a word that was used to distinguish younger, migrating communities from the 'old men' who stayed behind, or the Karamojong, derived from *aikar* 'to stay behind' and *imojong* 'the old men'.[44] While there is much about this period of political and economic transition that we do not understand, it is generally acknowledged that a critique of central authority accompanied Teso's aspiring 'youth'.[45]

Ideas about mobility were reworked into strategies of organisation. Between 1957 and 1962, Catholic activists in DP, writing from the Mill Hill Mission of Toroma, orchestrated meetings at multiple locations. Assembly sites in Soroti included the *Lukiiko* Hall, the African Club, a garden between the post office and cinema, and a large mango tree near the main market.[46] From these locations, the party sought to remedy what the Ganda DP leader Paul Ssemogerere had controversially called 'apathy' in Tesoland.[47] From their mango trees and Catholic mission, the party structured speaking tours throughout areas that included Amuria, Bukedea, Serere, Usuk, Kaberamaido, and Kalaki.[48]

---

[42] A. W. Otionomo, Katakwi, Letter to the Editor, *Uganda Argus*, 1 June 1957.
[43] SDA District Commissioner Files Schools: Mohammedan (Muslim)/African Education/24 Provincial Commissioner, Eastern Province, 13 November 1956.
[44] J. C. D. Lawrance, *The Iteso*, pp. 8–10.
[45] Sherman W. Seldon, 'Curing Tales from Teso', *Journal of the Folklore Institute*, 13 (1976), 137–54.
[46] SDA/Democratic Party/Varied Correspondence.
[47] 'DP Hits at Teso "Apathy"', *Uganda Argus*, 30 July 1962.
[48] SDA/Democratic Party/15 Secretary D.P. Teso Branch to District Commissioner,

To reinforce local canvassing, Benedicto Kiwanuka toured Tesoland in late 1961 and early 1962.[49] But his visit flopped. If anything, Kiwanuka's tour undermined the success of the party. Even Teso members of DP raised complaints about Kiwanuka's speeches in private correspondence between party executives and Kiwanuka. The speeches, they noted, were conducted in Luganda, which prevented voters from understanding what he was arguing.[50] For ordinary Iteso, Kiwanuka's persona resembled an earlier generation of Ganda chiefs, who used Luganda to dictate southern political interests. Like Apolo Kaggwa and Semei Kakungulu, Kiwanuka did not seem especially interested in appropriating local cultural practices. His tours also coincided with a string of arsons against Anglican churches in Kumi, allegedly carried out by DP Catholics. In response, one UPC youth wing activist commented in the national press: 'Religious rivalry in the district had never been so bad.'[51]

The politics of opposition associated with DP was rejected in eastern Uganda. Although Catholics constituted the majority of the population in Teso, DP was unable to secure Teso's national elections. In the principal parliamentary elections of 1961 and 1962, UPC outpolled DP in Teso by 22,038 votes and 10,715, respectively.[52] DP activists and Kiwanuka, like an earlier generation of colonial chiefs, were viewed as too 'boisterous'. The strategy of rotating meeting points was not enough to disassociate DP and Benedicto Kiwanuka from the long history of Buganda's political and cultural blunders in the area.

Why did DP fail to carry the Catholic vote in Tesoland? First, Obwangor, a son of the soil, advocated for a type of republicanism that left DP activists without a compelling political narrative. These communities believed he would move Tesoland into the forefront of national politics. While Tesoland had been a significant producer of cotton and cattle in the colonial economy, it was politically marginalised until the early 1960s. In turn, there was not a compelling reason for ordinary Teso Catholics to join a party that was associated with Ganda Catholics, Benedicto Kiwanuka in particular. Despite the region's Catholic associations, it was hard to imagine that local interests could be championed by Ganda politicians, and Kiwanuka was unable to dissociate himself from an earlier generation of Ganda colonial administrators. Shared

---

et al., 25 July 1958.
[49] 'Mr. Kiwanuka in Teso campaign', *Uganda Argus*, 22 January 1962.
[50] BKMKP/Democrat II Dem-Cor 1/President DP, Teso Branch, to Benedicto Kiwanuka, 25 October 1961.
[51] 'Church burned – religious rivalry blamed', *Uganda Argus*, 18 September 1961.
[52] Welbourn, *Religion and Politics in Uganda*, Table 3.

Catholic identity ultimately proved no match for ethnic loyalties and persuasive local political narratives.

Competing Royalisms in Toro

As DP struggled to build political alliances in eastern Uganda, they were simultaneously working to capitalise upon royalist dissent in western Uganda. As we will now show, the papers of Benedicto Kiwanuka and colonial reports complicate a Protestant or revivalist reading of 1960s western Uganda. Catholic conversion had long been associated with political dissent and royalist critique in the politics of western Uganda. In time, the Toro kingdom's critique of Rwenzururu secession was enveloped in conversations about Catholic identity and the life of DP.

On the eve of independence, September 1962, the Ugandan administrators F. C. Ssembeguya, G. O. B. Oda, and J. M. Okae were asked to 'inquire into and report to the Governor on the underlying reasons for the recent disturbances amongst the Baamba and Bakonjo of Toro District and to make recommendations in the light of their investigations'.[53] The disturbances in question had been the result of mounting political tensions between the kingdom of Toro and the Rwenzururu movement, whose activists sought to secede both from Toro and the nation of Uganda. Drawing from their field work, the three suggested that '[e]xtremely large crowds collected to submit evidence in the outlying areas of Toro Kingdom'.[54] The report concluded that there had been no fewer than sixty-eight acts of violence and intimidation – in August and September alone – in the separatist counties of Busongora, Bunyangabu, Bwamba, and Burahya.[55] During their work, the triumvirate collected written memoranda from 172 interest groups, which ranged from single-authored petitions to letters produced by thirty-four signatories.[56] Their work also included conducting semi-structured interviews throughout the kingdom.[57]

The political vocabulary with which Toro elites described their kingdom's ethnic minorities mirrored radical Hutu discourses in late 1950s Rwanda.[58] Separatists in Toro, the report noted, 'complained of the arrogant and

---

[53] 'Report of the Commission of Inquiry into the Recent Disturbances amongst the Baamba and Bakonjo People of Toro' (Entebbe: Government Printer, 1962), p. 1.
[54] Ibid.
[55] Ibid., pp. 19–20.
[56] Ibid., pp. 22–3.
[57] In ten days, they conducted approximately seventy-nine interviews (ibid., p. 24).
[58] J. J. Carney, *Rwanda Before the Genocide: Catholic Politics and Ethnic Discourse in the Late Colonial Era* (New York: Oxford University Press, 2014), p. 91.

high-handed behaviour of the Batoro'.[59] Drawing from the natural world, Toro royalists described Baamba and Bakonjo as 'apes, baboons, gorillas, insects, dogs, flies and pigs'.[60] Dissenters showed how their communities were forced to use the Rutoro language in courts, schools, and churches, as opposed to their local languages. Minorities, they continued, were refused scholarships, medical care, and due representation in the *Rukurato*, or parliament, of Toro.

More broadly, though, the committee became immersed in a complicated arena of competing historical claims. The committee noted, 'in the complaints raised by the Baamba/Bakonjo very many references were made to the historical origins of the Kingdom'.[61] In gatherings as large as 4,000, Baamba/Bakonjo 'made claims concerning their independence from the Omukama before the advent of the British administration'.[62] Dissenters explained with great historical detail how their lands 'had never been subject to conquest at the time of Kabarega'.[63] The Toro monarchy had emerged during the 1820s, when the economic and political reach of Bunyoro-Kitara was waning.[64] A Nyoro prince, Olimi I, set about establishing a separate kingdom. British and Ganda administrators backed Toro's secession to undermine Bunyoro's economy and political power. The Toro king Rukirabasaija Daudi Kasagama Kyebambe III secured separate status from Bunyoro. He then extended Toro's authority to govern and tax throughout the Rwenzori region with the backing of the colonial government (Figure 2.2). Toro's peripheral political historians contested the legitimacy of this early colonial settlement.

In his study of the East African Revival, Derek Peterson shows how Toro's Protestant revivalists advocated for the political hegemony of the kingdom of Toro. Peterson sees the acts of violence that were unfolding in western Uganda as a largely Protestant affair between royalists and revivalists on the one hand – who supported the integration of the Konzo and Baamba ethnic minorities into the Toro kingdom – and separatists on the other – whose religious motivations were more parochial or traditional. He shows how secessionist claims were created and historically animated by local societies, including

---

[59] 'Report of the Commission of Inquiry into the Recent Disturbances amongst the Baamba and Bakonjo People of Toro', p. 10.
[60] Ibid.
[61] Ibid., p. 1.
[62] Ibid., p. 5.
[63] Ibid., p. 5.
[64] For a detailed account of this period, see Shane Doyle's discussion on political reform and conquest in nineteenth-century Bunyoro: Shane Doyle, *Crisis & Decline in Bunyoro: Population & Environment in Western Uganda, 1860–1955* (Oxford: James Currey, 2006), pp. 42–93. See also Kenneth Ingham, *The Toro Kingdom in Uganda* (London: Methuen & Co. Ltd., 1975), pp. 1–88.

Figure 2.2 *Omukama* Rukirabasaija Sir George David Matthew Kamurasi Rukidi III, with British governor, Sir Frederick Crawford, c. 1960. *British National Archives CO 1069/200/21.*

the Bakonzo Life History Research Society, which 'showed Konzo and Amba people to be autochthons, natives who had inhabited the Rwenzori Mountains since ancient times'.[65] Where secessionist historians showed how the kingdom of Toro was indebted to its peripheral communities, who had protected Toro's kings in the mountains during the time of Kabalega's expansion wars, 'Toro's royal historians gilded their monarchy with the trappings of antiquity, representing themselves as allies of their British rulers'.[66] But claims about integration and separation were rooted in far-reaching antagonisms that existed between Protestant and Catholic communities, which is overlooked in Peterson's otherwise sapient study.

The White Fathers established the first Catholic mission in Toro in 1895. The location of their mission was Virika, in the outskirts of what would become the colonial town of Fort Portal.[67] In no area of Uganda did religious conversion follow political loyalties more closely than it did in Toro. The Toro monarchy was fledgeling during the early 1900s. To legitimate the rise of royalist power in the region – and the chiefly apparatus that accompanied it – Toro

---

[65] Peterson, *Ethnic Patriotism and the East African Revival*, p. 269.
[66] Ibid., pp. 253, 266.
[67] Yves Tourigny, *So Abundant a Harvest: The Catholic Church in Uganda, 1879–1979* (London: Darton, Longman and Todd, 1979), p. 58.

elites prayed Protestant prayers. They supported the work of British, Ganda, and Toro evangelists. Broadly, communities that shunned the resurgence of royalist power in the region became baptised Catholics. As Louise Pirouet pithily noted in her history of Christianity in Toro: 'The political opportunists became Protestant; the disgruntled, Catholics.'[68] Indeed, *Omukama* Kyebambe III's discriminatory treatment of Catholics, whom he refused to appoint to chieftaincies, raised considerable concern among Protestant administrators. At one point, colonial officers considered replacing Toro's king with his brother, who was far less hostile toward the region's Catholics.[69]

When Benedicto Kiwanuka and the Democratic Party organised in western Uganda, it was not without reason that they strategically scheduled meetings with Rwenzururu patriots. In September 1959, during a tour in the neighbouring kingdom of Ankole, Kiwanuka's itinerary showed that he went to great lengths to 'see important people and groups comprising leaders, prominent members, sympathisers, and those likely to join the party' (Chapter 4).[70] Meetings were organised each day in large hourly blocks. The itinerary for 23 September noted: 'We shall visit important people and hold a public meeting at 12.00 noon after which we shall leave for Fort Portal.' In Fort Portal, by contrast, it was important for Kiwanuka to speak with an ordinary group of separatists 'assembled on the evening we arrive'.[71] By prioritising Rwenzururu activists, Kiwanuka hoped that DP's politics of opposition would attract populist support from among dissenters in Toro. Kiwanuka believed that separatists would rework the nationalism of DP to bolster their aspirations for secession.

Unsurprisingly, then, Kiwanuka's relationship with the Toro monarchy was contentious. During the early 1960s, Kiwanuka refused to attend a party to honour a leading Toro Prince, Stephen Karamagi, the son of *Omukama* Rukidi III. Like *Kabaka* Muteesa II, Karamagi was a graduate of the University of Cambridge. He embraced and embellished the ornamentalism that characterised the cocktail parties of high society in Uganda's royal courts. Spurning such etiquette, Kiwanuka simply noted: 'I shall not find it possible to attend this party [in honour of the prince] because I shall be on my tour of the Protectorate at that time.'[72] Kiwanuka saw himself as a serious state-builder, undeterred by the trappings of parochial royalists.

---

[68] Pirouet, *Black Evangelists*, p. 55.
[69] Ingham, *The Toro Kingdom in Uganda*, pp. 82–4, 107–8.
[70] BKMKP/Ben Personal/Deputy Treasurer of DP, Kampala, to Provincial Leader, 14 September 1959.
[71] Ibid.
[72] BKMKP/Personal Correspondence of Chief Minister/Benedicto Kiwanuka to

Kiwanuka's elusiveness raised suspicions among Toro royalists, which was compounded by the fact that he was a subject of Buganda, whose government was at that time advocating for its own secession. It was not always easy for Toro elites to disentangle Kiwanuka's politics from the larger ambitions of the kingdom of Buganda. Leaders in Toro insinuated that Kiwanuka might be working as an operative on behalf of the *kabaka* in the region. The disruption of Toro politics by Buganda's king and Buganda's party activists, the prime minister of Toro maintained, would result in civil war. As the *katikkiro* of Toro asserted: 'Civil war must be prepared for by the people of Uganda at the dawn of independence if the Baganda persist in trying to impose the Kabaka as ruler of a self-governing Uganda.'[73]

Because Toro elites associated Kiwanuka with the political will of Buganda, Kiwanuka was ultimately compelled to 'call on the Omugabe of Toro'.[74] Toro's royal historians knew well how Buganda had undermined Bunyoro in the past by supporting their kingdom's secession. They were now worried that the government of Buganda – through the likes of Kiwanuka – would undermine the Toro kingdom by supporting Rwenzururu secession. Where Kiwanuka did not work to distance himself from his Ganda associations in Tesoland, the potential imminence of large-scale violence in western Uganda placed greater pressure on Kiwanuka to assuage concerns that the kingdom of Buganda was formally backing the emergence of the kingdom of Rwenzururu.

In contrast to DP, UPC in Toro was primarily a pro-monarchy party, at least until the mid-1960s. Its activists in the early 1960s, like Toro's ruling government, accused DP of supporting the secessionist politics of Rwenzururu's patriots. There were numerous reasons for this. When the colonial government finally produced their report on disturbances in the region, it did not go unnoticed that accusations of discrimination in the church were 'only supplied regarding the Church of Uganda and no details were given for the Roman Catholic Church'.[75] More specifically, the government of Toro 'blamed the Democratic Party and in particular Mr Kiwanuka'.[76] Government interlocutors argued that Kiwanuka's support of a separate district of Sebei, which was a contested polity in eastern Uganda, 'put the idea into the minds of the people and that when he toured the Toro District in his pre-election campaign

---

Prince Stephen Karamagi, 9 August 1961.
[73] 'Katikiro of Toro Warns Buganda', *Uganda Argus*, 13 August 1960.
[74] BKMKP/Information Department/Prime Minister's Events, 15 March 1962.
[75] 'Report of the Commission of Inquiry into the Recent Disturbances amongst the Baamba and Bakonjo People of Toro', p. 9.
[76] Ibid., p. 11.

he gave the impression that he would grant a separate district for the Baamba and Bakonjo'.[77]

Leaders in UPC generated critiques that expanded the claims of the colonial investigation. In March 1961, the Toro intellectual and UPC representative John Babiiha forwarded a detailed letter to the county chiefs of Toro and the king. With the devastating secession of Katanga in mind, Babiiha warned that the 'catastrophe of the Congo befalls Uganda'.[78] He passionately argued that Kiwanuka was conspiring with the government of Buganda and Rwenzururu patriots to abolish Toro – or at the very least, bring Toro under the political authority of Buganda. For Ganda patriots, he argued, and members of DP in particular, Uganda's nationalist moment was an opportunity to solidify Buganda's control of the region:

> I am informing you that Toro is in great danger because of DP which was non-existent here in Toro, but was brought in by the candidates who stood for DP – men who are great deceivers because they know what the leader of DP said in London in the month of October, 1960 that the Kabaka is the one who would rule Uganda.[79]

The Uganda People's Congress, by contrast, wished to assure the kingdom that every monarch 'shall have undisturbed peace (freedom) in his kingdom'. Babiiha continued:

> You should inform the Gomborora [sub-county] chiefs of the danger of DP. The parties of Buganda, DP, UNC, UNP and Progressive Party are working in concert to secure a unitary Government over which the Kabaka will rule without the existence [of] any other Mukama. This device they have received from Ethiopia.
>
> I am informed that if DP is in power, they will take away the Gombororas, Sazas, the Katikiros and the Secretary Generals, and then Ben Kiwanuka as Prime Minister will install Baganda as Regional Administrative Officers and Buganda the great country will rule the Uganda nation.[80]

By comparing Ethiopia with the kingdom, or country, of Buganda, UPC activists reinforced the expansionary ambitions of Buganda throughout the region.

---

[77] Ibid.

[78] BKMKP/Information Department/J.K. Babiiha, Chairman of the National Governing Council of Uganda, Uganda Peoples Congress, to All Saza Chiefs [of Toro], Rukirabasija Omukama, et al., 16 March 1961. Babiiha referenced the Congo's struggle to prevent the secession of Katanga, whose legislatures declared a republican state in July 1960 under the presidency of Moïse Tshombe.

[79] Ibid.

[80] Ibid.

Like the Ethiopian empire, they concluded, Ganda state-builders wished to incorporate less powerful, smaller kingdoms under their rule.[81] Royalists had but one sensible option: 'Vote UPC candidates only.'

Ultimately, however, unlike in eastern Uganda, UPC was initially unable to outmanoeuvre DP. While DP did not openly support secession,[82] Benedicto Kiwanuka and the party did offer tremendous support toward the cause of Toro's dissenting subjects. They distributed leaflets throughout Toro, inviting communities to learn 'the correct orientation of our politicians and we hope in Uganda's political emancipation'.[83] It was the hope of the party to 'discuss local grievances' and bring about 'valuable cooperation'. From the Catholic school St Leo's College, Kyegobe, Fort Portal, the publicity secretary of the party, Paul Ssemogerere, reminded party leaders: 'We are the only party who have so boldly come out on that point [in placing] the Head of State squarely into the hands of the people of Uganda (where it so fittingly lies).'[84] The language of 'emancipation' appealed to many of Toro's rowdy subjects. During the 1962 parliamentary elections, DP secured 22,001 votes to UPC's 13,259.[85]

The Democratic Party's victory was also the outcome of extensive strategising during a period when activists in the area feared persecution and death at the hands of Toro's royalists. As one DP supporter in Fort Portal reflected to Kiwanuka: 'We are pledged to do what's right and what we believe. Should we be slaughtered for the sake of goodness, so be it.'[86] In Rwenzururu, DP activists had to be equally cautious, especially after Uganda's independence. One Mutoro activist in the party, who identified himself as Benedicto R., indicated that he feared for his life and property while conducting party work in Bwamba and Busongora.[87]

The frequency of violence by 1964 had noticeably disrupted the ability of DP to operate safely outside of Fort Portal. As one letter noted: 'But quite

---

[81] For further discussion on the emergence and secession of tributary kingdoms in post-war Ethiopia, see Donald L. Donham, *Marxist Modern: An Ethnographic History of the Ethiopian Revolution* (Berkeley: University of California Press, 1999).
[82] 'DP "aims at Toro peace"', *Uganda Argus*, 3 December 1962.
[83] BKMKP/Ben Personal/Paul Semogerere, DP Memo, Fort Portal, 3 November 1959.
[84] BKMKP/Ben Personal/Paul Ssemogerere to Mr Mpima, St. Leo's College, Fort Portal, 20 December 1959. Underscore is Ssemogerere's.
[85] Welbourn, *Religion and Politics in Uganda*, Table 3.
[86] BKMKP/Personal Correspondence/DP Activist, Fort Portal, to Benedicto Kiwanuka, 5 March 1960.
[87] BKMKP/Hon The Chief Justice – Ranch Scheme/Benedicto R., DP Branch Chairman, Bwamba, to Paul Ssemogerere, 8 December 1963.

naturally the unrest in Busongora etc. must have interfered with [DP's] plans for free operations in the area.'[88] Benedicto Kiwanuka drew attention to the proliferation of violence in the area to criticise the leadership of UPC and the government's controversial role in the Congo, which concerned the acquisition of gold during the ongoing Katanga crisis. In one press comment, Kiwanuka observed:

> The Rwenzururu men in Toro are still active and the Prime Minister should know that killings in Toro by Bakonjo, Batoro, Bamba and Police continue to-day because of his inability to deal with the problem adequately. The life of a Mutoro or a Mwamba is as precious as that of a Congolese. As Prime Minister of Uganda Mr. Obote should confront these problems first before he wastes time and energy over matters which form no part of the responsibility of his office.[89]

By the time that activists in Rwenzururu were using overt violence to defend the interests of their imagined community in western Toro, Kiwanuka's support was less explicit than it had been four years earlier.

As small-scale guerrilla operations continued throughout the mid-1960s, the party struggled to maintain its structural integrity. The UPC and Toro governments worked aggressively to militarily and politically undermine regional dissent. Also, as the political legitimacy of kingdoms became a more prominent national question throughout the 1960s, erstwhile critics of the Toro monarchy now backed the kingdom to compete with the regional monarchies of Bunyoro, Ankole, and Buganda. Political mobilities provided by both the ruling UPC and the Toro monarchy were ultimately too attractive to resist. Party organisers identified a number of key additional challenges confronting DP, including the lack of financial support from Kampala and the closure of branches in each of Toro's counties.[90] When a number of Toro's DP representatives joined UPC in 1964, the Catholic president of DP in Toro, Cypriano W. Rusoke, scathingly noted:

> No body of the DP has converted. This is cheap politics played by political lunatics in Toro. The UPC in Toro is so tremendously divided and weak that it is now announcing names of people on the Radio, that God had never created. [...] The country should rest assured that the UPC in Toro is a dying horse and

---

[88] BKMKP/Not Marked 3/Paul Ssemogerere to Mr Francis Mugarura, Kilembe Mines, 8 September 1964.
[89] BKMKP/Uganda Versus (Unmarked Folder)/Benedicto Kiwanuka, Press Comment, 16 January 1965.
[90] BKMKP/Confidential 2/George S. Ruguma, assistant publicity secretary, Toro Kingdom, 'Problem Facing the Toro Branch', n.d.

we shall let it die a natural death. One can go about deceiving some people for some time but one can never deceive all the people for all the time.[91]

The language of 'political lunatics' underscored the unsettling character of disruptive Protestant politics. But the strategy worked, as UPC maintained its control of the area through the rest of the decade.

Conclusion

By the early 1960s, Catholic politics in eastern and western Uganda looked similar insofar as Benedicto Kiwanuka aimed to move beyond the perception that he was a strong advocate for Buganda's seceding monarchy. But differences abounded. In Teso, Catholic activists, who traced their religious genealogies through the Mill Hill missions of eastern Uganda, saw themselves as important interlocutors in a region torn by religious polarities. By the mid-1960s, Obwangor and other leading UPC Catholic intellectuals were comfortable joining the opposition, DP, when political power became too centralised and chiefs acquired too much authority under the UPC government. Egalitarian sensibilities compelled many of Teso's activists, regardless of their party association. In Toro in western Uganda, Catholic communities had long been associated with the critique of royalist political authority. The Democratic Party was overtly associated with critics of the Toro state and, more broadly, as supporters of the secessionist claims of Baamba and Bakonjo historians. In time, DP was unable to successfully maintain its hold on power in western Uganda, which it seemed to gain steadily by the late 1960s in eastern Uganda.

In Uganda's nationalist historiography, Catholic political mobilisation is overwhelmingly associated with DP, where UPC is viewed as a Protestant and, to a lesser extent, national Muslim party. In eastern Uganda, these associations do not hold. To suggest that DP was strictly a Catholic party fails to consider how Catholics outside of Buganda aligned with varying political movements to advocate for regional representation and economic development. Further, in Uganda's nationalist histories, Benedicto Kiwanuka is often cast as a Catholic republican who staunchly opposed the influence of kingdoms in the life of public politics. Kiwanuka, it is maintained, was especially critical of the idea of Buganda's secession, which is why *Kabaka Yekka* worked to systemically derail DP on the eve of independence (Chapter 5). Rethinking the history of Catholic dissent in western Uganda is important because it shows

---

[91] BKMKP/Not Marked 3/Cypriano W. Rusoke, DP President, Toro, Press Statement, 1 September 1964.

that Kiwanuka capitalised on the emergence of the populist Rwenzururu kingdom to secure electoral victory.

Kiwanuka clearly did not view all monarchical secessions similarly. As we will show in the next chapter, Catholic politics in Bunyoro and Kigezi raised a different set of questions and complications, each rooted in much longer histories of Catholic political violence. Where Buganda's historiography has often underscored the discriminatory force of Protestant power – or its benefits – the long political histories of southern Bunyoro and political life on the Kigezi-Rwanda border illustrate how Catholic activism became intertwined with varying religious and democratic revolutions at the beginning and end of colonisation.

CHAPTER 3

Catholic Violence and Political Revolution in Bunyoro and Kigezi

> Political unrest in Kigezi, Western Province, has led to three incidents of crop slashing in villages near Kakale. Police said that the crops belonged to members of the Democratic Party who had refused to join the Uganda Peoples Congress.
>
> ~*Uganda Argus*, 20 March 1962

In the last chapter, we showed how sectarian politics in late colonial eastern Uganda did not conform with conventional, southern historiographies. The Catholic activist Cuthbert Obwangor advocated for decentralised forms of political participation that championed local networks, inspired by the egalitarian ethos of the Mill Hill Mission and the histories of regional mobility. This cluster of priorities contrasted with DP's centralising project in the area, which Teso activists associated with the long history of Ganda chauvinism in the region. In western Uganda, by contrast, DP was associated with the unravelling of one form of central political authority and replacing it with another. Kiwanuka and his party were closely aligned with the Rwenzururu secessionist movement, whose Catholic dissidents challenged the Protestant legitimacy of the Toro monarchy. In contrast, UPC championed the royalist cause of the Toro kingdom.

This chapter explores the intersection of Catholic and Protestant politics in colonial Bunyoro and Kigezi. It argues that politics in colonial southern Bunyoro complicate conventional interpretations of Protestant power in Uganda. As far as many Nyoro patriots were concerned, it was Baganda Catholics who had 'eaten' the counties (the 'Lost Counties') of Mubende, not the likes of Semei Kakungulu or the powerful Protestants Apolo Kaggwa and Hamu Mukasa. The controversial legacies of Catholic chiefs in southern Bunyoro obstructed Catholic cosmopolitanism in central Uganda. Kiwanuka backed the return of Bunyoro's 'Lost Counties' to assuage political tensions among the region's Catholic communities and to create national alliances.

Kiwanuka's sympathies toward the region were consistent with the views of his wife's family, whose history was interconnected with Nyoro claims in the region. Kiwanuka's position was also inspired by the historical research of the Mubende Banyoro Committee, a Nyoro historical society that argued for the return of the 'Lost Counties' to Bunyoro. Kiwanuka's efforts were largely unsuccessful; intra-Catholic violence persisted throughout the late colonial period, and DP would be unable to claim the success of negotiating the reallocation. The 'Lost Counties' did not return to Bunyoro until January 1965, under the leadership of Milton Obote.

Where DP was associated with the restoration of land to the kingdom of Bunyoro, it was associated with the unravelling of royalist authority along the Uganda-Rwanda border. In the south-western district of Kigezi, the colonial state reinforced older nodes of central authority in the region. The Democratic Party, by contrast, was affiliated with the Hutu republican revolution in Rwanda, whose capital was only eighty kilometres away from Kigezi's southern border. Catholic and Protestant contestations were interconnected with political changes unfolding in the kingdom of Rwanda, and debates surrounding the creation of ceremonial heads in late colonial south-western Uganda were firmly rooted in both the revolution unfolding in Rwanda and efforts to strengthen royalist authority in Uganda's historic kingdoms. By reinforcing the central authority of the region's kingdoms, UPC sought to build alliances and expand their national authority. By bolstering the authority of centralised kingdoms, it was initially hoped that Protestant monarchies would exhibit loyalty toward UPC – a politics of gratitude or reciprocity. It was only after this strategy failed that the Obote government became increasingly hostile toward kingships.

Catholic Authority in Southern Bunyoro

Between the eighteenth and nineteenth centuries, the Bunyoro-Kitara empire dominated eastern Africa's politics and economies. For reasons that were both ecological and political, the empire's authority began to wane by the late nineteenth century. Shane Doyle has shown how droughts in the region adversely impacted health, agricultural production, livestock management, and demographic expansion from the late eighteenth century onward.[1] The geography of Bunyoro opened the kingdom's frontiers to external rivalries in ways that were without parallel in the region. Along the northern frontier of the kingdom, the Anglo-Egyptian military was expanding its sphere of influence in

---

[1] Shane Doyle, *Crisis and Decline in Bunyoro: Population and Environment in Western Uganda 1860–1955* (Oxford: James Currey, 2006), pp. 11–41.

the area. The kingdom of Toro had declared its independence from Bunyoro on the western front. To the south, the kingdom of Buganda, with the backing of the British Government, orchestrated military raids in the southern area of Kitara: the area that would become known as the 'Lost Counties'.

One of the contradictions of Uganda's early colonial empire was that when the Nyoro counties of Bugangaizi and Buyaga – or Mubende – were incorporated into Buganda, they were brought under the authority of Ganda Catholics. Shane Doyle shows that the English military administrator, Colonel Henry Colvile, hoped to allay earlier Catholic grievances concerning Protestant land allocations in Buganda by distributing Nyoro territories to Ganda Catholics. Colvile also wished to undercut the Catholic party's support of *Kabaka* Mwanga following the 1890s religious wars.[2] Henri Médard also suggests that Colvile, after preventing Catholic princes from assuming the kingship of Buganda, sought to mitigate Catholic grievances by awarding southern Bunyoro to Buganda's Catholic chiefs.[3]

When Buganda's Catholic chiefs migrated into the 'Lost Counties', a term that did not enter into popular discourse until the interwar period, they were especially rapacious.[4] Many of the Catholic chiefs who controlled new territories had participated in the religious wars, which resulted in an abrasive style of governance.[5] Catholics also worried that unless they quickly accumulated subjects and land, they would be unable to justify their land holdings to the *Lukiiko*. It was not entirely clear if Buganda's Protestants would, once again, dispossess them of their lands. In consequence, Nyoro chiefs experienced massive displacement, and ordinary Banyoro were forced into indentured servitude under Ganda Catholics.

Indentured servitude was intertwined with the history of slavery in the region. As Richard Reid has shown, slavery was a prominent feature of public life in Bunyoro and Buganda throughout the nineteenth century.[6] The accounts of nineteenth-century European explorers claimed that 50,000 enslaved eastern Africans were utilised in Buganda's army, while others suggested that

---

[2] Doyle, *Crisis and Decline in Bunyoro*, p. 81.
[3] Henri Médard, *Le royaume du Buganda au XIXe Siècle: Mutations Politiques et Religieuses d'un Ancien Etat d'Afrique de l'Est* (Paris: Karthala, 2007), p. 179.
[4] Our interpretation follows Doyle, *Crisis and Decline in Bunyoro*, p. 82.
[5] For further discussion on military operations during this period, see John M. Gray, 'The Sieges of Bukumi, Mubende District, in 1898', *Uganda Journal*, 25 (1961), 65–85; A. D. Roberts, 'The "Lost Counties" of Bunyoro', *Uganda Journal*, 26 (1962), 194–9.
[6] Richard J. Reid, *Political Power in Pre-Colonial Buganda: Economy, Society & Welfare in the Nineteenth Century* (Oxford: James Currey, 2002), pp. 113–19.

the average Muganda possessed approximately 100 enslaved Ugandans.[7] Holly Hanson has persuasively argued that the expansion of the kingdom of Buganda was possible due to the creation of *ebitongole* chieftaincies, whose subjects were predominantly war captives.[8]

Early Catholic politics inherited the legacies of regional slavery. Christopher Wrigley has shown how the Catholic capital of Buddu – or the 'place of the enslaved' – was first described as Bwiru, or the place of cultivators (*abairu*).[9] Buddu – or Bwiru – was at the centre of disputed land and labour between Buganda and Bunyoro until the late nineteenth century,[10] when the area became populated by large numbers of Ganda Catholics.[11] Up until 1900, Catholics remained far more reluctant than their Protestant counterparts to liberate enslaved labourers in Buddu and southern Bunyoro.[12]

Despite the problematic inequities that surrounded Catholicism in southern Bunyoro due to slavery, Nyoro chiefs converted in large numbers to navigate the development of newer types of spiritual and political authority. Due to the influence of local converts and missionaries, additional chiefs and communities converted to Catholicism throughout central Bunyoro. At the same time, Protestant administrators – Britons and Baganda – treated Nyoro elites with contempt. Before the outbreak of the First World War, Nyoro Catholic chiefs had revolted in protest in a movement known as the Nyangire uprising of 1907. As a consequence of the movement, forty-nine Nyoro Catholic chiefs were exiled by the colonial government and replaced by Ganda Protestants.[13]

The immediate cause of the uprising was disproportionate land allocations that benefited Ganda administrators, both Catholic and Protestant, followed by the imposition of Luganda in Nyoro churches, schools, and administrative centres. The colonial archive maintains dozens of petitions and complaints drafted by Bunyoro's exiled Catholics following the uprising, which included

---

[7] Ibid., p. 116.

[8] Holly E. Hanson, 'Stolen People and Autonomous Chiefs in Nineteenth-Century Buganda: The Social Consequences of Non-Free Followers', in *Slavery in the Great Lakes Region of East Africa*, ed. by Henri Médard and Shane Doyle (Kampala: Fountain Publishers, 2007), pp. 161–73.

[9] Christopher Wrigley, *Kingship and State: The Buganda Dynasty* (Cambridge: Cambridge University Press, 1996), p. 218.

[10] Médard, *Le royaume du Buganda au XIXe Siècle*, p. 108.

[11] John M. Waliggo, 'The Catholic Church in the Buddu Province of Buganda, 1879–1925' (unpublished PhD, University of Cambridge, 1976), pp. 80–81.

[12] Henri Médard argues that Protestant converts were more willing to release enslaved labourers because they were trying to cultivate tactical alliances with British emancipationists: *Le royaume du Buganda au XIXe Siècle*, p. 150.

[13] Doyle, *Crisis and Decline in Bunyoro*, p. 101.

burning Ganda huts and destroying Ganda crops in southern Bunyoro. While the petitions' themes vary to some extent, they commonly appealed to God's mercy to influence government policy.

Throughout the early twentieth century, Nyoro chiefs frequently employed the idea of 'mercy' to contest regional politics. One chief, Nikodemu Kakoko Mutaibwa, reworked confessional liturgy to frame his petition, which underscored the place of 'mercy' in political mediation:

> To my master Mr Judge Carter. [...] I inform you about my case, remember the mercy of God and help a prisoner so that I may not be sent to other lands. [...] Have mercy and have me brought before you and the Commissioner and hear everything that took place in Bunyolo, help me one person to speak. God will reward you. Do not abandon my father and my master. It would be well were I placed under one of the Baganda (chiefs) in Uganda or under a European and remain in his hands. I cling to your chair of justice.[14]

Zabuloni Kirose, another deportee, also appealed to God's mercy before Uganda's principal judge:

> To my master Judge Carter. How are you Sir? Now Sir, I ask you to help me. You are the Judge of all lands, why are we being taken away without (having the opportunity of) informing you as to the person who has committed an offence against the Government. [...] Sir, remember the mercy of our God.[15]

Appeals for God's mercy fundamentally framed how Catholics – including the White Fathers and Ugandan converts – mediated and critiqued public authority. The petitions of the period show how local converts reworked the Sacred Heart tradition that developed in France following the Revolution and the Franco-Prussian War.[16] Throughout the nineteenth century, French Catholics developed numerous songs, including the 'Canticle of the National

---

[14] UNA/Secretariat Minute Papers A43-25G/Nikodemu Kakoko Mutaibwa, Petition, Entebbe, 21 October 1907.

[15] UNA/Secretariat Minute Papers A43-25G/Zabuloni Kirose, Petition, Entebbe, 21 October 1907.

[16] For additional commentary on the importance of the Sacred Heart tradition in French mysticism, see the spiritual biography of the seventeenth-century nun, Saint Margaret Mary Alacoque, whose visions and reforms shaped Catholic practice throughout western Europe. Martha Mel Edmunds' work, for instance, shows how Sacred Heart devotion shaped the production of religious and Bourbon architecture throughout the early modern period. See: Martha Mel Edmunds, 'Gabriel's Altar for the Palace Chapel at Versailles: Sacred Heart and Royal Court in Eighteenth-Century France', *Journal of the Society of Architectural Historians*, 65 (2006), pp. 550–77.

Vow' and the 'Catholic Marseillaise', to solicit the intervention of a 'merciful' and 'conquering' God. The song was quickly adopted by Catholic pilgrims throughout the country, in places including Paray-le-Monial,[17] near Auvergne, where the Ugandan missionary Léon Livinhac was born during the mid-nineteenth century. The idea of mercy was politically translatable in both France and Bunyoro, both of which had experienced the ruptures brought about by military and religious violence.

By the late 1950s, Mubende's population was overwhelmingly Catholic. According to the 1959 government census, Catholics constituted 65 per cent of the population. The percentage of Catholics in Mubende outnumbered any area in Buganda, including Buddu.[18] Be that as it may, Catholic solidarities across the Bunyoro-Buganda border remained underdeveloped and, at times, volatile. Nyoro Catholics throughout Bunyoro, including the 'Lost Counties', distanced themselves politically from Ganda Catholics. Conflict over political boundaries restricted pan-Ugandan Catholicism.

Lost Lands and Historical Recovery

While Catholic cosmopolitanism had its limitations, members of DP worked to strengthen regional political alliances on the eve of independence. One of the most penetrating reflections on religious politics and the 'Lost Counties' was offered by N. K. Rugemwa, a DP representative for North Mubende. Rugemwa penned a lengthy memo to Uganda's constitutional conference, during which he argued for Bunyoro's re-annexation of the counties.[19] The memo is informed by extensive historical research. It begins by asserting that the '[p]erpetuation of the present Anglo-Buganda's colonial rule in the lost counties will lead to the unavoidable strife which may, and conceivably will lead to civil war'. Rugemwa cites at length Uganda's nineteenth-century records, which show how Bunyoro's trouble began when Ganda Catholics swallowed the counties. One extended section noted:

> It is revealed in [...] Omukama of Bunyoro's petition to H.M. The Queen on the Lost Counties issue that on 19th November, 1896 Mr. E. J. L. Berkeley reported the following to the Marquis of Salisbury in a despatch numbered 113:

---

[17] Raymond Jonas, *France and the Cult of the Sacred Heart: An Epic Tale for Modern Times* (Berkeley: University of California Press, 2000, p. 219.
[18] 'Uganda Census 1959: African Population' (Entebbe: Statistics Branch, Ministry of Economic Affairs, 1961), p. 44.
[19] BKMKP/DP Correspondence Personal/'Uganda Constitutional Conference', Memo by Hon N. K. Rugemwa, Representative for North Mubende: Restoration of the "Lost Counties" to Bunyoro' [c. early 1961].

'I proceeded to explain the distribution of these territories between two religious parties as made by Col. Colvile, would be maintained, namely, the district (marked as South Unyoro) bounded to the North By Ngusi river, to the west by the south-east shore of Lake Albert, to the south by Muzizi river and to the east by Kitumbwi river, would go to the Catholics and the territory lying to the east thereof, viz., bounded to the North by the Kafu River, to the east by the Nile and to the south by Buganda (as heretofore) would go to the Protestants.' The aforementioned was the despatch that sealed off the freedom of many hundreds of thousands of Banyoro, the inhabitants of the Lost Counties from year 1896 to the present date.[20]

The petition cited the resignation of the British administrator, Mr Pulteny, who had protested against the decision 'that South Unyoro is to be handed over to the Roman Catholics'. The two-page report concluded by outlining the adverse cultural impact of Buganda's colonisation of the area: Runyoro was forbidden in courts, schools, and churches, Kinyoro songs and dances were forbidden, and Ganda customary law was strictly enforced.

Rugemwa's line of interpretation followed the argumentative work of the patriotic historical society, the Mubende Banyoro Committee (MBC), which Nyoro patriots established during the mid-1950s to campaign for Bunyoro's reunification. More than any other organisation in late colonial Uganda, it was the MBC that asserted that Uganda should not secure self-rule or independence until Bunyoro's counties were returned. Drawing from St Matthew's Gospel (7:26–7), one of the movement's intellectuals noted: 'If self-rule were given to Uganda before the restoration of the counties to Bunyoro-Kitara, it would be "attempting to build the future sovereign state of Uganda upon a murram [clay or dirt] foundation".'[21]

In the press, MBC writers used theological analysis to critique Ganda imperialism. Writing from Nairobi, the MBC sympathiser Harry Gayonga asked, 'Are Baganda the only angels and Banyoro the only devils'?[22] The letter argued that ending 'black imperialism' should be prioritised over condemning 'white imperialism'. He compared Ganda chiefs in the 'Lost Counties' with Kenya's white settlers in the highlands of Kenya, and demanded that 'Buganda settlers, if they want to stay in Mubende must either combine with MBC and fight for the return of the counties or we, the legitimate owners of Mubende, shall rule and tell them to pack up for Buganda'.[23]

[20] Ibid.
[21] 'Mubende Statement on Constitution', *Uganda Argus*, 5 November 1959.
[22] Harry Gayonga, Letter to the Editor, Nairobi, *Uganda Argus*, 10 February 1960.
[23] Ibid.

Mubende Banyoro Committee writers spent considerable time repurposing early historical accounts of Uganda, including the writings of Apolo Kaggwa and Thomas' and Scott's history of Uganda.[24] Writers were quick to point out that the 'Lost Counties' contained the royal burial grounds of Bunyoro's kings. One editorialist, who self-identified as a 'Hopeful Mubendean', called for the immediate return of the 'counties [that] contain the tombs of the Abakama of Bunyoro and the two hills where traditional accession ceremonies used to be performed'.[25] In response to a letter that had questioned Nyoro migration in the area, the MBC organiser Christopher Atwoki, writing from Masaka, sarcastically questioned one Ganda patriot:

> In his letter [a Muganda] said that Banyoro living in Mubende were just immigrants from Bunyoro. May I know what kind of history books he reads before writing this misleading ideas [sic]? Kasolo, what about those tombs of late Bunyoro kings lying in Mubende? Did those immigrants form another kingdom or Bunyoro did not have enough land for their burial?[26]

As one activist, M. B. Siyawa, summarised: 'one can realize that Mubende was not part of Buganda and will never be.'[27]

Public claims about Ganda oppression in southern Bunyoro accompanied acts of violence and intimidation in ways that resembled the Nyangire uprising during the early 1900s.[28] Nyoro patriots demanded that all Banyoro stop trading at markets owned or managed by Baganda. According to one police report, Banyoro in Mugalama, Buyaga, were warned that their crops would be slashed and burned if they did not cooperate.[29] In Mayira, Buyaga, a group of eight armed Banyoro were accused of attacking a Nyoro chief's home in the evening, during which they slashed sixty-two banana trees and thirty-five coffee trees.[30] In Musale, protesters destroyed a Nyoro chief's forty-two cassava plants, in addition to twenty-nine banana trees and sixteen coffee trees. Village *Lukiiko* halls were burned, as were kitchens, exterior pit latrines, and

---

[24] K. L. N. Kamuhanda, Letter to the Editor, *Uganda Argus*, 7 August 1956; Mubendian, Buyaga, Letter to the Editor, *Uganda Argus*, 10 August 1956. See: H. B. Thomas and R. Scott, *Uganda* (London: Oxford University Press, 1935).

[25] Letter to the Editor, Hopeful Mubendean, *Uganda Argus*, 16 November 1957.

[26] Letter to the Editor, Christopher Atwoki, Masaka, *Uganda Argus*, 14 January 1960.

[27] M. B. Siyawa, Kakumiro, Letter to the Editor, *Uganda Argus*, 19 July 1961.

[28] For additional correspondence about Nyoro feelings about Ganda oppression, see: Marungu Sajjabbi, Kakumiro, Letter to the Editor, *Uganda Argus*, 2 January 1960; George Mpabaisi, Letter to the Editor, *Uganda Argus*, 23 January 1960.

[29] 'Intimidation Campaign in Mubende', *Uganda Argus*, 4 November 1960.

[30] Ibid.

schools.³¹ Attacks were often accompanied by letters 'that warned chiefs to stop cooperating with Baganda'.³² By November 1960, the colonial administration, at the urgency of the Buganda Government, declared Mubende a disturbed area.³³ Throughout southern Uganda, the MBC was proscribed, and in June 1962, the *Lukiiko* announced that the *kabaka*'s government in Mubende had unanimously passed a resolution banning the MBC.³⁴

In 1962, competing factions throughout Buganda and Bunyoro advocated intensely to secure the fate of the 'Lost Counties'. By January, the government had launched a special investigation in Mubende – often referred to as the Molson Commission – which eventually culminated in the 1964 'Lost Counties' referendum.³⁵ When the Privy Council Commissioners arrived in Mubende to collect testimony, they were greeted by Nyoro patriots and members of *Kabaka Yekka* (KY). The two factions had positioned themselves in opposition near the building. The national press suggested that hundreds of Banyoro brandished covered spears, while performing a battle dance; KY responded with counter dances.³⁶ As dances of intimidation unfolded, members from each of the two parties shouted competing slogans and waved partisan flags. Nyoro activists shouted that 'the counties belong to Bunyoro'; members of KY marched with placards that asserted: 'There are no "Lost Counties". We live in peace in Buganda.' With Bunyoro flags in hand, patriots' placards announced: 'We hate black colonialism. Bunyoro's heart is here.'³⁷

The kingdom of Bunyoro, for its part, had already taken measures to reclaim the 'Lost Counties'. In late 1961, the government of Bunyoro – the *Rukurato* – passed a resolution to reclaim the territories. With precise historical reference, they noted that the shortsightedness of British policy was on display for the world to see, asking interested observers to review 'the British Foreign Office declaration of June 30, 1896, which appeared in the *London Gazette* on July 3, 1896'.³⁸ The *Gazette* showed that the 'Territory of Unyoro, together with that part of the British sphere of influence lying to the west of [Buganda] and Unyoro which has not hitherto been included in the Uganda Protectorate, is

---

³¹ Ibid.
³² Ibid.
³³ 'Mubende trouble saza a disturbed area: CID sent in', *Uganda Argus*, 3 November 1960.
³⁴ 'Mubende Group Banned', *Uganda Argus*, 18 June 1962.
³⁵ *Presiding Officers' Instructions 1964: Referendum, Buyaga and Bugangazzi Counties* (Entebbe: Government Printer, 1964).
³⁶ 'Spears and Dancing for "Lost Counties" Team', *Uganda Argus*, 23 January 1962.
³⁷ Ibid.
³⁸ 'Rukurato Sunday meeting decides: Midnight tomorrow Bunyoro "Seizes" Lost Counties, Move Follows Declaration of 1896', *Uganda Argus*, 17 October 1961.

placed within the limits of that Protectorate[.]'[39] With one empire withdrawing from Uganda, it was now time to return lost land to another: Bunyoro-Kitara.

For Bunyoro's Protestant king, *Omukama* Tito Winyi IV, it was difficult to imagine the 'Lost Counties' dispute in ways that did not recall the early, controversial role of Buganda's Catholic chiefs. In turn, during the late 1950s and early 1960s, the kingdom's government reinforced the Protestant lineage of the monarchy, which it did to assert regional authority in the southern part of the kingdom and to complicate any legitimacy that Buganda possessed by underscoring its historic relationship with the Anglican church.

In late 1959, Winyi supported the production of the first mural to be painted in a Protestant church in Uganda, which was placed in a church in the royal capital of Hoima.[40] The mural was thirty-two feet long and ten feet in height. It chronicled the story of the early Christian church in Palestine in the setting of Bunyoro. It depicted five scenes: Jesus' miraculous feeding of the multitude, Christ's triumphal entry into Jerusalem during Passover, the crucifixion, the conversion of St Paul in Damascus, and a minister preaching the gospel. In the mural, Banyoro are set against a background of Nyoro traditional homes in the village.

The mural was consecrated during a moment when the Nyoro Government was criticising Catholics for creating confusion in Uganda. Following an address by Bunyoro's prime minister, during which he discussed 'the evil of muddling politics with religious differences' and the role of the Catholic Church in causing instability in Bunyoro,[41] one Nyoro Catholic in Bujumbura, Paulo Gahwerra, argued that the '*Katikkiro* of Bunyoro's speech in the *Rukurato*, Hoima [...] cannot pass unchallenged'.[42] He continued:

> The whole of this part of the speech was designed to discredit one religious community, the Catholic community. Mr Kwebiha, the *Katikkiro*, said that certain people who had proved a failure in life and that, because of their unsettled minds, were causing confusion, whereas he and his Cabinet are confusing the country and muddling politics with religion by their injustice. The people he was implying are not only fighting for their own rights but for the rights of the whole community, and they will fight till the *Katikkiro*'s Government shows justice in this country.

The assertion of Protestant, monarchical power in Bunyoro during the 'Lost Counties' dispute is insightful. The royalist government of Bunyoro

---

[39] 'Foreign Office, June 30, 1896', *London Gazette*, 3 July 1896.
[40] 'Mural Consecrated in Bunyoro Church', *Uganda Argus*, 25 November 1959.
[41] '"Religious ill-feeling" in Bunyoro', *Uganda Argus*, 6 November 1959.
[42] Paul Gahwerra, Letter to the Editor, *Uganda Argus*, 21 November 1959.

viewed Catholic politics and DP with suspicion. In the same speech, Bunyoro's *katikkiro* argued that DP, those 'people who were travelling at night spreading seeds of religious ill-feelings in the country must know that they were digging a grave for Bunyoro'.[43] As opposed to being grave diggers for the kingdom's burial, Hoima's royalists saw themselves as faithful mediators of the story of God's redemption in Uganda. The commissioning of the Hoima mural showed that the history of God's salvation now intersected with Bunyoro's past. Where Catholics were accused of being night travellers, and early instigators of political confusion in the 'Lost Counties', the Protestant monarchy operated in daylight. This would enable all to see that the kingdom might be resurrected through unification and the singing of national and patriotic anthems, which Winyi ordered to be performed during the mural's consecration.[44] The mural was created when it was politically advantageous for royal Protestants to assert their authority over lands that been seized by British and Catholic powerbrokers.

Ganda Patriots and Benedicto Kiwanuka's Project of Restoration

In contrast to Bunyoro's royalist state-builders and the MBC, ethnic patriots in Buganda fiercely opposed annexation. During the early 1960s, KY activists produced hundreds of articles, marches, placards, and commissioned centres to ensure that Buganda did not lose the counties. Buganda's *Lukiiko* openly resisted returning the counties. In one report, the kingdom asserted that 'Buganda will never agree to any recommendations from the Privy Council Commission into the "lost counties" dispute that gives any part of the kingdom to Bunyoro'.[45] Buganda's Catholic *Omulamuzi* (chief justice), J. P. Musoke, called the entire movement to restore the counties into question, concluding that 'all that is being said by the Mubende Banyoro Commitee about the "lost counties" is sheer lies'.[46]

Baganda on the streets of Kampala embodied the same resistance. In early 1962, a group of no fewer than 500 KY demonstrators paraded throughout Kampala wearing bark cloth and *kkanzu*s, or long robes, displaying placards that stated that Buganda would return nothing to Bunyoro (Figure 3.1).[47] Throughout 1962, KY appealed to Baganda to emigrate into the 'Lost

---

[43] '"Religious ill-feeling" in Bunyoro'.
[44] 'Mural Consecrated in Bunyoro Church'.
[45] '"We'll Never Give Counties Away"', *Uganda Argus*, 3 February 1962.
[46] 'Lost counties claim is lies – *Omulamuzi*', *Uganda Argus*, 1 September 1961.
[47] 'Counties "protest" march', *Uganda Argus*, 26 January 1962.

Figure 3.1 Throughout 1962, Ganda patriots protested Bunyoro's reacquisition of the 'Lost Counties'. *Uganda Argus*, 27 January 1962.

Counties'.[48] 'Jolly Joe' Kiwanuka organised a banana campaign, during which persecuted Baganda in the 'Lost Counties' would receive necessary support.[49] Once in Mubende, Baganda were to coordinate their efforts through the party's Mubende office, whose purpose was to 'defend the "lost counties"'.[50] The office was sanctioned by the Buganda Government, which reminded southern Ugandans that '[w]e shall all die instead of allowing the dismemberment of our Kingdom'.[51] In turn, reports indicated that Ganda cohorts as large as one hundred patrolled Mubende and Buganda's northern border with pangas (machetes) and spears, often slashing DP crops and threatening Baganda who supported DP.[52]

Ganda mobilisers during the period returned to the 1890s to generate shared memories among Ganda patriots and to produce public slogans and songs. One activist, Eddie Kayole, who was based in Masaka, reminded Baganda that they had conquered Bunyoro during the 1890s. Kayole then asked: 'What is the idea of making a war, if the conquests are to be returned?'[53] Ganda warriors had 'fought with King Kabalega and conquered him and [we] got the "lost counties" after the "lost blood"'. Kayole continued:

[48] 'Yekka Plan for Mubende', *Uganda Argus*, 23 April 1962.
[49] Ibid.
[50] '"Prepared to Defend Lost Counties"', *Uganda Argus*, 23 June 1962.
[51] Ibid.
[52] 'Violence mounts against DP men', *Uganda Argus*, 1 March 1962.
[53] Eddie Kayole, Masaka, Letter to the Editor, *Uganda Argus*, 14 January 1960.

[O]n the journey to the battle-field we went singing, '*Banange munywere. Omunyoro omukuule asitudde. Omunyoro owakabindi asitudde.*' Every Muganda still remembers that song. After the war, no doubt, we had a full right of claiming the whole of Bunyoro Kingdom as our conquest. So we even expected thanks from Banyoro for having preserved them as a kingdom – if they realised it. But seeing that they have failed to realise such a favour done to them we can resume the claim of the whole of Bunyoro Kingdom and the next thing they will hear is that they are under the sway of our hand. Let them ignite their own fate. In the meantime, let Banyoro not bite their tongues, but let them get hold of their pens and begin.[54]

The force of Kayole's argument drew from late nineteenth-century medical and farming vocabularies. In English, the song reads: 'Friends be firm (*Banange munywere*). The uprooted Munyoro is charging (*Omunyoro omukuule asitudde*). The Munyoro with the small windpipe is charging (*Omunyoro owakabindi asitudde*).' *Omukuule*, the uprooted one, in the verb form, *kukuula*, meant to extract or pull a tooth. It referenced an irregular dental configuration or the development of cavities, which warranted extraction for the purpose of preserving the other teeth, preventing abscess, or reducing pain. The term was also used to describe the practice of uprooting weeds in a garden to produce higher crop yields.

Ganda patriots, like Kayole, argued that Bunyoro during the late nineteenth century had become unstable, its subjects uprooted. By claiming the southern section of the kingdom, Buganda's chiefs – including Catholics – saw themselves stabilising the region, in much the same way as tooth extraction normalises the teeth or mouth, or uprooted weeds improve the beauty and production of a garden. When Kayole argued that stubborn Banyoro should not 'bite their tongues', but take out their pens and begin writing, he suggested that Banyoro should author letters and songs of gratitude toward Buganda. By removing the 'Lost Counties', a decaying tooth, Buganda was preserving the larger political structure of Bunyoro – the teeth – from rotting or biting the tongue. Following political orthodontics, Banyoro could now speak – or write – the praises of Buganda.

During the late colonial period, it was common for Ganda patriots to emphasise the moral necessity of Buganda's ownership. During the formal inquiry into the 'Lost Counties', the *ssaza* chief of Bugerere, S. B. Kigozi, argued that 'Bunyoro should be grateful [...] to the Baganda, who invited the missionaries to preach the Gospel, not only in Buganda but in other parts of the country,

[54] Ibid.

including Bunyoro'.⁵⁵ It had been Baganda, he continued, who had first 'provided administrators to establish proper administration in Bunyoro'.⁵⁶ The Ganda physician E. D. Kafero, similarly, after extensive travel in Bunyoro 'had discovered that the Banyoro did not like to work and that was a handicap to the development of their Kingdom'.⁵⁷ Kafero was morally compelled to direct 'the people of Buganda to go and develop their District'.⁵⁸

The Democratic Party and Benedicto Kiwanuka struggled to navigate Ganda patriots' demands to maintain the 'Lost Counties'. The overwhelming majority of DP's representatives supported the return of the 'Lost Counties' to Bunyoro, which only exacerbated tension and acts of intimidation and violence against DP campaigners. The DP representative for Mubende North, N. K. Rugemwa, argued that 'there had been continual outbreaks in the district since last year, because there was no democracy, no freedom of speech, and no good administration because all of the local Chiefs had become politicians.'⁵⁹ Rugemwa argued that '[f]or the last 60 years the people have been subjected to Buganda rule against their will'. In order to preserve 'good orderly government and democracy, all the Baganda Chiefs should be removed'.⁶⁰

The extent to which politics during the period was characterised by fear and intimidation warrants emphasis. Baganda chiefs' crops were regularly slashed or burned in the 'Lost Counties' throughout late 1961 and all of 1962.⁶¹ Between 22 February and 12 March alone, there were no fewer than seventy-two reported cases of intimidation, arson, or malicious damage to property.⁶² Nyoro protesters were frequently arrested, requests for additional police officers common, and Nyoro dissenters assassinated Baganda chiefs with arrows.⁶³ As one Nyoro placard read: 'return our counties Lords, prevent war, who would like to see widows and orphans.'⁶⁴

---

⁵⁵ '"Bunyoro should be grateful to Baganda"', *Uganda Argus*, 31 January 1962.
⁵⁶ Ibid.
⁵⁷ Ibid.
⁵⁸ Ibid.
⁵⁹ 'Appeal for calm in Mubende', *Uganda Argus*, 19 July 1961.
⁶⁰ Ibid.
⁶¹ 'Six cases of crop slashing in Mubende', *Uganda Argus*, 25 October 1961; 'Baganda Chiefs' Crops Chopped in Mubende', *Uganda Argus*, 18 January 1962.
⁶² '5 Banyoro jailed for damaging property', *Uganda Argus*, 12 March 1962.
⁶³ See, for example: 'Mubende – 33 are Jailed', *Uganda Argus*, 3 March 1962; 'Rioters jailed at Mubende', *Uganda Argus*, 23 March 1962; 'Mubende Incidents', *Uganda Argus*, 25 March 1962; '33 Go to Jail for Assembling', *Uganda Argus*, 27 March 1962; 'New Outbreaks of Violence', *Uganda Argus*, 31 March 1962; 'More police for Mubende', *Uganda Argus*, 1 May 1962; 'Arrow Kills Chief', *Uganda Argus*, 27 June 1962.
⁶⁴ '"Bunyoro ready to fight over counties"', *Uganda Argus*, 18 January 1962.

The pervading sense of fear placed activists and state administrators in a position where they were apprehensive about releasing any report on the counties, being concerned that it would only create further instability.[65] The extent to which parties could dampen violence and temper grievances became a key point of debate in gaining public legitimacy. Namely, who was best equipped to end the violence and intimidation? To this end, DP called for a safety pledge by September 1961, which followed a series of confrontations between Nyoro patriots and DP's Baganda members in Mubende.[66] Because of DP's association with Catholicism, some Nyoro patriots threatened to extract or remove DP from the area, in ways that echoed Kayole's earlier argument about teeth. In response to these threats, one DP writer in Hoima stated: 'DP is firmly rooted despite malicious and false allegations and the opponents of DP may be convinced that it will not be easily eradicated.'[67] Representatives of DP continued to argue that UPC was ill-equipped to resolve the conflict, while also asserting that KY was responsible for the proliferation of regional violence.[68]

Benedicto Kiwanuka believed that by returning Mubende to Bunyoro, he would unify Catholics in the area and entrench DP's role in unifying the country on the eve of independence. To this end, Kiwanuka organised a special tour throughout Mubende in March 1962, which included visiting the Officer-in-Charge for the counties and 'areas where men of the Special Force units are operating'.[69] It had been Kiwanuka's hope to capitalise on the moment. Following the tour, he concluded that Mubende 'presents the gravest security problem in the country today',[70] which was 'too deep-rooted to be left to the remedy of police activity and the imposition of curfews'.[71] Kiwanuka noted that the 'Lost Counties' must be returned and fully resolved before securing independence.[72] Failure to act, he continued, simply illustrated 'the kind of

[65] '"Fear Leads to Delay of Counties Report"', *Uganda Argus*, 27 March 1962.
[66] 'Mubende's DP man wants "safe conduct" pledge', *Uganda Argus*, 1 September 1961. Some Nyoro patriots accused DP of supporting Buganda, while Ganda patriots accused DP of supporting the return of the counties.
[67] Yakobo Kabeihobeiho, Hoima-Kitoba, Letter to the Editor, *Uganda Argus*, 17 May 1961.
[68] '"Let down by UPC"', *Uganda Argus*, 25 October 1961; 'Premier attacked over Lost Counties Issue', *Uganda Argus*, 24 May 1962.
[69] 'Prime Minister visits Mubende: Governor to meet Mengo Ministers', *Uganda Argus*, 13 March 1962.
[70] BKMKP/Federal Status/'Statement by the Prime Minister', 14 March 1962.
[71] 'Mubende unrest calls for commission of inquiry – Kiwanuka', *Uganda Argus*, 2 December 1960.
[72] 'Mubende is the Gravest Problem – Premier', *Uganda Argus*, 15 March 1962. See also 'United Front Needed for London – DP', *Uganda Argus*, 28 August 1961.

complacency reigning in Mengo circles'.⁷³ Kiwanuka was challenged to build solidarities with local Catholic Banyoro, even as the initiative ostracised him further from the government of Buganda. For DP to gain traction in Bunyoro, Kiwanuka had to prove that he was a different sort of Ganda Catholic chief than those of an earlier generation.

Kiwanuka drew from multiple arenas of inspiration to develop solidarity with Banyoro patriots. First, Benedicto was the husband of Maxencia, a Munyoro raised in the 'Lost Counties'. As Albert Bade has shown, Maxencia's father was a prince of the Bachwezi dynasty that governed the Bunyoro empire.⁷⁴ Their family's political authority had been undercut by the redistribution of Bunyoro's southern frontier. Family ties fostered for Benedicto a familiarity with the contentious character of Baganda Catholics in the area.

Second, Kiwanuka's papers show that he studied pamphlets and petitions produced by the MBC, whose authors, as we have begun to see, challenged historical accounts that privileged Buganda's ownership of southern Bunyoro. Kiwanuka's personal papers contain the influential pamphlet, '*Uganda Kwefuga ne Mubende Kwefuga: Mubende wants Freedom*', or 'Uganda for Independence and Mubende for Independence'.⁷⁵ The one-page circular drew from the metrics of time and the natural world to offer a forceful critique of Ganda chiefs in Bunyoro.

> The Baganda are saying that Whites should leave. But we Banyoro are saying that all of the Baganda should say 'goodbye'. The clock has ticked, the power should be with us the native [...]. Our language which the Baganda weakened must now be taught in schools and in all worshipping places and to be used in all offices. How many of our people are convicted for offences and how many of our children fail exams because of being forced to use the language which is not ours? [...] The sixty years that we have been paying taxes to the Buganda government, we have been rats' children on which the dogs' children feed!!⁷⁶

---

⁷³ 'Mubende is the Gravest Problem – Premier'.
⁷⁴ Albert Bade, *Benedicto Kiwanuka: The Man and His Politics* (Kampala: Fountain Publishers, 1996), p. 8.
⁷⁵ BKMKP/Om. A. Sebaggala e Gulama/'*Uganda Kwefuga ne Mubende Kwefuga: Mubende wants Freedom*' [c. 1961].
⁷⁶ *Abaganda bagamba nti Abazungu bagende. Naffe Abanyoro tugamba nti Abaganda mweraba! Essawa ekoonye obuyinza bwaffe okudda mu mikono gyaffe. [...] Olulimi lwaffe Abaganda lwe baadibya luteekwa kaakano Okuyigirizibwa mu masinzizo gonna, n'okukozesebwa mu Offices zonna. Abantu baffe bameka abasingibwa emisango, n'abaana baffe bameka abagwa ebigezo buli mwaka olwokuwalirizibwa okukozesa olulimi olutali lwaffe? [...] Emyaka enkaga (60) gye tumaze nga tuwa omusolo mu Gavumenti y'e Buganda, twafuuka abaana ba wammese abakuza ab'Embwa!!*

The writers reminded their readers – including Baganda – that '[i]n our culture God created us as Banyoro' and that to deny that one is a Munyoro 'is an abuse of God who created you as a Munyoro'! The letter continued with a theological interpretation of ethnic identity:

> God, the owner of heaven created us as real Banyoro. He gave us this nation, the language and good prestigious traditions. God created within us a spirit of fighting for our nation, including all the things that he gave us. Therefore, at this time: the land, rivers and mountains, the rocks, trees and plants, animals and birds, insects and other creatures are crying to God to return them to Bunyoro where he created them in the beginning of this nation of the Kingdom of Bunyoro Kitara.[77]

According to Kiwanuka, historical and theological claims demanded concrete, immediate political action. It was for this reason, then, that Kiwanuka talked extensively about the need for morally compelling, decisive leadership. In his writings on the 'Lost Counties' in a 1962 political manifesto, drawing from *Uganda Kwefuga ne Mubende Kwefuga*, Kiwanuka reflected extensively on the importance of political principle. 'Lack of principle', he asserted, 'is always a bad thing.'[78] And its absence had resulted in '[t]he present vacillation over the Lost Counties issue'.[79] The 'Lost Counties' constituted a problem, due to 'indecision',[80] which had to be solved with immediate urgency.[81] The future stability of Uganda could not be guaranteed without returning the 'Lost Counties'.

For his position on unification, Ganda patriots accused Kiwanuka of failing to resolve the impasse over the 'Lost Counties'.[82] The Legal Officer for Buganda, Fred Mpanga, publicly commented that the *kabaka* and *Lukiiko* were shocked by Kiwanuka's comments, which had been problematically offered after being in Mubende merely 'for a matter of hours'.[83] Mpanga also argued that Kiwanuka's statement undermined the legitimacy of the Ugandan police force in Mubende. Kiwanuka's position on Mubende pressured the government of Buganda to intensify their efforts to completely remove him from national politics. He was a liability.

---

[77] Ibid.
[78] RDA 904.4 Benedicto Kiwanuka, 'Uganda Elections–1962', p. 42.
[79] Ibid.
[80] Ibid.
[81] Ibid., p. 45.
[82] 'Speak out on counties, Chief Minister is asked', *Uganda Argus*, 1 February 1962.
[83] 'Mengo Hits at Premier's Visit to Mubende', *Uganda Argus*, 16 March 1962.

In the case of the 'Lost Counties', the premonitions of Kiwanuka were predictive. Just after independence, the *Lukiiko* was forced to reach out to the Obote government to request expanding the police force in Mubende.[84] Kiwanuka's campaign and independence did not resolve political tensions in the 'Lost Counties'. As one writer concluded in 1963, communities in southern Bunyoro continued to experience 'sufferings and humiliation which are being continually inflicted upon them by Buganda administrators'.[85] Following the 1964 Referendum, during which Banyoro voted to re-unify with Bunyoro, Uganda's monarchical president, *Kabaka* Edward Muteesa II, refused to ratify the outcome. On charges of constitutional abrogation, Milton Obote militarily removed Muteesa from power in 1966. Two years later, while Benedicto Kiwanuka was conducting political canvasing and visiting his wife's family in Mubende, a lorry collided with a vehicle carrying members of the family, resulting in the death of Kiwanuka's son, Benjamin Musajjakawa.[86] Kiwanuka never emotionally recovered from the loss of his son. He withdrew from Mubende politics and did not talk about the 'Lost Counties' in public again. Mubende had cost Kiwanuka his premiership and a son.

Populist Republicanism and Revolution in South-western Uganda

In southern Bunyoro, Benedicto Kiwanuka found himself in the middle of a fierce struggle over competing Catholic allegiances. He aligned with Nyoro patriots to stabilise national politics, which further ostracised DP in Buganda. In south-western Uganda, the role of DP was equally contentious. On the one hand, different ethnic communities throughout the region associated the party with the republican politics of Grégoire Kayibanda. In addition to trying to unify competing ethnic communities under the umbrella of DP, the party prioritised the populist interests of ordinary Bafumbira and Bakiga Catholics. In response, UPC heightened their political support of Bahororo, Bakiga elites and Batutsi refugees, especially after 1959.[87] The combination of the politicisation of Rwandan emigration and party competition for ethnic loyalties resulted in considerable sectarian violence throughout the region.

---

[84] 'Not enough police for Mubende', *Uganda Argus*, 6 November 1962.
[85] 'Bunyoro urges: Act now on counties', *Uganda Argus*, 10 January 1963.
[86] BKMKP/In Memoriam/Gurcharan Dass Construction Ltd. to Mr and Mrs Kiwanuka, 13 August 1968.
[87] Broadly, DP activists of the period hoped to appeal to ordinary cultivators in south-western Uganda, particularly among the Fumbira and Kiga ethnic communities, who inhabited much of the region.

Uganda's south-western religious and political history was interconnected with Rwanda's republican revolution in the late 1950s, during which Grégoire Kayibanda's *Parti du Mouvement de l'Emancipation Hutu* (Parmehutu), with significant assistance from the Belgian colonial state, toppled the region's ancient Tutsi monarchy. Rwanda's social revolution resulted in extensive Tutsi refugee emigration and concerns related to border security in Uganda. Throughout the late 1950s and early 1960s, the *Uganda Argus* chronicled Rwandan-related violence and the movement of numerous peoples across the Rwandan-Kigezi border, including Belgian soldiers, Batutsi refugees, and Bahutu patriots.[88] Incidents in Uganda included Tutsi militias burning the homes of Bahutu migrants in Uganda; and Bahutu pursuing Batutsi refugees across the border.[89]

Immigration in south-west Uganda, however, had a much older history. By the early 1920s, as Grace Carswell has shown, large numbers of Rwandan and Bakiga labourers passed through – or left – Kigezi on their way to work on farms in Buganda. She suggests that by 1924, nearly 65.4 per cent of migrants in Buganda were from or passed through the Western Province.[90] The work of Audrey Richards and P. G. Powesland on migrant labour in Buganda similarly showed that by September 1924, 447 out of 2,268 (19.7 per cent) migrant labourers travelling into and from Buganda were from Rwanda, with additional workers from Bunyoro, Toro, and Ankole.[91] Margaret Fallers' work showed that Banyarwanda and Banyankole comprised 26 per cent of the population in mid-1950s western Buganda.[92]

The processes of maintaining the integrity of local economies during the colonial period bolstered the political control of Kiga elites and individualised

---

[88] For example: 'Belgians Enter Kigezi', *Uganda Argus*, 10 November 1960; 'Refugees Pour In', *Uganda Argus*, 23 October 1962.

[89] Accounts included: 'Bahutu burn houses in Kigezi Raid', *Uganda Argus*, 20 March 1961; 'Police arrest man with Rifle', *Uganda Argus*, 25 December 1961. One article worryingly noted: 'Many people from the Congo and Ruanda-Urundi are crossing into Uganda, without being subject to immigration or customs checks. They are entering Uganda at Katuna, 15 miles from Kabale, where there is a road from Ruanda which has no Uganda border post' ('Loophole in Border Control', *Uganda Argus*, 19 January 1961).

[90] Grace Carswell, *Cultivating Success in Uganda: Kigezi Farmers and Colonial Policies* (Athens: Ohio University Press, 2007), p. 184.

[91] P. G. Powesland, 'History of the Migration in Uganda', in *Economic Development and Tribal Change: A Study of Immigrant Labour in Buganda*, ed. by Audrey I. Richards, 2nd edn (Nairobi: Oxford University Press, 1973), pp. 17–51 (p. 29).

[92] Margaret Chave Fallers, *The Eastern Lacustrine Bantu (Ganda and Soga)* (London: International African Institute, 1968), p. 27.

land markets.[93] The development of a colonial administration, in turn, substantially underscored the authority of Bakiga, Bahororo, and Baganda chiefs – who regulated farming cultivation, taxation, bride wealth, and famine reserves – over the majority of Fumbira and Kiga farmers.[94] Carswell goes so far as to suggest that European colonisation constituted the 'first time men could be appointed with power over non-family members, and over people from different clans and lineages'.[95]

The contested histories of ethnicity, class, migration, and land ownership informed religious voting practices. At the time of the Hutu revolution, Kigezi's religious demographics favoured Protestant communities and the region's Bakiga and Bahororo chiefs. The 1959 census indicated that of persons sixteen years and over, 69,000 were Catholic, and 99,000 were Protestant.[96] Despite a larger Protestant population, though, election projections for both 1961 and 1962 were nearly split between DP and UPC, as evidenced by the 1961 Kigezi District Council elections, during which DP and UPC secured twenty-four seats each.[97] Where UPC initially struggled to secure voter turnout, DP's aggressive canvasing strategies among Catholic farmers resulted in favourable outcomes.

In many ways, party membership did mirror religious loyalties. When Fred Welbourn conducted his research on religion and politics in late colonial Uganda, he found that activists in both Kigezi and Ankole often referred to their political party to describe religious identities. As he noted: 'More than one report – from both missionaries and anthropologists – was received of men in Ankole and Kigezi who, when asked, "What is your religion?", replied, "UPC". In one instance the question was pressed: "I meant, 'have you been baptized?'" – and the answer was "Yes! We're UPC".'[98]

Tensions between religious factions played out in administrative centres and in rural villages. There were extensive efforts to control the District Council, whose responsibilities included regulating the distribution of revenues. Throughout the early 1960s, the council was boycotted, mostly by DP, whose members argued that they were being discriminated against.[99] Kigezi's

---

[93] Carswell, *Cultivating Success in Uganda*, pp. 1–3.
[94] Ibid., p. 13.
[95] Ibid., p. 15.
[96] 'Uganda Census, 1959: African Population' (Statistics Branch, Ministry of Economic Affairs), p. 76.
[97] '"Dead-heat" in Kigezi election', *Uganda Argus*, 10 February 1961.
[98] Fred B. Welbourn, *Religion and Politics in Uganda: 1952–1962* (Nairobi: East African Publishing House, 1965), p. 41.
[99] 'DP Members Absent as District Council Meets', *Uganda Argus*, 13 June 1962; 'Kigezi Council Dissolved', *Uganda Argus*, 4 November 1962.

District Commissioner saw the region's religious rivalries as impeding political progress and economic development. Before a full town hall, one newspaper article summarised: 'The District Commissioner said that Kigezi had had an unhappy history over recent years of rivalry and friction between the two religious groups, which had marred the orderly progress of the district.'[100] He concluded by stating: 'I cannot but condemn the action of DP in refusing to attend today's meeting.'[101]

Beyond the politics of town centres, there were tensions and acts of violence and intimidation. Uganda's late colonial landscapes were accentuated by hundreds of parades and public dances and festivities. Parties often used each other's colours to identify political allegiances. In Kigezi, DP and UPC campaigned intensely with their respective colours: for DP, green and white; for UPC, red and black. Activists donned hats and dyed *kkanzu*s in party colours.[102] Patterns and colouration also enabled parties to organise targeted protests and to identify parade organisers. On one occasion, for instance, in the village of Kabahesi, Ndorwa county, less than ten kilometres north of the Rwandan border, a public brawl erupted after 'members of one political party staged a victory parade of drumming and dancing through the village'.[103]

Members of DP throughout Kigezi complained regularly about the demands that Protestant chiefs and pro-UPC communities placed on them. The demands of communal labour were often raised as a topic of grievance. In July 1959, the assistant provincial organiser of DP in western Uganda penned a lengthy letter of complaint to the secretary general of the Kigezi District Council.[104] The letter was produced in a style that modelled an investigative report and, revealingly, the prologue to St Luke's Gospel.[105] The letter began:

> I promised to give you a full account of the grieving facts which my Party and I have noticed during our stay in the following counties: Kinkizi, Rujumbura

---

[100] 'Opening of Kigezi Council Boycotted by DP members', *Uganda Argus*, 28 February 1961.
[101] Ibid.
[102] 'Kigezi elects new Council today', *Uganda Argus*, 8 February 1961.
[103] 'Kigezi Speaker warns DO Absentees', *Uganda Argus*, 2 March 1961.
[104] BKMKP/Loose Papers/Assistant Provincial Leader's Organizer, Uganda Democratic Party, to Secretary General, Kigezi District Council, 28 July 1959.
[105] The prologue of Luke's Gospel is investigative: 'Since many have undertaken to compile a narrative of the events that have been fulfilled among us, just as those who were eyewitnesses from the beginning and ministers of the word have handed them down to us, I too have decided, after investigating everything accurately anew, to write it down in an orderly sequence for you, most excellent Theophilus, so that you may realize the certainty of the teachings you have received' (Luke 1:1–4, New American Bible translation).

and Rukiga. In these lines I wish to present true fact which unfortunately all relate to the mistreatment of people by their chiefs and which can be checked in one way or another.[106]

The writer concluded by arguing that Uganda's colonial order had empowered pastoralists in Kigezi to exploit farmers,[107] in much the same way as colonialists had favoured Batoro in Fort Portal and Batutsi in Rwanda. After explaining how local chiefs forced members of Kigezi's communities to work communally for *pulani* or *burungi bwansi*, the good of the nation, he observed that the labour of nation-building – which included providing chiefs with *matooke* (plantain-like banana staple), hens, eggs, milk, and beer – fell mostly to poor farmers:

> To us, it appears to be gross injustice for only a certain class of people to be forced to carry out this [sic] 'pulani' affairs whereas another is put in a privileged position of non-participation. In Rujumbura, for instance, all Bahima do not participate in 'Pulani'. Elsewhere, rich people and families of local chiefs are exceptions to the scheme. Do you think that this is a fair way of social development?[108]

By the end of the 1950s, DP had begun to challenge the legitimacy of Bakiga and Bahororo Protestant elites as part of a larger campaign to support Catholic political representation in Kigezi. The party worked to associate UPC elites with the older militarisation policies that had once resulted in the formation of the Mpororo and Igara states,[109] and regional colonisation during the 1900s. In consequence, DP was viewed as a political sympathiser of Grégoire Kayibanda's Parmehutu in Rwanda. The Uganda People's Congress, by contrast, worked to centralise regional authority around the political

---

[106] BKMKP/Loose Papers/Assistant Provincial Leader's Organizer, Uganda Democratic Party, to Secretary General, Kigezi District Council, 28 July 1959.
[107] Similar arguments regarding ethnic and religious associations were unfolding in Ankole (Chapter 4). See S. R. Karugire, *A Political History of Uganda* (London: Heinemann Educational Books, 1980), pp. 160–61.
[108] 417 BKMKP/Loose Papers/Assistant Provincial Leader's Organizer, Uganda Democratic Party, to Secretary General, Kigezi District Council, 28 July 1959.
[109] The communities of south-western Uganda had once been organised into a series of centralised states, including the Mpororo kingdom. As Jan Vansina has shown, there were numerous monarchical projects in the precolonial regions surrounding Lakes Edward, George, and Albert. Between the eighteenth and nineteenth centuries, an interconnected economy of cattle, labour, salt, metal, and spiritual knowledge shaped the political topographies of Rwanda's and western Uganda's Great Rift Valley (Jan Vansina, *Antecedents to Modern Rwanda: The Nyiginya Kingdom* (University of Wisconsin Press, 2005), pp. 109–25).

priorities of Bakiga, as well as those of Batutsi elites arriving from Rwanda, who aligned themselves politically with Bahororo and Bakiga activists for protection. Having arrived as refugees, both Batutsi and Bahutu stood as candidates in council elections.

Fred Welbourn persuasively argued that Kigezi activists compared Benedicto Kiwanuka with Kayibanda for two reasons.[110] First, while the Tutsi monarchy represented a particular class of Catholic elites, Kayibanda saw himself instituting populist notions of Catholic equality, ideas with which DP was associated in Uganda. When political activists in Kigezi heard Benedicto Kiwanuka assert, 'we shall fight and win our independence and recognition as free peoples of the world',[111] it was generally held that he was furthering Kayibanda's push for a 'liberating democracy' for the Hutu: *'Notre peuple a opté pour la démocratie, pour une démocratie libératrice'*, 'Our people have opted for democracy, for a liberating democracy'.[112] The suspicion of similarity between the two was confirmed, argued UPC observers, by DP's use of a clenched fist, which Parmehutu also used. Second, in lower council elections, DP supported all nominated Hutu candidates. Batutsi and Bahororo Catholics, by contrast, struggled to attract similar support; in no documented case did DP select a Tutsi candidate over an independent Hutu.

While Benedicto Kiwanuka and DP were increasingly associated with republican politics in the area, UPC doubled their efforts to centralise chiefly authority. The Ganda intellectual Abubakar Mayanja – who engineered the political alliance between UPC and *Kabaka Yekka* – argued that the Kigezi Appointments Board should be principally comprised of Bakiga chiefs.[113] The Appointments Board regulated the administration of chieftaincies and government representatives, and it was Mayanja's hope that by filling vacancies with Protestant Bakiga, and Catholic Batutsi to a lesser extent, UPC would dampen the expanding political influence of Catholic populists.[114]

---

[110] Welbourn, *Religion and Politics in Uganda*, p. 40.
[111] 'Forward to Freedom: Being the Manifesto of the Democratic Party', p. 3.
[112] '*Le Président Kayibanda, vous parlé: discours prononcé par Son Excellence Mr. Gr. Kayibanda, Président de la République Rwandaise*', 26 Octobre 1960, devant l'Assemblée Législative, p. 7. A copy of this speech is maintained in the Auxiliary Library of Stanford University.
[113] BKMKP/Ben Personal/P.K. Ssemogerere to Editor, *Uganda Argus*, 17 October 1959.
[114] It is not entirely clear why Mayanja was appointed by UPC to manage its electoral strategies in Kigezi. We do know that his father incorporated Rwandan labourers to manage the agricultural work of their family farm in Zziba (Jonathon L. Earle, *Colonial Buganda and the End of Empire: Political Thought and Historical Imagination in Africa* (Cambridge: Cambridge University Press, 2017), p. 161).

One DP critic, J. N. Nkubayamahina, argued that Mayanja's push for the ethnic centralisation of administrative power would problematically disrupt local alliances between the region's various linguistic communities. After referencing Mayanja, he noted: 'Surely it is just amazing that the Council turned a deaf ear to the warning given against difficulties of imposing Rukiga on the other tribes.'[115] Party leader Paul Ssemogerere responded similarly:

> It was all very well for Mr. A. Mayanja [...] to voice complaints against the 'imposition of the Kigezi Appointments Board upon the people of Kigezi' [...]. Mr Mayanja indulges in a reckless victimization of innocent prominent peoples in Kigezi and, in consequence, is liable to provoke tribalism (much as he denies it) and foment trouble among Kigezi people apparently for the sake of gratifying certain admirers, he might find himself the hero of an undesirable cause and on the very verge of doing cheap politics.[116]

Mayanja's supposedly cheap politics, though, compelled Bakiga elites to support UPC. One writer noted that the 'goodness of having our official [Rukiga] language is self-evident in that you can express your political feelings in the whole country without any difficulty'.[117] The Kiga writer U. K. Ntandayarwo expressed his heartache at the very thought of Kinyarwanda or Runyankore being prioritised over Rukiga:

> As a typical Mukiga I very strongly oppose the suggestion put forward by a certain migrant from Fort Portal who has smashed my heart saying that Runyaruanda language should be used as a native language of Bakiga. [...] How should the Runyaruanda language be imposed upon the whole population of Kigezi due to a small proportion of Banyaruanda, the inhabitants of Congo, just in the corner of Kigezi, to come out and be the majority of Bakiga country. I should be obliged to say that Banyaruanda are immigrants of Kigezi.[118]

Uganda People's Congress activists argued that DP, which was willing to support a liberal cosmopolitanism, would be unsatisfied until the authority of Kiga and Bahororo powerbrokers was completely undermined.

As in Rwanda, violence in Kigezi was enmeshed in debates about ethnic representation. The burning of DP homes and crops was frequently discussed in the press and in confidential party correspondence between Benedicto

---

[115] J. N. Nkubayamahina, Letter to the Editor, *Uganda Argus*, 2 January 1960.
[116] BKMKP/Ben Personal/P.K. Ssemogerere to Editor, *Uganda Argus*, 12 October 1959.
[117] E. H. Rutaganikayo, Letter to the Editor, *Uganda Argus*, 14 April 1960.
[118] U. K. Ntandayarwo, Jinja, Letter to the Editor, *Uganda Argus*, 21 January 1960.

Kiwanuka, government administrators, and Kigezi's sub-branches.[119] The Catholic activist Geoffrey Kitago, who self-identified himself as 'a citizen of Kigezi', argued to the *Argus*' readers that the composition of the Appointments Board 'has not only been unfair on religious basis as some people say, but is also becoming a danger on tribal sides'.[120] The responsibilities of the Appointments Board included appointing the region's representatives in Uganda's national parliament. Kitago wished to make 'it quite clear to the Government that we are fighting for lasting peace, freedom of the people and natural right of the Kigezi people'.[121] Democratic Party counsellors, after arguing that the government needed to conduct interviews with 'Protestants, Pagans, Moslims [sic] and Catholics', noted that 'if the Government decides to support the [Protestant] trouble makers of Kigezi in order to secure superficial settlement, the development of Kigezi is at stake. A good Government always supports the good people.'[122]

The Democratic Party complained that UPC was undermining their work in Kigezi by organising forgery campaigns and explicit acts of violence. An unidentified group of DP supporters criticised the work of the colonial government, which, they claimed, only intervened 'under the instigation of the Protestants of Kigezi District'.[123] Supporters of DP observed that UPC and their government allies convened 'a lot of night meetings which were held in the District'. During these meetings, anonymous letters were produced 'in the name of Catholics and mostly pretending to say that they were prepared by Catholics and by the Present Chairman of the Appointments Board'. The letters were designed to underscore the volatile character of DP. It was the concern of the cohort that forgery would 'be a source of the worst trouble that the country has ever seen'.[124] In addition to fabricating letters, the DP Branch President of Kigezi, Michael Baffire, argued that UPC openly informed the District Commissioner that it would commit open acts of violence against DP members.[125] With concern, he reflected: 'I wish to emphasize that the Uganda

---

[119] See, for instance: BKMKP/Confidential 2/'Resumed Meeting of the District Council', 7 May 1960; BKMKP/Govt. House. Copies of Minutes/R. P. Towle, District Commissioner, Kigezi, to Secretary General, Kigezi District Council, 14 June 1960.
[120] Geoffrey Kitago, Letter to the Editor, *Uganda Argus*, 22 June 1960.
[121] BKMKP/Govt. House. Copies of Minutes/Kigezi District Councillors to Minister of Local Government, 16 June 1960.
[122] Ibid.
[123] BKMKP/Govt. House. Copies of Minutes/Undesignated, Kigezi, to the Governor, 17 June 1960.
[124] Ibid.
[125] BKMKP/Om A. Sebaggala e Gulama/Micheal [sic] Baffire, Democratic Party Branch President, Kigezi District, 24 March 1960.

Democratic Party, Kigezi Branch regrets with great concern of the indifference and weakness of both the Protectorate and the Kigezi Local Government in taking sufficient measures against the irresponsible spirit that is growing among certain sections of the Public in Kigezi.'

For UPC activists, by contrast, DP was viewed as a party of public disruptors. When Benedicto Kiwanuka travelled throughout Kigezi, he and his team of campaigners used 'loud-speakers' to boisterously proclaim the messages of the party.[126] In late 1960, DP activists disrupted an audience of 400 UPC supporters at an afternoon rally, which resulted in outbursts, disturbance, and arrests.[127] Local activists in both parties struggled to respond to allegations of violence, disruption, and intimidation. The secretary general of Kigezi, F. T. Kitaburaza, noted that it was concerning that 'new forms of hatred should come into the country at a time that all the authorities were working together to eliminate the old cancer of religious ill feelings'.[128] The Anglican Bishop of Uganda, Leslie Brown, and the Catholic Bishop of Mbarara, Jean Marie Ogez, issued a joint statement, which they required their priests and leaders to read in each of Kigezi's respective Protestant and Catholic churches.[129] Their letter underscored the disruptive character of Kigezi's sectarian politics: 'We consider it a scandal and a disgrace that religion should be the basis of bitter political rivalry'.[130]

When voting finally occurred in Kigezi for the national government, a remarkable 90 per cent voter turnout was expected.[131] As one newspaper report noted: 'In parts of rural Kigezi, men and women have been busily engaged in erecting strong barricades round polling stations in preparation for the expected rush of voters.'[132] By the time that votes were counted, UPC had secured 91,493 votes to DP's 89,885.[133] In response, DP filed an astonishing 6,297 formal complaints throughout the district.[134] This followed an earlier barrage of complaints by DP regarding voter registration in Kigezi. In 1958, there had been 1,269 complaints filed concerning the registration of

---

[126] BKMKP/Democrat II Dem-Cor 1/President, DP Kigezi Branch, to Benedicto Kiwanuka, 29 November 1960. See also BKMKP/Sundry Corresp. + Lukiiko Matters/DP Kigezi Organiser to Benedicto Kiwanuka [c. late December 1958].

[127] 'Two D.P. Officials sent to Jail at Kabale', *Uganda Argus*, 30 January 1961. See also 'Party supporter clash in Kigezi', *Uganda Argus*, 2 January 1962.

[128] 'Call to End Violence in Kigezi', *Uganda Argus,* 21 March 1960.

[129] 'End Violence in Kigezi, Bishops Urge', *Uganda Argus*, 9 April 1960.

[130] Ibid.

[131] 'Barricades', *Uganda Argus*, 22 March 1961.

[132] Ibid.

[133] Welbourn, *Religion and Politics in Uganda*, Table 3.

[134] '6,297 Claims in Kigezi Registers', *Uganda Argus*, 15 February 1962.

electors. The second highest district to launch complaints was Bukedi, where only forty-one charges were filed.[135] Despite their efforts, though, as one UPC activist concluded, the 'death knell' for DP had been sounded in Kigezi.[136]

Once in power, UPC supported the centralisation of regional authority.[137] For the political inheritors of the region's precolonial kingdoms, including Kiga and Hororo chiefs, the public legitimisation of power entailed creating a ceremonial head for the region, which was pursued publicly as early as August 1962.[138] For supporters of UPC, the party's victory heralded the possibility of resurrecting older ceremonies of power and kingship. As one republican dissenter lamented: 'Nothing could be more pathetic than the move being taken by the Kigezi District Council to install a ceremonial head.'[139] The Democratic Party's political priorities, by contrast, leaned toward linguistic and ethnic cosmopolitanism in the region, not bolstering political tribalism.[140]

Conclusion

The history of religious politics in late colonial southern Bunyoro enables us to understand how competing Catholic political interests were at the centre of the 'Lost Counties' dispute. After the religious civil wars in 1890s Buganda, Catholic chiefs asserted administrative control of southern Bunyoro. Following existing practices in both Buganda and Bunyoro, this first generation of colonial chiefs controlled enslaved labourers well into the early 1900s. The history and politics of the family of Maxencia Kiwanuka were firmly rooted in the rise and decline of the Bunyoro empire, particularly along its southern frontier. Influenced by his family connections and the work of Nyoro historians, Benedicto Kiwanuka hoped that by supporting the return of Mubende to Bunyoro, he would both unify Catholics and bolster DP's vision for the national unification of Uganda.

---

[135] C. P. S. Allen, Supervisor of Elections, 'Uganda Legislative Council Elections, 1958: A Report on the First Direct Elections to the Legislative Council of the Uganda Protectorate' (Entebbe: Government Printer, 1958), p. 45.
[136] E. N. Bisamunyu, Kabale, Letter to the Editor, *Uganda Argus*, 17 August 1961.
[137] 'Unitary rule best – Kigezi committee', *Uganda Argus*, 26 November 1960.
[138] 'Kigezi move for Ceremonial Head', *Uganda Argus*, 1 August 1962.
[139] Sezi T. Rugwira, Kampala, Letter to the Editor, *Uganda Argus,* 16 August 1962.
[140] This language borrows from John Lonsdale's seminal work on moral ethnicity and political tribalism: John Lonsdale, 'Moral Ethnicity and Political Tribalism', in *Inventions and Boundaries: Historical and Anthropological Approaches to the Study of Ethnicity and Nationalism*, ed. by Preben Kaarsholm and Jan Hultin (Roskilde: International Development Studies, Roskilde University, 1994), pp. 131–50.

Prior to 1966, UPC in south-western Uganda was largely viewed as a pro-royalist party, as it was in Toro. Like their colonial predecessors, some argued, UPC believed in strong, centralised governments, which on the ground easily translated into supporting local kingships and autochthonous state-builders. This was a key strategy for creating and controlling political reciprocities. In stark contrast, Benedicto Kiwanuka and DP were associated with Bakiga farmers, and Hutu revolutionaries in Rwanda. It was only after the 1967 constitutional crisis and subsequent abolition of Uganda's kingdoms that public memory shifted, during which communities began to recast UPC as a republican party that had long aimed at destroying the state's precolonial kingdoms. Benedicto Kiwanuka sought to imagine a Kigezi polity that was open to various ethnic participants. It was a vision with which '[r]epresentatives should be elected on a territorial basis instead of a tribal basis'.[141] He had hoped that, '[i]n this way tribalism will be checked and it will be possible for the country to make use of every able citizen'.[142] On the ground, though, politics were more complicated – and more violent. The Democratic Party was ultimately unable to break the political back of south-western Uganda's Protestant state-builders and their UPC allies.

The previous two chapters have attempted to show how religious politics worked differently in Tesoland, Toro, Bunyoro, and Kigezi. By accentuating the varying iterations of Catholic politics throughout the country, we have attempted to complicate the politico-religious essentialisms that have informed Uganda's nationalist historiography. In the following two chapters, we redirect our gaze toward Catholic political competition between DP activists in Acholiland and Ankole, and within Buganda. Following the 1962 election, as we show in the following chapter, DP was split over the personality and poor performance of Kiwanuka. Party debates highlighted competing centres of Catholic authority in Acholiland and Ankole. In Chapter 5, we show how Benedicto Kiwanuka's liberal vision competed with several Catholic alternatives circulating in late colonial Buganda.

---

[141] BKMKP/Ben Personal/'Points from the memorandum and policy statement of the Democratic Party', Fort Portal, November 1959.
[142] Ibid.

CHAPTER 4

Acholi Alliances and Party Insurrection in Ankole

> The Democratic Party Acholi Branch suggests a strong stand behind the leadership of Ben [...] They say any change in the party's Leadership now because of Bagorogoza's heckling would do more harm than good to the unity of the Party and will create a precedence which may in the long run be detrimental to the party and scandalous.
>
> ~DP Party Report, late 1962[1]

In the previous two chapters, we have shown how DP and UPC struggled to straddle the interiority of regional politics. Catholic intellectuals in 1950s Tesoland aligned with UPC because they were concerned that DP would reinforce the authority of Baganda activists in the region. In western Uganda, UPC cultivated an alliance with Toro state-builders, both of whom associated the Catholic Church and DP with the movement for the secession of Rwenzururu. Benedicto Kiwanuka and DP in south-western Uganda were believed to be part of an emerging revolutionary republicanism throughout Rwanda and the region. In the 'Lost Counties' in southern Bunyoro, Benedicto Kiwanuka struggled to demonstrate that he was not a successor of an older generation of Ganda Catholics who had governed the area with contempt.

In this chapter, we wish to refocus the geographies of Ugandan nationalism by underscoring the development of sectarian politics in the northern region of Acholiland. In Uganda's nationalist historiography, Acholi politics is frequently described in terms of its proximity to the colonial military.[2] Scholars such as Aidan Southall looked to northern Uganda to historicise the militarisation – and, in turn, destabilisation – of public life in postcolonial Uganda.[3]

---

[1] BKMKP/Govt. House. Copies of Minutes, Etc./DP Party Report [c. late 1962].
[2] Gardner Thompson, *Governing Uganda: British Colonial Rule and Its Legacy* (Kampala: Fountain Publishers, 2003), pp. 32–35.
[3] Aidan Southall, 'General Amin and the Coup: Great Man or Historical

In ways that do not sit comfortably with Uganda's nationalist historiography, though, we argue that there was a concerted effort among Acholi intellectuals to upend or provincialise the political and financial economies of southern and central Uganda by the late 1950s.[4] The Acholi poet and aspiring UPC activist Okot p'Bitek used the national press, novels, and poetry to criticise Uganda's urban spaces and labour economies, particularly in Buganda and Busoga. In works such as *Song of Lawino* and *Song of Ocol*, p'Bitek offered blistering critiques of the Catholic Church's influence on domesticity in Acholiland. Daudi Ocheng (Ochieng), like p'Bitek, was educated at the elite Ganda preparatory school, King's College, Budo, after which he studied at the University of Wales. His politics took a different path, however. During the early 1960s, Ocheng was a pre-eminent political organiser for the Ganda patriotic party, *Kabaka Yekka*. Okot p'Bitek and Daudi Ocheng pursued two different projects during Uganda's late colonial moment – one overtly republican; the other royalist. Yet both reinforced Protestant political hegemony, and both demonstrated a striking distaste for and distrust of DP and its Catholic influences.[5]

Second, this chapter shows how Catholic and Protestant politics played out differently in northern Uganda. Regional political violence in colonial Acholiland was propelled by Protestant and Catholic sectarianism prior to the First World War. In time, Protestant and Catholic animosities expressed themselves through Uganda's two major late colonial political parties, DP and UPC. Benedicto Kiwanuka and DP marshalled Acholiland's Catholic majority to contest the influence of Protestant activists in the region. In 1962, the party successfully prioritised electoral victory in Acholiland, which they saw as a bellwether for national political success. In contrast, DP failed to contest West Nile, assuming that the Province's dominant Catholic population would turn out for them. Their sectarian assumptions would prove vain, helping to tip the national elections to UPC.

In the south-western kingdom of Ankole, the leadership of DP gained considerable ground by the early 1960s. Protestant Bairu (originally 'cultivators') sought to restructure political authority in the kingdom around rural

---

Inevitability?' *The Journal of Modern African Studies*, 13 (1975), 85–105. Similarly, Phares Mutibwa's history of Uganda's civil war underscores the adverse impact of the Acholi army on citizens' rights across Uganda (Phares Mutibwa, *Uganda Since Independence: A Story of Unfulfilled Hopes* (Trenton, NJ: Africa World Press, 1992), p. 71).

[4] Our understanding of provincialisation borrows from Dipesh Chakrabarty, *Provincializing Europe: Postcolonial Thought and Historical Difference* (Princeton, NJ: Princeton University Press, 2007).

[5] Patrick W. Otim, 'Local Intellectuals: Lacito Okech and the Production of Knowledge in Colonial Acholiland', *History in Africa*, 45 (2018), 275–305.

agriculturalists. The *omugabe* (king of Ankole) backed Benedicto Kiwanuka and the Democratic Party, who were supported by the kingdom's Catholic Bairu. This was designed to enable the region's ruling Bahima and Bahinda clans, whose political authority in the region was interconnected with cattle economies, to maintain their hold on power.

Ultimately proving successful, in 1961 DP appointed the kingdom's first Catholic *enganzi* (Prime Minster), John Kabaireho, who quickly set about dismantling the work of UPC, *Kabaka Yekka*, and their Ankole counterpart, *Omugabe Wenka* (King Only). The emergence of DP in Ankole accentuated the leadership of Basil K. Bataringaya and Isidoro Bagorogoza, whose alliance wished to remove Benedicto Kiwanuka from power in 1962. To maintain his hold on the party, Kiwanuka looked north. With the backing of Acholi's delegates, Kiwanuka maintained his leadership of the party. By reassessing the interlocking histories of party alliances in Ankole and Acholiland, this chapter problematises the geographical assumptions that have guided Uganda's political history writing, which has tended to compartmentalise northern and southern Uganda into distinctive arenas of activism.

Ethnicity and Religious Authority in Acholiland

Historians of northern Uganda dispute the role that centralised authority played in Acholiland. Ronald R. Atkinson argues that Luo-speaking communities in northern Uganda began to imagine themselves as an interconnected political body before the late eighteenth century.[6] Building upon his field work from the late 1960s and early 1970s, Atkinson maintains that the idea of a unified polity emerged over time in response to the expansion of royal authority in Bunyoro-Kitara, which compelled northern Uganda's autonomous communities to adopt Nyoro regalia – such as drums and spears. Political and economic relations with Bunyoro propelled the formation of new political institutions as well, including dynastic authority or *rwot*-ship. More recent historians, including Charles Amone and Okullu Muura, argue that Arab traders (from Khartoum, not Zanzibar), or *Kutoria*, were the first to use the term 'Acholi'. Prior to the eighteenth century there were approximately fifty-six chiefdoms that spanned no fewer than four political zones.[7] When *Kutoria* reached northern Uganda, they interacted extensively with members of the

---

[6] Ronald R. Atkinson, *The Roots of Ethnicity: The Origins of the Acholi of Uganda Before 1800* (Philadelphia: University of Pennsylvania Press, 1994).

[7] Charles Amone and Okullu Muura, 'British Colonialism and the Creation of Acholi Ethnic Identity in Uganda, 1894 to 1962', *Journal of Imperial and Commonwealth History*, 42 (2013), 239–57.

Ganyi chiefdom, whose dialect was similar to the language of Luo-Shilluk communities in Sudan. The pronunciation of 'Shulli' resembled 'cooli' or 'Acoli'.[8]

Early colonial administrators – of both the Anglo-Egyptian Condominium and southern Uganda – believed that by incorporating Acholiland into the Uganda Protectorate they would successfully end the transportation of enslaved central and northern Ugandans to Khartoum, including enslaved Acholi sold in Bunyoro.[9] British and Baganda military administrators used the leverage of military violence to secure political treaties with Acholi chiefs, whose jurisdictions were smaller than imagined by their southern administrators, who were accustomed to working through the expansive hierarchies of Buganda. Colonial Acholiland was administered through the headquarters of Gulu, the abbreviated form of Agullu.[10] The Sudanese stations of Gondokoro and Nimule, and West Nile station at Wadelai were 'moved inland to a healthier and more central position among the Acholi tribe'.[11]

Colonial Acholiland constituted the largest territory in Uganda outside of Buganda.[12] To manage the region, British and Baganda administrators instituted draconian measures to abolish hereditary authority and older forms of communal labour. As Jan Jørgensen shows, administrators introduced steep fines and codes of imprisonment after the First World War to force Acholi farmers to both produce cotton and provide surplus migrant labourers. In 1923, only 4,700 acres of cotton were produced in Acholiland. Within seven years, cotton acreage had increased to 38,500.[13] Beyond farming cotton, large numbers of Acholi served as migrant labourers in Bunyoro and Tesoland.[14] In addition to farming cotton and finger millet, Acholi worked in numerous vocations. According to one survey conducted in 1950, half of Acholi migrants

---

[8] In the written Acholi language, 'c' is pronounced 'ch', which has resulted in the variant spellings, Acoli/Acholi.

[9] Henri Médard, 'Introduction', in *Slavery in the Great Lakes Region of East Africa*, ed. by Henri Médard and Shane Doyle (Kampala: Fountain Publishers, 2007), pp. 1–37 (p. 19); Shane Doyle, 'Bunyoro & the Demography of Slavery Debate: Fertility, Kinship & Assimilation', in *Slavery in the Great Lakes*, Médard and Doyle, pp. 231–51.

[10] Amone and Muura, 'British Colonialism and the Creation of Acholi Ethnic Identity in Uganda'.

[11] 'Colonial Reports – Annual Report for 1904–5' (London: Printed for His Majesty's Stationery Office, Darling & Son Ltd., 1905), p. 28.

[12] BKMKP/Taxation on [...] BA Costs/B.W. Langlands, 'Nationalism, Regionalism, Federalism: The Geographical Basis to some Conflicting Political Concepts in East Africa', Department of Geography, Makerere University College, n.d.

[13] Jan Jelmert Jørgensen, *Uganda: A Modern History* (New York: St. Martin's Press, 1981), p. 98.

[14] Ibid., p. 110.

(based on a study of 194 workers) were engaged in unskilled labour. The survey also showed that 15 per cent were employed as soldiers, with an additional 15 per cent working as policemen, prison guards or game wardens.[15] As we will see more fully when we turn to the literature of Okot p'Bitek, migrant labour was a key area of political reflection among Acholi activists during the mid-1950s.

Religious change accompanied shifting economies and mobility. As we showed in Chapter 1, Catholicism in West Nile, Acholiland, and Lango was introduced by the Verona Fathers of the Sacred Heart of Jesus, or the Combonis, so named after the Order's Italian founder, Daniel Comboni. The Combonis arrived in northern Uganda in 1910, and later came into conflict with their Protestant rivals. Louise Pirouet argued that the Verona Mission in northern Uganda was pursued for nearly five decades before it was finally established, which meant that 'the [Acholi] mission mattered more to [the Verona] than to CMS for this important psychological reason'.[16] As Henni Alava has also shown, Comboni missionaries already knew Nilotic languages from their decades of experience in Sudan, and they arrived in northern Uganda during a temporary withdrawal of CMS from the region.[17] These factors combined to give Catholics a demographic advantage in the region. By the late 1950s, approximately 39 per cent of Acholi's population were registered Catholic; Protestants constituted 33.1 per cent.[18]

Patrick Otim's work on the intellectual history of Acholiland shows how Protestant and Catholic conversion and parochial education disrupted local politics. Throughout the 1910s and 1920s, political violence was a common occurrence between Acholi Catholics and Protestants. In response to growing sectarian violence, the Entebbe government passed a zoning law in 1915, which mandated that Catholics and Protestants build their schools two miles apart.[19] The Acholi writer, Santo Oyet, recalled that Protestant schools had taught Acholi students to 'hate Catholics and never submit to them'.[20] The Acholi historian, Lakana Onek, also noted in his biography, *Kwo-na Ikare Macon*, how the training of the Church Missionary Society had 'creat[ed] hatred

---

[15] Ibid., p. 122.
[16] M. Louise Pirouet, *Black Evangelists: The Spread of Christianity in Uganda, 1891–1914* (London: Collings, 1978), pp. 144–5.
[17] Henni Alava, '"There is Confusion." The Politics of Silence, Fear and Hope in Catholic and Protestant Northern Uganda', unpublished PhD, University of Helsinki, 2017, pp. 48, 56.
[18] Fred B. Welbourn, *Religion and Politics in Uganda: 1952–1962* (Nairobi: East African Publishing House, 1965), Table 3.
[19] Otim, 'Local Intellectuals', p. 302.
[20] Ibid.

among people'.[21] Throughout the colonial period, aspiring Catholic chiefs in Acholiland were placed into Protestant schools, as 'the Catholic Church could not groom chiefs'.[22] These anti-Catholic sensibilities would shape the thinking of two of Acholiland's most prominent intellectuals, Okot p'Bitek and Daudi Ocheng, as we will now explore.

The Contrasting Protestant Political Visions of Okot p'Bitek and Daudi Ocheng

Not surprisingly in light of this history, religious and party associations were mostly sectarian in Acholiland.[23] Two of the foremost activists to emerge out of late colonial Acholiland were Okot p'Bitek and Daudi Ocheng, both of whom rose through the educational hierarchies of the Anglican church. In time, both pursued competing intellectual horizons for navigating the ongoing presence of religious sectarianism in Ugandan politics. Neither overcame their distrust of Catholic politics in general, and DP in particular. The two also developed drastically different approaches for responding to the force of Ganda patriotism on the eve of independence: p'Bitek radically opposed Buganda's bid for secession or special status; Ocheng became one of the fiercest defenders of Ganda political rights.

Okot p'Bitek was born in Gulu in 1931 into a prominent Protestant family.[24] He attended the CMS secondary school, Gulu High School, before completing his secondary studies at the elite Ganda preparatory school, King's College, Budo. After two additional years of teacher training in Mbarara, he returned to Gulu to conduct the Anglican choir at Sir Samuel Baker's School. During the late 1950s and early 1960s, p'Bitek completed courses at the Universities of Bristol, Wales (Aberystwyth), and Oxford. After returning from the United

---

[21] Ibid.

[22] Patrick W. Otim, 'Forgotten Voices of the Transition: Precolonial Intellectuals and the Colonial State in Northern Uganda, 1850–1950' (unpublished PhD, University of Wisconsin-Madison, 2016), p. 83.

[23] Jan Jelmert Jørgensen shows how party identities were structured around both religion and clan solidarities: *Uganda: A Modern History*, pp. 195–9. See also A. G. G. Gingyera-Pincycwa, *Issues in Pre-Independence Politics in Uganda: A Case-Study on the Contribution of Religion to Political Debate in Uganda in the Decade 1952–62* (Kampala: East African Literature Bureau, 1976).

[24] This paragraph draws from the insights of: G. A. Heron, 'Introduction', in *Song of Lawino Song of Ocol* (Long Grove, IL: Waveland Press, Inc., 2013), pp. 1–33; Oga A. Ofuani, 'The Traditional and Modern Influences in Okot p'Bitek's Poetry', *African Studies Review*, 28 (1985), 87–99; Tanure Ojaide, 'Poetic Viewpoint: Okot p'Bitek and His Personae', *Callaloo*, 27 (1986), 371–83. We are also grateful for the insights of Patrick H. Otim.

Kingdom, p'Bitek joined Makerere College in Kampala. He soon began working with the Ugandan Cultural Centre, where he established his reputation as a leading poet and cultural writer in eastern Africa.

Throughout the late 1950s, p'Bitek was an active writer and contributor to the national press. His political aspirations culminated in the intention to stand for parliament as a UPC candidate in the early 1960s. He retracted, though, after deciding to return to Oxford to work on Acholi and Langi oral histories.[25] His political writings at the time of independence examined two topics: first, the moral and economic plight of Acholi labourers in Buganda and Busoga, which he interrogated in the 1953 novel, *Lak Tar Miyo Kinyero Wilobo*, or *White Teeth make us Laugh on Earth*; second, the degeneracy of the Catholic Church in Acholiland.

White Teeth is a historical fiction that explores the coming of age of Okeca Ladwong, or Atuk, in colonial Uganda. Atuk is in love with Cecilia Laliya, whose family demands an exorbitant bridewealth before the two's relationship can continue. With little opportunity to accumulate capital in Acholiland, though, Atuk imagines the possibility of obtaining wealth in Buganda, or 'Bananaland'.[26] He soon sets off by bus to Kampala, or the 'town of magic',[27] for the first time in his life. Along the way, he encounters different languages and the varying colours of school uniforms. The bus reaches Kampala by night, the lights and splendour of which mesmerised Atuk:

> At last Kampala came into sight! It was eight in the evening when we entered the town. Lights were like stars in the clear sky: some were red like large glowing logs; others blue and yet not blue, white and yet not white; others twinkling like fireflies. Kampala at last! The night was not dark and yet there was no moon. It was like daytime![28]

Beyond the allure of the lights, Atuk finds himself in a city where there are few places to rest, limited resources, theft, regular confrontations with the police, and people with poor manners. Atuk is unable to secure employment in Kampala, which forces him to travel to Jinja to work on the sugar plantations in Kakira. Atuk reflects on the realities of immobility and class:

---

[25] p'Bitek's research resulted in his seminal work on Acholi and Langi conceptions of *Jok*, or spirit (Okot p'Bitek, 'The Concept of Jok among the Acholi and Lango', *Uganda Journal*, 27 (1963), 15–30).
[26] Okot p'Bitek, *White Teeth*, trans. by Okot p'Bitek and Lubwa p'Chong (Nairobi: Heinemann, 1989 [1953]), pp. 32, 39.
[27] Ibid., p. 42.
[28] Ibid., 43.

> When I was at home in Acoli, I had heard people say that there were very many jobs in Kampala, with very good pay. When I came to Kampala, I found there were many jobs alright but there were very many unemployed workers too. I searched and searched in vain for a job for a long time! Finally, I had only five shillings left in my pocket. [...] The good jobs with big pay in Kampala were for those who were well educated.[29]

Kampala, far from being a city of magic, as he once believed, was a 'hard city', a place where 'relatives reject their kins'.[30]

Atuk's fate does not improve in the sugar fields of Busoga. After one too many harsh encounters with labourers and landowners, Atuk concludes that he must return home before dying or being robbed again. The return home is a sombre affair, which compels Atuk to think about the limits of economic and political mobility for non-Baganda in southern Uganda. He recalls the beauty of home: 'Which place on earth was sweeter than home? When people are returning home, they are filled with great happiness. [...] no matter how many friends you may have in a land not of your own, home is still sweet, is still best, is still home'.[31] But the colonial city had robbed Atuk even of this most basic comfort. Home no longer afforded the same psychological or emotional comforts. Atuk realises that he is now returning 'home to a nightmare, to die a slow, painful death of poverty and hardship'.[32] He concludes: 'I am taking my bones home, as we say. I am resigning myself to the cruel fate I was born to: to see suffering all my life.'[33]

Okot p'Bitek's literary reflections on Buganda in 1953 informed much of his political commentary in the national press. While Buganda might afford wealth to some, it was equally a place of dire poverty, tears, disease, evil people, and frightened vagabonds.[34] Disavowing any conception of Ganda exceptionalism, it is rather unsurprising that p'Bitek authored rousing letters in the press that lambasted Ganda patriots and Buganda's move toward secession. The most pressing need in late colonial Uganda, p'Bitek maintained, was undermining the political authority of the government of Mmengo, whose feudalists prevented ordinary Ugandans from participating in party politics.[35] As p'Bitek argued:

---

[29] Ibid., p. 74.
[30] Ibid., p. 75.
[31] Ibid., p. 101.
[32] Ibid., pp. 102–3.
[33] Ibid., p. 103.
[34] Ibid., p. 78.
[35] Okot p'Bitek, 'A Bold New Start in Uganda', *Uganda Argus*, 4 January 1960.

The decline of Mengo's prestige and power should now become rapid, and the reactionaries face imminent and final collapse in the face of the nationalistic movement that has now engulfed the entire continent. The political parties in Uganda must now work relentlessly, concentrating their forces in the stronghold of feudalist Buganda Lukiko and government, which is clearly bankrupt in their policy, to win away the people of Buganda. For the building of a democratic Uganda, and for the welfare of the whole population all progressive forces in Uganda must unite.[36]

Nationalists had one objective: to unify to end the pretentious patriotism of the kingdom of Buganda. By the mid-1960s, just as Obote was constitutionally abrogating Uganda's precolonial kingdoms, p'Bitek pushed his argument further, expressing disdain for each of Uganda's monarchies:

> You loyal Muganda
> Dressed in white *kanzu* [white, long robe],
> I see you kneeling
> Before another man,
> Trailing your *kanzu*
> In the mud,
> Like a priest
> But serving an altar of man
> Not God;
> You man from Bunyoro
> And you from Toro
> What's wrong with your knees
> That you lie on your bellies
> Eating dust?[37]
> Are you earthworms?
>
> [...]
>
> What is uhuru [freedom/independence] to you?
> You Bairu from Ankole[38]

---

[36] Okot p'Bitek, 'It is a humiliating blow for the men of Mengo', *Uganda Argus*, 4 February 1960. Similar arguments are found in two editorials: Okot p'Bitek, 'Traditions in Uganda must be brought up to date', *Uganda Argus*, 18 June 1959; Okot p'Bitek, 'Only one Uganda – and Buganda is merely a part of it', *Uganda Argus*, 14 December 1960.
[37] The lyric calls attention to the prostration of subjects before kings.
[38] Okot p'Bitek, *Song of Lawino Song of Ocol* (Long Grove, IL: Waveland Press, Inc., 2013), p. 146.

Democratic Party writers were quick to note that p'Bitek's conflation of Ganda identity with political royalism ignored Benedicto Kiwanuka's national project. Writing from Makerere, the DP activist E. S. Kirenga responded to an editorial p'Bitek authored in the *Uganda Argus*, in which he had claimed that the government of Mmengo had either silenced or coopted all of Buganda's party nationalists by the late 1950s, to which Kirenga retorted:

> But there is one formidable nationalist leader, the most outspoken critic of Kintu's government who has not been turned into a loyal servant. That politician is Mr. Benedicto Kiwanuka. As a result of Mr. Kiwanuka's bravery, Uganda's unity is almost ensured and independence is near at hand. Elections to the Legco will now take place everywhere in Uganda. If the D.P. members in Buganda had not registered, Uganda's unity would be a mere dream, something only to be wished for. Uganda's independence would be many years off. This is why I regard Mr. Kiwanuka as the only true nationalist leader we have here.[39]

Kirenga's letter aimed to force p'Bitek to recognise that Buganda would have avoided national politics were it not for DP. In refusing to boycott the national elections, as Mmengo ordered, DP successfully pressured the government of Buganda to renege in order to defeat Kiwanuka and the party.

Unlike Kirenga, p'Bitek did not see DP or Benedicto Kiwanuka as particularly nationalist in their political outlook. In contrast, for p'Bitek, the party was merely an extension of the Catholic Church, whose presence in Acholiland warranted severe consternation. The poet's most robust critique of DP and its associations with Catholic morality in public life was *Wer pa Lawino*, or *Song of Lawino*. He began writing the poem during the height of sectarian contestations during the late 1950s. He completed it by the mid-1960s.[40]

The long poem tells the heart-breaking story of Lawino, whose life is subject to the harsh realities of domesticity under the critical eye of a stern Catholic husband, Ocol. As the poem begins, Ocol is drawn to Lawino's beauty. She recalled the early days of their courtship:

> When Ocol was wooing me
> My breasts were erect.
> And they shook
> As I walked briskly,
> And as I walked
> I threw my long neck
> This way and that way

[39] E. S. Kirenga, 'Freedom is near at hand', *Uganda Argus*, 28 December 1960.
[40] Ofuani, 'The Traditional and Modern Influences in Okot p'Bitek's Poetry', p. 88.

> Like the flower of the *lyonno* lily
> Waving in a gentle breeze.[41]

In time, though, Lawino understands that she has regrettably attracted the affection of an austere Catholic, who looks upon Acholi culture with disdain:

> He [Ocol] says my mother is a witch,
> That my clansmen are fools
> Because they eat rats,
> He says we are all Kaffirs [nonbelievers].
> We do not know the ways of God,
> We sit in deep darkness
> And do not know the Gospel,
> He says my mother hides her charms
> In her necklace
> And that we are all sorcerers.

The readers see that Lawino is relentlessly ridiculed because she does not know how to properly cross herself according to Catholic custom. Lawino also does not understand why the Acholi gloss, *Rubanga*, is used to describe the Catholic God. The term was the name of a spirit that caused tuberculosis of the spine, which prompted Lawino to describe Mary as the Mother of the Hunchback.[42] As the poem continues, Lawino is perplexed by the unsettling behaviour of the Verona Fathers, who drink excessively and gaze intensely at women's breasts.[43] When questioned, a priest 'threatens you with his beard'![44] The teachers of religion, she concludes, 'hate questions'.[45]

The structure of the poem hinges on Chapters 10 and 11. Chapter 10, *The Last Safari to Pagak* [place of death or no return], is a scathing critique of Roman Catholicism. The irascible Ocol ridicules Acholi hygiene, hospitality, medicinal herbs, relics, and parenting practices. Lawino reaches the conclusion that her husband rejects and will continue to reject her: 'My husband rejects me/Because he says/That I am a mere pagan/And I believe in the devil.'[46]

The extended religious critique takes a political turn in Chapter 11, *The Buffalos of Poverty Knock the People Down*. Here p'Bitek offers a damning condemnation of the Democratic Party, for which Ocol is a local organiser. The following stanzas – Lawino's lament – warrant extended citation:

---

[41] p'Bitek, *Song of Lawino Song of Ocol*, p. 47.
[42] Ibid., pp. 75, 86–7, 93–4.
[43] Ibid., p. 81.
[44] Ibid., p. 88.
[45] Ibid., p. 90.
[46] Ibid., p. 101.

With the coming
Of the new political parties,
My husband roams the countryside
Like a wild goat;

[...]

He says
They are fighting for Uhuru
He says
They want Independence and Peace
And when they meet
They shout "Uhuru!" "Uhuru!"
But what is the meaning
Of Uhuru?

He says
They want to unite the Acoli and Lango
And the Madi and Lugbara
Should live together in peace!
He says
The Alur and Iteso and Baganda
And the Banyankole and Banyoro
Should be united together
With the Jo-pa-Dhola and the Toro
And all the tribes
Should become one people.

[...]

My husband is the leader
Of the Democratic Party.
When they greet each other
They shake their fists.

[...]

Ocol dislikes his brother [a UPC supporter] fiercely,
His mother's son's hatred
Resembles boiling oil!
The new parties have split the homestead
As the battle axe splits the skull!

[...]

Is this the unity of Uhuru?
Is this the Peace
That Independence brings?

[…]

He [Ocol] shouts
His brother will bring Communism!
I do not know
What this animal is!

He says
The Congress Party [UPC]
Will remove all Catholics
From their jobs
And they will take away
All the land and schools and will take people's wives
And goats, and chickens and bicycles,
All will become the property
Of the Congress people.

[…]

When Ocol's brother replies,
He sound[s] like the dance-drums
In the late evening.
He says
The Democratic Party
Is the Party for Padrés
The Party for fools and blockheads.
He says Catholics have numb heads
They hear everything from the Italian Fathers!
He says
The Democratic Party
Will sell the land
To poor white men
Refugees, who came to this country
Saying they have come to teach
The white man's religion
When they have no teaching certificates

[…]

> Where is the Peace of Uhuru?
> Where the unity of Independence?
> Must it not begin at home?
> And the Acoli and Lango
> And the Madi and Lugbara
> How can they unite?
> And all the tribes of Uganda
> How can they become one?
>
> I do not understand
> The meaning of Uhuru![47]

For p'Bitek, the legitimacy of any political party, especially DP, was gauged by its impact on domesticity. Far from being a force for national unification, as Kirenga had aloofly noted at Makerere, DP – a party for 'priests', 'fools' and 'blockheads' – divided families, communities, and states. If Ocol and DP accomplished anything in Acholiland, it was 'the death of the homestead'.[48] And with the destruction of the family unit would come the destruction of Acholi culture and the stillbirth of a nation.

Like, p'Bitek, Daudi Ocheng (or Ochieng) was born into a prominent Protestant home in Gulu.[49] After attending the Anglican school, Gulu Primary, Ocheng joined Budo Junior School. Ocheng completed his secondary education at King's College, Budo, where he and *Kabaka* Edward Muteesa II began a lifelong friendship. After graduating King's College, Ocheng attended Makerere and the University of Wales in Aberystwyth, before launching a political career as an independent candidate in Kampala, where he later defeated Benedicto Kiwanuka's bid for a seat in the National Assembly.[50] By the mid-1960s, Muteesa and Ocheng lived together, and Ocheng served as Muteesa's official advisor.[51] The two remained inseparably close until Ocheng died in 1966.

---

[47] Ibid., pp. 103–07. This extended citation is used with the kind permission of Waveland Press, Inc.

[48] Ibid., p. 110.

[49] Elizabeth Laruni, 'From the Village to Entebbe: The Acholi of Northern Uganda and the Politics of Identity, 1950–1985' (unpublished PhD, University of Exeter, 2014), pp. 171–72; 'Ochieng, Obote never saw eye-to-eye', *New Vision*, 1 February 2007.

[50] 'Mr. Ocheng to contest Kampala seat', *Uganda Argus*, 4 November 1960; 'Mr. Ocheng elected', *Uganda Argus*, 19 December 1963.

[51] 'Why Dr. Obote, a man I once knew well, seized my kingdom', *Sunday Telegraph*, 3 July 1966.

Ocheng was the most consequential Acholi activist in late colonial Uganda. He spoke fluent Luganda,[52] eventually becoming the secretary general of KY. Ocheng's driving interest was economic policy.[53] His writings during the late 1950s and early 1960s were mostly concerned with development.[54] But it was his role in KY and in negotiating the political alignment between the government of Buganda and UPC that is frequently recalled in popular historical memory.[55] For Ocheng, DP symbolised the undoing of Uganda's Protestant political order and the autonomy of Buganda, from which he and his family had benefited. The unification of KY and UPC was the surest way to prevent DP from ruining what had been a worthy political pursuit. The government of Uganda was legitimate to the extent that it preserved the country's pre-colonial kingdoms. As Ocheng reminded Milton Obote: 'it is the duty of the Government you now lead to protect not only the CONSTITUTION BUT ALSO THE POSITIONS OF OUR HEREDITARY INSTITUTIONS IN UGANDA.'[56]

One of the more insightful documents into Ocheng's political project was produced by KY during the mid-1960s, shortly before he died: *'Yekka Party: Yentandikwa Daudi Ocheng Amaliridde Okubunyisa Yekka Nokujja mu Gavumenti mu 1967,'* 'It is the Beginning: Daudi Ocheng is Determined to Popularise Yekka and Come into Government in 1967'.[57] In the document, the readers are told that Milton Obote had struggled to understand how to forge an alliance with Buganda, until Ocheng served as a mediator:

> He [Obote] spent seven sleepless nights, until he met Daudi Ocheng, born in Acoli. Obote found Ocheng at Uganda Club and informed him of his intentions to reach Mmengo. Ocheng then told Obote: 'You have come to the head because in Mengo, that is where I beat dogs and they bark.'[58]

Under Ocheng's counsel, the kingdom of Buganda 'decided to support someone from northern Uganda [Obote] and not a fellow Muganda [Kiwanuka]' because Kiwanuka had 'warned his supporters against supporting the ideas

---

[52] Laruni, 'From the Village to Entebbe', p. 172.
[53] 'Ocheng is new Deputy Finance Minister', *Uganda Argus*, 7 November 1960.
[54] Daudi Ocheng, 'Economic Forces and Uganda's Foreign Policy', *Transition*, 6/7 (1962), 27–29; Daudi Ocheng, 'Development in Buganda', *Uganda Argus*, 17 November 1962.
[55] 'Daudi Ochieng was a nationalist – Katikkiro', *Daily Monitor*, 3 June 2016.
[56] MUA KY/2 Daudi Ocheng, Secretary General, Kabaka Yekka, to Milton Obote, 27 September 1965. Capitalised lettering is Ocheng's.
[57] ICS/PP.UG.KY.7 O.S.L. Tomusange, *Yekka Party: Yentandikwa Daudi Ocheng Amaliridde Okubunyisa Yekka Nokujja mu Gavumenti mu 1967'*.
[58] Ibid., p. 2.

of their own nation Buganda'.⁵⁹ By refusing to support Buganda's secession, DP had 'separated itself from the general concerns of Buganda and was thus alienated like the proverbial soldier ant'.⁶⁰

In contrast, Acholi politicians looked upon Daudi Ocheng with suspicion. Elizabeth Laruni's research on 1950s Acholiland shows how northern activists of the period were wary of Ocheng, whose father was ridiculed for encouraging a son of Acholiland to learn Luganda. One retired member of the civil service recalled:

> When he [Ocheng] visited here he would come and go as he liked nobody cared and nobody bothered him. Ocheng's father was very enlightened. At that time the Acholi thought he was a traitor. Why send your kids to learn Luganda? I personally refused to learn the language in Makerere, the Baganda were so proud of their language. I was in the Capital of Uganda, why should I learn Luganda?⁶¹

A separate interlocutor stated: 'Daudi became a member of the Lukiko. He spoke excellent Luganda. At independence he became a member of KY after the Kabaka nominated him and Ocheng became completely on that side.'⁶² Unlike p'Bitek, Ocheng supported the power and legitimacy of Uganda's kingdoms, especially Buganda. While Acholi looked upon Ocheng's Luganda acquisition with scepticism, language fluency demonstrated an admirable royalist patriotism among Ganda elites and populists.

DP and UPC Rivalries in Northern Uganda

It was easy for Catholics in Acholiland to look around and see a distinctly Protestant pattern of political rulership governing Uganda. After all, some argued, it had been two northern Protestants, Milton Obote and Daudi Ocheng, who guaranteed the UPC-KY alliance, thereby preventing DP, the 'Catholic party', from coming to power. In the past, Protestant chiefs in Acholiland played a distinctive, controversial role in the police force and the collection of taxes.⁶³ In ways that complicated p'Bitek's and Ocheng's perspectives, Acholiland's Catholic writers underscored the Protestant monopolisation of political posts. In the Acholi Catholic magazine, *Lobo Mewa*, one writer commented:

---

⁵⁹ Ibid., p. 1
⁶⁰ Ibid.
⁶¹ Laruni, 'From the Village to Entebbe', pp. 172–3.
⁶² Ibid., p. 172.
⁶³ Otim, 'Forgotten Voices of the Transition', pp. 223–76.

The dispute concerning religion in Uganda is not over doctrinal differences but about jobs and scholarships. The Catholics feel aggrieved and wonder why such important posts like that of a county chief [...] are held by Protestants. For evidence of this unfairness try to find out about the major African officials like Ministers, the Kabaka, the Mukama, the Mugabe and many different grades of chiefs. [...] Note the small number of Catholics among them.[64]

By pursuing electoral victory in Acholiland, DP aimed to crack the foundation of Protestant authority throughout the country. As the DP historian Lwanga Lunyiigo argued, the electoral victory of DP on the eve of independence had 'a domino effect on the other districts. The party captured the *Eishengero* (parliament) of Ankole District in 1960 and the Bukedi District Council at the beginning of 1961 and was neck and neck with the UPC in the Kigezi District Council elections'.[65] It was believed that by securing Acholiland, DP would demonstrate that it was a national party and legitimate alternative to Protestant governance. The party's propagandists claimed that DP would fight for all religious communities, unlike the Protestant parties.

The Democratic Party appealed to young Acholi voters and potential activists by awarding scholarships. The Gulu Diocese of the Verona Mission had created eighty-nine primary schools in Acholiland by 1961, twice as many as in Lango.[66] Comboni schools educated 11,913 Acholi students. There were additionally eleven junior secondary schools and forty-three high school students.[67] Under DP leadership, Acholi received the second highest apportionment of scholarships for university education: Buganda received 114, compared to Acholiland's twenty-eight. Busoga received the third highest with twenty-seven appointments.[68]

The party prioritised scholarships to bolster national legitimacy. In the party's political manifesto, 'Forward to Freedom', the founders argued that the 'provision of education is the most constructive means through which the people of Uganda can solve their own problems'.[69] The party developed a ten-year program which supported 'indigenous cultures through music, art,

[64] Quoted in S. R. Karugire, *A Political History of Uganda* (London: Heinemann Educational Books, 1980), p. 135.
[65] Lwanga Lunyiigo, *Short History of the Democratic Party*, p. 45.
[66] There were forty-nine Verona primary schools in Lango. (Democrat II Dem-Cor-1/'Statistical Report: Gulu Diocese'). While the report is not dated, it accounts for numbers up until 1961.
[67] Ibid.
[68] BKMKP/Chief Minister's Office/Secretary, Central Scholarships Selection Committee to Prime Minister, 9 April 1962.
[69] ICS PP.UG.DP.39 'Forward to Freedom: Being the Manifesto of the Democratic Party', 11 April 1960, p. 9.

language and other forms of spontaneous expression'.[70] Once DP secured the 1961 election, Kiwanuka began lobbying aggressively to secure scholarships for Ugandans. One of the more high-profile arrangements was with the Kennedy administration in October 1961, during which Kiwanuka, J. H. Obonyo (Acholi South East), and Hon E. B. Bwambale (Toro South) secured 300 scholarships (Figure 4.1).[71] Internal memos in the US State Department show that the British Government had helped to arrange the meeting. For the Kennedy administration, it was hoped that Kiwanuka 'could play an important role in such [an eastern African federation] and would probably act as a brake on any tendency within the federation to court friendship with the Communist Bloc'.[72] The Democratic Party did not miss the opportunity – they championed the party's success by scheduling a number of stories and interviews in the *Uganda Argus*.[73]

To undermine the DP scholarship strategy and its appeal for northern Ugandan supporters, UPC supporters in Acholiland and Milton Obote, their Langi leader, worked to highlight cultural and regional similarities between Langi and Acholi constituents.[74] Such comparisons were made during a time when plans were underway to connect Lira and Gulu by railway.[75] In March 1962, one month prior to the parliamentary elections, Obote spoke in Gulu, where he tried to convince voters that UPC was backed in Jinja, Mbale, Bugiri, and Kampala.[76] Unity among Acholi and Langi communities, it was claimed, would set a model for national unity. Before a fanfare of forty dancing troupes, Obote, with an entourage of Langi delegates, admonished the audience to join UPC 'in the last stages of the struggle for the unity and Independence of Uganda'.[77]

The UPC case for regional solidarity did not translate into electoral victory in Acholiland. In one of the tightest elections in the country, DP secured

---

[70] Ibid., p. 10.
[71] Albert Bade, *Benedicto Kiwanuka: The Man and His Politics* (Kampala: Fountain Publishers, 1996), p. 57.
[72] JFKPOF-125-007-p0005/Confidential/'Memorandum for Mr. McGeorge Bundy', 11 October 1961.
[73] 'Chief Minister Sees Kennedy and Dean Rusk', *Uganda Argus*, 19 October 1961; 'Mr. Kiwanuka Promised U.S. Aid', *Uganda Argus*, 21 October 1961.
[74] Laruni, 'From the Village to Entebbe', p. 105.
[75] 'Study on Gulu-Nile Rail Link', *Uganda Argus*, 15 January 1962; 'Northern Rail Extension Will be Open in September: Railway's Big March to the North', *Uganda Argus*, 30 June 1962; '"An Act of Faith in the North": Lira Rail Link Opens', *Uganda Argus*, 24 September 1962.
[76] '"No Need for Fear"', *Uganda Argus*, 13 March 1962.
[77] Ibid.

Figure 4.1 Shortly after the respective national elections in Uganda and the United States brought two Catholic leaders to power, Benedicto Kiwanuka, with Hon J. H. Obonyo (Acholi South East) and Hon E. B. Bwambale (Toro South), discussed student sponsorships with John F. Kennedy, 17 October 1961. The DP championed international scholarships to bolster their party's legitimacy in national politics. *John F. Kennedy Library.*

34,126 votes, compared to UPC's 33,985. There were a number of reasons why UPC did not win the April 1962 election. First, despite cultural and linguistic similarities across late colonial Acholiland and Lango, the religious disparities were considerable. Lango was a Protestant stronghold, constituting approximately 45.9 per cent of their population; Catholics comprised around 23.3 per cent of Lango.[78] This was the largest religious disparity of any district in Uganda. Second, the DP scholarship strategy in Acholiland had effectively persuaded younger Catholic voters that their regional interests would indeed be prioritised by Kiwanuka's government. Third, on the eve of the election, UPC Acholi Branch had not reached an agreement on its candidates, which caused confusion among potential supporters.[79]

---

[78] Welbourn, *Religion and Politics in Uganda*, Table 3.
[79] 'Confusion over a Candidate: Puzzle for Voters in Acholi', *Uganda Argus*, 23 April 1962.

The Uganda People's Congress, however, was far more successful in the Catholic region of West Nile, which, behind Lango, possessed the highest disproportionate religious demographics in the country. The population was registered at approximately 45.8 per cent Catholic, 23.8 per cent Protestant, and 9.3 per cent Muslim.[80] During the parliamentary election in West Nile, though, DP secured only 42,738 votes, compared to UPC's 43,504.[81] This result was especially embarrassing since DP had won its very first Legislative Council seat in the region in 1958.[82]

Why did DP electorally fail in West Nile? Kiwanuka mistakenly assumed that the party would secure West Nile due to its religious demographics. In turn, he spent very little time or money canvasing in the area. The DP District Organiser in West Nile, V. J. Opoti, worried about the lack of attention that the party paid toward West Nile. He argued that DP had failed to prioritise the area, unlike UPC, which was aggressively organising public meetings. In one letter to Kiwanuka, Opoti commented:

> The members of your party in this district are earnestly asking me whether I could arrange with you in order that you should send somebody from the headquarters, like the National Party Organizer or the Secretary-General to visit the district and hold meetings here and there. Such visits are frequently arranged by the U.P.C. leaders over here and they are usually impressive to the public. I think the same impression will be given to our followers and sympathizers if at all you could kindly send somebody here soon in the month of July.[83]

In what may have been his only campaign stop in West Nile, Kiwanuka simply argued that UPC and KY had 'brought about considerable misery in many families, including death of both Africans and non-Africans'.[84] The DP national leadership did not have a coherent or compelling vision for supporters in West Nile. They learned a difficult lesson that religious demography did not ensure political destiny. Sectarian loyalties had their limits.

Once UPC secured West Nile, there were considerable complaints made by Catholics and party leadership about discrimination. In one party report, Peter T. K. Mulwanyi, the DP principal party organiser in Buganda, talked extensively about the Protestant monopolisation of posts in West Nile. In one section, Mulwanyi stated: 'Mr. Musisi [a political activist] knows that Mr. Ben

---

[80] Welbourn, *Religion and Politics in Uganda*, Table 3.
[81] Ibid.
[82] 'National Congress Success at Polls', *Uganda Argus*, 27 October 1958.
[83] BKMKP/Correspondence/V. J. Opoti to Benedicto Kiwanuka, 22 June 1960.
[84] BKMKP/Information Department/Press Release of Benedicto Kiwanuka, 10 April 1962.

cannot apply for a UPC job, and he knows that even if he would apply and it's granted to him, that would not have erased the deed done in West Nile when all of the Catholics in the government were fired.'[85] He continued:

> If Mr. Kiwanuka or Mr. Ssemogerere get jobs, that cannot satisfy all of the Catholics who were fired from jobs because of their religion. Since Mr. Musisi is the one pleading for these issues, he should come out straight and tell if the Catholics were not fired in West Nile because of their Catholicism. And to tell if the same issue did not happen in Kigezi recently.[86]

Following the surprising DP loss in West Nile, Kiwanuka did not address the region in his most extensive political document of the period, '1962 Uganda Elections'. His next public commentary on the area did not emerge until 1965, when he accused the Obote government of smuggling Egyptian and Chinese arms into the Congo – through the West Nile region – to support Christophe Gbenye's uprising.[87] But in between West Nile and Lango, in Acholiland, DP had succeeded in establishing its stronghold in the area. In time, as we will now show, Kiwanuka would need to return to Acholiland to maintain his control over the party (Figure 4.2).

Party Schism and DP Monarchism in Ankole

Following DP's defeat in the 1962 elections, Ankole members no longer believed that Benedicto Kiwanuka was well suited to lead DP after independence. The DP representative for Ankole, Basil K. Bataringaya, was appointed Leader of the Opposition in the National Assembly. With considerable backing throughout Ankole and the party, Bataringaya contested Kiwanuka's overall party leadership in October 1962. Bataringaya's backers argued that 'Kiwanuka is anathema',[88] a theological term used to describe a heretic who should be cast out. It was maintained that the 'Democratic Party was dead

---

[85] BKMKP/Not Marked 3/Peter T. K. Mulwanyi, 15 October 1964: *'Mw. Musisi amanyi nti Mwami Ben tayinza kusaba UPC mulimu, era akimanyi nti ne bwe yandibadde ng'agusabye ne gumuweebwa ekyo si kyandiggyewo kikolwa kyakolebwa mu West Nile Abakatoliki bonna abaali bali ku mirimo mu Gavumenti yaayo bwe baagobe-bwe awatali nsonga.'*

[86] Ibid. *'Mw. Kiwanuka bw'afuna omulimo oba Mw. Ssemogerere ekyo si kimatiza buli Mukatoliki yenna eyagobebwa ku mulimu olw'eddiini ye. Mw. Musisi asabibwa nga bwe yetantalise ebintu bino addemu busimbalale nti Abakatoliki sibagobwanga mu West Nile olw'Obukatoliki bwaabwe era nti ne mu Kigezi sibaliiyo abagobeddwa mu nsangi zino olw'ensonga y'emu.'*

[87] BKMKP/56–69/Benedicto Kiwanuka Press Comment, 16 January 1965.

[88] BKMKP/Govt. House. Copies of Minutes, Etc,/Terms of Reference/Part IV, p. 5.

Figure 4.2 J. H. Obonyo and Acholi celebrate Kiwanuka's premiership, Lugogo Stadium, 1 March 1962. *Benedicto Kiwanuka Papers.*

and that the party may rise again and only when there is an immediate change of leadership'. Internal complaints against Kiwanuka were extensive: 'politically shortsighted, stubborn and incorrigible'.[89] Another party leader asserted that Kiwanuka was 'more of a mercenary than a dedicated member of the Democratic Party and therefore no longer the man to lead'.[90]

[89] Ibid., p. 6.
[90] Ibid. Kiwanuka was accused of being a mercenary because 'he has not got the people he leads at heart and it is alleged that since the Democratic Party followers

Isidoro Bagorogoza, who supported Bataringaya, was Kiwanuka's strongest adversary. He had marshalled a following of thirty-four delegates to support Bataringaya's bid.[91] Bagorogoza's authority in the party was associated with the Catholic mission of Kitanga in Kabale.[92] He also served as the leader of DP in Ankole and Kigezi.[93] Bagorogoza offered the party's executive a three-page speech calling for Kiwanuka's termination.[94] He argued that Kiwanuka had paid members of the party to advocate for his presidency, including Bagorogoza himself.[95] The speech focused on ten criticisms, which ranged from Kiwanuka's lack of sociability to the frightening character of his speeches.[96] The failure of the party in the predominantly Catholic area of West Nile was underscored, before the speech concluded with a dire warning and the promise of renewal: 'Our Party is dying. Let us look ahead and organize anew. If Ben resigns people may backbite us at first, but before this year ends there will definitely be a revival of the Democratic Party.'[97]

The development of a party revolt among western Ugandan delegates reflected the particular power that DP possessed in Ankole. Ankole's colonial kingship had been confronted with numerous obstacles. The kingdom was populated by two economic classes – the *Bairu* (planters or agriculturalists) and *Bahima* (pastoralists) – whose history has dominated Ankole's religious and political historiography. The Ankole historian Samwiri Rubaraza Karugire argued that the 'Bairu were entirely agriculturalists from which activity they provided for their needs', where the 'Bahima [...] were cattle keepers [...] who did not engage in any other activity unrelated to their cattle on which they

---

were tortured and murdered in various corners of Buganda he has never paid a visit to any scene'.
[91] 'Kiwanuka told "get out"', *Uganda Argus*, 8 November 1962.
[92] BKMKP/Confidential 2/Permanent Secretary, Ministry of Health, to I. Bagorogoza, 28 August 1962.
[93] BKMKP/Govt. House. Copies of Minutes, Etc./Bagorogoza to Members of the Executive Committee, n.d.
[94] Ibid.
[95] Ibid. Kiwanuka allegedly paid Bagorogoza 700 East African Shillings to ensure his support.
[96] Ibid. The full list included (in abbreviated form): 1. His speeches frighten people; 2. Kabaka does not like him; 3. Why did he confirm the Kyabazinga [titular head of Busoga] knowing that there was to be another Constitutional Conference?; 4. He speaks proudly, that he has money [vehicles], wife, etc.; 5. He is not sociable; 6. Ben has no diplomacy; 7. He does not co-operate with his colleagues. He works alone; 8. Bribery at elections; 9. Agenda not followed; 10. He does not fight for people when in danger. He only cries.
[97] Ibid.

depended for their living'.[98] In the past, the nomenclatures were largely used to describe economic status, which could change in the life of an individual or community. But during the colonial period – resembling colonial Rwanda – economic classifications took on novel racial and political associations that were previously not as pronounced.

By the time that the Ankole Agreement was signed in 1901, which formalised the kingdom's status in the Uganda Protectorate, political power was associated with the royal Bahima clan, the Bahinda. Soon after, the Bahinda clan underwent a political crisis surrounding the assassination of Harry George Galt, who was the sub-commissioner of the Western Province. Ankole's powerful *enganzi* (prime minister), Nuwa Mbaguta, aspired to revolutionise Ankole in much the same way as Apolo Kaggwa had in Buganda.[99] Mbaguta was a member of the royal clan of the former kingdom of Mpororo, whose territory had been mostly assimilated into colonial Ankole. Writers of the period generally held that the assassination of Galt – orchestrated by the *omugabe* and members of the royal family – was intended to undermine Mbaguta's authority. The plot, though, did not go according to plan. Colonial reports show that the Ankole Agreement was suspended until 1912, and extensive fines were imposed on Ankole. The colonial annual report following the assassination stated: 'The local authorities were reprehensibly indifferent or inefficient in their conduct throughout the investigations into the circumstances of the crime, and the powers of local government were suspended, a fine upon the country being since imposed.'[100]

The overwhelming majority of Bahinda rulers fled from Ankole after the assassination.[101] The subsequent vacuum of royal authority meant that *Omugabe* Kahaya II (r. 1895–1944) and Mbaguta struggled to maintain control over the region. But it also meant that competition for political legitimacy increased. By the late 1930s, an administrative council in Buganda was tasked with identifying an eligible Muhinda to succeed. When *Omugabe* Gasyonga II (r. 1944–67) assumed the throne, he was hardly known in Ankole.[102] Numerous Bairu activists, who had obtained colonial education, worked to increase the political and tenure rights of farmers. Unlike Buganda, Bunyoro,

---

[98] Karugire, *A Political History of Uganda* p. 139.
[99] M. Louise Pirouet, *Historical Dictionary of Uganda* (London: The Scarecrow Press, 1995), pp. 154–55; 245–7.
[100] 'Colonial Reports – Annual' (1905–06), p. 27.
[101] Martin R. Doornbos, *Not All the King's Men: Inequality as a Political Instrument in Ankole, Uganda* (The Hague: Mouton Publishers, 1978), pp. 71–2.
[102] Ibid., p. 72.

and Toro, the *omugabe* was treated more like a chief than a king – by both British administrators and Nkore subjects.[103]

Political competition was compounded by religious conversion. Numerous studies on the history of religions in Ankole have showed how Bahima elites and a smaller percentage of Bairu were active campaigners for the Native Anglican Church. This meant that over three-quarters of Ankole's colonial chiefs were Protestant.[104] In contrast, the majority of Bairu became Catholics, following the work of the White Fathers and Ganda catechists such as Yohana Kitagana.[105]

The emergence of anticolonial politics in 1950s Ankole threatened to undo the authority of an already weakened kingship. The principal critics of the monarchy were Protestant Bairu, including the UPC campaigner, Grace Ibingira, who argued that Bairu had successfully mastered colonial education and accumulated more ministerial posts in Kampala than their Bahima rulers. Such arguments seemed to have build on older ideas about class mobility. The emergence of the activism of Protestant Bairu placed the Protestant leadership of the kingdom as well as Catholic Bairu in a precarious position. Both Samwiri Karugire and Martin Doornbos have persuasively argued that DP's success in Ankole was an outcome of the collective interests of the Protestant ruling family and Bairu Catholics, both of whom sought to bolster their tentative positions against their Protestant rivals.[106]

By the early 1960s, with the backing of the Ankole monarchy, DP worked aggressively to undermine UPC, KY, and *Omugabe Wenka*, the Ankole counterpart of KY. In 1960, DP gained control of the Ankole parliament, the *Eishengyero*. In 1961, they appointed the kingdom's first Catholic *enganzi*, John Kabaireho, which caused the UPC members of the house to walk out in protest.[107] The national press during this period is full of numerous accounts of DP passing sweeping land reforms to empower Catholic communities and the jurisdiction of the *omugabe*.[108] These accounts paralleled numerous

---

[103] Ibid., p. 98.

[104] Ibid., p. 124. County numbers were at 87.5 per cent; Sub-County, 86 per cent; Parish, 77.4 per cent. Catholic numbers were predictably smaller: County, 12.5 per cent; Sub-County, 14 per cent; Parish, 22.6 per cent. There were no Muslim or 'Pagan' chiefs registered.

[105] Pirouet, *Black Evangelists*, pp. 110–42; Deogratias M. Byabazaire, *The Contribution of the Christian Churches to the Development of Western Uganda 1894–1974* (Frankfurt: Peter Lang, 1979), pp. 50–54.

[106] Karugire, *A Political History of Uganda*, p. 160–61; Doornbos, *Not all the King's Men*, pp. 87–95, 129.

[107] *Uganda Argus*, 16 September 1961.

[108] See coverage in *Uganda Argus* on 2 October 1957 and 2 November 1957. Also: 'D.P. majority in Ankole Eishengyero', *Uganda Argus*, 12 November 1960.

cases where the *Eishengyero*'s UPC membership faced recurring obstruction, resulting in numerous walkouts.[109] In the run-up to the national elections, Kabaireho routinely ordered the arrest of opposition members. He was especially hostile toward the associates of KY, who were overtly critical of Ankole's alliance with DP.[110] In one statement, Kabaireho asserted: '[A]nyone propagating Kabaka Yekka in Ankole by shouting the Kabaka Yekka slogan, making Kabaka Yekka signs, wearing its badges and flying Kabaka Yekka flags, selling badges or convening meetings will be guilty of an offence and may be prosecuted.'[111]

In the election of 1962, DP secured 109,426 votes to UPC's 99,295.[112] The rise of DP in Ankole coincided with the Ankole Agreement of 1962, which the *omugabe* hailed as symbolising a new historical era of Ankole power and autonomy.[113] Gasyonga II's constitutional power and his family's claim to power could no longer be questioned by Protestant Bairu. The Agreement stated:

> 2. (1) The Omugabe shall enjoy all the titles, dignities, and preeminence that attach to the office of Omugabe under the law and custom of Ankole.
>
> (2) The Omugabe, the Omwigarire (Queen) and members of the Royal Family that is to say, descendants of Omugabe Rwebishengye (*Abanyinginya n'Abanyiginyakazi*), shall enjoy their customary titles and precedences.
>
> (3) The Omugabe shall take precedence over all persons in Ankole [...].[114]

The signing of the Agreement attracted an audience of 7,000 people at Kakyeka Stadium in Mbarara.[115] During the presentation, claims about historical periodisation were made. In one address, Ankole's history was divided into three periodisations: a precolonial period when Ankole's kings ruled with supremacy; British Protection; and the Age of the Agreement of 1962.[116] Sitting on the platform were representatives of DP, including Benedicto Kiwanuka. Where DP had been associated with republicanism throughout

---

[109] 'U.P.C. members quite Eishengyero', *Uganda Argus*, 26 November 1960; 'U.P.C. Walk out again from *Eishengyero*', *Uganda Argus*, 8 November 1961.

[110] 'Yekka men detained', *Uganda Argus*, 23 February 1962; 'Dictatorship warning from Kabaka Yekka', *Uganda Argus*, 14 March 1962; R. Mukasa, 'No Yekka hostility in Ankole', *Uganda Argus*, 20 March 1962.

[111] 'Chiefs told of Ankole ban on Kabaka Yekka', *Uganda Argus*, 8 March 1962.

[112] Welbourn, *Religion and Politics in Uganda*, Table 3

[113] 'Ankole enters a new era says Omugabe', *Uganda Argus*, 31 August 1962.

[114] 'The Ankole Agreement, 1962' (Published by Authority), p. 9.

[115] Ibid.

[116] Ibid.

the country and especially in neighbouring Kigezi, Ankole stood out for its DP royalism. The party – under the regional leadership of the Bairu intellectual Basil Bataringaya – were responsible for empowering the authority of the monarchy in ways that it had not enjoyed for sixty years. According to UPC critics, Ankole had become the 'only D.P. island in the country'.[117]

Acholi Loyalties and Leadership Contests

The development of DP leadership in Ankole would require Kiwanuka to rely upon the support of Acholi delegates to maintain his control of the party. When Bataringaya advocated for new party leadership, it was the culmination of class shifts unfolding in Ankole. If Catholic Bairu had successfully navigated Ankole's Protestant machinery, they saw themselves able to lead all of Uganda and certainly the party. But despite the unprecedented power and success of DP in Ankole, Bataringaya's insurrection in 1962 failed. He was unable to secure the backing of the Acholi delegates, who worried that a fracture between Buganda (symbolised in Kiwanuka's leadership) and Ankole-Kigezi (embodied in the Bagorogoza-Bataringaya alliance) would be the party's undoing. The DP's post-independence report of 1962 stated:

> The Democratic Party Acholi Branch suggests a strong stand behind the leadership of Ben [...] They say any change in the party's Leadership now because of Bagorogoza's heckling would do more harm than good to the unity of the Party and will create a precedence which may in the long run be detrimental to the party and scandalous.[118]

To counter the emerging regional power of DP in Ankole, Acholi diplomats lobbied to restructure the party's constitution:

> The Democratic Party Acholi Branch had a lot to say about the party constitution. It stated that many of our shortcomings were due to the loop holes in the constitution and they had this much to say – 'unless and until an over-all revision is made in the constitution quickly there would appear little that can be done to save the party from colapsing [sic]'.[119]

The Acholi delegates' principal concern was that under Benedicto Kiwanuka's leadership, the party required regional decisions and appointments to be approved through an executive body based in Kampala. The new proposal,

---

[117] 'Ankole must not be a "D.P. Island"', *Uganda Argus*, 12 November 1962; 'Ankole is "Only D.P. Island in the Country', *Uganda Argus*, 23 January 1963.
[118] BKMKP/Govt. House. Copies of Minutes, Etc./DP Party Report [c. late 1962].
[119] Ibid.

which was approved, allowed district branches to introduce party motions and to approve their own representatives. The idea was to create a system to efficiently streamline the appointment of delegates who were accountable to their own constituents, as opposed to a Kampala-based executive. But by enabling stronger regional representation, Acholi delegates bolstered their position in the party, which they could then use to challenge the Ankole delegates. In short, the move streamlined Acholiland's authority in the national party. With the backing of Acholi activists, Kiwanuka maintained his leadership over the party; Batarinyaya was once again appointed secretary-general. The rivalry, however, lasted throughout the 1960s.

In November 1963, Benedicto Kiwanuka and the DP Acholi Branch, under the leadership of Atwoma T. Okeny, Martin Okelo, and J. H. Obonyo, organised a tour in Acholiland. The purpose of the tour was twofold. First, Kiwanuka owed his continued presidency of the party to Acholi delegates. A tour extended to him the opportunity to exhibit gratitude. Second, party organisers were anxious to secure a number of upcoming District Council elections. One letter written by the Acholi executive stated: 'It is hoped that Acholi District shall be well served should you concede to this arrangement as the District faces two District Council bye-elections in the near future.'[120]

Kiwanuka visited seven of the key political areas across Acholiland, culminating in a leaders' conference at a war memorial. By the end of the week, according to one report in the national press, Kiwanuka spoke on no fewer than twenty-seven occasions.[121] His talks focused on the government's decision to lower coffee and cotton prices. Obote defended the measure by arguing that he was flooding international markets with Ugandan commodities. Kiwanuka asserted that the measure undercut the earning capacity of Acholi farmers.[122] Kiwanuka also castigated the UPC government for 'spending money on television instead of on more schools and medical centres', which called attention to the recent establishment of the Uganda Broadcasting Corporation (UBC). Democratic Party diplomats argued that UBC was the propaganda wing of UPC. To the press, Kiwanuka shared that his speeches had been well received across Acholiland, compelling supporters to lavish him with a decorated elephant tusk, an ostrich egg, chickens, baskets, and pottery.[123] Following his

---

[120] BKMKP/Confidential 2/Atwoma T. Okeny to President General, Democratic Party, 1 November 1963; BKMKP/Wot Pa Ladit President General Pa Democratic Party Mr. B. K. M. Kiwanuka [...]'; Programme Bibedo Kit Man'.
[121] 'Kiwanuka on Coffee Prices', *Uganda Argus*, 19 November 1963.
[122] Ibid.
[123] Ibid.

canvassing and the work of Acholi organisers, DP continued to secure seats on the District Council in Acholiland into the mid-1960s.[124]

As Kiwanuka bolstered his support throughout Acholiland, Acholi MPs and the DP leadership were being hammered by the UPC government in Kampala, which had deployed police officers to follow Acholi MPs and senior leadership, especially J. H. Obonyo (South East Acholi) and Paul Ssemogerere,[125] both of whom were accused of travelling regularly to Toro to support Rwenzururu separatists (Chapter 2). The question of police escorts was raised on the floor of the parliament by Alexander Latim, who represented North West Acholi. Latim's commentary resulted in a shouting match between UPC parliamentarians and Members of the Opposition (DP). Felix Onama, the Minister of Internal Affairs, asserted that Obonyo and Ssemogerere were 'in some way connected with the irresponsible elements causing trouble in Toro'.[126] The fighting did not dissipate until Cuthbert Obwangor (Chapter 2) addressed Latim, assuring him that 'there were no persons "restricted" in Toro'.

With increasing government pressure and lingering internal party divisions, DP was unable to command the loyalties of all its parliamentarians throughout the 1960s. Unreconciled with Kiwanuka's faction of the party, Bataringaya, with five members of DP, ultimately crossed the floor and joined UPC on 31 December 1964 (Chapter 6).[127] Despite the backing of Acholi delegates, Kiwanuka and DP could not control its Ankole delegates. The national image of the party never recovered.

Conclusion

This chapter has explored Acholi and Ankole politics, and their impact on national life in late colonial Uganda. Acholi writers and activists offered numerous visions of political authority, which reflected a longer history of regional competition throughout northern Uganda. While the majority of Acholi were Catholic, the region produced a number of pre-eminent Protestant intellectuals. The most consequential of them, Okot p'Bitek, was deeply cynical of urban economies in 1950s Uganda. He was especially critical of the influence of the Catholic Church on public life and rural domesticity in Acholiland. For his part, Daudi Ocheng used the existing political infrastructure of the kingdom

---

[124] BKMKP/Confidential 2, President General, Benedicto Kiwanuka to Prime Minister, 20 May 1964.
[125] 'M.P. linked with Toro "irresponsible" elements', *Uganda Argus*, 7 November 1963.
[126] Ibid.
[127] Lwanga Lunyiigo, *A Short History*, pp. 74–7.

of Buganda to advance his own career in national politics. Where p'Bitek was aligned with UPC, Ocheng helped give birth to DP's principal opponent in Buganda, *Kabaka Yekka*.

We have also examined the role of DP in the expansion of monarchical authority in late colonial Ankole. To undermine the emerging powerbase of Protestant Bairu communities, the ruling monarchy of Ankole and Bairu Catholics aligned under the political leadership of the Democratic Party. The alliance enabled Catholic communities to strengthen their own position on the eve of independence, while bolstering the authority of *Enganzi* Kabaireho and *Omugabe* Gasyonga II against their Protestant detractors. One of the outcomes of the success of DP in Ankole was that its leadership, seen in the likes of Basil K. Bataringaya and Isidoro Bagorogoza, was well positioned to overthrow Benedicto Kiwanuka. In 1962, Bataringaya and his supporters attempted just such a soft coup. But Kiwanuka's support in Acholiland remained strong. With Acholi support, Kiwanuka maintained control of the party, although DP would never fully recover from these internal leadership divisions.

Ankole and Acholiland constituted two competing visions of leadership for the party. These visions were shaped by distinctive political contexts. In Acholiland, DP activists responded to both the Protestant nationalisms of p'Bitek and Obote, while also confronting the Ganda royalism of Daudi Ocheng. In Ankole, Catholics aligned with the ruling Protestant monarchy in order to prevent UPC and KY from securing control of the area. Acholi and Ankole party members soon found themselves at loggerheads over the party's future. Because of worries over a northern-southern divide in the party, Acholi members were able to make the case for Kiwanuka's continued leadership of the party. But the factions never fully reconciled.

Even as Kiwanuka struggled to mediate competing DP interests in northern and western Uganda, in Buganda he faced Catholic political alternatives to his own Christian democracy and liberal nationalism. In the following chapter, we analyse two such alternatives – the political radicalism of Semakula Mulumba, and the conservative royalism of Aloysius Lubowa. There were no fewer than three Catholic political projects at work in Buganda.

CHAPTER 5

Catholic Patronage and Royalist Alternatives in Buganda

> Benedicto Kiwanuka had intended to 'crush me' [...]! But he was unfortunate because the God of justice prevented the malicious deeds.
>
> ~Semakula Mulumba[1]

> This is where Benedicto Kiwanuka found himself in difficulties in Buganda. Because Buganda was administratively very strong at that time. [...] Many Catholics did not go with him.
>
> ~ Aloysius D. Lubowa[2]

In the previous chapter, we explored competing political agendas between the DP branches of Acholiland and Ankole. As Uganda neared independence, Benedicto Kiwanuka's leadership was undermined by delegates in Ankole. In late colonial Buganda, Catholic democratisation engendered different political possibilities and competition for Catholic constituents throughout the kingdom. As Carol Summers has shown, Catholic debates about public power in late colonial Buganda were intertwined with older ideas about mobility, authority, and inclusion.[3] In his quest to push for a liberal democratic nationalism, Benedicto Kiwanuka found himself in direct opposition with two of Buganda's

---

[1] UM 'Benedicto Kiwanuka *Kirumira Mpuyibbiri*', 29 March 1960: *'Benedicto yali ayayanira okugenda okummenyera mu Kooti ng'amenya mu jjenje ekkalu! Naye kyokka, eky'okusalirwa gy'ali, Katonda Omwenkanya yalungamya abaali bakulembeddwamu omwoyo ogw'ekkabyo n'effutwa.'*

[2] Interview, Jonathon L. Earle with A. D. Lubowa, Maya, Mpigi, 23 November 2009.

[3] Carol Summers, 'Catholic Action and Ugandan Radicalism: Political Activism in Buganda, 1930–1950', *Journal of Religion in Africa*, 39 (2009), 60–90.

most influential late colonial Catholic politicians: the former Catholic seminarian Semakula Mulumba, formerly Brother Francis; and Aloysius Darlington Lubowa, the chief justice (*omulamuzi*) of Buganda. Lubowa was the most politically influential Catholic royalist in late colonial Buganda.

We begin this chapter by exploring Kiwanuka's and Mulumba's fraught relationship, and the larger fissures in Buganda's Catholic community that their relationship embodied. The tumultuous relationship between these two Catholic intellectuals shows how southern Ugandan activists struggled to control Catholic patronage and patriarchal authority. Kiwanuka's approach to public politics was acutely masculine, contributing to DP's failure to empower women's political movements. Mulumba threatened traditional Catholic religious hierarchies, including that of Bishop Joseph Kiwanuka, the epitome of Ganda clerical authority. To undermine Catholic priestly authority further, Mulumba supported the controversial career of Matia Kigaanira Ssewannyana, a Catholic lay person who became a priest for Kibuuka, the Ganda god of war. We then turn to A. D. Lubowa. In the late 1950s, it was symbolically and electorally important for Kiwanuka to secure the backing of the Catholic county of Buddu, and Buganda's Catholic counties more broadly. Ultimately, though, the government of Buganda and *Kabaka Yekka* carried Buddu and the majority of Buganda. For Catholic royalists, such as Lubowa, the obligation to serve Buganda's kingship outweighed the authority of Uganda's newfangled political parties – even if the DP membership was predominantly Catholic. In ways that challenge Uganda's nationalist historiography, the majority of Catholics in Buganda supported KY, not DP. The triumph of political royalism in Buganda fragmented the kingdom's Catholic communities, which obliged Joseph Kiwanuka, Archbishop of Rubaga, to intervene with a circular letter.

Benedicto Kiwanuka was one of a number of elite Catholic men in late colonial Buganda who reworked their Catholic identity to create and recast political authority in the kingdom. Kiwanuka did not control Catholic political identity, and it was not a foredrawn conclusion that Catholic activists would adopt Kiwanuka's particular brand of democratic nationalism. Kiwanuka, though, was a threat to Uganda's religious order. Claims about religious authority and Catholic ideation fundamentally shaped unfolding debates about ethnic loyalty and patronage. The government of Buganda, in response, directed the weight of its administrative authority and resources toward the systematic dismantling of DP. Political Catholicism was a highly regulated, fraught enterprise. Duress fostered the notion that DP was a political movement for persecuted activists, a theme we will develop in the final chapter.

Semakula Mulumba and the Betrayals of Christian Leadership

Semakula Mulumba was one of southern Uganda's most controversial politicians throughout the late 1940s and 1950s. He was raised in a devout Catholic home in Buganda following the First World War, which inspired him to pursue seminary and priesthood early in his life. By the late 1940s, though, Mulumba had become fully involved in the creation of the dissenting movement, the Bataka Union (BU), which branded itself as the moral and political guardians of Buganda's clan heads.[4] Following a long tradition of Ganda imperial citizenship, Mulumba lobbied in Great Britain on behalf of BU throughout the 1950s. His activism constituted what Carol Summers has called, 'Catholic radicalism',[5] or a politics that refused to extend deference to Anglican and Catholic leadership. Mulumba was especially wary of Bishop Stuart of the Church of Uganda and Benedicto Kiwanuka.

Mulumba was a visceral critic of the Anglican Church of Uganda (COU), which he saw as destroying Buganda's authentic culture and economy. Among the COU's many culpabilities, Mulumba maintained, it had supported the illegitimate creation of private land holdings in Buganda (*mailo*) when Anglican dignitaries and Buganda's Protestant chiefs signed the Uganda Agreement of 1900. Like an earlier generation of Bataka activists during the 1920s, Mulumba argued that the creation of private land holdings undermined the authority of the kingdom's clan heads (*abataka*), who historically negotiated land, burial practices, labour, and royal authority in the kingdom. Mulumba was also quick to note that the Church of Uganda controversially supported the remarriage of Lady Irene, who, as Buganda's *nnamasole* (queen mother), did not customarily pursue matrimony following the death of a king – in this case, the passing of *Kabaka* Chwa II.[6] During the late 1940s, as well, the Anglican church supported the marriage

---

[4] The best review of the political ideals of Bataka Union is: Carol Summers, 'Grandfathers, Grandsons, Morality, and Radical Politics in Late Colonial Buganda', *The International Journal of African Historical Studies*, 38 (2005), 427–47.

[5] Carol Summers, 'Catholic Action and Ugandan Radicalism', p. 61.

[6] For the long history of the politics of queen mothers and the early 1940s controversy see Nakanyike B. Musisi, 'Women, "Elite Polygyny," and Buganda State Formation', *Signs*, 16 (1991), 757–86; Holly E. Hanson, 'Queen Mothers and Good Government in Buganda: The Loss of Women's Political Power in the Nineteenth Century', in *Women in African Colonial Histories*, ed. by Jean Allman, Susan Geiger, and Nakanyike Musisi (Indiana University Press, 2002), pp. 101–34; Kevin Ward, 'The Church of Uganda and the Exile of Kabaka Muteesa II, 1953–55', *Journal of Religion in Africa*, 28 (1998), 411–49.

of *Kabaka* Muteesa II and Damali Kisosonkole, with whose clan, the *Nkima*, Buganda's kings did not customarily wed.[7]

In his critique of Anglican power, Mulumba rejected the conventional pleasantries that regulated manners in imperial high society.[8] In 1948, the Bishop of Uganda, Cyril Stuart, invited Mulumba to join him for a meal in Westminster at the Royal Empire Society. In his letter of decline, Mulumba questioned the legitimacy of the COU, noting that Uganda was, after all, 'the Land of the Black Martyrs'.[9] Mulumba then used the language of sexual violence to question Protestant legitimacy in Uganda: 'The Church of England and the British Government are the mother and the father of their daughter, Uganda. Indeed, it makes one feel most uncomfortable to think of a mother who screens her husband while he rapes their own charming little daughter of 6!'[10] Mulumba's comment called attention to the creation of Uganda in 1894 and the signing of the Uganda Agreement six years later. For Ganda elites and readers with Victorian sensibilities, Mulumba's claim was disturbing. It accentuated the fabrication of Uganda by indicating that the state's invention was analogous to sexual violence. While the Church of Uganda gave motherly birth to Uganda in 1894, it was a child simultaneously violated by a belligerent father – the colonial state in 1900.

The statement also was an inflammatory indictment of endogamy in Ganda politics, seen most clearly in the *kabaka*'s marriage in 1948. For Ganda patriots of the 1940s, including Mulumba, much of what was at stake in the marriage controversies of the period was the erasure of climbable hierarchies. By supporting the remarriage of royal women, and by allowing particular clans with common pasts and genealogies to marry, the balance of political power was thrown off-kilter. Mulumba asserted that the development of clanship imbalances had resulted in 'overwhelming calamity', which warranted Bishop Stuart's immediate resignation.[11]

---

[7] Carol Summers, 'All the Kabaka's Wives: Marital Claims in Buganda's 1953–5 Kabaka Crisis', *Journal of African History*, 58 (2017), 107–27.

[8] For further insights into the history and politics of manners in colonial Uganda see Carol Summers, 'Radical Rudeness: Ugandan Social Critiques in the 1940s', *Journal of Social History*, 39 (2006), 741–70. David Cannadine offers a broader conversation on the politics of class in the British Empire in *Ornamentalism: How the British Saw Their Empire* (London: Penguin, 2002).

[9] BNA CO 537/3593 Semakula Mulumba to Bishop C. E. Stuart, 26 July 1948. Mulumba does not specify if he had in mind Uganda's Christian martyrs, broadly, or only the martyrs of the Catholic Church.

[10] Ibid.

[11] Mulumba's preoccupation with royal conjugality drew from, among other sources, older historical claims made by his clan, *Lugave* or Pangolin (Anteater).

Mulumba drew from the gospels to highlight the political duplicity of Anglican leadership:

> There is only one course open for you to take. You must resign; and your Superior will be wise in accepting your resignation. A new Bishop, with a more supernatural outlook, will be of assistance to your Superior in restoring order and peace in the present chaos and disturbances. [...] My Lord, 'you cannot serve two master[s], God and mammon', the Church and the State. You cannot be a servant of the Church of God, and, at the same time, the servant of a godless State, You cannot be an [honourable] Minister in the Church of England, and, at the same time, a so-called [legal] agent of the British Government in Uganda. My Lord, you must resign; you cannot get away from it.[12]

In the same letter, Mulumba reminded Stuart about the death of Bishop James Hannington, the Anglican missionary who was executed by order of *Kabaka* Mwanga in 1885. The bishop was murdered for entering the kingdom's eastern border, which Mwanga associated with military invasion. Mulumba could 'still remember Bishop Hannington's stubbornness'.[13] Far from being a praiseworthy Protestant martyr, Hannington deliberately disregarded 'the traditions and customs of the country to enter Buganda by the Eastern Busoga side where our Kabaka, in the early days, used to get his food products and cattle, and keep some of his wives'.[14] Hannington had egregiously believed that 'Christian views dispensed him from obedience to our Kabaka'. Stuart was asked to consider, in turn, the fact that 'Christianity did not shield him from the spears of our Kabaka's executioners, anyway'. Protestant power and privilege were not insurmountable. Given the fact that Mulumba's letter was penned in the shadow of the public assassination of Buganda's Protestant

---

The *Lugave* clan was one of Buganda's oldest clans in Buganda; it predated the monarchy. Neil Kodesh has shown how Pangolin clan historians shaped some of the earliest accounts of the Buganda kingdom. When the first king of Buganda, *Kabaka* Kintu, established his authority over the clans of Buganda, he did so with the assistance of Mukiibi, the Pangolin clan leader. It had been Mukiibi that helped Kintu conquer the python-king Bemba. The expanding royal authority of Kintu resulted in the proliferation of national gods, each of whom asserted authority over local spirits and healing practices. It had been Mukiibi, and his assistants, Nfudu and Kigave, who defeated Bemba and restored social calm. Throughout the clan's long history *Lugave* activists returned to the distant past to show how their clan had played an essential and unique role in the creation of kingship. See Neil Kodesh, *Beyond the Royal Gaze: Clanship and Public Healing in Buganda* (Charlottesville: University of Virginia Press, 2010), pp. 48–50.

[12] BNA CO 537/3593 Semakula Mulumba to Bishop C. E. Stuart, 26 July 1948.
[13] Ibid.
[14] Ibid.

prime minister, Martin Luther Nsibirwa, which occurred in 1945 by the main entry of Namirembe Cathedral, it seems that Mulumba fully intended Stuart to read his historical commentary as a threat of assassination.

Mulumba, though, was not simply interested in calling the morality of a Protestant empire into question. His public career illuminates larger debates that were unfolding among Ganda Catholics over patronage. As Carol Summer has convincingly argued, Mulumba was equally preoccupied with the (in) equity of Catholic hierarchies in Uganda. As she notes, even as Mulumba 'protested major international injustices, such as cotton price manipulation, police killings, and violations of treaties, he continued to care about the position of the teaching brothers who received little respect from priestly White Fathers who dominated Catholic hierarchical politics'.[15]

Semakula Mulumba became one of Benedicto Kiwanuka's most vocal critics. In early 1960, Mulumba penned a manifesto that included 248 accusations against Kiwanuka. The criticisms were sweeping, ranging from claims that Benedicto Kiwanuka was organising the Church's bishops to disassociate with Mulumba to allegations that Kiwanuka had physically prevented both Mulumba and the trade unionist Ignatius Musazi from entering into *Kabaka* Edward Muteesa II's apartment in London during the king's exile.[16]

In the manifesto, Mulumba, with much gusto, began by arguing that only Benedicto Kiwanuka could rouse him to publicly castigate a Ugandan or African associate: 'Ever since I launched the struggle to turn the powers of leadership over to the hands of you, the nationals, I have never attacked a fellow blackman! I never fight a fellow blackman, unless it is that person who provokes me!'[17] For Mulumba, Benedicto Kiwanuka's sole purpose was 'for his political party or for the Catholic priests and others to pursue the task of convincing all of you people that "Mulumba is a liar"'.[18] Mulumba expressed his worry that 'the Democratic Party has been ordered by the Catholic priests secretly to fight Mulumba'.[19]

The 'lies' and accusations referenced by Mulumba recalled a series of debates that unfolded in the Catholic newspaper, *Munno*, and in public forums around Kampala, where Catholic members of the Democratic Party accused

---

[15] Summers, 'Catholic Action and Ugandan Radicalism', pp. 83–84.
[16] UM Semakula Mulumba, 'Benedicto Kiwanuka Kirumira Mpuyibbiri', 29 March 1960, paragraphs 70, 186.
[17] Ibid., paragraph 2: *Kasokedde ntandika olutalo olw'okuzza obuyinza obufuga ensi mu mikono gyamwe abantu aberere, nnetekera etteeka lyengoberera mu kulwaana kwange: Sirumba Muddugavu munnange! Sirwanagana na Muddugavu munnange, wabula nga ye anumbye!*'
[18] Ibid., paragraph 9.
[19] Ibid., paragraph 11.

Mulumba of redirecting Catholic patronage away from Uganda's priests and toward himself.[20] In turn, Mulumba spent a considerable amount of space in the opening pages of his manifesto reflecting on his own biography and the biography of his father. Mulumba reminded Ganda Catholics that it had been his father, Sagini Meja [Sergeant Major] Alipo Mulumba, who first helped the White Fathers move from the Mombasa coast into the interior of Buganda. In time, during the First World War, Mulumba's father 'saved the lives of the Catholic priests who went with him with the British to fight the Germans in Tanganyika'.[21] Among his many accomplishments, Alipo Mulumba allegedly saved the White Fathers of Katigondo Seminary from starvation during the 1940s. Semakula Mulumba argued that Catholic infighting was the result of coordinated efforts to centralise Catholic authority in the state on the eve of independence by Kiwanuka and priests.

Mulumba's reflections suggest that the Catholic conceptual preoccupation with *amazima n'obwenkanya*, 'truth and justice', the slogan of the Democratic Party, was not simply a way to call into question Protestant power in the colonial state, as is largely suggested in Earle's initial work on the subject.[22] By contrast, it was within the moral economy of Catholic disputation that arguments about 'truth and justice' were strongest. Mulumba reflected extensively on the topic of 'truth and justice' in relation to Catholic patronage and authority. He noted: 'The words of Benedicto Kiwanuka about Mulumba [...] are the words of the Catholic priests! They cannot accuse me of anything in truth and justice!'[23] It was within the discursive context of 'truth and justice' that Mulumba went to such lengths to question the moral legitimacy of Benedicto Kiwanuka's leadership and the significance of the Catholic priesthood.

Mulumba called on all Catholic priests to question Kiwanuka's ill motives. Priests were obliged to understand Benedicto beyond the surface, to know him, as Mulumba did, 'fully in truth and [in] his heart'.[24] Kiwanuka was a man of 'uncontrollable rage, jealousy and envy, treachery and hypocrisy,

---

[20] See *Munno*, May–December, 1958.
[21] Ibid., paragraph 16.
[22] Jonathon L. Earle, *Colonial Buganda and the End of Empire: Political Thought and Historical Imagination in Africa* (Cambridge: Cambridge University Press, 2017), pp. 185–97.
[23] Mulumba, 'Benedicto Kiwanuka Kirumira Mpuyibbiri', paragraph 30: '*Ebigambo bya Benedicto Kiwanuka muMulumba [...], bigambo bya Basosoloti! Bo eya'amazima n'eby'obwekanya bye bandisaanye okunziramu, tebabirina n'akamu kokka!*'
[24] Ibid., paragraph 32.

and one who uses others to achieve his selfish ends'.[25] To support his diatribe, Mulumba recounted his shared history with Kiwanuka, which warrants extended citation:

> To swear upon the living God, I very much loved Benedicto Kiwanuka throughout the time when he was in England [as a student and working with the *kabaka*]! I trusted him! I opened up my heart to him! It was only Benedicto who called me and I never hesitated! Who ever wanted to see me had to see Benedicto Kiwanuka first! There was nothing that Benedicto asked me to do and I failed! When he was the Secretary of Uganda Students in England, he invited me to speak in their gatherings! Benedicto led me to the *kabaka* in London. Benedicto also led me to Dr Kalibbala [principal diplomat during the Namirembe Negotiations, which guaranteed Muteesa II's return from exile] when he had come to England to speak about what they did with Wankoko (Hancock)! Benedicto brought Mr. Matayo Mugwanya to me [Buganda's former Catholic *omulamuzi*, Minister of Justice]! I do not eat food in other places, when I can avoid it, but I ate at Benedicto's home together with his friends. I trusted him, I loved him.
>
> [...]
>
> On his first Christmas in England, Benedicto Kiwanuka feasted at my place [...]. When I think of what he has done to me in Uganda, I see that I shared a chicken dish with Judas Iscariot. When Benedicto Kiwanuka was about to return to Uganda, his wife became sick. The sickness became serious and it was evident that she needed an operation in a hospital. But at that time Benedicto wanted to conduct a tour in Europe, so that he may tell others on his return that "I went here and there," like now he enjoys the opportunity to be asked by the priests to narrate his tour of Canada and USA to the ordinary Catholics. His wife's operation was a priority [...]. The doctors told him that she had to be operated while unconscious. But he chose to go for a tour at the expense of his sick wife who was awaiting the difficult ordeal of operation! Benedicto neglected his wife at that time, when any woman would need her husband to be near her, to counsel her, to give her whatever she wants in her sickness. That is a responsibility of a married man who received the vows of love, help and treatment in times of sicknesses, in happy and sad times, sickness and life! That responsibility originates from the Sacrament of Holy Matrimony, of Marriage!

---

[25] Ibid., paragraph 33.

But a person of Benedicto's education, who is always 'prayed for' by the priests, day and night, neglected all those because he had to achieve what he aimed at![26]

What are we to make of Mulumba's account? At one level, it evokes feelings of despondency surrounding the loss of friendship. It recounted the tragic falling out of close friends, who once lived in community with common purpose. With deep longing and nostalgia, Mulumba recalled a bygone era, a time when two comrades shared meals, homes, and holidays together.

At another level, it is a story of betrayal, a chronicle of how a once-loyal subject of the *kabaka* and faithful husband lost himself in the causes of the Catholic Church and the making of a modern nation. It echoes the story of Judas' decision to betray Jesus Christ prior to the crucifixion. For Mulumba, Kiwanuka had rejected all that was decent and good in Ganda society, namely its kingship and the importance of communal and filial solidarity. But why precisely had Kiwanuka compromised his principles of Ganda patriotism and patriarchy? In Mulumba's eyes, the Church and its priests compelled Kiwanuka to pursue a nefarious path. Contrary to what Kiwanuka and the Catholic leadership of DP would have its members believe, the Catholic Church was not an instrument of mass action and anticolonial resistance against a predominantly Protestant establishment. If anything, the Catholic Church deceived its congregants into believing that the project of state-building was a worthy cause in the first place, and that national ambition should be prioritised over domesticity. We shall return to gender and patriarchy more fully momentarily.

Mulumba asserted that Catholics, as the name Buddu suggested, represented an enslaved and enslaving class in Buganda. Far from being a political liberator, Kiwanuka was associated with a religion that tyrannised the minds and mobilities of its converts. Mulumba noted: 'Benedicto Kiwanuka still desires an embrace from the priests. That is still a big problem for Catholics. Time has come for Catholics to fight the chains of slavery.'[27] Mulumba's statement in Luganda was a wordplay. Strictly speaking, the sentence called for Catholics to break the chains or shackles of those who are in slavery, '*Abakatoliki obudde butuuse okukutula empingu ez'obuddu ng'abasajja*'! More generally, though, it evoked earlier ways of thinking about the Catholic county of Buddu as 'the place of slaves'. In colonial Buganda, Buddu signified the cultural heart of Catholicism (Chapter 1). By calling on Catholics to fight to liberate those enslaved in chains, Mulumba was asking Catholics to contest the political hierarchies of their own Church. The Catholic Church, with its

[26] Ibid., paragraphs 38, 47, 49, 50, 51.
[27] Ibid., paragraph 97.

ensconced position in Buddu, was complicit in the enslavement of Baganda. Discourses about nineteenth-century slavery in Uganda echoed long into the twentieth century.

Patriarchal Authority and Women's Political Mobilisation

Religious leadership was shaped by gendered conceptualisations of public responsibility and debates about patriarchal authority. As we have begun to see, Mulumba spent considerable time thinking carefully about Kiwanuka's marriage. After Mulumba had talked about Kiwanuka's marital negligence in his public circular, he devoted several paragraphs that recounted the details of a medical surgery that Kiwanuka's wife, Maxencia, required. Throughout the night of Maxencia's operation, Mulumba recounted, she was vomiting. In the morning, she called two Baganda politicians living in London, Mbazira and Ndawula, pleading: 'Please come for me before I die!'[28] After Mbazira and Ndawula recognised the seriousness of Maxencia's medical condition, 'they decided to call the Mutaka [Mulumba]'![29] Mulumba recounted: 'The telephone call came when I was working, and I told them to wait until I finished the Bataka's letters. When I took those letters to the post office, I took Mrs Kiwanuka at my home and informed my doctor to come and treat her.'[30] At length, Mulumba continued:

> I found Mrs Kiwanuka in severe pains, almost having brain damage. Ndawula and Mbazira helped to put her in my car, went with us to the post office and then helped to take her into my home. From there, I took her to the doctor who diagnosed her and secretly told me that she was in deep pains, and even her brain was unstable! I returned with Mrs Kiwanuka to my home and she took the medicine which the doctor had given us. I ordered my white secretary, a lady, to take her to the visitors' room where she would sleep!
>
> At 12:00 midnight, my doctor came to see how the sick person was fairing. He gave her more medicine. He told me that the medicine she had to use was too expensive! I said 'don't mind, all I want is this woman to be healed. Her husband is away'. The night was not good. I had many worries in my heart! But I forced myself to have the nerve. I dedicated the life of Mrs Kiwanuka to God. In the morning, I went and brought all of the medicine which the doctor had prescribed, and I gave them to the sick person. After that, I rested.

[28] UM Semakula Mulumba, 'Benedicto Kiwanuka Kirumira Mpuyibbiri', 29 March 1960, paragraph 53.
[29] Ibid., paragraph 54.
[30] Ibid.

[...]

After some days, Mrs Kiwanuka helped herself in the house, and she could even cook tea for us. One evening before I had gone to sleep, my telephone rang and it was Benedicto Kiwanuka! I told him, "your wife had almost died! But do not worry much, come with all of your things and stay here with her at my home". When he came, he had a bath, changed clothes, ate and we narrated everything to him. With that he was filled with rage, wanting to sue the hospital! I asked him, "what is your accusation"? We are in a foreign country, you will bring shame on us. You left your wife in danger and went out to visit. How will you defend that in court?[31]

Mulumba's story was an assertion of patriarchal self-importance. In the account, a negligent Kiwanuka abandoned his wife, who would have likely died had it not been for the care, patience, and patrimony of the Mutaka, Semakula Mulumba. Mulumba portrayed himself as possessing the ability to balance medical practices – and the confidence of doctors, who conveyed their secret knowledge to him – with his international political responsibilities (Figure 5.1). Unlike Kiwanuka, Mulumba cared for the sick and vulnerable, while simultaneously serving Buganda's elders and clan leaders. Mulumba presented himself to his readers as a sacrificial patriarch, who even possessed authority over British women. Under his care and instruction, sick Ugandan women became empowered to customarily serve tea to men and house guests. Where Benedicto Kiwanuka responded in anger to his wife's sickness, Mulumba was a calm mediator and defender of filial responsibility.

Mulumba's musings also underline the reality that DP remained an overwhelmingly masculine project. Although the party ran female candidates in the 1962 elections, and Kiwanuka supported the enshrinement of women's right to vote in the 1962 Constitution,[32] DP still struggled to recruit and include female activists. Party material rarely demonstrated a commitment to marshalling female Catholics within the party. As one DP historian observed: 'The DP had failed to penetrate [...] the councils of women and other such organisations.'[33] In part, this reflected a broader discrepancy in the political mobilisation of Anglican women versus Catholic women in Buganda. As Aili Tripp and Sarah Ntiro have shown, Anglican Mothers' Unions were first established in 1908 and had eighty-eight branches throughout the Uganda

---

[31] Ibid., paragraphs, 55–8, 62–3.
[32] Aili M. Tripp, *Women and Politics in Uganda* (Madison: University of Wisconsin Press, 2000), p. 40, p. 46.
[33] Samwiri Lwanga Lunyiigo, *A Short History of the Democratic Party* (Rome: Foundation for African Development, 1984), p. 73.

Figure 5.1 Mulumba delivered this image to Kiwanuka. Mulumba's handwritten description on the back of the photograph reads: 'Semakula Mulumba speaking in Trafalgar Square at a demonstration organised by "Kenya Committee" on 23rd August 1953, to protest against the collective punishment and indiscriminate killing of Africans by white settlers in Kenya'. *Benedicto Kiwanuka Papers.*

Protectorate by 1926. During the *kabaka* crisis of 1953–55, Mothers' Union leaders formed the *Banakazadde Begwanga* (Mothers of the Nation), who formally reprimanded Andrew Cohen for deporting the *kabaka* without their consultation. In contrast, the Catholic Women's Clubs of Uganda did not start on a local level until 1952, and they were not established nationally until 1959, although Catholic women were involved in the ecumenical and pan-ethnic Uganda Council of Women.[34]

Kiwanuka's private papers show that his views on women's social roles had been shaped considerably by his service during the Second World War in Egypt and Palestine. In 1944, while stationed in Egypt, Kiwanuka wrote to the editor of the Luganda newspaper *Matalisi*, which was funded by the East African Railways and Harbours in 1912.[35] He reflected at length on the practice of bridewealth in Buganda.[36] In the letter, Kiwanuka argued that bridewealth should be abolished in Uganda because it hindered women from marrying and producing children. For Kiwanuka, brideprice 'prevents the multiplying of people in a country. Because a poor person cannot marry and therefore cannot produce children'.[37]

Kiwanuka's case for the elimination of dowry sought to bolster patriarchal authority. As Holly Hanson has shown, by the end of the nineteenth century, extensive exchanges of obligation and reciprocity in Buganda regulated the practice of engagement and marriage. 'In marriage', Hanson argues, 'women exchanged hard work for social esteem: a woman whose hoe handle broke because it had been worn by hard use received the gift of a goat from her husband.'[38] During the early colonial period, communities maintained the expectations of extensive obligation. In his work on the customs of the Baganda, Apolo Kaggwa observed that men – in addition to providing butter,

---

[34] A. M. Tripp and Sarah Ntiro, 'Women's Activism in Colonial Uganda', in *The Women's Movement in Uganda: History, Challenges, and Prospects*, ed. by Aili Mari Tripp and Joy C. Kwesiga (Kampala: Fountain, 2002), pp. 25–6, 31–2; Tripp, *Women and Politics in Uganda*, pp. 34–38.

[35] Christiane Meierkord, Bebwa Isingoma, and Saudah Namyalo, 'Towards Assessing the Space of English in Uganda's Linguistic Ecology: Facts and Issues', in *Ugandan English: Its Sociolinguistics, Structure, and Uses in a Globalising Post-Protectorate*, ed. by Christiane Meierkord, Bebwa Isingoma, and Saudah Namyalo (Amsterdam: Johns Benjamins Publishing Company, 2016), pp. 19–50 (p. 37).

[36] BKMKP/In Memorian/Benedicto Kiwanuka to Ssebo Mukunganya, 29 January 1944.

[37] '*Zizlyiza okwala kw'abantu mu Ugwanga. Kubanga omuntu bw'aba omuyinike oba omwavu nga tasobola kuwasa tasobola kuzaala.*'

[38] Holly E. Hanson, *Landed Obligation: The Practice of Power in Buganda* (Portsmouth, NH: Heinemann, 2003), p. 30.

clothes, and *matooke* (cooking bananas) – frequently provided the wife's family with 'five jars of beer, two cows, two goats (known as good morning), two bundles of barkcloth, two baskets of salt, and five thousand cowry shells'.[39] Kiwanuka concluded by arguing that poorer boys should not have to pay in excess of 50 East African shillings for dowry, which was significantly less than what was commonly required.[40] By reducing brideprice, Kiwanuka undermined the importance of extensive networks that were often necessary to ensure that an appropriate amount of gifts were provided by a man and his clan to his wife and his wife's family. At the same time, Kiwanuka did not envision reducing or removing maternal responsibilities – it was fully expected that women would continue to serve and provide in ways that were consistent with the past. Benedicto Kiwanuka's views also reflected those of his bishop in Masaka, Joseph Kiwanuka, who, as early as 1942, publicly condemned the 'selling of our daughters' into marriage.[41] As we will see, Bishop Kiwanuka's authority was hardly uncontested in late colonial Buganda.

Contesting Priestly Authorities

Despite the masculine priorities that informed Kiwanuka's case for the elimination of dowry, Mulumba continued to see him – and Catholic leaders in general – as politically weak. For Catholic priests to forego their cultural and biological responsibilities to reproduce was problematic enough. For

---

[39] Apolo Kaggwa, *Ekitabo Kye Mpisa Za Baganda (The Customs of the Baganda)*, ed. by May M. Edel, trans. by Ernest B. Kalibala (New York: Columbia University Press, 1934), p. 99. See also Karin Pallaver, '"The African Native Has no Pocket": Monetary Practices and Currency Transitions in Early Colonial Uganda', *The International Journal of African Historical Studies*, 48 (2015), 471–99.

[40] A. W. Southall and P. C. W. Gutkind's work on colonial Kampala shows that even among poorer labourers in Kampala, it would have been common to pay around 120 shillings to fulfil parental demands for brideprice (Aidan W. Southall and Peter C. W. Gutkind, *Townsmen in the Making: Kampala and Its Suburbs* (Kampala: Uganda Bookshop for the East African Institute of Social Research, 1956), p. 86). Skilled traders, including tailors, butchers, and carpenters, earned between 200 and 500 shillings per month (ibid., p. 142). High rent for a downtown shop was around 100 shillings per month. One Ganda clerk reported that his monthly salary was 167 shillings, 17 shillings of which went to food and 55 to rent (ibid., pp. 163–4).

[41] Quoted in John Mary Waliggo, 'Archbishop J. Kiwanuka and the Vision of Integral Development', in John Mary Waliggo, *The Man of Vision: Archbishop J. Kiwanuka* (Kisubi: Marianum Press, 1991), 38–9. Waliggo argues that this 1942 intervention was far more controversial than Kiwanuka's better-known 'Church and State' letter, to be discussed later in this chapter.

Kiwanuka, who had a wife and children, to neglect patriarchal responsibilities was even more scandalous. In a political world supposedly lacking in masculine leadership, Mulumba argued that Baganda should emulate the bravery of the Catholic spirit priest, Matia Kigaanira Ssewannyana.

Buganda needed masculine heroism, Mulumba asserted, not the impotent leadership of Benedicto Kiwanuka and Catholic priests. In late 1961, Mulumba published and circulated a series of letters on the history of heroism, which he sold as a pamphlet for one East African Shilling.[42] The title read, '*Okuzukusa obuzira bwa Baganda abedda bwebalina*', or 'To awaken the bravery of the Baganda, which they had in the past'.[43] The verb, *okuzukusa*, was closely related to the Christian language of resurrection, '*okuzuukira/okuzuukiza*' – it described an awakening after deep slumber. The first letter in the pamphlet, '*Obuzira Bwaffe Abaganda*', 'The Heroism of we Baganda', was forty-five paragraphs, or nine pages in length. It was specifically addressed to the Catholic Brother and *Mutaka* (clan head), Sebugulu. The letter is an extensive biographical reflection on the importance of heroism or bravery in the life of public politics. It also intended to produce shock value. Mulumba began by recounting the bravery of his father and his father's generation. 'Our fathers', Mulumba argued, 'were heroes!' He reflected:

> It always made me happy [growing up] to hear about their battles and heroism! And I also loved the songs which the brave men sang: 'This is where we passed, putting on dirty shorts!' And I also loved the Baganda names [that warriors adapted] which conveyed braveness: 'animal-men' [*basajjansolo*], 'They will return only with the skull' [*Balizzakiwa*], 'The nation is bought with corpses' [*ensi-egula-mirambo*]!

Far from evoking a peaceful, gradual transition toward self-rule, Mulumba underscored the history of supernatural authority,[44] violence, and state-building.

Following his interest in *basajjansolo*, Mulumba championed the spiritual authority of one of the most controversial activists of the period, the prophet Matia Kigaanira Ssewannyana, a baptised Catholic who politically rebranded himself as the eighteenth-century Ganda god of war, Kibuuka, during the

---

[42] For further discussion on the politics of heroism or honour (*ekitiibwa*), see John Iliffe, *Honour in African History* (Cambridge: Cambridge University Press, 2005), pp. 161–80.

[43] MUA KY Box 2/*Bya Semakula Mulumba Omubaka w'Abataka mu Bungereza*, '*Okuzukusa obuzira bwa Baganda abedda bwebalina*', late 1961.

[44] The power of *basajjansolo* was associated with *misambwa*, spirts that appeared in the form of an animal, especially a leopard.

exile of *Kabaka* Muteesa II. In a period of national crisis, this god possessed Kigaanira, who worked as a lorry driver. After becoming possessed, Kigaanira travelled to historically significant sites that chronicled the earlier career of Kibuuka. At Kigaanira Kibuuka's shrines, a colonial officer was killed and the prophet, who allegedly possessed spiritual authority over the natural world, commanded Baganda to stop paying colonial taxes. His prophecies were proclaimed with a snake around his neck, and often from trees, which recalled the death of the eighteenth-century god after whom Kigaanira was renamed. The eighteenth-century Kibuuka had plummeted onto a tree and died after being shot by Banyoro warriors. The twentieth-century iteration of Kibuuka was believed to speak to *Kabaka* Muteesa II through the power of the wind.[45]

Kibuuka's activism was covered extensively in the Luganda Catholic press.[46] Mulumba asserted that it was the work and supernatural power of the prophet, not Archbishop Kiwanuka and his cohort of Anglican and Catholic elites, that secured Muteesa's return from exile in 1955. But far from instigating a populist Catholic movement, Mulumba's claims animated strong opposition. For one Mpigi-based Catholic writer, Balikanda, Mulumba's claim that Kibuuka had secured Muteesa's return by consulting spirits and a national hero-god was absurd. He responded fiercely:

> Now you [Mulumba] seem confused. In your letters you and your followers say that Kiganira is right and that he was the one who made the *Kabaka* return from exile. That whatever Kiganira said on the tree was correct! Dear Mulumba when will you ever stop that deceit? Kiganira mobilised people to evade paying taxes, and to believe that the foreigners were the principal enemies of the *kabaka*'s return.[47]

Balikanda was especially concerned about Mulumba's criticism of Archbishop Kiwanuka. He commanded Mulumba to 'leave our bishop alone'.[48] Mulumba's letters had caused Balikanda to have 'missed a heart beat'. Balikanda reminded *Munno*'s Catholic readers that Mulumba was an unsuccessful ordinand, 'a brother who failed to fulfil his vows and that shows that he did not have a thorough training in priesthood'. Mulumba was not to

---

[45] For Kigaanira's fuller biography see Jonathon L. Earle, 'Political Activism and Other Life Forms in Colonial Buganda', *History in Africa*, 45 (2018), 373–95.

[46] 'Kibuka n'Abamu ku Bagoberezi be Bali Mu Mikono gya Babuyinza!', *Munno*, 16 February 1955; 'Kiganira Aliwoza 28 February', *Munno*, 23 February 1955; 'Kiganira ate aliwoza 26 April', *Munno*, 2 March 1955; 'Abakwatirwa e Mutundwe ne Kigânira basibiddwa myâka', *Munno*, 5 April 1955; 'Ogwa Kiganira be banne guli mu Koti nto', *Munno*, 27 April 1955.

[47] *Munno*, 9 May 1958.

[48] Ibid.

be taken as an authoritative arbiter of Ganda politics; he was not 'an informed person on Catholic religion, like Bishop Kiwanuka'. For Balikanda, one could only conclude that Mulumba's approach to Ganda affairs was pro-communist and spiritually suspect:

> Words of this kind stink of communism. And I strongly pity you, because one day you will face the wrath of God for teaching things that are incorrect to the souls of people. I don't think that you can win that case, but only by repenting. You will face a great difficulty, Semakula! Believe it or not, one day God will put you in a furnace'.[49]

Like Balikanda, Ben Kiwanuka used the Catholic press to delegitimise Mulumba. Kiwanuka wanted all of Buganda's Catholics to understand that Mulumba spent his time in the United Kingdom criticising the Catholic Church and Catholic priests. Because of Mulumba, the faithful abandoned the Church because they believed that the priests practised poor manners: '*ng'abantu baleseyo okusoma olw'okubanga mbu Abasaserdoti bayisa bubi nnyo*', 'people stopped attending church because the (Catholic) priests were behaving badly'.[50] Kiwanuka also argued that Mulumba failed to serve Buganda's clan leaders. In particular, Kiwanuka reminded readers that the Bataka had sent musical instruments and a drum to the *kabaka* in exile, which Mulumba was instructed to play before Muteesa II. Not only did Mulumba fail to have the instruments played; he did not visit the *kabaka* for two months, if not more (*N'ebirala*). In turn, Mulumba was not a champion of social responsibility in the kingdom: 'he [was] a great liar [who] can even make one believe a very obvious lie'.[51]

At one level, during a time when the Democratic Party was working to gain populist support throughout the state, Mulumba disrupted the pleasantries and elitist visions of Catholic patronage in Buganda. To colonial administrators and Anglican priests, he questioned the integrity of the Church of Uganda's missionaries and martyrs. To Catholic audiences, he argued that Benedicto Kiwanuka had abandoned filial responsibility due to the prayers and compulsion of Catholic priests. Masculine politics among Catholics reinforced a social environment where the party was ineffective in bolstering women's movements. For Mulumba, the political interests of Catholics would best be served by the likes of Kigaanira Ssewannyana, not Archbishop Kiwanuka. Ultimately, Benedicto Kiwanuka and his allies successfully discredited Mulumba's radicalism, insofar as Mulumba's vitriol did not directly translate into political

---

[49] Ibid.
[50] 'B. Kiwanuka', *Munno*, 22 March 1960.
[51] Ibid.

disassociation or violence in Buganda against members of DP. At the same time, Kigaanira's ministry seems to have both propelled and reflected the currents of populist royalism reshaping Ganda politics as independence neared. Kiwanuka would not be as successful in overcoming the political work of Aloysius Lubowa.

Kabaka Yekka and the Catholic Royalism of Aloysius Lubowa

Semakula Mulumba was not the only Catholic activist who contested Ben Kiwanuka's influence in Buganda. *Omulamuzi* Aloysius Darlington Lubowa was Buganda's most influential Catholic royalist. His argumentative abilities – and commitment to Buganda's political hierarchy – presented a roadblock for Kiwanuka's bid to attract the kingdom's Catholic voters. His work also ensured that the majority of Buganda's Catholics backed the royalist party, *Kabaka Yekka*, not DP.

Aloysius Lubowa was born in 1927 into a staunch Catholic home. By the mid-1950s he was a prominent journalist with the Iranian-owned Luganda press, *Matalisi*, which was subsidised by the East African Railways and Harbours.[52] For his work in the Uganda national press, Lubowa was selected to cover the coronation of Queen Elizabeth II in June 1953. After returning from Westminster, Lubowa co-founded the popular Luganda newspaper, *Uganda Eyogera*, 'Uganda Speaks', which he used to advocate for the return of *Kabaka* Muteesa II from exile in London, and to shame Catholic chiefs who did not raise funds for Muteesa's welfare. By the late 1950s, Lubowa secured a principal seat in the *Lukiiko* for the Protestant county of Kyaddondo. As a representative of the *Lukiiko*, Lubowa was one of Buganda's key negotiators during Uganda's constitutional conferences in London in the early 1960s. Lubowa and his Catholic colleague, Leonard Basudde, also served as lead advisors for Buganda's Protestant prime minister, Mikaeri Kintu (Figure 5.2).

In retrospective interviews, Lubowa emphasised that the *Lukiiko* was very sceptical of political parties in Buganda, even if individual members held party cards.[53] Lubowa, for instance, recalled that he was an early member of the Uganda National Congress. But the general collective culture of Mmengo was wary of parties, which they believed 'would interfere with Buganda's position' if they acquired too much power. For Lubowa, political parties were useful to the extent that they instigated economic protest. But they were not designed to

---

[52] The following biographical account and quotations are from an interview that Earle conducted with A. D. Lubowa in the latter's home in Maya, Mpigi, on 23 November 2009.

[53] Earle conducted multiple interviews with Lubowa between 2009 and 2016.

Figure 5.2 Ministers of the kingdom of Buganda (left to right): Minister of Local Government, A. D. Lubowa; Minister of Justice, L. Basudde; Prime Minister, M. Kintu. Uganda Independence Conference, Marlborough House, June 1962. *Royal Commonwealth Society COI/A/610. Reproduced by kind permission of the Syndics of Cambridge University Library.*

supplant the authority of the *kabaka*'s government. As Lubowa asserted, the ministers of Buganda 'did not want political parties, they wanted the *Lukiiko* [...] to possess internal power'.

Lubowa recalled that scepticism toward national political parties was not exclusively conjured in the parliamentary halls of Bulange. Throughout Buganda, musicians authored songs that lauded the *Lukiiko*'s authority. One tune, he sang, asserted: 'The clan elders have rejected political parties; We want people to be behind the *Lukiiko*.' As Lubowa saw it, this was an idyllic moment in Ganda politics, before things fell apart in the mid-1960s. 'Whatever Mmengo stood for [it went very quickly to the grassroots].' For Lubowa, the late 1950s and early 1960s were a time when ordinary Baganda were protected subjects under the authority of the kingship, and Baganda did not want to do anything to compromise the authority of the *Lukiiko*, which had secured Buganda's privileged status in Uganda for over fifty years.

In reality, though, loyalties had to be won. Political hierarchies worked to the extent that they capitalised upon the emotional topographies of the period. Lubowa's royalism was a product of the exile and return of *Kabaka* Muteesa

II, which fundamentally altered the course of Ganda politics. Up until his exile, Muteesa II was largely perceived as an Anglophile playboy king, whose marriage with a member of a 'forbidden' clan was surrounded with controversy.[54] When Muteesa returned in late 1955, it set in motion powerful currents of royalist populism throughout the kingdom. Parties emerged and collapsed to the extent that they successfully navigated these currents.

Lubowa used *Uganda Eyogera* to publicly shame Catholic chiefs for failing to support the exiled *kabaka*. In one article, the Catholic chief of Buddu, the Pokino, was ridiculed for obstructing fundraisers to support Muteesa:

> The Pokino has declared at Bukoto, Masaka, that he will deal seriously with people found collecting for the Kabaka's subsistence. Better things were expected of this chief who was appointed by the Kabaka. Kabaka Muteesa II is our undoubted King who is suffering in exile for us, and we are determined to give him every assistance. Anyone who wishes us to forget our Kabaka is doing it in vain and must be laughed to scorn.[55]

By the time that Muteesa II returned, Catholic political leaders, who feared being shamed in the press or in public gatherings, orchestrated demonstrations of loyalty to Muteesa. Catholics in Mawokota were among the first to volunteer to clean the *kabaka*'s palace.[56] And when the *kabaka* visited Mawokota in December, shortly after his return, Catholic subjects accused the Kayima (*ssaza* chief of Mawokota) of betraying Muteesa.[57] If Catholic chiefs were going to maintain their posts in the emotional climate that followed the exile, they would need to be far more effusive than in the past.

Lubowa maintained that Catholics had a responsibility to uphold the integrity of Buganda and the *kabaka*. Only kings and their parliaments were equipped to govern the affairs of state. For Lubowa, DP signified the erosion of royalist political authority in Buganda. Until the government of Buganda could guarantee the special status of the kingdom and the *kabaka* in a postcolonial Uganda, Mmengo ordered all Baganda to avoid any national election, the first of which occurred in 1961. As we showed in the Introduction, though, Benedicto Kiwanuka and DP rejected the government of Buganda's boycott of the national elections. Ganda patriots argued that Kiwanuka became Uganda's

---

[54] Summers, 'Radical Rudeness', p. 743; Earle, *Colonial Buganda and the End of Empire*, pp. 111–14.

[55] 'Does the Pokino wish the people to forget the Kabaka?', *Uganda Eyogera*, 26 February 1954. The English translation was produced by the Uganda Information Department.

[56] *Uganda Post*, 14 September 1955.

[57] *Gambuze*, 6 December 1955.

first prime minister by disregarding the authority of Mmengo. But for Lubowa, the real issue was that Kiwanuka was attempting to replace one regime of hierarchical authority with another. In his mind, Kiwanuka and DP were misguided prophets, and it was imperative to silence them as quickly as possible. The political interests of Ganda Catholics – and Baganda more generally – would be best served by championing the cause of the kingdom of Buganda, not national political parties.

Shortly after DP secured the 1961 election, party activists across Buganda's political spectrum organised or joined the newly founded royalist party, *Kabaka Yekka*. But it was not only Protestants, Muslims, and 'neo-traditionalists' who worked under the auspices of KY. Catholics too were equally supportive of the early mantra of KY: 'Out with the Democrats! Protect the throne!'[58] The point warrants emphasis. In Uganda's nationalist historiography, KY is unanimously viewed as an anti-Catholic party. Fred Welbourn showed how KY's first General Secretary, S. K. Masembe-Kabali, openly asserted that the purpose of KY was 'to keep the Catholics out'.[59] Both Anthony Low and I. R. Hancock argued that KY's leadership was unquestionably anti-Catholic.[60] But such accounts do not explain why so many ordinary Catholics and Catholic activists backed KY.

At one level, it was necessary for the leadership of KY to appeal to Catholic voters and powerbrokers, from Lubowa to Augustine Kamya, who worked together to establish the Uganda National Movement.[61] The executive minutes of KY show that numerous Catholics were members of the central committee, including Lubowa, Francis Walugembe, and Latimer Mpagi.[62] At the

---

[58] Audrey I. Richards, 'Epilogue', in *The King's Men: Leadership and Status in Buganda on the Eve of Independence*, ed. by Lloyd A. Fallers (London: published on behalf of the East African Institute of Social Research by Oxford University Press, 1964), pp. 357–95 (p. 82).

[59] Welbourn, *Religion & Politics in Uganda*, p. 26.

[60] D. A. Low, *Political Parties in Uganda 1949–62* (London: University of London Athlone Press, 1962), p. 54; I. R. Hancock, 'Patriotism and Neo-Traditionalism in Buganda: The Kabaka Yekka ('The King Alone') Movement, 1961–1962', *The Journal of African History*, 11 (1970), 419–34. Such assumptions have been repeated by political scientists writing on Uganda's history, such as Giovanni Carbone's claim that 'KY also came into being as what could be described as an anti-Catholic coalition' (Giovanni Carbone, *No-Party Democracy? Ugandan Politics in Comparative Perspective* (Boulder, CO: Lynne Rienner, 2008), p. 15).

[61] M. S. M. Kiwanuka, 'The Uganda National Movement and the Trade Boycott of 1959/60: A Study of Politics and Economics in Uganda on the Eve of Independence' (Cambridge CAS: (676.1): Box 320, n.d.), p. 2.

[62] 'Kabaka Yekka (No. 2)', Secret Report, c. November 1961. We wish to thank Apollo Makubuya for providing us with a copy of the executive minutes.

same time, Lubowa maintained that Catholic devotees would secure their future rights by investing in the life and priorities of the kingdom. At a time when some Ganda Protestant patriots were accusing Catholics of betraying the *kabaka*, Lubowa argued that Catholic royalists were needed more than ever to protect the security of their coreligionists.

To this end, Lubowa travelled throughout London and Buganda to advocate for the kingdom's special status in national politics and the importance of the platform of KY.[63] With the backing of Mmengo, Lubowa commanded county (*ssaza*) chiefs in the Catholic counties of Buddu, Busujju, Buvuma, Mawogola, and Mawokota to resist DP and back KY. Catholic county chiefs then commanded sub-county chiefs (*ggombolola*) and parish (*muluka*) chiefs to do likewise.[64]

It is difficult to overstate the success of Lubowa's campaign, which took advantage of Catholic initiatives to demonstrate loyalty to the *kabaka*. As Lubowa stated: 'the general rank-in-file in Buganda did not come with him [Benedicto Kiwanuka].'

> Even Catholics [did not follow Kiwanuka]! Because [in] those days, Buganda of Mmengo influence [all over Buganda] was so strong that once they [*bakopi*] sensed that whoever was talking to them did not enjoy full support of Mmengo (or the *Lukiiko*); [...] they fell back. Do you understand what I mean? The rank-and-file – the normal *bakopi* in the villages – the moment they sensed that Mr AD Lubowa, although he speaks very sweetly, very nicely, but he doesn't enjoy the full support of the *Lukiiko*, or the Buganda Government's sentiments, they did not join. [...] This is where Benedicto Kiwanuka found himself in difficulties in Buganda. Because Buganda was administratively very strong at that time. [...] Many Catholics did not go with him. You see?[65]

Lubowa's claims are borne out by the electoral evidence. During the election boycott of 1961, no county in Buganda registered over 2.66% of the population.[66] Voter registration for the 1961 election was abysmal in each of Buganda's principal Catholic counties: Buddu, 2.66%; Busujju, 0.37%;

---

[63] 'Kabaka flies to London: "Aim to Remove Uncertainty"', *Uganda Argus*, 15 August 1960; 'Lukiko Will Hear Report on London Conference', *Uganda Argus*, 29 August 1960; 'Lukiko Votes in Favour of Secession', *Uganda Argus*, 24 September 1960; 'Lubowa sure of Solution', *Uganda Argus*, 15 February 1961; 'Parties Merge in Support of Kabaka Yekka', *Uganda Argus*, 11 November 1961; 'We will fight for unity – Lubowa', *Uganda Argus*, 8 March 1962.

[64] Interview, Jonathon L. Earle with A. D. Lubowa, Maya, Mpigi, 23 November 2009.

[65] Ibid.

[66] Voter registration was higher in the 'Lost Counties' of Bunyoro.

Buvuma, 0.49%; Mawogola, 0.59%; Mawokota, 1.12%.[67] Once KY formed in June 1961, Catholics filled the membership registries and delegates' address forms to demonstrate loyalty to the throne.[68] In consequence, DP was unable to marshal majority support in any of Buganda's Catholic counties during the 1962 elections, which Buganda did not boycott. The low percentages of DP support are indicative of Lubowa's success: Buddu, 22%; Busujju, 10%; Buvuma, 45%; Mawogola, 14%; Mawakota, 22%.[69] Whatever its reputation as the 'Catholic party', DP failed to secure majority Catholic regions of Buganda, continuing the outcomes we noted in both Tesoland and West Nile.

The Political Intervention of Archbishop Joseph Kiwanuka

With so many Catholics joining KY – and frequent political violence committed against DP Catholics (Chapter 6) – Joseph Kiwanuka, newly appointed as Archbishop of Rubaga in Kampala, issued a pastoral letter to fellow Catholics entitled 'Church and State: Guiding Principles'. Issued on 23 November 1961, 'Church and State' became the most controversial Catholic pastoral letter in modern Uganda. Archbishop Kiwanuka began this circular by lamenting the 'wounded Catholic neighbours' who had approached him since September.[70] For the Archbishop, their injuries had stemmed from their opponents' convictions that 'You are a traitor to the Kabaka and to your country'. Archbishop Kiwanuka noted that not all Catholics were targeted but only those who supported DP.[71] Even Archbishop Kiwanuka himself had been verbally accosted, accused with other Catholic bishops of being 'the people who do not want Buganda to receive what belongs to her' and of underwriting DP movement. 'What are you Bishops looking for here? You don't like the Kabaka! Wait until tomorrow and go to welcome Benedicto!'[72]

---

[67] Fred B. Welbourn, *Religion & Politics in Uganda* (Nairobi: East African Publishing House, 1965), Table I.
[68] The membership registries are held with the Masembe-Kabali Papers in Africana Archives of Makerere University: MUA/KY2/#4-KY List.
[69] Welbourn, *Religion & Politics in Uganda*, Table I. The sub-county returns were reproduced in *Uganda Argus*, 24 February 1962.
[70] RDA Archbishop Joseph Kiwanuka, 'Church and State: Guiding Principles', 18 November 1961, p. 3.
[71] The Archbishop stated, 'There are also Catholics who registered as members of the Uganda People's Congress and the Uganda National Congress, however none of them are molested' (ibid., p. 3).
[72] Ibid., pp. 2–3. Archbishop Kiwanuka noted that critics continually accused the bishops and DP Catholics of opposing 'what belongs to Buganda' without explaining the deeper meaning. One could posit that this referred to the Lost Counties.

In response, Archbishop Kiwanuka sketched a political vision that resembled the modern constitutional monarchy of the UK,[73] as well as the conclusions of the Namirembe Conference and Hancock Commission in which he himself had played a critical role.[74] In summary, for the Archbishop, Buganda's political present and future lay not with 'absolute Monarchy' but rather with a combination of 'Democracy', 'Constitutional Monarchy', and 'Aristocracy (*Bakungu*)'. As the Archbishop stated, 'the forms of government may change', and if properly executed, 'Democracy does not destroy Kingship'.[75]

Regarding the elections of 1962, Archbishop Kiwanuka urged Catholic voters to take into consideration each party's attitudes toward religion, rejecting any party which 'says it will debar religion from government, or rob the Church of her schools, or throw religion out of schools'.[76] He reserved special opprobrium for parties making 'pagan' offerings, critiquing Mulumba and *Kabaka Yekka* by condemning the practice of 'composing so-called prayers for the Kabaka in which, in fact they invoke all the "Balubale" [precolonial gods] of the pagans of old'.[77] Catholics were 'forbidden to join such a party', and also should not join a party 'which is seen inciting people to do wrong to others'.[78] Implicitly affirming Lubowa's claims, Archbishop Kiwanuka admitted that many Catholics were among those pushing this agenda: 'I am deeply surprised to see that there are Catholics who still called themselves Catholics, and still joining such parties which bring back paganism, and they not only commit themselves entirely to such parties but also go round inciting others to

---

[73] In the only appendix of 'Church and State: Guiding Principles', Archbishop Kiwanuka provided a one-page defence of constitutional monarchies. The appendix reworked the language of the Namirembe Agreement of 1955, which resulted in Muteesa's return from exile: 'When a country with a king reaches the stage where its government is ruled by its people such a country may still want to keep its kings and for that reason it takes its kings out of politics. When political parties are established in a country, if the king still mixes up in politics the kingship is on the way to digging its own grave. We have the example of other countries to prove that, and therefore Buganda showed clear-sightedness when she decided on the Constitutional Monarchy.'

[74] D. A. Low, *Buganda in Modern History* (Berkeley: University of California Press, 1971), p. 123.

[75] J. Kiwanuka, 'Church and State', p. 6, p. 9.

[76] Ibid., p. 16. This criticism was likely directed at UPC's platform which called for a much larger state role in the funding and operation of religious schools, a promise Obote's government fulfilled in 1963.

[77] Ibid., p. 16. Earlier in the letter, the Archbishop argued that since *Kabaka Yekka* and *Mwoyo gw'Eggwanga* ('Heart of the Nation') had 'never produced a Manifesto' and 'are not recognised by government', they 'cannot be considered as parties [of] which you would become members' (p. 15).

[78] Ibid., p. 16.

join them'.⁷⁹ In contrast, for the Archbishop, properly formed Catholic voters should be open to choosing selfless, God-fearing leaders of 'high moral character' who will 'fight' for religion's role in government and the nation. The rhetoric here, including the Archbishop's exhortation that voters should 'choose people who struggle for truth and justice, people who will everywhere help Buganda and Uganda to unite and to stand together as brothers', endorsed DP and Benedicto Kiwanuka in principle if not in name.⁸⁰

It was the Archbishop's epilogue, however, that would attract the most scathing criticism from Ganda royalists. Kiwanuka castigated KY for pulling the king into electoral politics. 'Those "Kabaka Yekka" and the others who flatter themselves that they are the defenders of the Throne and of the King, are the ones who will spoil our royalty by dragging the king in the backwash of politics.' The Archbishop even warned the *kabaka* against overt politicisation. 'When a King supports one party he shows himself as being no more the king of all his people, but only of that section of his people of which he says, "These are my men who really care for me, and among whom I am hiding."'⁸¹ In a closing salvo, the Archbishop minced no words in ordering Catholics to reject KY: 'Compete in parties which are known; but for such slogans as "Kabaka Alone", "we are behind the throne", "we back the Lukiko", keep away from them'.

Not surprisingly, *Kabaka* Muteesa II was not happy with the Archbishop's intervention. On the night the letter was released on 23–24 November 1961, the *kabaka* sent police to arrest him. Kiwanuka had already left the country for a fundraising trip in the USA, so Mmengo officials instead arrested and interrogated Fr Joseph Ssebayigga, the parish priest of Rubaga Cathedral. Armed with stones, pangas, and axes, hundreds of DP Catholics gathered for a midnight protest. The Vicar General and future Archbishop of Kampala, Fr Emmanuel Nsubuga, dissuaded the Catholic crowd from marching on Mmengo, and Ssebayigga was released in the early morning hours of 24 November.⁸²

In the meantime, *Kabaka Yekka* castigated the Archbishop's letter. Its publicity secretary Abu Mayanja critiqued the Archbishop's lofty claims about ecclesial authority: 'We believe the state and the Government should have supreme power and we do not subscribe – as the Chief Minister seems to do

---

[79] Ibid.
[80] Ibid., pp. 19–20.
[81] Ibid., pp. 21–2.
[82] Willy Mukasa, 'The day Kabaka Muteesa "beat up" the Catholic Archbishop', *Weekly Topic*, 31 January 1992, p. 9, consulted in 'Bendicto Kagimu Mugumba Kiwanuka: A Martyr of Truth and Justice', Proposal to open process for beatification in Archdiocese of Kampala (Kampala: N.P., 2014), Appendix 29. See also 'Kabaka Orders Arrest of Prelate: Crowds gather to protest at Rubaga', *Uganda Argus*, 25 November 1961.

– to the idea that the church should have supreme authority over the state.'[83] In response, KY produced its own letter, '*Kabaka Yekka*: A Thought on His Grace the Archbishop of Rubaga and Metropolitan Letter', the cover of which showed the *kabaka* 'with his Holiness Pope Pious [sic] XII in the V[a]tican in 1958'.[84] The seven-page circular, which sold for 50 shillings, was structured around precise political verdicts, including: '*Kabaka*ship keeps Buganda together', 'He who disunites will be Condemned', 'Archbishop's Letter causes disunity', 'Letter irresponsible', 'Unnecessar[y] to preach hatred', 'Unwise to base political parties on religious differences', and 'Baganda will not take the Archbishop's letter seriously'. It asserted that if 'the party supported by the Roman Catholic Church comes into power [DP] that will be the end of this Kingdom. We have been warned'.[85] Baganda were commanded to serve the Queen Ant (*Nnamunswa*) [*Kabaka*], who would destroy the Termite-killer (*Nnabe*) [DP].[86] Throughout 1962, the Archbishop was physically threatened, and his residence was burgled on his first night back in Uganda.[87] Even as the *kabaka* de-escalated the public conflict in late 1962, overall relations between Muteesa and Archbishop Kiwanuka remained poor until the latter's death in February 1966.[88]

Far from extricating DP Catholics from their political quandary in Buganda, the Archbishop's intervention appeared to worsen their situation. As we will explore in the next chapter, DP Catholics suffered even worse political violence and intimidation in the months leading up to the 1962 elections. Ultimately, it was the Catholic royalists who secured KY's victory. Abu Mayanja argued that the Roman Catholic hierarchy was backing DP to the detriment of Buganda. It was precisely in response to this sort of discourse that Lubowa exhorted

---

[83] 'Kabaka Yekka "Won't Honour Secret Pact"', *Uganda Argus*, 16 December 1961. Echoing medieval theology as well as Pope Leo XIII's *Immortale Deo* (1885), Archbishop Kiwanuka had argued that 'the jurisdiction of the Church over man is much higher in dignity than that of the State, since the Church, works in the supernatural order for the eternal welfare of souls' (Kiwanuka, 'Church and State', p. 12).

[84] ARP 14/4 'Kabaka Yekka: A Thought on His Grace the Archbishop of Rubaga and Metropolitan Letter' [late 1961].

[85] Ibid., p. 7.

[86] Ibid.

[87] 'Archbishop's home burgled', *Uganda Argus*, 13 March 1962.

[88] For nearly a year, Archbishop Kiwanuka refused to attend Buganda Government events due to *Kabaka* Muteesa's refusal to apologise for his treatment of Fr Ssebayigga ('Archbishop's boycott, unless...', *Uganda Argus*, 16 August 1962). The Archbishop and the *kabaka* did not meet in person until late September 1962 (see the frontpage photo in *Uganda Argus*, 24 September, noting how the *kabaka* and the Archbishop finally met to discuss 'recent misunderstandings').

Catholics to demonstrate that they too were loyal to the throne. After KY's triumph in the election of 1962, Catholic loyalties could no longer be questioned as they were in the past. For his work in advocating for Mmengo and KY, Lubowa was appointed *omulamuzi* in 1964. He remained highly active in Buganda politics throughout his long career.

Conclusion

There were multiple Catholic political projects circulating in late colonial Buganda. Some were clearly more popular than others. Benedicto Kiwanuka and DP allies sought to vitiate Semakula Mulumba's call for patriotic Baganda to question the authority of both Protestant and Catholic hierarchical traditions. The activism of Kibuuka Kigaanira both reflected and contributed to a rising royalist populism of the late 1950s, on the coattails of which Mulumba attempted to ride. By successfully channelling the currents of the time, A. D. Lubowa's campaign for royalist authority was electorally effective. Where Mulumba may have exhibited patriotic vitriol, Lubowa was administratively positioned to implement concrete strategy. The majority of Buganda's Catholics boycotted the 1961 election and then backed KY in 1962.

But electoral victory came at a very high cost. The DP-KY division in Buganda was even more divisive among Catholic communities than it was in deepening Catholic-Protestant-Muslim fault lines. In this respect, we suggest that intra-Catholic competition was a catalyst for the formation of KY. When Archbishop Kiwanuka intervened with his political circular, he was enormously concerned about intra-Catholic hostilities. One of the key outcomes of political violence was that DP demanded that British colonial officials and the *kabaka*'s government stop acts of political intimidation. At the same time, Benedicto Kiwanuka urged his own followers to embrace the role of martyrs rather than lash back, preparing themselves to 'die for justice' as necessary.[89] As we show in the following chapter, DP's self-image as a 'persecuted party' and Kiwanuka's preoccupation with martyrdom only increased throughout the 1960s, culminating in his assassination in 1972.[90]

---

[89] Kiwanuka quoted in 'DP warning on election violence', *Uganda Argus*, 14 February 1961. See also 'DP to defy election 'threats'', *Uganda Argus*, 14 February 1961.
[90] 'DP Leader tells meeting his party is persecuted', *Uganda Argus*, 26 November 1960.

CHAPTER 6

'I offer today my body and blood': Violence, Resistance, and Martyrdom

> But as for myself I am going to leave my protection to God. If it pleases Him for me to die let it be. I shall do my work at His place. The only question is to be prepared at all times.
>
> ~Benedicto Kiwanuka, undated[1]

In a speech to parliament on 7 January 1964, only fifteen months after independence, Prime Minister Milton Obote formally endorsed a one-party political system. Pointing to the regional models of Jomo Kenyatta's Kenya African National Union (KANU) and Julius Nyerere's Tanganyika (later Tanzania) African National Union (TANU), Obote argued that a one-party state does not inevitably prevent criticism or the free expression of opinion. Dismissing political opposition as a bourgeois, 'capitalist' notion imported from the colonial West, the prime minister announced that Uganda 'had rejected capitalism once and for all', and he castigated Uganda's opposition – the Democratic Party (DP) – for being 'subversive and irresponsible'.[2] For Obote, UPC could and should be the vehicle for representing the political interests of all Ugandans.

Benedicto Kiwanuka did not delay in his response. In a press release issued the next day, Kiwanuka exhorted his DP supporters and his fellow Ugandans to embrace a politics of resistance. For Kiwanuka, Obote's statement merely confirmed his long-standing suspicion that the prime minister harboured ambitions of serving as 'prime minister for life', aided and abetted by a UPC that championed 'deceipt [sic], nepotism, and self-aggrandisement'.[3] In contrast, Kiwanuka and DP had made a covenant with democracy: 'We, as a group, are wedded to democracy, and we are wedded for all time'. Ultimately, Uganda

---

[1] BKMKP/Not Marked 6/Benedicto Kiwanuka handwritten note, undated.
[2] 'Socialism must govern', *Uganda Argus*, 8 January 1964.
[3] BKMKP/Confidential 2/Benedicto Kiwanuka, 'Socialism and One-Party Rule', 8 January 1964. Subsequent quotations are from this document.

was a 'free nation', and the Ugandan people would not stand idly by while a 'group of power-hungry men take this away from us. We will die rather than give in.' In Eucharistic overtones reflective of Catholic theology, Kiwanuka placed himself in the *persona Christi*, offering his life as a political martyr to Uganda in the face of creeping dictatorship.

> If Dr. Obote intends to use force to achieve his object then I tell him that we will resist. I offer today my body and blood, and there are a lot more who will follow my example. This is our country and here we must remain and die. We have freedom and we will die free men rather than remain alive slaves. A one-party system turns the whole mass of people into slaves of the big dictator – and we will never accept it.[4]

Over the next eight years, Benedicto Kiwanuka not only spoke out but embodied his rhetoric of resistance and martyrdom, suffering arrest, imprisonment, and, in 1972, death at the hands of Obote's successor, General Idi Amin Dada. At the same time, the increasingly marginalised DP conceived itself as a persecuted movement in the 1960s, struggling to retain a relevant public voice as UPC subsumed Uganda's political space.

To contextualise the 'political martyrdom' of Kiwanuka and DP, we focus in this final chapter on the themes of intimidation, resistance, and violence that dominated the final decade of Kiwanuka's life. First, building on the analysis of Ganda political royalism explored in the last chapter, we examine the trajectory of political violence that dogged DP during the 1961–62 electoral period. Overlooked or underplayed in much of Uganda's nationalist historiography,[5] anti-DP persecution was a primary vehicle of political

---

[4] Ibid.

[5] A. B. K. Kasozi sees the mid-1960s as the origin of Uganda's political violence and doesn't mention anti-DP intimidation or violence in the 1950s and 1960s (A. B. K. Kasozi, *The Social Origins of Violence in Uganda, 1964–1985* (Montreal: McGill-Queen's University Press, 1994). T. V. Sathyamurthy describes Kiwanuka as 'volatile and pompous' and agrees that Mmengo elites 'regarded the elevation of a *mukopi* to the position of Chief Minister of Uganda as a personal affront', but he does not discuss the electoral intimidation or violence against DP (T. V. Sathyamurthy, *The Political Development of Uganda: 1900–1986* (Brookfield, VT: Gower, 1986), pp. 392–6). Richard Reid's more recent thematic history discusses the contestation of political visions in late colonial Uganda but omits anti-DP violence (Richard J. Reid, *A History of Modern Uganda* (Cambridge: University of Cambridge Press, 2017), pp. 313–29). Contemporaneous works written in the early 1960s were more blunt. Writing in 1962, D. A. Low admitted that KY looked to 'destroy the DP in Buganda' by 'calling upon Protestant and anti-Catholic sentiments' (Donald A. Low, *Political Parties in Uganda 1949–62* (London: University of London Athlone Press, 1962), p. 54). Writing in 1963, Audrey Richards

intimidation in the two years leading up to independence. Second, we analyse the initial post-independence period, during which DP constituted Uganda's formal parliamentary opposition. In the context of Obote's and UPC's growing state authoritarianism, Kiwanuka and his DP allies embraced a theopolitical discourse of martyrdom in ways that elicited the religious historiographies of the late nineteenth century (Introduction). Such discourses accentuated prophetic resistance, uncompromising commitment to the principles of 'truth and justice', and an embracing of redemptive suffering in a spirit of eschatological hope.[6] Kiwanuka used the idea of martyrdom in the context of excessive violence to engender spiritual solace and to empower distraught party members, locating DP within the Catholic tradition of the Uganda Martyrs with the empowering conviction that God would redeem the just. Third, we examine the final eighteen months of Kiwanuka's life that culminated in his September 1972 assassination. Initially, Kiwanuka saw Idi Amin as 'God's agent', his January 1971 military coup fulfilling Kiwanuka's hopes for Uganda's deliverance from Obote. Ultimately, Amin would not be the agent of Uganda's salvation but rather of Kiwanuka's own death and Uganda's further descent into authoritarian oppression and political violence.

Electoral Boycott and the Proliferation of Political Violence

The cause of political royalism discussed in Chapter 5 resulted in far-reaching episodes of political violence against members of DP. Convinced that Buganda's 'special status' would not be preserved after independence, the kingdom of Buganda called for all Baganda to boycott the 1961 national elections. On 30 August 1960, following the DP decision to protest the boycott, DP members were expelled from the *Lukiiko* while hundreds of protesters denounced Kiwanuka as a 'traitor' to the *kabaka*; one DP member was 'physically ejected and manhandled' by the crowd.[7] Baganda who registered to vote faced death threats, the slashing of their coffee trees, and the burning of their homes. Over 100 police reports on political intimidation were filed between September and November 1960. Even the colonial elections commissioner, R.

---

claimed that 'Democratic Party candidates showed great courage in standing for the [1962] elections at all, in view of the threats of violence against them' (A. I. Richards, 'Epilogue', in *The King's Men: Leadership and Status in Buganda on the Eve of Independence*, ed. by L. A. Fallers (London: Oxford University Press, 1964), p. 364).

[6] In Christian theological discourse, the term 'eschatology' refers to beliefs concerning the 'last things' such as ultimate human destiny, divine judgement, the fate of the world, and the afterlife.

[7] 'Yelling Crowd Besieges Bulange', *Uganda Argus*, 30 August 1960.

C. Peagram, spoke out on the violence in November, lamenting the low voter registration numbers which he attributed to 'the peculiar circumstances of Buganda, in which intimidation and fear took so big a part in the ordinary lives of peaceful citizens'.[8]

For his part, Joseph Kiwanuka framed the crackdown as part of a broader persecution of Catholics. In a September 1960 pastoral letter – his final as Bishop of Masaka before his appointment as Archbishop of Rubaga – Joseph Kiwanuka lamented the accusations against the Catholic Church and exhorted Masaka Catholics to continue to publicly identify with their faith, reminding his flock that the Buganda Martyrs were also falsely accused of hating the *kabaka* and their country. For the bishop, Catholics should not take vengeance on their enemies, but neither should they remain quiet when the truth needs to be spoken.[9] But attacks on DP only grew worse as the March 1961 Legislative Council (Legco) elections approached, and Buganda's muted 'secession' fizzled. In an effort to stop further voter registrations, a 75 per cent majority of the *Lukiiko* passed a resolution condemning registrants as 'traitors to Buganda who have rebelled against the Kabaka and the *Lukiko*' and promising that those who disregarded their directions 'would never be able to build a home in Buganda'.[10]

Initially, the widespread voter boycott in Buganda actually helped DP's political fortunes, as we began to show in Chapter 5. Only 3.5 per cent or 35,000 of Buganda's one million eligible voters registered for the March elections, but almost all were DP supporters, thus carrying Buganda's Legco seats. Combined with DP's competitive showing in the rest of Uganda, Kiwanuka's party scored an unexpected upset over Obote's UPC, taking fifty of Uganda's eighty-eight Legislative Council seats despite losing the overall popular vote to UPC.[11] The Catholic newspaper *Munno* celebrated the DP triumph as Obote blamed the Catholic Church for his defeat, attributing UPC's loss to 'the active participation of a religious denomination'.[12] Kiwanuka promised a rapid

---

[8] 'Thousands too afraid to register', *Uganda Argus*, 17 November 1960. See also 'Electors threatened in campaign against registration', *Uganda Argus*, 1 September 1960.

[9] '*Mukozese Amagezi – Mugoberere Obuntubulamu*', Pastoral Letter by Bishop Joseph Kiwanuka, Bishop of Masaka, *Munno*, 6 September 1960. The title can be translated as 'Use Wisdom and Be Prudent'.

[10] 'Legislative Council electors would be traitors – Lukiko', *Uganda Argus*, 7 February 1961.

[11] UPC outpolled DP 488,334 to 407,416 in 1961 elections, or 54 per cent to 46 per cent (Low, *Political Parties in Uganda*, p. 46).

[12] '*Ewangudde Nnyo; Okujaganya Kunene Nnyo*' ('D.P. has won greatly; there are massive celebrations'), *Munno*, 27 March 1961; 'We Wish Them Luck: Obote',

timeline for independence, comments which *Uganda Argus* noted came as he exited Palm Sunday Mass at Rubaga Cathedral – a not-so-subtle reminder of Kiwanuka's and DP's Catholic connections.[13]

However, even as their leaders controlled more levers of domestic power at the national level, DP members continued to face overt political intimidation in Buganda. In April 1961, the *Lukiiko* temporarily expelled two ministers, two county chiefs, and fourteen members who had participated in the elections.[14] In May, a Ganda farmer was imprisoned for threatening to kill a man for being a member of DP.[15] In July, two Ganda men were jailed for 18 months for attacking a DP supporter for voting in the elections.[16]

The violence grew worse after Kiwanuka's ultimately futile stand against indirect elections in Buganda at the Lancaster House conference in London in September–October 1961.[17] In mid-October, a mob of KY supporters marched on DP homes, and in November thousands of coffee and banana trees belonging to DP sympathisers and Bugisu Cooperative Union members were slashed with crowds chanting, 'We shall kill you because you are traitors of this country.'[18] Acts of violence included the burning of Catholic schools

---

Uganda Argus, 27 March 1961. This echoed critiques Obote had made in late 1960. At the first annual conference of UPC in September 1960, Obote denounced the 'twin sins of tribalism and religious association in politics' and instructed religious leaders to 'take their hands off of politics' and 'concentrate on religion'. ('Keep out of politics, church told: Mr. Obote's warning at party conference', *Uganda Argus*, 19 September 1960).

[13] 'Election Results: Independence the Prime Aim', *Uganda Argus*, 27 March 1961.
[14] 'Baminister Babiri Bagobeddwa mu Lubiko', *Munno*, 8 April 1961.
[15] 'Threatened DP Man', *Uganda Argus*, 30 May 1961.
[16] 'Two Jailed for Attack on DP Man', *Uganda Argus*, 9 July 1961.
[17] Direct elections to parliament were instituted throughout Uganda with the exception of Buganda, where the *Lukiiko* was allowed to appoint MPs. Kiwanuka briefly led a DP walkout from the Lancaster talks over British acquiescence to indirect elections. He continued to lambast this decision in his post-election commentaries, attributing much of the blame to an 'organised campaign by Church leaders here who are working against me and my Party', namely retired Anglican Archbishop of Canterbury Geoffrey Fisher (RDA '1962 Uganda Elections', p. 17). The Kiwanuka-Fisher correspondence is included in several different folders of Kiwanuka's private papers (BKMKP/Federal Status/ 'Archbishop Fisher Benedicto Kiwanuka Correspondence', 2–10 October 1961). On the Lancaster House debates and Kiwanuka's resistance, see 'London: Election Plans Agreed', *Uganda Argus*, 2 October 1961 and 'D.P. quits London talks', *Uganda Argus*, 3 October 1961.
[18] 'Crop-Slashers at Work Again', *Uganda Argus*, 18 November 1961; 'Yekka Mob marched on DP homes', *Uganda Argus*, 22 November 1961.

that were affiliated with the party,[19] the theft of animals,[20] and threatening party members with decapitation.[21] The term used to describe these acts was '*okutiisatiisa*', 'to intimidate', or 'intimidation', which in its basic form meant to 'instill fear'. The desired outcome was to create '*bajenjeeka*', or 'those who are timid', 'inactive', or 'rootless'.[22]

As the February 1962 *Lukiiko* elections approached, anti-DP intimidation increased. Highlights included KY's burning DP's flag in effigy; the beating, arrest, and imprisonment of five DP members, allegedly on the *kabaka*'s orders; and the burning of two Catholic schools with threats of worse actions if Benedicto Kiwanuka was elected.[23] In total, forty incidents of anti-DP, KY violence were reported to police headquarters in Kampala in early 1962, including arson, death threats, assault, theft, the slashing of trees, and even the three-day house arrest of a DP supporter while a KY crowd chanted 'Kabaka Yekka victory' outside his house.[24]

The story of the DP activist Gilbert Mulindwa is illustrative of the violence that was unfolding in Buganda. Mulindwa's home was destroyed in the village of Nantabuliriwa in the Protestant county of Kyaggwe for participating in the electoral strategies of DP.[25] The letters that remain in the colonial archive depict a harrowing ordeal, during which the local parish chief in Nantabuliriwa marshalled 750 KY patriots to surround Mulindwa's home. The crowd, according to Mulindwa, was accompanied by a Buganda Government police officer who donned a hat that promoted the party image of KY.[26] As Mulindwa noted, the police officer paraded a '[badge] of spears and shield on his fez cap and

---

[19] '*Ekyokerezi ku Ssomero*', *Taifa Empya*, 7 February 1962.
[20] 'Yekka men deny stealing goat', *Uganda Argus*, 3 August 1962; 'Yekka man stole two DP cows', *Uganda Argus*, 8 November 1962.
[21] 'Chief threatened to "chop off" DP men's heads', *Uganda Argus*, 2 February 1962.
[22] R. A. Snoxall, *Luganda-English Dictionary* (Oxford: Clarendon Press, 1967).
[23] 'Public Hanging', *Uganda Argus*, 10 January 1962; '5 DP Men "beaten up and arrested"', *Uganda Argus*, 16 January 1962; 'Rubaga school is fired', *Uganda Argus*, 7 February 1962; 'School burnt down', *Uganda Argus*, 26 February 1962.
[24] 'Violence mounts against DP men', *Uganda Argus*, 1 March 1962; 'Yekka men held after assault', *Uganda Argus*, 5 March 1962.
[25] Kyaggwe was in many respects the spiritual capital of Protestantism in Buganda. The powerful Protestant chief Hamu Mukasa, who donated land for the development of B/Uganda's pre-eminent Anglican training school, Bishop Tucker Theological College, governed its territory in the early colonial period. From Kyaggwe, local converts strategised the Protestant conversion of Uganda (John V. Taylor, *The Growth of the Church in Buganda: An Attempt at Understanding* (London: SCM Press, 1958).
[26] BNA CO 822/2425 Gilbert Mulindwa to Governor of Uganda, 4 April 1962.

had big [knives] with him'.²⁷ The chief and police officer announced that it was now time for the *kabaka*, the king of Buganda, to 'kill the red ant', '*Kabaka atta nabbe*', a phrase that was used to intimidate members of DP throughout the early 1960s.²⁸ One group entered into the home and apprehended all of the men, who were accused of being DP sympathisers; they were escorted to a local jail and incarcerated on charges of treason. The women and children ran into a nearby forest. A group of KY supporters then used iron bars to demolish the home, after which the doors and windows were set on fire. Mulindwa himself was severely beaten. As he recalled, the attack 'weakened my life and c[u]t short my lifetime as I am 41 years of age. Two fingers of my left hand are also disabled and I do not feel myself to be well in my head as I am no longer in the usual state of my brain'.²⁹ In other accounts, Mulindwa described in detail 'the blood that streamed all over me'.³⁰ Mulindwa requested for the colonial government to 'evacuate me to some other place where I shall get peaceful sleep other than living in fear always. I have no[thing] I can do now because during the day time I have to sleep and at night I am on guard for my family where I can hardly sleep'.³¹

To illustrate the violent character of the assault to colonial officials, Mulindwa supplied an unsettling photograph with one of his letters (Figure 6.1). In it, he is wearing a white, un-tucked, button-up shirt, with the sleeves rolled up. Mulindwa is holding his right hand up as a closed fist, the hand gesture of DP. A large white bandage circumnavigates Mulindwa's head. The front of the shirt is splattered with blood, especially the area of the chest. His two smallest fingers on the left hand are contorted due to the pain and immobility that he described in a number of the letters. For DP activists in Kyaggwe,

---

²⁷ BNA CO 822/2425/6 Gilbert Mulindwa to Colonial Secretary, 6 April 1962.
²⁸ Ibid. The proverb that accosters shouted, *Kabaka atta nabbe,* was widely circulated as an eponymous pamphlet throughout Buganda (ICS PP.UG.KY '*Kabaka atta Nabbe*', c. early 1962). The proverb assured Baganda that the king would kill the ants that attack the termite mound: the kingship of Buganda. The pamphlet was written in response to a DP manifesto authored in Luganda, '*Ettu ly'Ebisubizo n'Enkola ya D.P. (Manifesto ya Democratic Party)*', 'The Package of the Promises and Systems of Governance of DP: The Manifesto of the Democratic Party'. In the KY pamphlet, royalists argued that *Manifesto ya Democratic Party* revealed that DP had one principal objective: to place a Catholic commoner (*mukopi*), Benedicto Kiwanuka, above the king of Buganda. The language – *okuwan'gama ku Mpologoma Ssabasajja Kabaka wa Buganda* – conveyed the idea of Benedicto Kiwanuka forcing himself into a chair or seizing the throne of the king of Buganda.
²⁹ Gilbert Mulindwa to Governor of Uganda, 4 April 1962.
³⁰ Gilbert Mulindwa to Colonial Secretary, 6 April 1962.
³¹ BNA CO 822/2425 Gilbert Mulindwa to Colonial Secretary, 7 July 1962.

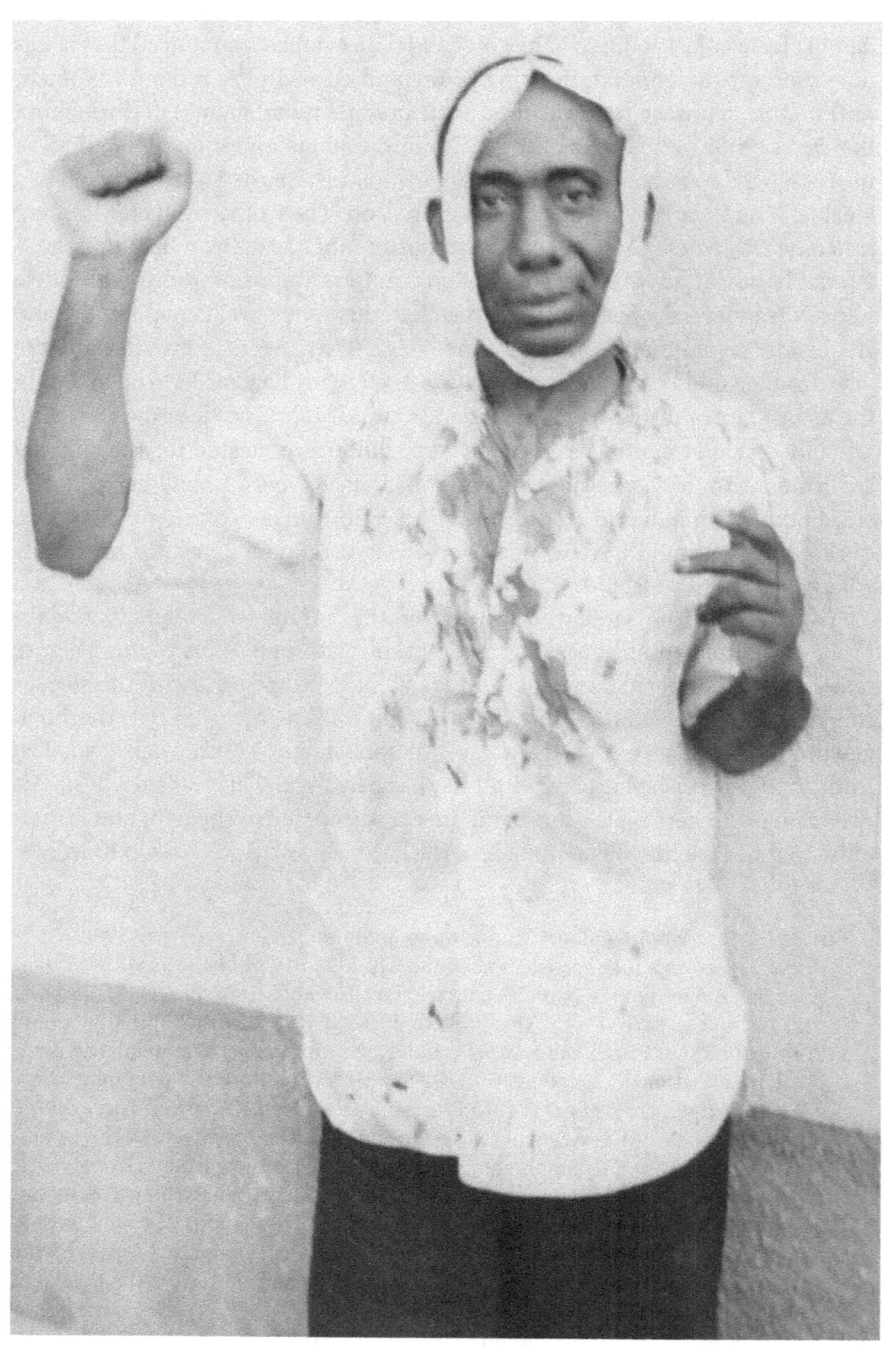

Figure 6.1 DP activist Gilbert Mulindwa poses with the party's closed fist following an attack on his property, April 1962. *British National Archives CO 822/2425.*

Mulindwa was but one of the 2,000 DP activists systemically targeted in February during local elections to the *Lukiiko*.[32] The case of Mulindwa, it was argued, 'clearly shows how the Buganda Government was in support of these acts that we of the D.P. should be wiped out completely in Buganda during the days between 24th, 25th and 26th February, 1962'.[33]

Tactics of intimidation had their desired effect. In the late February *Lukiiko* elections, *Kabaka Yekka* swept to power, winning sixty-three of the sixty-six seats in Buganda.[34] If DP had a moral victory, it was the voters who registered but abstained, voted against KY, or did not register at all – a total of 41 per cent of the electorate.[35] Given Britain's Lancaster compromise to allow Buganda to indirectly elect their National Assembly members from the *Lukiiko*, KY's dominant victory was an ill portent for DP's prospects in the forthcoming April 1962 national elections.

Not surprisingly, Benedicto Kiwanuka attributed his party's defeat to electoral intimidation. In his own extensive 1962 commentary on the elections, Kiwanuka highlighted how the chiefs' control of the electoral process enabled them to threaten voters, naming incidents where electoral officials sealed and resealed ballot boxes and vowed to burn or behead those who 'voted for the hoe' (a prominent DP symbol). Kiwanuka ultimately sent twenty-two pages describing irregularities to the colonial governor, Sir Walter Coutts, on 15 March.[36] Kiwanuka also attributed much of the blame for electoral violence to Britain's decision to allow indirect rather than direct elections for the National Assembly in Buganda.

> What is it that has emerged as the practical result of the indirect elections system being introduced into Buganda? The whole of our liberty is gone. In Buganda you must now belong to the Kabaka-Yekka Party or you are the enemy of the Kabaka; and if you are the enemy of the Kabaka you should be tried for treason and executed! As simple as that. The whole country is now under mob rule. That is why houses are demolished in broad daylight; crops slashed;

---

[32] BNA CO 822/2425/8 Gilbert Mulindwa to Secretary of State for the Colonies, 21 June 1962.

[33] Gilbert Mulindwa to Governor of Uganda, 4 April 1962.

[34] Samwiri Lwanga Lunyiigo, *A Short History of the Democratic Party 1954–1984* (Rome: Foundation for African Development, 1984), p. 63. DP's only victories were in the 'Lost Counties', the former territories of Bunyoro, which Kiwanuka had assiduously courted (see Chapter 3).

[35] 'Yekka sweep into power: influence by chiefs alleged by DP', *Uganda Argus*, 24 February 1962; Low, *Political Parties in Uganda*, p. 55.

[36] RDA '1962 Uganda Elections', pp. 26–7. In this document, Kiwanuka provided both a summary of these charges (pp. 35–9) and a detailed listing of them (pp. 46–61).

men butchered like sheep; women raped; priests tied up and beaten; people threatened in every possible way without hearing any kind of murmur from the Government at Mengo.[37]

In the face of all this, Kiwanuka continued to exhort DP supporters to retain hope, arguing that they 'did not have a fair game' in the *Lukiiko* elections but would stand better odds in national elections in which Ugandans would surely stand for 'democracy' rather than 'slavery'.[38] The party also continued to propagate a message of resistance in the face of persecution. 'The Democratic Party will fearlessly continue its noble cause for undiluted democracy no matter what resistance it encounters and no matter from how high a circle such resistance may be emanating'.[39] For Kiwanuka, DP opponents' resort to violence ultimately revealed weakness – namely a lack of conviction that they could peacefully convince people to vote for their party. Just as Jesus had been 'persecuted by His own people', so DP was being persecuted by their fellow Baganda. The results would be similarly calamitous for all involved.[40]

In his speech at the formal institution of self-rule on 1 March 1962, Kiwanuka transposed these views to the national stage. Commenting on Uganda's anticolonial struggle to achieve self-rule, Kiwanuka again fell back on the discourse of resistance and martyrdom:

We are determined to die than to give up the freedom which we have received today. [...] Many people went to prison for long terms of imprisonment – many died; many lost property which they will never recover; others lost their jobs which resulted in the disintegration of their families; others suffered physical pain against the agents of power against whom we were fighting.'[41]

Critics of Kiwanuka, including British colonial officials, noted that few if any Ugandans had died in an anticolonial struggle against the British.[42] Yet for Kiwanuka and DP, the past eighteen months had been a period of tremendous political intimidation, which for Kiwanuka had been aided and abetted by the feeble leadership and active acquiescence of the British colonial governor

---

[37] Ibid., p. 19.
[38] 'Kabaka Yekka clinch their victory: Challenge to rest of Uganda', *Uganda Argus*, 26 February 1962.
[39] 'DP men assaulted and persecuted', *Uganda Argus*, 26 February 1962.
[40] RDA '1962 Uganda Elections', p. 43.
[41] 'Uganda's struggle ends', *Uganda Argus*, 2 March 1962.
[42] A. C. Duffield, 'Mr. Kiwanuka's speech caused resignation', *Uganda Argus*, 17 March 1962. Such dismissals overlooked Bataka activists who had died in detention in the 1940s.

and hostile civil servants.[43] Ultimately, Kiwanuka's rhetoric and even his late switch to support full federal status for Uganda's four kingdoms were not enough to prevent a UPC-KY victory in Uganda's National Assembly elections in April. Uganda People's Congress won thirty-seven seats to DP's twenty-two, although DP narrowed the overall voting gap with UPC from 1961.[44] Whatever his disappointment, Kiwanuka gracefully conceded defeat: 'I wish my friend Dr. Obote the best of luck'.[45] Kiwanuka remains the only Ugandan prime minister or president to peacefully hand over power to a democratically elected successor.

'DP is ready to die': The Rhetoric of Resistance during the Obote Government

In the days following the National Assembly elections, anti-DP violence continued unabated. A KY mob chased a DP supporter into the bush and killed him, later raping his wife; armed UPC supporters drove DP members out of their homes in three different communities.[46] In the aftermath of these incidents, Kiwanuka issued an appeal to the new UPC government to prosecute the perpetrators, warning that 'he might not be able to restrain his followers if provocation continued'.[47] Kiwanuka again appealed to DP followers to stay true to their principles and to resist the politics of intimidation. 'Our motto of truth and justice is bound to win in the end [...] We shall resist with all our might any attempt from any quarter to exterminate our party.'[48] In June, DP leaders continued to protest ongoing violence and death threats against Kiwanuka, attributing most of this to KY supporters and the *kabaka*'s government.[49] In several incidents, DP retaliated against its opponents, such as in

---

[43] For example, Kiwanuka issued an angry condemnation of British elections supervisor R. C. Peagram for allowing KY chiefs to supervise elections in Buganda. Shortly after this 1 March speech, he demanded that Peagram be fired, to no avail (BKMKP/Elections/Benedicto Kiwauka to Governor of Uganda Walter Coutts, 12 March 1962).

[44] Nationwide, UPC outpolled DP in March 1961 elections by over 80,000 votes (488,334 to 407,416). In the April 1962 elections, UPC defeated DP by around 60,000 votes (545,324 to 484,324 votes). (Low, *Political Parties in Uganda*, 46; Lwanga Lunyiigo, *Short History*, p. 65).

[45] 'DP Government Resigns', *Uganda Argus*, 28 April 1962.

[46] 'DP man killed by crowd', *Uganda Argus*, 2 May 1962.

[47] 'End these threats against DP – Kiwanuka', *Uganda Argus*, 3 May 1962

[48] Ibid.

[49] 'Violence must stop, says DP', *Uganda Argus*, 8 June 1962; 'DP prefer death to deceit', *Uganda Argus*, 19 June 1962; 'Violence condoned says DP', *Uganda Argus*, 23 June 1962.

Kiwanuka'a home village of Kisabwe where DP supporters killed a man and threatened to 'wipe out KY supporters' from the region.[50]

Even as the UPC government distanced itself from such acts of overt violence, Obote also spoke of the need for 'anti-subversive laws' that would target anti-government plotting, such as an alleged DP arms shipment from Rwanda supposedly facilitated by Catholic priests in Kigezi.[51] Other UPC representatives went further: one MP from Obote's home region of Lango described DP as a 'cancer in the nation'.[52] For Kiwanuka, this was part of a broader UPC plot to 'liquidate' DP and turn Uganda into a one-party dictatorship.[53] For Obote and UPC, in contrast, DP's declining national profile and languishing public support would take care of the job for them. This judgement seemed confirmed in October 1962 when only ninety delegates showed up for the DP annual meeting, a far cry from the six hundred who had attended a year earlier. In turn, Kiwanuka faced his first significant leadership challenge, led by the prominent Ankole Catholics Basil Bataringaya, the leader of the parliamentary opposition, and Isidoro Bagorogoza (Chapter 4).[54]

It was at this sparsely attended DP annual conference that Kiwanuka finally collapsed emotionally. After calling for a minute of silence to honour two murdered DP supporters,[55] Kiwanuka sat back down at his table and wept profusely. He then rose and, drawing on the rhetoric of Abraham Lincoln's Gettysburg Address, exhorted DP members to be ready to offer their own lives for the causes of freedom and liberty:

> These men have died for us. Let us therefore be here dedicated to the great task remaining before us, that from these two dead men we take increased devotion to that cause for which they gave their last full measure of devotion, that we here resolve that these men shall not have died in vain [...] I intend to fear nobody in this political battlefield. I was born a man and a man I shall

---

[50] 'Minister in Trouble Area', *Uganda Argus*, 6 December 1962.
[51] BKMKP/Personal Confidential/S. W. Munabi, 'Uganda People's Congress Press Release', September 1962; 'DP 'shocked' by Obote's warning, *Uganda Argus*, 31 August 1962; 'Mr. Chemonges replies for D.P.', 4 September 1962; 'DP denies arms plot allegation', *Uganda Argus*, 5 September 1962; 'Premier repeats warnings', *Uganda Argus*, 27 September 1962. Kiwanuka threatened a libel lawsuit against the government for making these claims.
[52] 'Get rid of the opposition – M.P.', *Uganda Argus*, 17 November 1962.
[53] 'DP denies arms plot allegation', *Uganda Argus*, 5 September 1962.
[54] 'DP annual meeting', *Uganda Argus*, 26 October 1962.
[55] On KY's October 1962 fatal beating of DP supporter Francisco Kanani, see 'DP man walked 9 miles after attack', *Uganda Argus*, 23 July 1963.

die, and I say to you all now that it is better to give even life itself than to succumb to the wishes of an evil man.[56]

Kiwanuka's emotive plea for political martyrdom helped resuscitate his own political prospects. Supported by DP's Acholi delegates (Chapter 4), he won two-thirds of the subsequent conference vote for DP president-general, fending off Bataringaya's bid to replace him as party leader. As Kiwanuka triumphantly proclaimed in the aftermath of his reelection, 'DP is reborn'.[57] Yet for Kiwanuka, political resurrection never fully emerged from the shadows of suffering and death. As he wrote near the end of his 1962 elections commentary, those who want to work for democracy in Uganda 'should be prepared even for death itself', and DP 'shall not rest until our principles have been firmly established both in Buganda and Uganda [...] This is the spirit in which we shall ever fight, struggle, and if necessary, die, but, in the end, triumph'.[58] For Kiwanuka, the apostles of democracy must be prepared for persecution and martyrdom, trusting that their sufferings would ultimately redeem the nation.

In 1963–64, the Democratic Party settled into its role as a minority opposition movement. It was an increasingly lonely affair. In UPC's own political eschatology, the party planned to rule Uganda 'until Jesus comes'.[59] In contrast, DP lacked the parliamentary numbers to offer a substantive check on the government's ambitions. In an effort to boost the opposition, Kiwanuka even reached out to his old nemeses in *Kabaka Yekka*, calling for a merger of their parties and contesting a *Lukiiko* seat on a KY ticket in hopes of getting elected indirectly to the National Assembly.[60] Although he emphasised the importance of political opposition being 'constructive' rather than 'subversive',[61] Kiwanuka also continued to accentuate the themes of persecution and martyrdom. In a press conference in July 1963, he accused the government of tapping his phones and planning to arrest him.[62] In December 1963, he helped organise a mass protest in Katwe of coffee prices that led to a melee with police

[56] 'Ex-premier weeps for dead men', *Uganda Argus*, 29 October 1962.
[57] 'DP is reborn says leader', *Uganda Argus*, 30 October 1962.
[58] RDA '1962 Elections by B. Kiwanuka', p. 44.
[59] K. K. K. Karegyesa quoted in 'Ankole is only DP island in the country', *Uganda Argus*, 23 January 1963.
[60] Kiwanuka ran against Daudi Ocheng (Chapter 4); Ocheng crushed Kiwanuka in the indirect election to the National Assembly in December 1963 ('Mr. Ocheng elected', *Uganda Argus*, 19 December 1963). Kiwanuka's decision to contest the *Lukiiko* seat cost him support within his own party, especially after years of railing against indirect elections and KY's intimidation tactics ('3 more cross over: Dispute over DP leadership', *Uganda Argus*, 6 June 1964).
[61] 'DP Chief's New Year Message', *Uganda Argus*, 2 January 1964.
[62] 'Mr. Kiwanuka speaks', *Uganda Argus*, 15 July 1963.

and his arrest and overnight detention.[63] As discussed at the beginning of this chapter, Obote's decision in January 1964 to publicly endorse a one-party system added further fuel to Kiwanuka's determination to resist. In his words, 'DP is ready to die in a fight to oppose dictatorship by one man'.[64]

The intertwining themes of political martyrdom and resistance found common cause with key elements of the broader Ugandan Catholic community in 1964. In July, Kiwanuka and DP West Nile representative Gaspare Oda accused the central government of complicity in the firing of dozens of Catholic chiefs and civil servants due to their Catholic identity and perceived support for DP, calling for an official commission of inquiry into religious identity and the civil service.[65] Protesting Obote's new state education policy, 2,500 Catholics gathered at the Clock Tower in Kampala on 12 July to demand the resignation of the UPC education minister, Dr Luyimbazi Zake.[66] Three weeks later, 40,000 Catholics gathered at Namugongo – the future site of the Uganda Martyrs' shrine – to protest UPC education policy and UPC opposition to a recent schools accord signed between the Catholic Church and the Buganda Government. In his homily, Mgr Joseph Ssebayigga – the priest who had been arrested in Archbishop Kiwanuka's place in November 1961 – called for 'justice' for Catholic civil servants in northern Uganda. Reflecting the centrality of the martyrs' tradition in Catholic Uganda, Ssebayigga also invoked the 'Uganda Martyrs to help Catholics in their present and future struggles against humiliation and injustice'.[67]

The Uganda Martyrs would soon have an even larger intercessory platform. At the beginning of September, Pope Paul VI announced that he would canonise the twenty-two Catholic Buganda Martyrs in St Peter's Church in Rome on 18 October 1964. These would be the first canonisations of his reign and the first formally recognised Catholic saints from sub-Saharan Africa.[68] Ugandan Catholics celebrated their church's arrival on the world stage over the next

---

[63] 'Ben Kiwanuka Arrested', *Uganda Argus*, 5 December 1963; 'Kiwanuka's home searched', *Uganda Argus*, 6 December 1963.

[64] 'DP to fight Lango Council elections', *Uganda Argus*, 21 January 1964. The party's fortunes temporarily rebounded as they won city and local council elections in Jinja and Kampala in February 1964, successes which Kiwanuka attributed to Ugandans' opposition to a one-party system ('DP jubilant at election successes', *Uganda Argus*, 22 February 1964).

[65] 'Dismissed because of religion', *Uganda Argus*, 11 July 1964; 'DP chief on sackings: More soon in West Nile', *Uganda Argus*, 27 July 1964.

[66] 'Sack minister, say Catholics', *Uganda Argus*, 13 July 1964.

[67] '40,000 Catholics at special mass', *Uganda Argus*, 3 August 1964.

[68] 'Buganda Martyrs to be Canonised in October', *Uganda Argus*, 12 September 1964.

five months. Masses and benedictions were celebrated for days surrounding the canonisation date. In an ecumenical gesture, Archbishop Kiwanuka invited Anglican Archbishop Leslie Brown to attend the ceremony in Rome. In Uganda, the months-long festivities culminated with a February 1965 Mass that drew 40,000 to Nakivubo Stadium in Kampala, including Obote, Brown, the Tanzanian Cardinal Laurent Rugambwa, and the Vatican's head of evangelisation and mission.[69]

If the Ugandan Catholic Church was enjoying a global moment in late 1964 and early 1965, the same could not be said for the Democratic Party. In January 1965, Basil Bataringaya and five other DP MPs crossed the aisle to join UPC. Shortly thereafter, Obote announced that there was no longer an 'official opposition party in the National Assembly nor constitutional provision for a Leader of the Opposition'.[70] This was more than opportunistic rhetoric; DP was down to ten MPs after failing to convince KY's fourteen MPs to join forces with them.

Unable to play much of a constructive role in opposition, DP again fell back on the rhetoric of resistance to address international and domestic politics. Kiwanuka criticised the recently established Organisation of African Unity (OAU) for overlooking electoral intimidation in Uganda, while publicity secretary Paul Ssemogerere organised a series of public meetings calling on DP members to 'resist dictatorship' and 'resist totalitarianism'.[71] Opening a new DP branch in Busoga, Kiwanuka's wife Maxencia promised that 'DP will never die because it was built on the truth'.[72] Returning to his 'gospel' of democracy, Benedicto Kiwanuka predicted that '1966 will be a year in which the people of Uganda will have finally to make up their minds as to whether this country will enjoy the full benefits of democracy or will suffer the scourges of a dictatorship'.[73]

Uganda's 1966 crises are well known and well attested elsewhere (Introduction). Key events included the attempted 22 February UPC cabinet putsch against Obote; Obote's subsequent suspension of the 1962 Constitution and elimination of *Kabaka* Edward Muteesa's presidential office, following his refusal to ratify the outcome of the referendum that returned the 'Lost

[69] 'Uganda masses mark Canonisation', *Uganda Argus*, 13 October 1964; 'Ugandans are canonised', *Uganda Argus*, 19 October 1964. 'Canonisation Climax: 40,000 at Nakivubo', *Uganda Argus*, 8 February 1965.
[70] '6 DP Men Join UPC', *Uganda Argus*, 1 January 1965; 'KY and DP Reply', *Uganda Argus*, 4 February 1965.
[71] BKMKP/Confidential 2/'Benedicto Kiwanuka Press Comment on Congo Situation', 16 January 1965; 'Aim of DP meetings', *Uganda Argus*, 26 February 1965.
[72] 'DP will never die – Mrs. Kiwanuka', *Uganda Argus*, 8 September 1965.
[73] ICS PP.UG.DP.37 'Benedicto Kiwanuka, DP Press Release, 1 January 1966'.

Counties' to Bunyoro; the April 'pigeonhole' constitution, accompanying suspension of the 1967 elections; the establishment of a state of emergency in Buganda; and the May 'Battle of Mmengo' in which Colonel Idi Amin's soldiers torched the *kabaka*'s palace at Mmengo, forcing Edward Muteesa to go into hiding and then, via Burundi, seek exile in the UK.[74]

Early in the crisis, on 1 March, Obote met with DP opposition leaders Latim, Ssemogerere, and Oda to try to convince them of the necessity of his actions. Unconvinced, the DP leaders described Obote's actions as a 'coup against his own government'.[75] Kiwanuka's rhetoric went much further as he posited that Obote's decision to suspend the 'sacred' constitution put him in league with Hitler, Mussolini, and Ghana's Kwame Nkrumah, promising that the people stood ready to 'fight for their Constitution [...] We prefer death to being your slaves'.[76] Although DP parliamentarians initially took an oath of allegiance to the new constitution the day after its promulgation on 16 April,[77] DP's central executive came out forcefully against it two weeks later. Calling for a new constitutional conference and immediate elections, DP again framed its opposition role in terms of resistance and a willingness to undergo redemptive suffering that would ultimately help deliver the fruits of freedom to Uganda.

> It is absolutely impossible to rule merely with the gun and without the consent of the people. Suppression is no solution. Let the whole world take note that the Democratic Party will resist and offer anything to fight dictatorship in this country. Whether this fight will mean death or imprisonment, persecution or torture in any form, the Democratic Party will ever remain vigilant, and a day will come when this country – when all people of Uganda regardless

---

[74] Ironically in light of their previous tensions, *Kabaka* Edward Muteesa apparently received support from the Catholic parish at Rubaga during his initial escape. Then Vicar General (future Archbishop and Cardinal) Emmanuel Nsubuga and Fr Joseph Ssebayigga were interrogated about this in June 1966 (Kathleen Lockard, 'Religion and Political Development in Uganda, 1962–72', unpublished PhD thesis, University of Wisconsin-Madison, 1974, p. 234). The story has also lingered in Catholic oral history in Uganda. In the words of local Catholic scholar Br Anatoli Wasswa, 'they [the priests] gave him [the *kabaka*] wine, dressed him as a priest and sent him out of the country' (Anatoli Wasswa, interview with Carney, Bunga, Kampala, 30 June 2015).

[75] 'Obote's action saved many lives', *Uganda Argus*, 2 March 1966.

[76] BKMKP/Confidential 2/'Kiwanuka public letter to Obote', 3 March 1966. He wrote in the immediate aftermath of a February 1966 military coup that toppled Nkrumah, a coup justified in part due to a 1964 constitutional provision establishing Ghana as a one-party state with increased powers of detention.

[77] 'Opposition MPs agree to take new oath', *Uganda Argus*, 18 April 1966.

of their creed or tribe will truly enjoy freedom and all the other fruits of their hard-won independence.[78]

Eschatological deliverance felt more and more like a dream deferred, however. Instituted by Obote during the violence of May 1966, the state of emergency in Buganda continued into 1967 with no end in sight. Although opposition parties were still legal, DP was not allowed to hold press conferences or public rallies, and Obote's government used detention laws to imprison without trial opponents of the regime.[79] The 1967 elections – the elections DP had banked on to revive its party's fortunes – were postponed after the passage of the 1966 constitution. For all intents and purposes, Uganda had become a functional one-party state by the end of 1966.

Yet far from conceding defeat, DP leaders continued to contest public politics. In November 1966, Kiwanuka threatened to call for rebellion if the state of emergency did not end soon: 'I shall withdraw my hand which hitherto has restrained many a man who wanted to take unconstitutional measures to remedy what they considered to be wrongs done to them by the Government. As I said before you are only 92 as against 7 million citizens.'[80] Echoing the St Crispin's Day speech of Henry V, as recounted by Shakespeare, DP publicity secretary and Kiwanuka confidant Paul Ssemogerere (Figure 6.2) called on delegates at the party's 1966 annual conference to persevere in 'the glorious fight for democracy':

> If it is killings, how many of our people have been killed because they believed in Democracy? If it is imprisonment how many of our people have been falsely arrested and imprisoned? And how many thousands of innocent people have been dismissed from their jobs, denied employment, bursaries or scholarships or had their taxes unfairly assessed and yet have endured all this injustice? Yet suffering has not been confined to Democrats alone. The common man everywhere has in one way or other suffered from the misconduct of the present government.[81]

---

[78] ICS PP.UG.DP.5 Latim & Ssemwogerere, 'DP and Obote's Constitution', 3 May 1966. Kiwanuka echoed these sentiments in a London speech on 7 May by calling for immediate national elections and a constitutional convention (BKMKP/Confidential 2/'London Speech to UGASSO on Ugandan Political Situation', 7 May 1966, p. 6).

[79] 'DP Chief wants rally ban lifted', *Uganda Argus*, 1 September 1966; 'Emergency Extended', *Uganda Argus*, 19 November 1966; ICS PP.UG.DP.19 A. A. Latim, 'DP Statement', 18 March 1967; Joshua B. Rubongoya, *Regime Hegemony in Museveni's Uganda: Pax Musevenica* (New York: Palgrave Macmillan, 2007), p. 41.

[80] BKMKP/Uganda Versus/Benedicto Kiwanuka, 'DP Response to State of Emergency', 14 November 1966.

[81] ICS PP.UG.DP.14 Paul Ssemogerere, 'DP Speech to Annual Delegates', 17

Figure 6.2 Paul Ssemogerere, pictured here with Benedicto Kiwanuka, served as the DP's publicity secretary throughout the late 1950s and 1960s. *Benedicto Kiwanuka Papers.*

Here, Ssemogerere rhetorically melded DP suffering with the suffering of Uganda's people. 'Our people' is no longer just the 'Democrats', but all the people of Uganda. In turn, 'the voice of the people is the voice of God', noted Ssemogerere in a public letter in May 1967, a theological claim which had long been recycled in European political thought (*Vox populi, vox Dei*).[82] Like the exiled people of Israel in the Bible, DP needed to cultivate patience and hope as it suffered through its own captivity. In Ssemogerere's words, 'Let us remain confident, for the day of redemption is fast approaching'.[83]

The Democratic Party's day of political redemption, however, remained elusive. A more substantive constitution was passed in 1967, delaying parliamentary elections until at least 1972. The state of emergency in Buganda remained in place. The government even took aim at the institutional Catholic Church by expelling nine Comboni missionary priests from northern Uganda for allegedly aiding southern Sudanese rebels.[84] While UPC officials toured Uganda trumpeting the government's achievements, DP vainly petitioned for the right to hold political meetings or rallies. Finally, in May 1968, Kiwanuka, Latim, and the DP national executive issued a blistering rebuke of 'Machiavellian and undemocratic' UPC policies that 'seriously offend against all established tenets of democracy'.[85] Here they highlighted the new constitution's inclusion of detention without trial, the centralisation of power in the hands of the president, and Uganda's general slide toward a

---

September 1966. Kiwanuka and DP Executive Committee echoed this language in a December press release. 'The Democratic Party will face up to the greatest persecution and suffering, as it has done in the past, rather than give up the glorious fight for democracy' (ICS PP.UG.DP.24 DP Executive Committee on Obote and Elections, 15 December 1966).

[82] Alain Boureau, 'L'adage vox populi, vox dei et l'invention de la nation anglaise (VIIIe–XIIe siècle)', *Annales. Histoire, Sciences Sociales*, 47 (1992), 1071–89.

[83] ICS PP.UG.DP.4 Paul Ssemogerere, 'DP Letter', 13 May 1967.

[84] BKMKP/News Items/'Expulsion of Priests Raises Problems', *Daily Nation*, 20 January 1967; 'We're Innocent, say expelled Uganda priests', *Daily Nation*, 20 January 1967. See also *Munno*, 20 January 1967. Far from an outspoken critic of Obote's government in the 1960s, even newly appointed Kampala Archbishop Emmanuel Nsubuga issued a strong rebuttal. 'Catholics in Uganda, and perhaps all over the world, are deeply perturbed by the sudden decision of the government to expel from this country ten Roman Catholic priests [...] Such conduct does not show that there is harmony between the State and the Church although Government leaders appear to be courteous to the church and her leaders in Uganda' ('Kampala Archbishop Condemns Expulsions', *Daily Nation*, 21 January 1967).

[85] BKMKP/Secretary of State Correspondence/'Statement by the National Executive', 17 May 1968.

'totalitarian state'.[86] It was a sign of DP's diminished political status, though, that such accusations did not produce much of a government reaction.

Kiwanuka kept up the rhetorical barrage in 1969. In March, he publicly decried what he described as 'discrimination based on religion, political belief and tribe' as well as a culture of political intimidation marked by detention without trial, the banning of public or private DP meetings, and emergency regulations, claiming that 'people live in fear of apprehension from their beds'.[87] For Kiwanuka, Obote's invoking of Ugandan national brotherhood conveniently overlooked the government's decisions to abolish the kingdoms and what Kiwanuka described as 'the mutilation of Buganda', namely the extension of parliamentary terms 'against the wishes of the people' and the overall 'suppression of political opponents'.[88] Citing the Gospel of Matthew's strident 'woe to you' narratives against the Pharisees, Kiwanuka accused UPC of hypocrisy for opposing authoritarian white rule in Rhodesia while Ugandans were 'rotting in prison without trial'. Again, Kiwanuka challenged the usage of Africanist discourse to occlude ongoing political intimidation in the postcolonial world (Chapter 1): 'Is prison life sweet to an African if he is thrown into it by a fellow African, and bitter if he is thrown into it by a European racist?'[89]

Kiwanuka would soon find out. The Obote government did not immediately react to his March 1969 salvo, likely out of concern for the potential impact on Pope Paul VI's upcoming visit to Uganda in July, the first of a Catholic Pope to sub-Saharan Africa. After Kiwanuka firmly rejected a proposal by UPC to merge the two parties,[90] the Obote government cracked down. On 6 September, Kiwanuka was taken from his sickbed at his home on Masaka Road and arrested, with Paul Ssemogerere, on charges of libel and 'publishing a seditious document intended to bring hatred or contempt or to excite disaffection against the present Government, the President, and the Constitution'.[91]

---

[86] Ibid.
[87] ICS PP.UG.DP.11 'Kiwanuka Response to Obote's Communication', 8 March 1969, p. 1.
[88] Ibid., p. 7.
[89] Ibid., p. 12. Kiwanuka explicitly cited Matthew 23:27 here: 'Woe to you, scribes and Pharisees, you hypocrites; because you are like to whited sepulchers, which outwardly appear to men beautiful but within are full of dead men's bones and of filthiness.'
[90] BKMKP/Confidential 2/Benedicto Kiwanuka to EMK Mulira, 25 August 1969. Again, Kiwanuka resorted to inflammatory rhetoric as he questioned how he could possibly merge with a party and leader who had overseen 'corruption, tribalism, vandalism, squandering of public funds, political cowardice, and exploitation of the masses by those on top'.
[91] ICS PP.UG.DP.31 '1969 Uganda vs. Kiwanuka and Ssemwogere'. See also 'DP Leader Pleads Not Guilty', *Uganda Argus*, 10 September 1969.

Police searched DP headquarters, and 150 other DP members were imprisoned over the next several weeks, including a group in Masaka arrested for wearing DP's white and green colours.[92] Kiwanuka was so sick that he spent his initial days of detention under police guard at Mulago Hospital.[93] However, he was ultimately acquitted of the government's charges and released in October.

Far from tempering Kiwanuka's rhetoric, his arrest and trial seemed to give him new energy. He used the occasion of Uganda's Independence Day commemoration to describe 'the seven years of UPC rule since independence [as] nothing but a record of injustice, arbitrary rule, and broken promises'. Likewise, this seventh anniversary came, he argued, at a moment when 'tyranny and political persecution dictate Government policy' with over 200 political prisoners languishing in jail.[94] For this reason, Kiwanuka announced that DP would not commemorate Ugandan independence in 1969. 'We find it difficult to go out to celebrate when our fellow freedom fighters – virtually all of them completely innocent – are, purely out of spite and hate, suffering from the most inhuman treatment in prison.'[95]

Two months later, Kiwanuka again joined his fellow DP 'freedom fighters' in the gaol. In the immediate aftermath of the attempted assassination of Obote in Gulu on 19 December 1969, Kiwanuka was arrested on alleged conspiracy charges.[96] His case was never brought to trial as he languished in prison for thirteen months. Allowed an occasional 'through-the-glass' conversation with his wife, he spent much of detention in solitary confinement, suffering psychological if not physical torture.[97] In prison he claimed to find common cause with how 'Jesus was misinterpreted and maltreated when he was speaking the truth'.[98] Like Jesus, Kiwanuka's misinterpretation and maltreatment would culminate in what he – and many of his supporters – saw as his own martyrdom.

---

[92] BKMKP/Minister without Portfolio Cotton and Coffee/Paul Ssemogerere, 'DP Leaders Detention', 30 September 1969.
[93] ICS PP.UG.DP.1 A.A. Latim, 'Ben's Arrest', 17 September 1969.
[94] ICS PP.UG.DP.13 'Kiwanuka Press Statement on Uganda's 7th Anniversary', 7 October 1969.
[95] Ibid.
[96] BKMKP/Confidential 2/Benedicto Kiwanuka Detention Notice, 22 December 1969.
[97] 'Maxensia Zulbango Kiwanuka Testimony', Uganda Commission of Inquiry into Violation of Human Rights, 1988, pp. 6584, 6594; Maurice Kagimu Kiwanuka, interview by Carney, Rubaga, Kampala, 6 July 2017.
[98] Albert Bade, *Benedicto Kiwanuka: The Man and His Politics* (Kampala: Fountain, 1996), p. 145.

'Children of Mother Mary never die': Idi Amin and the Killing of Benedicto Kiwanuka

At various points throughout the 1960s, Benedicto Kiwanuka revealed a vivid sense of his own vulnerability. The death threats and anti-DP violence that marked the 1961 and 1962 elections left their wounds, building on a personality keenly attuned of any perceived slight, whether real or imagined. Kicked out of his government housing in late 1962, he built a new home on Masaka Road marked by seven-foot high walls and barbed wire. Asked to explain these security features, Kiwanuka bluntly responded, 'I do not think the threats against me have been exaggerated, but I will be safe here'.[99] Later in the decade, he purchased life insurance and bought a gun.[100] In his private notes, Kiwanuka ruminated on his own death. 'But as for myself I am going to leave my protection to God. If it pleases Him for me to die let it be. I shall do my work at His place. The only question is to be prepared at all times.'[101] As discussed throughout this chapter, the discourse of Kiwanuka and DP throughout the 1960s was deeply shaped by themes of suffering, persecution, and anticipation of death.

Initially, however, the *coup d'état* of General Idi Amin Dada on 25 January 1971 portended much better tidings. If Kiwanuka's 1969 arrests and detention as a political prisoner inculcated a lived experience of suffering, Amin's decision to free Kiwanuka and other political detainees seemed to represent the long-delayed 'day of deliverance' that DP had predicted throughout Obote's rule. In the days and weeks following the coup, DP leaders were gushing in their gratitude toward the general who professed that he 'feared no man on this earth apart from God'.[102] Despite the undemocratic nature of a military coup, Alex Latim, secretary-general of DP, praised Amin as the 'Liberator of our freedom in Democracy'.[103] A week after his release from detention, Kiwanuka thanked Amin for having 'saved the country from totalitarianism, tyranny, corruption, and nepotism', describing him as the 'agent of Almighty God'.[104] He went even further in a March 1971 speech at a dinner hosted by Amin.

---

[99] 'Kiwanuka playing it safe', *Uganda Argus*, 5 November 1962.

[100] BKMKP/Insurance-Life-General/various correspondence; BKMKP/Arms/J. D. Turyagenda, for Permanent Secretary of the Ministry of Internal Affairs, to Benedicto Kiwanuka, 8 February 1968.

[101] BKMKP/Not Marked 6/Benedicto Kiwanuka handwritten note, undated.

[102] This became one of Amin's trademark phrases, but his first utterance came in a meeting with Anglican and Catholic bishops days after the coup (see *Munno*, 1 February 1971).

[103] ICS PP.UG.DP.22 Latim to Amin, 13 February 1971.

[104] BKMKP/Elections/Benedicto Kiwanuka to General Idi Amin Dada, 4 February 1971.

Comparing the 'wild jubilation' in Uganda at the fall of Obote to Europe's celebrations at the end of the Second World War, Kiwanuka made the astounding claim that Obote's crimes surpassed those of Adolf Hitler: 'But then, although Hitler was admittedly a wicked man, he did not reach, in my view, the dimensions in wickedness of the man who masqueraded here as the champion of the common man'.[105] Condemned to die by their 'diabolical enemy' Obote, the Ganda prisoners' release from prison 'meant real resurrection'.[106] In essence, Amin had become Uganda's Mosaic agent of a new Exodus, as the ex-detainees wrote in a public letter to Amin: 'Remembering always, that as the Biblical Moses delivered the Jews out of Pharaoh's bondage, so have you delivered the people of Uganda out of captivity and enslavement under Obote.'[107] Such obsequies also revealed Kiwanuka's continuing ambitions to be a political player in postcolonial Uganda.

Kiwanuka was soon rewarded for his fealty to the 'agent of Almighty God'. In June 1971, Amin announced Kiwanuka's appointment as Chief Justice of the Supreme Court; Kiwanuka was the first Ugandan to serve in this office.[108] According to the later testimony of his wife Maxencia, Kiwanuka was reluctant to accept the position but ultimately acquiesced to Amin's 'begging' and his friends' entreaties.[109] Whatever his ambivalence, Kiwanuka dove into the new job with his typical vigour. He announced that he intended to meet with all local magistrates in Uganda to address problems of tardiness, drunkenness, lack of impartiality, and delayed judgements. He also promised to protect Ugandans against government abuses, 'not allowing you to be thrown into prison at the whims of an Executive as had happened in times past'.[110]

This reassertion of principle, accompanied by Kiwanuka's trademark 'sense of righteousness' and commitment to the 'straight ways of justice',[111]

---

[105] ICS PP.UG.DP.21 'Kiwanuka speech on ex-detainees', 7 March 1971, pp. 1–2.
[106] Ibid., p. 2. Showing just how far Kiwanuka had moved from his supposedly non-negotiable principles of democracy and the rule of law, he claimed in this speech that 'there is no known principle in international law upon which the rejection of your Government can be based by any nation at the moment'.
[107] ICS PP.UG.DP.23 'Letter from ex-detainees to Amin', 7 March 1971.
[108] Prior to Kiwanuka, two British litigants and the Nigerian jurist, Egbert Udo Udoma, served as Uganda's first postcolonial chief justices.
[109] 'Maxencia Zulbango Kiwanuka Testimony', pp. 6572–3, 6585. She claimed that she opposed her husband's taking this position and later said that Amin ordered Kiwanuka to host and pay for a celebration of his own appointment to the Supreme Court.
[110] BKMKP/Folder 56–69/Acting Chief Justice Ben Kiwanuka, Address at International Conference Center, 7 July 1971.
[111] These descriptors are taken from a personal letter from Kiwanuka's longtime confidant, Fr Tarcisio Agostoni, who also posited that 'this work [of Chief Justice]

also planted the seeds of an emerging split with Amin. In September 1971, an Indian landowner approached Kiwanuka to protest government plans to appropriate his sugar plantation for a new Sango Bay airstrip. Hearing word of this meeting, Amin's cabinet officials murmured that 'Kiwanuka should be watched'.[112] In February 1972, a Ministry of Health official sought legal advice from Kiwanuka after his family was arrested at gunpoint by military police.[113] Amin also personally distanced himself from Kiwanuka. Although the two had shared a Christmas dinner with Kiwanuka's family in 1971, they rarely fraternised in 1972. Amin rejected Kiwanuka's invitation to his silver jubilee wedding anniversary, and Kiwanuka refused to attend most public ceremonies after being snubbed at a government meeting in late 1971.[114] In the meantime, Kiwanuka expanded his life insurance policy.[115]

When the *Uganda Argus* was printed on 21 August 1972, the front cover announced, 'All Asians Must Go'. Upon receiving his copy, Kiwanuka read closely. The original copy is preserved in Kiwanuka's private collection (Figure 6.3), with annotated blue ink marks showing what captured the Chief Justice's attention. The thickness of the annotated markings increased in the middle of the second paragraph, where the writer called Kiwanuka specifically into question, implicating both his Catholicism and the Indian alliances he had cultivated in recent years:

> The President also charged that a few Ugandan Africans, including some high-ranking Government officials in Masaka District, are in the pockets of the outgoing Asians and the imperialists and are opposed to the move to expel them. One such official holds a very high position in the Government and is known

---

fits you more also for your uncompromising sense of religion' (BKMKP/Mr. Kiwanuka Personal/Agostoni to Kiwanuka, 4 July 1971).

[112] BKMKP/Not Marked 5/Benedicto Kiwanua Memo, 'Secret', 24 September 1971.

[113] BKMKP/Private Correspondence/Alfred Munduku to Benedicto Kiwanuka, 12 January 1972. Kiwanuka forwarded this correspondence to Amin, requesting that he inform Kiwanuka of his response (BKMKP/Private Correspondence/Benedicto Kiwanuka to Idi Amin Dada, 8 February 1972).

[114] Bade, *Benedicto Kiwanuka*, p. 153. According to Kiwanuka, his decision to withdraw from public events stemmed from a personal slight – namely Amin's decision in October 1971 to seat Kiwanuka among other cabinet officials rather than in his own separate space as Chief Justice (BKMKP/Govt House Copies of Minutes/Benedicto Kiwanuka to President Idi Amin Dada, 31 August 1972). The story of Amin's rejection of Kiwanuka's wedding invitation was relayed by Maurice Kagimu Kiwanuka, speech at Benedicto Kiwanuka Memorial Lecture, High Court, Kampala, 21 September 2018.

[115] See life insurance correspondence in BKMKP/Uganda Versus/March 1972 and 26 May 1972 and BKMKP/Loose Papers, 22 June 1972 and 19 July 1972.

Figure 6.3 Kiwanuka opposed Amin's decision to expel Uganda's Asian communities. In this annotated newspaper clipping, Kiwanuka noticed that Amin had begun to use the press to cast Catholics as Asian sympathisers. *Uganda Argus,* annotated, 21 August 1972 in *Benedicto Kiwanuka Papers.*

to be the prime mover of this small pocket of opposition said the President. He is attempting to use this isue [sic] to divide the people of this country on a religious basis with the hope that he will achieve his selfish ends. The person concerned is known to the Government and in fact the Government has already lost confidence in him as a result of his dirty activities.[116]

Protesting these accusations in a personal letter to Amin, Kiwanuka denied that he 'engaged in any activities' opposing Amin's decision to expel the Asians and called on Amin to quell swirling rumours about his imminent arrest and death. Staring into the abyss, Kiwanuka again expressed his baseline conviction that God stood with him. 'For it is not death that I fear, for there is no one who has insurance against it, but the fact that we have reached this stage. [...] Let me hope, however, that the Almighty God will come in and vindicate the cause of the just.'[117]

As has been well attested elsewhere, Kiwanuka's decision to hear the case of British businessman Daniel Stewart sealed his final fate. Stewart had been arrested without trial and detained at Luzira military barracks. Over the strenuous opposition of the Amin government, the British High Commissioner requested that Kiwanuka hear the case. Kiwanuka concurred and granted Stewart a writ of *habeas corpus*, arguing that the executive branch should not dictate to the judicial branch.[118] By mid-September, rumours swirled that Kiwanuka's days were numbered. Close confidants, including his wife, Archbishop Nsubuga, Fr Clement Kiggundu (the editor of *Munno*), and Fr Agostoni, urged him to flee the country. Kiwanuka stood firm, however, insisting that 'nothing can happen to him without God's approval' and that 'we cannot allow our country to continue in this way because we are too threatened. If we have to die, let's die as martyrs rather than as cowards.'[119]

Kiwanuka would not have to wait long for his opportunity to become a political martyr. On the morning of Thursday, 21 September 1972, he partook

---

[116] BKMKP/Annotated Newspapers/'All Asians Must Go', *Uganda Argus*, 21 August 1972. Emphasis original.

[117] BKMKP/Govt House Copies of Minutes/Benedicto Kiwanuka to President Idi Amin Dada, 31 August 1972.

[118] Bade, *Benedicto Kiwanuka*, p. 156; Lwanga Lunyiigo, *Short History*, p. 88. Obote's and other exiles' unsuccessful invasion of Uganda in September 1972 also created the pretext for a crackdown of perceived enemies of the state. On the aborted invasion, see Donald A. Low, 'Uganda Unhinged', *International Affairs*, 49 (1973), 219–28 (p. 228); Kasozi, *Social Origins of Violence*, pp. 121–2.

[119] 'Bendicto Kagimu Mugumba Kiwanuka', p. 26; Bade, *Benedicto Kiwanuka*, p. 158. Kiggundu himself was killed by Amin's agents in January 1973. Kiggundu's successor as editor of *Munno* attributed Kiggundu's killing to his ongoing investigation of Kiwanuka's death (Simon Mwebe, interview with Carney, Kampala, Uganda, 12 July 2017).

in his daily practice of attending Mass at Rubaga Cathedral. A week earlier he had taken the unusual step of requesting and receiving the Catholic sacrament of anointing, a ritual only granted in cases of serious illness or in anticipation of death.[120] Shortly after 8 a.m., as Kiwanuka sat in his chambers, plainclothes intelligence officers with Uganda's General Security Unit confronted him at gunpoint. As he was forced out of the building and into the trunk of a waiting Peugeot car, he shouted in Luganda to one of his assistants, '*Matiya bantutte, naye abaana ba Maria tebafa*'! ('Mathias, they have taken me, but children of Mother Mary do not die'!)[121] The car sped off, and Kiwanuka was never seen alive again.

Conflicting accounts of the circumstances of Kiwanuka's death circulated in the months and years to come. In the immediate aftermath of Kiwanuka's disappearance, and under international pressure from figures like Kenyan President Jomo Kenyatta, Amin's government blamed Obote's agents, and Amin allegedly offered Kiwanuka his freedom if he would sign a document implicating Obote.[122] In the official 1975 government report on the disappearances between 1972 and 1974, the exiled former minister of foreign affairs, Wanume Kibede, was blamed for his death.[123] Maxencia Kiwanuka also alleged that Kibede had tried to summon Kiwanuka to night meetings on several occasions and threatened him in multiple phone calls, although she ultimately attributed responsibility for Kiwanuka's death to Amin.[124] For his part, Kibede denied involvement and claimed that Amin personally ordered Kiwanuka's arrest and execution.[125] In its 1978 report, Amnesty International also implicated Amin directly, arguing that Kiwanuka was killed in 'retaliation for his demands in favor of the independence of the judiciary and the right of

---

[120] Revealingly, the propagators of Kiwanuka's beatification cause equate his sacramental request to those of the Buganda Martyrs seeking baptism prior to their deaths in 1886. 'This is no different from some of the twenty-two Uganda martyrs like Saint Kizito, Saint Mbaga Tuzinde, Saint Gyaviira and others who yearned for baptism, knowing very well that it was to lead to their death' ('Bendicto Kagimu Mugumba Kiwanuka', p. 12).

[121] The account here is taken from two sources: 'Bendicto Kagimu Mugumba Kiwanuka', pp. 17, 24–30; Ugandan National Government, '1975 Commission of Inquiry into Disappearances. Subject No. 34: Benedicto Kiwanuka', pp. 112–13.

[122] 'Concern Over Chief Justice', *Uganda Argus*, 23 September 1972; '1975 Commission of Inquiry into Disappearances', p. 16; 'Bendicto Kagimu Mugumba Kiwanuka', p. 28.

[123] '1975 Commission of Inquiry into Disappearances', pp. 118–22. Kibede allegedly feared Kiwanuka's popularity within DP and his future political prospects.

[124] 'This was clear and open that Amin picked him up' ('Maxencia Zulbango Kiwanuka testimony', p. 6581).

[125] Ibid., pp. 124–5. This account was originally published in *Drum Magazine*, 4 October 1974.

habeas corpus'.[126] It is possible that Kiwanuka was tortured and then killed at Nakasero presidential lodge within days of his arrest, shot by Amin himself when he refused to sign the document blaming Obote for his arrest.[127] His body has never been conclusively identified.

Conclusion

Benedicto Kiwanuka was the most polarising and uncompromising Catholic activist in late colonial and early postcolonial Uganda. His liberal politics and refusal to comply with the electoral and monarchical project of Buganda's *Lukiiko* galvanised party alliances and led to extensive anti-DP violence in 1961–62. By the late 1960s, he was in prison under Obote. In 1972, General Idi Amin orchestrated his execution. Likewise, themes of persecution, martyrdom, and redemptive suffering profoundly shaped the political discourse of Kiwanuka and the Democratic Party in the 1960s. Such discourse partly reflected both Kiwanuka's conspiratorial personality and a DP self-identity that UPC's Grace Ibingira once described as 'persecution mania ridden'.[128] But as we have shown in this chapter, this corporate identity also emerged from a decade's worth of anti-DP political intimidation.

Four decades after his death, family and friends of Ben Kiwanuka initiated a formal effort to convince the Catholic Church to declare him as a Christian martyr and 'servant of God', the first step on the Catholic road to canonised sainthood. Kiwanuka was murdered nearly ninety years after the deaths of the Uganda Martyrs. The memory of both of these intersections continues to attract popular reflection throughout Uganda, as both have come to signify the costliness of principled politics in the making of modern Uganda. It is with the contested memory and legacy of 'St Ben' – and the overall importance of recovering DP's complicated history for scholarship on both Uganda and Catholic studies in Africa – that we now conclude our study.

---

[126] AFR 59/05/78 Amnesty International, 'Human Rights in Uganda Report', June 1978, p. 5. In this vein, the Ugandan judiciary continues to organise a memorial to Kiwanuka every year on the anniversary of his death.

[127] This was the conclusion shared by Maurice Kagimu Kiwanuka at the Benedicto Kiwanuka Memorial Lecture at High Court, Kampala, Uganda, 21 September 2018.

[128] 'Expatriates retired "over DP threats"', *Uganda Argus*, 8 November 1962.

Conclusion

> The Democratic Party will face up to the greatest persecution and suffering, as it has done in the past, rather than give up the glorious fight for democracy.
>
> ~Benedicto Kiwanuka & the DP Executive Committee, 15 December 1966.[1]

> I want to remind Ugandans that our liberation is near, this has all been done to us to intimidate us and other Ugandans. But they should overlook the sufferation [sic] we have gone through and keep their eyes on the prize – liberation. Sooner or later the oppressed shall be free and they should not be scared because the people we are scared of are more scared of us. They should continue asserting that our power is people power.
>
> ~Robert 'Bobi Wine' Kyagulanyi, Gulu High Court, 1 October 2018.[2]

This book has sought to resuscitate the power, breadth, and conflicting cross-currents of Benedicto Kiwanuka's and the Democratic Party's political project in independence-era Uganda. Although grounded in the Catholic community, Kiwanuka's cosmopolitan project moved beyond a sectarian defence of Catholic interests toward a broader commitment to a 'gospel of democracy' that could challenge entrenched sociopolitical hierarchies in the name of DP's credos of truth and justice (Chapter 1). Yet the success of DP's Catholic nationalist project varied regionally. In Tesoland (Chapter 2), DP's centralising project proved largely impotent in the face of the egalitarian

---

[1] ICS PP.UG.DP.24 'Kiwanuka & DP Executive Committee on Obote & Elections', 15 December 1966.

[2] 'Uganda's liberation is near, says Bobi Wine', *Daily Monitor*, 2 October 2018, www.monitor.co.ug/News/National/Uganda-liberation-near-Bobi-wine/688334-4787318-14sc2wgz/index.html, accessed 28 July 2020.

republicanism of Cuthbert Obwangor, the Catholic face of UPC in eastern Uganda. In contrast, DP found common cause with politically marginalised groups in western Uganda, whether Bafumbira and Bakiga communities in Kigezi, Rwenzururu patriots in Toro, or anti-Ganda Nyoro patriots looking to recover the 'Lost Counties' for Bunyoro (Chapter 3). Although it primarily advocated for democracy over hereditary monarchy, DP could prove flexible even on this point. Ankole remained a DP stronghold in part due to an alliance between Catholic Bairu peasants and the ruling Protestant *omugabe*, over and against an expanding Protestant class of elites (Chapter 4). Whether in Teso or Toro, DP's UPC rivals organised not just around anti-Catholicism, but also in response to lingering resentment of historical Ganda aggression and resistance to Ganda privilege in postcolonial Uganda. In this sense, our study demonstrates the importance of bringing multifaceted, regional lenses to late colonial history in Uganda rather than the Ganda-centric and southern perspectives that have often dominated earlier analyses of this era.

Whatever Fred Welbourn's influential musings, our study also problematises a facile linking of 'DP' with '*dini ya Papa*' (religion of the Pope) and 'UPC' with the 'United Protestants of Canterbury'.[3] Despite large Catholic demographic advantages in West Nile and Tesoland, DP lost the 1962 elections in these areas because it failed to campaign effectively and offer a compelling political platform for local voters. In contrast, whatever the literary power of Acholi poet Okot p'Bitek's anti-Ganda and anti-Catholic republicanism, DP's scholarship strategy and empowerment of local leaders helped establish Acholiland as a DP stronghold (Chapter 4). This alliance enabled Kiwanuka to retain power in the 1960s and facilitated the emergence of future Acholi DP leaders including Alex Latim and Norbert Mao, the president of the party at the time of writing. Even in DP's home region of Buganda, the Catholic vote proved fickle. Under the influence of powerful figures such as A. D. Lubowa, Buddu Catholics proved far more loyal to *Kabaka* Muteesa II and the *Kabaka Yekka* party, whatever the pro-DP exhortations of Archbishop Joseph Kiwanuka (Chapter 5). When one examines the DP political movement across the Uganda Protectorate in the late colonial period, one sees that the story is far more complicated than the simple 'Catholic-Protestant' tropes that have generally dominated the literature as well as post-1986 political discourse.[4]

---

[3] F. B. Welbourn, *Religion and Politics in Uganda 1952–1962* (Nairobi: East Africa Publishing House, 1965), p. 1.

[4] Yoweri Museveni's National Resistance Movement employed the sectarian labelling of DP and UPC to partisan effect in its efforts to legitimise its own 'no-party movement' in the late 1980s and 1990s. Such discourse also emerged in post-1986 popular histories in Uganda, such as James Tumusiime's claim that DP introduced

Yet DP's and Kiwanuka's Catholic roots and identity were never wholly subsumed by modern secularity. One sees the importance of Catholic identity emerging repeatedly on a discursive level: the rhetoric of Matthew's Sermon on the Mount shaped DP's political manifesto, while Fr Agostoni transposed the iconography of the Catholic Missal into DP's official symbol of 'truth' and 'justice' (Chapter 1). Likewise, Catholic religious networks remained critical for DP activists' mobilisation of voters throughout this period. In turn, the violence, persecution, and marginalisation that marked DP throughout the 1960s led Kiwanuka and other activists to embrace the martyrdom motifs that had been so influential in shaping Catholic self-identity in early colonial Uganda (Chapter 6). Not surprisingly in light of Kiwanuka's death and the violence of postcolonial Uganda politics, it is this memory of martyrdom that has lingered in both DP's and Uganda's memorialisation of Kiwanuka.

Memory and Memorialisation

Eleven years after Kiwanuka's disappearance, Paul Ssemogerere, his close confidant and successor as DP president-general, addressed the party's National Council meeting. He spoke in 1983 in the midst of an especially bleak period in Uganda's postcolonial history. The murder of Kiwanuka had signified the intensification of Idi Amin Dada's repressive regime (1971–79). Over 200,000 died during the final six and a half years of Amin's rule, many of them political and economic elites or Acholi and Langi soldiers seen as loyal to Obote.[5] Prominent victims included the Catholic layman Joseph Mubiru, the former president of the Bank of Uganda arrested the same week as Kiwanuka; Fr Clement Kiggundu, editor of the Catholic daily *Munno* who was killed in January 1973 in part for his investigations into Kiwanuka's death;[6] Archbishop Janani Luwum, the Anglican prelate whose outspoken criticisms of the government led Amin to have him executed in February 1977;[7] and DP leader

---

the 'politics of religious interests at the expense of other national considerations' (James Tumusiime, *Uganda 30 Years: 1962–1992* (Kampala: Fountain Press, 1992), 26).

[5] A. B. K. Kasozi, *The Social Origins of Violence in Uganda, 1964–1985* (Montreal: McGill-Queen's University Press, 1994), p. 4. On the Amin era, see Alicia C. Decker, *In Idi Amin's Shadow: Women, Gender and Militarism in Uganda* (Athens: Ohio University Press, 2014); and Derek R. Peterson and Edgar C. Taylor, 'Rethinking the State in Idi Amin's Uganda: The Politics of Exhortation', *Journal of Eastern African Studies* 7 (2013): 58–82.

[6] Simon Mwebe, interview with Carney, Kampala, Uganda, 12 July 2017. Mwebe was a close collaborator with Kiggundu and succeeded him as editor of *Munno*.

[7] 'Letter from the House of Bishops to President Amin, 12 February 1977', in

Alex Latim, hunted down by Amin's security forces in Gulu in March 1979.[8] The 1979 'liberation war', led by Ugandan expatriates and the Tanzanian army, forced Amin into exile. But Uganda's political violence only worsened in the resulting vacuum of power. Ssemogerere and DP contested and likely won Uganda's first democratic elections in eighteen years in December 1980. But with the backing of Tanzania President Julius Nyerere and the Tanzanian army, official results ushered Milton Obote and UPC into power again.[9]

By 1983, DP remained legal but suffered ongoing government harassment. Uganda was in its third year of the 'bush war' launched by Yoweri Museveni and the National Resistance Army (NRA), a conflict that in much of the country proved even bloodier than the Amin years, especially in the central 'Luwero Triangle'. Catholic institutions were particular targets of government crackdown during the early 1980s, in part due to perceived Catholic sympathy for DP and NRM and also due to the outspoken, anti-government opposition of the Ganda Archbishop of Kampala, Emmanuel Cardinal Nsubuga.[10]

In this difficult context, Ssemogerere encouraged his 'party of martyrs' to remain steadfast. Noting that many DP members were 'languishing in detention', DP's secretary-general called for members to stand in silence 'in memory of thousands of our fellow party men who have been killed because of the noble objects in which they believed and for which they lived in the greater interests of this country'.[11] Specifically naming Kiwanuka and Latim, Ssemogerere exhorted DP members to 'walk in the footsteps of their illustrious and courageous parliamentary predecessors in the darkest days of the

---

Edward Muhima, 'Fellowship of His Suffering: A Theological Interpretation of Christian Suffering under Idi Amin', unpublished PhD thesis, Northwestern University, 1982, pp. 149–50. On Luwum's ministry, opposition to Amin, and death, see Festo Kivengere, *I Love Idi Amin* (Old Tappan, NJ: New Life Ventures, 1977) and Margaret Ford, *Janani: The Making of a Martyr* (London: Lakeland, 1978).

[8] Samwiiri Lwanga Lunyiigo, *A Short History of the Democratic Party 1954–1984* (Rome: Foundation for African Development, 1984), p. 89.

[9] Kasozi, *Social Origins of Violence*, p. 143.

[10] Under Nsubuga's influence, the Catholic bishops' pastoral letters in the 1979–82 period were notably blunt and critical, highlighting specific government abuses (see RDA, Ugandan Episcopal Conference, 'I have heard the cry of my people', 11 November 1980; 'Be converted and live', 11 March 1981; 'In God We Trust', 25 December 1982). Uganda National Liberation Army (UNLA) soldiers raided Rubaga Cathedral and the Cardinal's residence on Ash Wednesday 1982, searching for NRM collaborators and evidence of church complicity (RDA D/1090/1, 'Press Statement of His Eminence Emmanuel Cardinal K. Nsubuga Concerning the Events of Ash Wednesday, 24 February, 1982 at Rubaga', 1 March 1982).

[11] RDA 916.3, 'Ssemogerere Opening Speech to National Council Meeting', 1 October 1983. Subsequent quotations in this paragraph are taken from this document.

1960s. They would not hesitate to stick to the DP principles and to speak out loud and clear for truth, for justice, for constitutionalism, for democracy, and for human rights'. Noting that DP was now an official member of the 'Christian Democratic International', Ssemogerere hastened to downplay any sectarian connotations, arguing that the word 'Christian' was a 'mere historical accident', and that DP would continue to be open to people of 'all religious affiliations'. Finally, even as he lamented what he called the 'rigged' 1980 elections, Ssemogerere proclaimed that DP's political mission remained the same – namely, to 'spread the gospel of national unity, of truth and justice and of peaceful and positive approach as well as of political co-existence with our opponents to all corners of Uganda and to all fellow citizens'.

Several recurring themes emerged in Ssemogerere's memorialisation of Kiwanuka and DP's founding generation. First, there is a strong emphasis on DP's identity as a party of suffering, victimhood, and martyrdom, a history that long predated the Luwero war. In this regard, for Ssemogerere, the political violence of the 1980s may have differed in intensity but not in kind to that of the 1960s. As in the past, 'the majority of victims of insecurity in Uganda are members of the DP'. Second, DP's political 'gospel' remained consistent – namely to speak for political truth, justice, democracy, and national unity, and to utilise 'positive and peaceful' means rather than violent revolution. Third, the spectre of religious tribalism lingered over DP, sparking defensive denials from party leaders yet also reflecting the party's continued association with the institutional Catholic Church.[12]

As had been the case in the 1960s, DP in the 1980s was passionate in opposition but struggled to gain actual political power. Ssemogerere remained head of the parliamentary opposition throughout the Obote II years (1981–85). In turn, he distanced himself from the NRA rebellion and agreed to serve in the Okello government that followed the military's ousting of Obote in July 1985. When the NRA conquered Kampala and took power on 26 January 1986 – nearly fifteen years to the day after Amin's coup – Ssemogerere and DP found themselves in a marginalised position. Although the subsequent NRA/NRM government incorporated Ssemogerere and several other key DP officials in an initial cabinet of national unity, the government's nearly twenty-year ban on political parties squelched any potential party revival, and DP never again reached its electoral zeniths of 1961 or 1980. In the meantime, key Catholic leaders defected to the NRM. For example, prominent Catholic scholar and

---

[12] For DP historian Lwanga Lunyiigo, the influence of the Catholic Church on the party became more pronounced in the early 1980s: Ssemogerere was very close to the church hierarchy, and priests openly joined the party (Lwanga Lunyiigo, interview with Carney, Kisubi, Uganda, 29 September 2018).

activist Fr John Mary Waliggo served on the 1995 constitutional revision, but he did so on behalf of an NRM government which he described as 'pro-life, pro-people, and pro-democracy, pro-reconciliation and pro-development'.[13]

As the unofficial head of a still-banned DP, Ssemogerere unsuccessfully challenged Museveni in the 1996 presidential elections, the first since NRM took power. Even after the restoration of multi-party politics in 2005, the Democratic Party faded further from the centre of political opposition in the 2000s and 2010s, overshadowed by new parties such as Kizza Besigye's and Mugisha Muntu's Forum for Democratic Change, and more recently by Robert 'Bobi Wine' Kyagulanyi's National Unity Platform. But as expressed in the epigraph to this chapter, in the quotation of Bobi Wine, whose sensibilities were shaped by his Catholic upbringing, DP's rhetoric – especially its commitment to the path of redemptive suffering and eschatological hope for popular political deliverance – remains alive and well in opposition discourse in Museveni's Uganda.

Even though his political party's fortunes have declined, Benedicto Kiwanuka continues to be memorialised in twenty-first century Uganda. In 2012, Kiwanuka's family and admirers initiated a formal effort to beatify him as a 'patron [saint] of Ugandan politicians'.[14] Combining personal testimonies, news articles, and biographical details, this 178-page canonisation petition emphasises Kiwanuka's personal religious devotion. Highlighted here is his attendance at daily Mass at Rubaga Cathedral, his ecumenical spirit in reaching out to Anglicans and Muslims, his willingness to forgive *Kabaka* Muteesa II by providing legal assistance after his exile, and his defence of priestly celibacy against a reform-minded priest at Makerere University.[15]

But the primary justification for beatifying Kiwanuka is the committee's claim that he should be classified as a martyr. The beatification proposal details the possible scenarios surrounding the manner of his brutal death. The

---

[13] John Mary Waliggo, 'The Role of the Christian Churches in the Democratisation Process in Uganda, 1980–1993', in *The Christian Churches and the Democratisation of Africa*, ed. by Paul Gifford (Leiden: Brill, 1995), pp. 205–24 (p. 213).

[14] Fr Denis Mayanja quoted in 'Bendicto Kagimu Mugumba Kiwanuka: A Martyr of Truth and Justice', Proposal to Kampala Archdiocese to open process for beatification (Kampala: N.P., 2014), p. 13. We are grateful to Ambassador Maurice Kagimu Kiwanuka and the organising committee for sharing these unpublished materials with us.

[15] 'Bendicto Kagimu Mugumba Kiwanuka', pp. 9–14, 20. The celibacy debate with Fr Aloysius Lugira is also found in BKMKP/Not Marked 6/B. Kiwanuka to Fr Aloysius Lugira, 5 February 1972. Lugira later left the priesthood, married, and retired in the USA. He contributed a letter supporting Kiwanuka's beatification cause ('Bendicto Kagimu Mugumba Kiwanuka', Appendix 24).

proposal also highlights the martyr's ethos that animated Kiwanuka, noting that 'whenever he believed in something, he had to die for it'.[16] Similarly, although Kiwanuka received warnings of his imminent arrest, he rejected friends' and associates' entreaties that he flee Uganda, arguing that he 'was not going to run away from the truth and that he would rather die for the truth and justice'.[17] In this regard, Kiwanuka is presented here not so much as a religious martyr persecuted for his devotion to the Catholic Church, but rather as a public witness to the common good and rule of law. In this regard, the Kiwanuka beatification cause reflects ongoing intra-Catholic debates over how to define the *odium fidei* ('in hatred of the faith') that is required for one to be formally classified as a Catholic martyr.[18] For its part, the local Ugandan Catholic Church has not issued a response on the Kiwanuka cause. Hierarchical reluctance may reflect a certain ambiguity about canonising political leaders, although the silence on Kiwanuka contrasts sharply with the enthusiasm of the Tanzanian church for the cause of Julius Nyerere (Figure C.1).[19]

If the Catholic Church is still reluctant to officially canonise 'St Ben', the Ugandan judiciary is doing its best to unofficially canonise Kiwanuka as the 'chief priest of the sacred sanctuary of justice'.[20] On the forty-sixth anniver-

---

[16] 'Bendicto Kagimu Mugumba Kiwanuka', p. 10. His wife Maxencia's words are also telling as she describes her husband as a 'kind of Spartan when it came to anybody trying to challenge or deflect him from what he considered to be a moral duty. He would rather die' ('Mrs. Ben Kiwanuka tells the truth', interview with V. P. Kirega-Gava, 1979, in 'Bendicto Kagimu Mugumba Kiwanuka', Appendix 33).

[17] Ibid., p. 28.

[18] Pope Francis' recent beatification and later canonisation of Salvadoran Archbishop Oscar Romero as a 'martyr' stands out here. Romero was assassinated in March 1980 by a government death squad. Since the government was made up of Roman Catholics, Romero would not typically have been considered a martyr. However, following a teaching that first emerged under Pope John Paul II, Romero's case exemplifies an expansion of the definition of martyr to include those killed *in odium caritatis*, or what John Allen calls a 'victim of those motivated by a hatred of charity' (John L. Allen, 'Beatification of El Salvador's Oscar Romero a Turning Point for Catholicism', May 16, 2015, https://cruxnow.com/church/2015/05/beatification-of-el-salvadors-oscar-romero-a-turning-point-for-catholicism, accessed 28 July 2020).

[19] Nyerere was recently declared a 'Servant of God' by the Vatican, the first step on the road to formal sainthood. Even the Ugandan Church has embraced Nyerere's cause. The 2017 Uganda Martyrs' Day celebrations began with prayers for Nyerere's beatification, and Museveni came out in favour of his beatification in 2018 (See: 'Nyerere beatification prayers at Namugongo', *New Vision*, 1 June 2017; 'Museveni prays for sainthood of Tanzania's Nyerere at Uganda Martyrs' celebration', *Africa News*, 3 June 2018).

[20] This was the description of Kiwanuka given in a poem dedicated to him at the

Figure C.1 During Uganda Martyrs' Day, June 2010, banners advocating for Julius Nyerere's canonisation were displayed in Namugongo. *Authors' personal photographs.*

sary of his death on 21 September 2018, Uganda's judiciary launched a new Benedicto Kiwanuka Memorial Lecture series and commissioned a bust of Kiwanuka to stand outside the High Court building in Kampala (Figure C.2). A solemn procession of judges and lawyers retraced Kiwanuka's final steps from his chambers to the parking lot where he was last seen. In a parade of speeches and tributes, former judges, politicians, and lawyers took turns praising Kiwanuka's commitments to the rule of law, impartial justice, and judicial independence.[21] In this vein, the Deputy Chief Justice, Alphonse Owiny-Dollo, described Kiwanuka's death as the 'triumph of the rule of law and justice over the abuse of power', calling Kiwanuka a 'martyr in defence of the rule of law'. Simon Peter Kinobe, president of Uganda's Law Society, highlighted Kiwanuka's refusal to grant impunity to state actors when they abuse human rights. The Chief Justice, Bart M. Katureebe, envisioned Kiwanuka's death through the prism of 'what can go tragically wrong if we deviate from constitutional principles'. The keynote speaker, former Chief Justice Samuel Wambuzi, linked Kiwanuka to the 'original murder' of Abel in Genesis 4:10–12. Like Abel, in Wambuzi's words, 'Benedicto Kiwanuka's blood continues to cry out from the ground, asking that his death not be in vain, and that his legacy of a fearless commitment to justice and the rule of law be protected as a national trust and heritage'. For Wambuzi, Uganda now needs to raise up 'many Kiwanukas' to bring an 'end to impunity for state actors' and the 'suffocation' of the judiciary due to underfunding and political intimidation.

With the strong support of Chief Justice Katureebe, the annual lecture series is scheduled to continue on the anniversary of Kiwanuka's death 'to act as a reference point for judicial offenders and other human rights defenders'.[22] In the meantime, Kiwanuka's bust will stand as a silent witness to his lifelong commitment to the DP principles of 'truth' and 'justice', looking over the High Court that served as the bookends for Kiwanuka's professional career, first as a young law clerk, and then as the Court's highest official.

Benedicto Kiwanuka Inaugural Memorial Lecture event, High Court, Kampala, Uganda, 21 September 2018. Subsequent quotations are taken from speeches given at this event, which was attended by Carney. Further tributes can be found in the September 2018 issue of *The Judiciary Insider* produced by the Ugandan Judiciary's Editorial Board.

[21] The 2018 ceremony is now available online: www.youtube.com/channel/UC1vZntKWjNCqVHB16y4IgWQ, accessed 7 August 2020.

[22] 'Judiciary to celebrate Ben Kiwanuka annually', *Judiciary Insider* (September 2018), p. 11.

Figure C.2 Chief Justice Kiwanuka's bust is on permanent display outside the High Court building in Kampala. *Authors' personal photographs.*

Remembering Kiwanuka and DP in Catholic Scholarship

The memory of Kiwanuka is clearly alive in both the Catholic Church and public life in Uganda. Why, however, should recovering and expanding this history matter more broadly to scholars working on questions of Catholic politics in Africa?

We suggest that the history of DP and Kiwanuka offers an original contribution to the historiography of Catholicism and politics in modern Africa. Through much of the late twentieth century, scholarly studies of Catholic Africa were largely internal ecclesiastical histories.[23] Over the past quarter-century, both anthropologists and political scientists have made notable contributions to Catholic social and political history on the continent.[24] And even more recently, multiple historians have offered finely grained, regional studies of Catholic politics in Africa.[25] We share the local and contextual focus of these recent monographs, as well as these scholars' recognition of the complex and variegated ways in which Catholic theology both shaped and reflected multiple streams of colonial and nationalist politics alike. However, we argue that the story of Kiwanuka and DP pushes the understanding of 'Catholic politics'

---

[23] John Baur, *Two Thousand Years of Christianity in Africa: An African History* (Nairobi: Paulines Publications Africa, 2009); Adrian Hastings, *The Church in Africa 1450–1950* (Oxford: Clarendon Press, 1994). Hastings was a former White Father missionary who spent much of the 1960s and 1970s in Uganda; Baur was also a White Father who taught church history for years in Nairobi. On explicitly Catholic political history, Ian and Jane Linden's influential body of work stands out (Ian Linden and Jane Linden, *Catholics, Peasants, and Chewa Resistance in Nyasaland, 1889–1939* (London: Heinemann, 1974); Ian Linden and Jane Linden, *Church and Revolution in Rwanda* (Manchester: Manchester University Press, 1977); Ian Linden, *The Catholic Church and the Struggle for Zimbabwe* (London: Longman, 1980).

[24] In anthropology, see Dorothy L. Hodgson, *The Church of Women: Gendered Encounters between Maasai and Missionaries* (Bloomington: Indiana University Press, 2005); Phyllis M. Martin, *Catholic Women of Congo-Brazzaville: Mothers and Sisters in Troubled Times* (Bloomington: Indiana University Press, 2009); Todd M. Whitmore, *Imitating Christ in Magwi: An Anthropological Theology* (London: T&T Clark, 2019). In political science, see Paul Gifford, *African Christianity: Its Public Role* (Bloomington: Indiana University Press, 1998) and Timothy Longman, *Christianity and Genocide in Rwanda* (Cambridge: Cambridge University Press, 2010).

[25] See Reuben A. Loffman, *Church, State and Colonialism in Southeastern Congo, 1890–1962* (New York: Palgrave Macmillan, 2019); Eric Morier-Genoud, *Catholicism and the Making of Politics in Central Mozambique, 1940–1986* (Rochester, NY: University of Rochester Press, 2019); Elizabeth Foster, *African Catholic: Decolonization and the Transformation of the Church* (Cambridge, MA: Harvard University Press, 2019).

beyond what has remained a largely ecclesiastical or institutional focus. The story of Catholic politics in Africa is not just about the church's engagement with the colonial or postcolonial state, or how clergy and missionaries formed rival ideological factions shaping church politics from below.[26] Nor is it simply about the fierce contestation between rival Catholic intellectual-cum-theological projects, or how ethnopolitical divisions undermined the Catholic Church's public ethical witness.[27]

In a sense, then, this book pushes analysis of Catholic politics beyond 'the Church' (if 'the Church' here is taken to primarily refer to the institutional Catholic Church, focusing on Catholic clergy, missionaries, and the hierarchy). Rather, we have demonstrated the distinctive and often divergent ways in which Ugandan Catholic laity, both politicians and voters, operated in the public sphere, and the creative and deeply contextual ways in which Catholic identities can link with and shape political identities. We have seen that Catholic political identity was far more diffuse and multifaceted than previously imagined, even in a country like Uganda with its deeply ingrained stereotypes of 'religious sectarianism' and supposedly monolithic religious voting blocs. We hope this volume will inspire historians of African Catholic politics to expand their analysis beyond the clergy and missionaries, church-state relations, or institutional politics to a deeper and broader consideration of lay Catholic identities in the public sphere. To paraphrase Kiwanuka, much can be learned from the 'well-intentioned men and women out to do good' who mobilised political movements at the dawn of independence.[28]

---

[26] The former argument carries through in the earlier work of Hastings (see his *A History of African Christianity, 1950–1975* (Cambridge: Cambridge University Press, 1979). The latter theme is taken up in Morier-Genoud's and Loffman's more recent monographs on Catholic politics in Mozambique and the Belgian Congo, respectively.

[27] For the first view, see Foster's *African Catholic* which focuses on the West African context. The latter view is emphasised in Carney's earlier work, *Rwanda Before the Genocide: Catholic Politics and Ethnic Discourse in the Late Colonial Era* (New York: Oxford University Press, 2014).

[28] 'D.P. Leader's Appeal', *Uganda Argus*, 30 September 1958.

Bibliography

Primary Sources

Archives

Audrey Richards Papers, London School of Economics (ARP)
The British anthropologist Audrey Richards was deeply interested in the politics and social organisations of Uganda in the 1950s and early 1960s, especially during her tenure at the East African Institute of Social Research. She served as its first director in 1950. Her private papers contain anti-Catholic propaganda of the early 1960s, in addition to correspondence with the Catholic intellectual and newspaper editor, Simon M. K. Musoke.

British National Archives, London (BNA)
The orchestration of public looting and political violence resulted in the authorship and circulation of hundreds of letters and petitions throughout the late colonial period. This included correspondence written by lamenting Catholics, such as Gilbert Mulindwa, and the Catholic radical Semakula Mulumba, who was a prolific letter writer. Correspondence is especially noted in the following files: CO 537 and 822.

Church of Uganda Archives, Birmingham
We drew from Anglican church records in south-western Uganda to understand how Protestant and Catholic identities informed border politics in that region and Rwanda. These records were accessed in both Birmingham and through the Divinity Library of Yale University, which maintains microfilmed copies of the original material.

Hamu Mukasa Library, Mukono, Uganda
Maintained by the Hamu Mukasa Foundation, the private library and papers of Hamu Mukasa include newspapers, annotated books, letters, and the administrative records of one of Uganda's most consequential chiefs and history writers of the twentieth century.

Institute of Commonwealth Studies, London (ICS)

The Institute of Commonwealth Studies houses two important collections that we reviewed closely. First, the chief political negotiator for the British Government during the exile of *Kabaka* Muteesa II (1953–55) – and of the 1955 Agreement – was Sir Keith Hancock, who served as a professor at the Institute. The papers and correspondence related to his work are filed as 'Buganda Papers'. The material includes hundreds of letters between Hancock and Ugandan activists, discussion and interview notes, committee notes, and newspaper clippings. Second, ICS holds copies of hundreds of political letters and pamphlets produced by Uganda's foremost political parties during the late- and postcolonial era, namely: Uganda National Congress, Democratic Party, Democratic Party Young Wing, Uganda People's Congress, Progressive Party, Uganda National Liberation Front, and National Resistance Movement. We drew especially from PP.UG.DP (Political Parties. Uganda. Democratic Party).

John F. Kennedy Presidential Library and Musuem, Boston (JFKOF)

The Presidential Library and Museum of John F. Kennedy holds memoranda and Intelligence Weekly Reviews that pertain to the diplomatic relationships between the United States and eastern Africa. The folders that we examined contain material surrounding Benedicto Kiwanuka's visit to Washington, DC, in October 1961 and Milton Obote's in October 1962.

Makerere University Africana Archives, Kampala (MUA)

Makerere University contains a large body of vernacular manuscripts and ephemera from the 1950s. Its holdings include boxes of material produced by *Kabaka Yekka* activists, notably pendants, committee minutes, letters, petitions, and speeches.

National Archives at College Park, Maryland (NARA II)

Throughout the 1950s and 1960s, the State Department of the United States expanded its presence and intelligence networks throughout sub-Saharan Africa. This resulted in the collection of political documents, and the production of CIA weekly summary reports and embassy reports, which were developed in conversation with prominent activists of the period. The American government was increasingly interested in Ugandan politics, in response to both its military's activity in the Congo and Milton Obote's Move to the Left. In addition to the CIA records, which can be accessed onsite – through a computer interface – we worked principally with Record Groups 59 and 84.

Rubaga Diocesan Archives, Kampala (RDA)

The Rubaga Diocesan Archives is one of the best organised historical repositories in Uganda. It holds the largest collection of Catholic material in the country, in addition to an impressive library that maintains a complete copy of Uganda's HANSARD. We reviewed much of the relevant material between the 1960s and mid-1980s, including the pastoral and political work of Archbishop Kiwanuka throughout the 1950s and 1960s. We were also able to review useful material on Catholic chieftaincies during the interwar period.

Soroti District Archives, Soroti, Uganda (SDA)

At the time of writing, the Soroti District Archives were located in a government building in Soroti, eastern Uganda, which was the district headquarters of colonial Tesoland. Following a restoration project organised by William Outa and a cohort from Centre College (Kentucky) in 2016, SDA was relocated to the Uganda National Archives in Kampala. The collection has been tremendously overlooked by historians of Uganda, as has Teso's political history more broadly. In the colonial period, the region was overlooked due to the preoccupation – if not obsession – with southern and western kingdoms. More recently, scholars have shifted their gaze northward, where the conflict of the Lord's Resistance Army (LRA) has attracted a growing body of political science literature. Between the colonial and postcolonial cracks of Uganda, though for different reasons, Teso has remained a vastly understudied region. In this project, though, we wanted to take Teso politics seriously. The minutes, reports, police investigations, and petitions located in SDA allowed us to identify some of the complexities that characterised the area during the late colonial period.

Uganda Museum, Kampala (UM)

While working through the library of the Uganda Museum, Earle located an uncatalogued manuscript, which was placed between two books. The manuscript – 'Benedicto Kiwanuka *Kirumira Mpuyibbiri*' – was authored by Semakula Mulumba in early 1960. It is a collection of 248 moral and political accusations made against Benedicto Kiwanuka.

Uganda National Archives, Kampala (UNA)

The Uganda National Archives (Kampala) holds a number of petitions written to the colonial government by Nyoro activists in the early 1900s. These letters provide important insights into how Ganda Catholics territorially dislocated Catholics of Nyoro heritage in the 'Lost Counties', and how Banyoro contested Ganda religious and political authority during the same period.

Personal Papers

Benedicto KM Kiwanuka Papers (BKMKP)

Kiwanuka's private papers are the largest collection of evidence used in this book. The papers are comprised of around 4,900 pieces of textual evidence, organised in eighty-three folders (the original folders). The collection also includes 900 pages of loose-leaf material. It also consists of several dozen books, some of which are annotated, and newspapers in English, Luganda, and Swahili. The course notepads that Kiwanuka used in law school are also preserved.

Ignatius K. Musazi Library

Ignatius Musazi's library and papers are the subject of Earle's previous work. In this monograph, we draw brief attention to Musazi's particular reading of *I Kings*, from which he developed ideas about the theological meaning of political party schemes.

Private Papers of Jonathon L. Earle and J. J. Carney

Across the last several years, we have accumulated digital and physical copies of hundreds of rare political and religious primary sources. These range from copies of photography to the Forum for Democratic Change's martyrdom flyers that circulated on Martyrs Day in 2010.

Interviews

Kajubi, William S., interviews with Earle, Kampala, 2 December 2009, 17 February 2010.
Kiwanuka, Maurice Kagimu, interview with Carney, Kampala, 6 July 2017.
Kiwanuka, Yusufu, interview (in Oded, *Islam in Uganda*, p. 328), Lwanjaza, Singo, 12 November 1967.
Lubowa, A. D., interview with Earle, Maya, Mpigi, 23 November 2009. Several additional interviews were conducted between 2009 and 2016.
Lwanga Lunyiigo, Samwiri, interview with Carney, Kisubi, 29 September 2018.
'Mrs. Ben Kiwanuka tells the truth', interview with V. P. Kirega-Gava, 1979, in 'Bendicto Kagimu Mugumba Kiwanuka', Appendix 33).
Mwebe, Simon, interview with Carney, Kampala, 12 July 2017.
Samioni, Kalikuzinga, interview (in Oded, *Islam in Uganda*, p. 342), Bulange, Mmengo, 31 January 1968.
Tyaba, L. Mathias and Simon Mwebe, interview with Earle, Kampala, 30 July 2010.
Wasswa, Anatoli, interview with Carney, Bunga, Kampala, 30 June 2015.

Speeches

Benedicto Kiwanuka Inaugural Memorial Lecture event, High Court, Kampala, Uganda, 21 September 2018.
Kayibanda, Grégoire, '*Le Président Kayibanda, vous parlé: discours prononcé par Son Excellence Mr. Gr. Kayibanda, Président de la République Rwandaise*', 26 Octobre 1960, devant l'Assemblée Législative.
Kimbowa, Charles M., 'Archbishop Joseph Kiwanuka as I Knew Him', 21st Archbishop Joseph Kiwanuka Memorial Lecture, 20 June 2013, Kampala, Uganda.
Kiwanuka, Maurice Kagimu, speech at Benedicto Kiwanuka Memorial Lecture, High Court, Kampala, 21 September 2018.

Zziwa, Margaret, 'Archbishop Kiwanuka and the Empowerment of the Girl-Child', 23rd Annual Archbishop Kiwanuka Lecture, Kampala, Uganda, 25 June 2015.

Newspapers and Periodicals (Principal Collections Consulted)

Daily Monitor

The *Daily Monitor* is Uganda's largest independent press. We used the press to follow contemporary DP politics.

Daily Nation

Founded during the era of Kenyan independence, the *Daily Nation* reports itself as selling over 46,000 copies per issue by the 1970s. To follow eastern African politics, Kiwanuka read the *Nation*. We reviewed the remaining issues in his personal library to explore the regional discourses circulating during the mid-1960s.

Drum Magazine

This South African production produced some of the most extensive photographic records of late colonial and postcolonial Uganda. Their holdings are now digitally accessible through Bailey's African History Archives (BAHA).

London Gazette

The *Gazette* was first published in 1665. Throughout the nineteenth and twentieth centuries, it documented Britain's domestic and international affairs, including colonial statutes and agreements in eastern Africa.

Munno

This is Uganda's historic Catholic press and the country's oldest newspaper. Benedicto Kiwanuka was also an avid reader of the press, with bound copies in his library that dated back to the 1930s. We drew liberally from this Luganda periodical to follow strands of Catholic political discourse.

New Vision

Mostly a pro-government newspaper, we used *New Vision* to contrast and complicate the coverage of *Daily Monitor*.

Taifa Empya and Uganda Post

Two of the leading Luganda presses during the independence era; we focused our review on the early 1960s. Hard copies are available for review in the Africana

Archives of Makerere University. We are especially grateful to George Mpanga for his work with these collections.

Uganda Argus

To enable our writing, we read the entirety of this English-language national press between 1955 and 1972 over the course of several months. We identified 5,685 digitised pages worth of material (articles that we digitised). From this, we cited no fewer than 276 articles in the book. The content includes letters to the editors, commercial advertisements, general news coverage, speeches, court hearings, and police investigation reports.

Published Primary Sources

Government Publications

AFR 59/05/78 Amnesty International, 'Human Rights in Uganda Report', June 1978.
Allen, C. P. S., Supervisor of Elections, 'Uganda Legislative Council Elections, 1958: A Report on the First Direct Elections to the Legislative Council of the Uganda Protectorate' (Entebbe: Government Printer, 1958).
'Annual Reports on the Kingdom of Buganda[,] Eastern Province[,] Western Province[,] [and] Northern Province for the Year ended 31st December, 1949' (Entebbe: Government Printer, 1950).
'Colonial Reports – Annual Report for 1904–5' (London: Printed for His Majesty's Stationery Office, Darling & Son Ltd., 1905).
'Colonial Reports – Annual Report for 1913–14' (London: Printed under the Authority of His Majesty's Stationery Offices by Barclay and Fry, Ltd., 1915).
'Colonial Reports – Annual Report for 1920 (April to December)' (London: His Majesty's Stationery Office, 1922).
'Presiding Officers' Instructions 1964: Referendum, Buyaga and Bugangazzi Counties' (Entebbe: Government Printer, 1964).
'Report of the Commission of Inquiry into the Recent Disturbances amongst the Baamba and Bakonjo People of Toro' (Entebbe: Government Printer, 1962).
'Report of the Uganda Independence Conference, 1962' (London: Her Majesty's Stationery Office, 1962).
'The Legislative Council (Elections Ordinance)' (Entebbe: Printed by the Government Printer, 16 October 1957), Article 89.
'Uganda Census 1959: African Population' (Entebbe: Statistics Branch, Ministry of Economic Affairs, 1961).
Uganda Commission of Inquiry into Violation of Human Rights, 1988.
Ugandan National Government, '1975 Commission of Inquiry into Disappearances'.
West, Henry W., *The Mailo System in Buganda: A Preliminary Case Study in African Land Tenure* (Entebbe: Government Printer, 1965).

Books

Agostoni, Tarcisio, *Every Citizen's Handbook: Building a Peaceful Society*, originally published in 1962 with a revised edition released in 1997 (Nairobi: Paulines Publications Africa).
Bible. Depending on the context of the citation, we use either the New Revised Standard Version (Oxford University Press), or the New American Bible, which is an English-Catholic translation produced following the Second Vatican Council.
Bweebare C., Byamugisha, *A Geography of Uganda: An 'A' Level Geography Approach with Field Work*, Revised edition (Kampala: Simplified & Low Priced Textbook Centre, 1994).
Churchill, Winston, *My African Journey* (Toronto: William Briggs, 1909).
Chwa II, Kabaka Daudi, *Why Sir Apolo Kaggwa, K.C.M.G., M.B.E., Prime Minister of Buganda, Resigned*, trans. by S. B. K. Musoke (Mengo, Uganda: Gambuze Press, 1928).
Crabtree, W. A., *Elements of Luganda Grammar: Together with Exercises and Vocabulary* (Kampala: The Uganda Bookshop, 1923).
Cunningham, J. F., *Uganda and Its Peoples: Notes on the Protectorate of Uganda Especially the Anthropology and Ethnology of Its Indigenous Races* (London: Hutchinson & Co., 1905).
Dawson, E. C., *James Hannington, First Bishop of Eastern Equatorial Africa: A History of his Life and Work, 1847–1885* (New York: Anson D. F. Randolph & Company, 1887).
Ddiba, J. L., *Eddini Mu Uganda*, 2 vols (Masaka, Uganda: St Liberatum Printing Press, 1967), II.
Encyclical Letter of Pope Pius XI: Divini Redemptoris (London: Catholic Truth Society, 1937).
Foote, Commander Andrew H., Lieut. Commanding U.S. Brig Perry on the Coast of Africa, *Africa and the American Flag* (New York: D. Appleton & Co., 1854).
Ford, Margaret, *Janani: The Making of a Martyr* (London: Lakeland, 1978).
Ibingira, G. S. K., *The Forging of a Nation: The Political and Constitutional Evolution to Independence, 1894–1962* (Kampala: Uganda Publishing House, 1973).
Johnston, Harry Hamilton, *The Uganda Protectorate: An Attempt to Give Some Description of the Physical Geography, Botany, Zoology, Anthropology, Languages and History of the Territories Under British Protection in East Central Africa, Between the Congo Free State and the Rift Valley and Between the First Degree of South Latitude and the Fifth Degree of North Latitude*, 2 vols (London: Hutchinson & Co., 1902), I.
Kaggwa, Apolo, *Bassekabaka be Buganda*, trans. By Semakula Kiwanuka (Nairobi, Dar es Salaam, Kampala: East African Publishing House).
——, *Ekitabo Kye Mpisa Za Baganda (The Customs of the Baganda)*, ed. by May M. Edel, trans. by Ernest B. Kalibala (New York: Columbia University Press, 1934).
——, *The Reign of Mwanga II (A Later Addition to Ekitabo Kya Basekabaka Be Buganda)*, trans. by Simon Musoke (Kampala: Typescript found in the University of Cambridge Library, 1953).

Kasirye, Joseph S., *Obulamu Bwa Stanislaus Mugwanya (The Life of Stanislaus Mugwanya)* (Dublin: Typescript found in Seeley Library, University of Cambridge, 1963).

Kiggen, Rev. Father J., *Ateso-English Dictionary* (London: St. Joseph's Society for Foreign Missions, 1953).

Kivengere, Festo, *I Love Idi Amin* (Old Tappan, NJ: New Life Ventures, 1977).

Lugard, Frederick, *The Rise of Our East African Empire: Early Efforts in Nyasaland and Uganda*, 2 vols (London: Frank Cass and Co., 1968), II.

Lwanga Lunyiigo, Samwiri, *A History of the Democratic Party: The First Thirty Years (1954–1984)* (Kampala: Fountain, 2015).

——, *A Short History of the Democratic Party*, ed. by Richard Muscat (Rome: Foundation for African Development, 1984).Mullins, J. D. and Ham Mukasa, *The Wonderful Story of Uganda* (London: Church Missionary Society, 1904).

Muteesa II, Kabaka Edward, *Desecration of my Kingdom* (London: Constable, 1967).

Mwebe, Simon and Anthony Sserubiri, *Ebyafaayo bya DP: 1954–1984* (Rome: Foundation for African Development, 1984).

Obote, A. Milton, *Myths and Realities: Letter to a London Friend* (Kampala: Consolidated Printers, 16 November 1968).

Obwangor, C. J., *Ideological Conflict in Uganda since Independence 1962–1989 (Position Paper on Uganda Constitutional Issues)* (Kampala: Uganda Constitutional Commission, 1989).

——, *Political Parties (Position Paper on Uganda Constitutional Issues)* (Kampala: Uganda Constitutional Commission, 1990).

p'Bitek, Okot, *Song of Lawino Song of Ocol* (Long Grove, IL: Waveland Press, Inc., 2013.

——, *White Teeth*, trans. by Okot p'Bitek and Lubwa p'Chong (Nairobi: Heinemann, 1989 [1953]).

Roscoe, John, *The Northern Bantu: An Account of Some Central African Tribes of the Uganda Protectorate* (Cambridge: Cambridge University Press, 1915).

Snoxall, R. A., *Luganda-English Dictionary* (Oxford: Clarendon Press, 1967).

Thomas, H. B., and R. Scott, *Uganda* (London: Oxford University Press, 1935).

Walser, Ferdinand, *Luganda Proverbs* (Berlin: Reimer, 1982).

Articles

The Church Missionary Gleaner, 1 July 1902, p. 103.

The Church Missionary Gleaner, 1 September 1903, p. 134.

'A Cycle of Prayer', *The Church Missionary Gleaner*, 1 October 1910.

'I have Purchased the Road with my Life', *Church Missionary Gleaner*, 1 October 1904.

Kasasira, Risdel, 'Ben Kiwanuka: The Chief Justice who died for justice', *Uganda Heroes* 1.1 July 2006 (consulted in 'Bendicto Kagimu Mugumba Kiwanuka', Appendix 31).

Maloba, Gregory, Jonathan Kingdon, and Rajat Neogy, 'Gregory Maloba Talks About His Childhood and His Growth as a Sculptor', *Transition*, 1963, 20–22.

Mukasa, Willy, 'The day Kabaka Muteesa "beat up" the Catholic Archbishop', *Weekly Topic*, 31 January 1992, p. 9, consulted in 'Bendicto Kagimu Mugumba Kiwanuka: A

Martyr of Truth and Justice', Proposal to open process for beatification in Archdiocese of Kampala (Kampala: N.P., 2014), Appendix 29.
Ocheng, Daudi, 'Economic Forces and Uganda's Foreign Policy', *Transition*, 6/7 (1962), 27–9.
Ogora, Lino Owor, 'Justice and Reconciliation Project: The Mukura Massacre of 1989' (JRP Field Note XII, Gulu, March 2011).
'Once a Slave', *Church Missionary Gleaner,* 1 September 1904.
p'Bitek, Okot, 'The Concept of Jok among the Acholi and Lango', *Uganda Journal*, 27 (1963), 15–30.
Pasha, Emin, 'The Diaries of Emin Pasha—Extracts I', ed. by John M. Gray, *Uganda Journal*, 25 (1961), 1–15 (p. 1).
——, 'The Diaries of Emin Pasha—Extracts VI', ed. by John M. Gray, *Uganda Journal*, 27 (1963), 143–61 (p. 53).
——, 'The Diaries of Emin Pasha—Extracts IX', ed. by John M. Gray, *Uganda Journal*, 29 (1965), 77–83.
Pope Pius XII, '*Fidei Donum*: On the present condition of the Catholic Missions, especially in Africa', 21 April 1957.
Richardson, Rev. A. E., 'The Tribes of the Egyptian Soudan', *Church Missionary Gleaner*, 1 January 1906.
'The Opening of Mombasa Cathedral', *Church Missionary Gleaner*, 1 September 1905.
'Uganda', *The Church Missionary Gleaner*, 1 September 1905.

Chapters in Edited Volumes

'Gelasius I', in *From Irenaeus to Grotius: A Sourcebook in Christian Political Thought 100–1625*, ed. by Oliver O'Donovan and Jean L. O'Donovan (Grand Rapids, MI: Eerdmans, 1999), pp. 177–9.
'Letter from the House of Bishops to President Amin, 12 February 1977', in Edward Muhima, 'Fellowship of His Suffering: A Theological Interpretation of Christian Suffering under Idi Amin', unpublished PhD thesis, Northwestern University, 1982.

Secondary Sources

Books and Monographs

Achebe, Chinua, *Things Fall Apart: A Novel* (New York: Anchor, 1994 [1959]).
Alighieri, Dante, *Dante's Inferno*, trans. by Henry Francis Cary, New Edition (New York: Cassell, Petter, Galpin & Co. [1805]).
Apter, David E, *The Political Kingdom in Uganda: A Study in Bureaucratic Nationalism*, 2nd edn (Princeton, NJ: Princeton University Press, 1967).
Atkinson, Ronald R., *The Roots of Ethnicity: The Origins of the Acholi of Uganda Before 1800* (Philadelphia: University of Pennsylvania Press, 1994).
Babou, Cheikh Anta, *Fighting the Greater Jihad: Amadu Bamba and the Founding of the Muridiyya of Senegal, 1853–1913* (Athens: Ohio University Press, 2007).

Bade, Albert, *Benedicto Kiwanuka: The Man and His Politics* (Kampala: Fountain, 1996).
Baur, John. *Two Thousand Years of Christianity in Africa: An African History*. Revised Edition (Nairobi: Paulines Publications Africa, 2009).
Bayart, Jean-François, *The State in Africa: The Politics of the Belly*, trans. by Mary Harper, Christopher Harrison, and Elizabeth Harrison (London: Longman, 1993).
Bruner, Jason, *Living Salvation in the East African Revival in Uganda* (Rochester, NY: University of Rochester Press, 2017).
Buchanan, Tom and Martin Conway, eds, *Political Catholicism in Europe, 1918–1965* (Oxford: Clarendon, 1996).
Byabazaire, Deogratias M. *The Contribution of the Christian Churches to the Development of Western Uganda 1894–1974* (Frankfurt: Peter Lang, 1979).
Cabrita, Joel, *Text and Authority in the South African Nazaretha Church* (Cambridge: Cambridge University Press, 2014).
Cannadine, David, *Ornamentalism: How the British Saw Their Empire* (London: Penguin, 2002).
Carbone, Giovanne, *No-Party Democracy? Ugandan Politics in Comparative Perspective* (Boulder, CO: Lynne Rienner Publishers, 2008).
Carney, J. J., *For God and my Country: Catholic Leadership in Modern Uganda* (Eugene, OR: Cascade, 2020).
———, *Rwanda Before the Genocide: Catholic Politics and Ethnic Discourse in the Late Colonial Era* (New York: Oxford University Press, 2014).
Carswell, Grace. *Cultivating Success in Uganda: Kigezi Farmers and Colonial Policies* (Athens: Ohio University Press, 2007).
Cavanaugh, William T., *The Myth of Religious Violence* (New York: Oxford University Press, 2009).
———, *Torture and Eucharist: Theology, Politics, and the Body of Christ* (Oxford: Blackwell, 1998).
Chadwick, Owen, *The Christian Church in the Cold War* (London: Penguin, 1992).
Chakrabarty, Dipesh, *Provincializing Europe: Postcolonial Thought and Historical Difference* (Princeton, NJ: Princeton University Press, 2007).
Cisternino, Mario, *Passion for Africa: Missionary and Imperial Papers on the Evangelisation of Uganda and Sudan, 1848–1923* (Kampala: Fountain, 2004).
Cody, Lisa Forman, *Birthing the Nation: Sex, Science, and the Conception of Eighteenth-Century Britons* (Oxford: Oxford University Press, 2005).
Cooper, Frederick, *Africa Since 1940: The Past of the Present* (Cambridge: Cambridge University Press, 2002).
Crowder, Michael, *West Africa under Colonial Rule* (Evanston, IL: Northwestern University Press, 1968).
Davidson, Basil, *Which Way Africa? The Search for a New Society*, 3rd edn (Harmondsworth: Penguin Books, 1971).
Decker, Alicia, *In Idi Amin's Shadow: Women, Gender, and Militarism in Uganda* (Athens: Ohio University Press, 2014).
Donham, Donald L., *Marxist Modern: An Ethnographic History of the Ethiopian Revolution* (Berkeley: University of California Press, 1999).
Doornbos, Martin R., *Not All the King's Men: Inequality as a Political Instrument in Ankole, Uganda* (The Hague: Mouton Publishers, 1978).

Doyle, Shane, *Crisis and Decline in Bunyoro: Population and Environment in Western Uganda 1860–1955* (Oxford: James Currey, 2006).
Earle, Jonathon L., *Colonial Buganda and the End of Empire: Political Thought and Historical Imagination in Africa* (Cambridge: Cambridge University Press, 2017).
Fallers, Margaret Chave, *The Eastern Lacustrine Bantu (Ganda and Soga)* (London: International African Institute, 1968).
Fanon, Frantz, *The Wretched of the Earth*, trans. by Constance Farrington (New York: Grove, 1963).
Faupel, J. F., *African Holocaust: The Story of the Uganda Martyrs* (New York: P. J. Kennedy, 1962).
Feierman, Steven, *Peasant Intellectuals: Anthropology and History in Tanzania* (Madison: University of Wisconsin Press, 1990).
Ferguson, James, *Global Shadows: Africa in the Neoliberal World Order* (Durham, NC: Duke University Press, 2006).
Foster, Elizabeth A., *African Catholic: Decolonization and the Transformation of the Church* (Cambridge, MA: Harvard University Press, 2019).
——, *Faith in Empire: Religion, Politics, and Colonial Rule in French Senegal, 1880–1940* (Stanford, CA: Stanford University Press, 2013).
Gale, H. P., *Uganda and the Mill Hill Fathers* (London: Macmillan, 1959).
Getz, Trevor R. and Liz Clarke, *Abina and the Important Men: A Graphic History*, 2nd edn (New York: Oxford University Press, 2015).
Gifford, Paul, *African Christianity: Its Public Role* (Bloomington: Indiana University Press, 1998).
Gilli, Aldo, *Daniel Comboni: The Man and his Message* (Bologna: Editrice Missionaria Italiana, 1980).
Gingyera-Pincycwa, A. G. G., *Issues in Pre-Independence Politics in Uganda: A Case-Study on the Contribution of Religion to Political Debate in Uganda in the Decade 1952–62* (Kampala: East African Literature Bureau, 1976).
Glassman, Jonathan, *War of Words, War of Stones: Racial Thought and Violence in Colonial Zanzibar* (Bloomington: Indiana University Press, 2011).
Hansen, Holger B., *Mission, Church and State in a Colonial Setting: Uganda 1890–1925* (London: Heinemann, 1984).
Hansen, Holger B. and Michael Twaddle, eds, *From Chaos to Order: The Politics of Constitution-Making in Uganda* (Kampala: Fountain, 1995).
Hanson, Holly E., *Landed Obligation: The Practice of Power in Buganda* (Portsmouth, NH: Heinemann, 2003).
Hastings, Adrian, *The Church in Africa 1450–1950* (Oxford: Clarendon, 1994).
——, *The Construction of Nationhood: Ethnicity, Religion and Nationalism* (Cambridge: Cambridge University Press, 1997).
——, *A History of African Christianity 1950–1975* (Cambridge: Cambridge University Press, 1979).
Hodgson, Dorothy L. *The Church of Women: Gendered Encounters between Maasai and Missionaries* (Bloomington: Indiana University Press, 2005).
Horn, Gerd-Rainer, *Western European Liberation Theology: The First Wave (1924–1959)* (Oxford: Oxford University Press, 2008).

Hunter, Emma, *Political Thought and the Public Sphere in Tanzania: Freedom, Democracy and Citizenship in the Era of Decolonization* (Cambridge: Cambridge University Press, 2015).
Ikegami, Eiko, 'Emotions', in *A Concise Companion to History*, ed. by Ulinka Rublack (Oxford: Oxford University Press, 2012), pp. 333–53.
Iliffe, John, *Honour in African History* (Cambridge: Cambridge University Press, 2005).
Ingham, Kenneth, *The Toro Kingdom in Uganda* (London: Methuen & Co. Ltd., 1975).
Isichei, Elizabeth, *A History of Christianity in Africa: From Antiquity to the Present* (Grand Rapids, MI: Eerdmans, 1995).
Jonas, Raymond, *France and the Cult of the Sacred Heart: An Epic Tale for Modern Times* (Berkeley: University of California Press, 2000).
Jones, Ben, *Beyond the State in Rural Uganda* (Edinburgh: Edinburgh University Press, 2009).
Jørgensen, Jan Jelmert, *Uganda: A Modern History* (New York: St. Martin's Press, 1981).
Kahangi, Gordon Kamugunda, *A History of East Africa: From Ancient to Modern Time* (Kampala: Wavah, 2006).
Kaiser, Wolfram, *Christian Democracy and the Origins of the European Union* (Cambridge: Cambridge University Press, 2007).
Kaiser, Wolfram and Helmut Wohnout, eds, *Political Catholicism in Europe 1918–45* (New York: Routledge, 2004).
Kanaaneh, Rhoda Ann, *Birthing the Nation: Strategies of Palestinian Women in Israel* (Berkeley: University of California Press, 2002).
Kantorowicz, Ernst, *The King's Two Bodies: A Study in Mediaeval Political Theology* (Princeton, NJ: Princeton University Press, 2016).
Karugire, Samwiri R., *A Political History of Uganda* (Nairobi: Heinemann, 1980).
Kasozi, A. B. K., *The Bitter Bread of Exile: The Financial Problems of Sir Edward Muteesa II during his Final Exile, 1966–1969* (Kampala: Progressive Publishing House, 2013).
——, *The Social Origins of Violence in Uganda, 1964–1985* (Montreal: McGill-Queen's University Press, 1994).
——, *The Spread of Islam in Uganda* (Nairobi: Oxford University Press, 1986).
King, Noel Quinton, A. B. K. Kasozi, and Arye Oded, *Islam and the Confluence of Religions in Uganda, 1840–1966* (Tallahassee, FL: American Academy of Religion, 1973).
Kiwanuka, Semakula, *A History of Buganda: From the Foundation of the Kingdom to 1900* (London: Longman, 1971).
Klaiber, Jeffrey, *The Church, Dictatorships, and Democracy in Latin America* (Maryknoll, NY: Orbis, 1998).
Kodesh, Neil, *Beyond the Royal Gaze: Clanship and Public Healing in Buganda* (Charlottesville: University of Virginia Press, 2010).
Kollman, Paul and Cynthia Toms Smedley, *Understanding World Christianity: Eastern Africa* (Minneapolis: Fortress Press, 2018).
Lavigerie, Charles Martial Allemand and Xavier de Montclos, *Lavigerie: la mission universelle de l'eglise*. Foi vivante 280 (Paris: Cerf, 1991).

Lawrance, J. C. D., *The Iteso: Fifty Years of Change in a Nilo-Hamitic Tribe of Uganda* (London: Oxford University Press, 1957).
Linden, Ian, *Global Catholicism: Towards a Networked Church* (London: Hurst, 2012).
——, *The Catholic Church and the Struggle for Zimbabwe* (London: Longman, 1980).
Linden, Ian and Jane Linden, *Catholics, Peasants, and Chewa Resistance in Nyasaland, 1899–1939* (Berkeley: University of California Press, 1974).
——, *Church and Revolution in Rwanda* (Manchester: University of Manchester Press, 1977).
Loffman, Reuben A., *Church, State and Colonialism in Southeastern Congo, 1890–1962* (New York: Palgrave Macmillan, 2019).
Longman, Timothy. *Christianity and Genocide in Rwanda* (Cambridge: Cambridge University Press, 2010).
Low, Donald A., *Buganda in Modern History* (Berkeley: University of California Press, 1971).
——, *Political Parties in Uganda 1949–62* (London: University of London Athlone Press, 1962).
Lwanga Lunyiigo, Samwiri, *Mwanga II: Resistance to Imposition of British Colonial Rule in Buganda, 1884–1899* (Kampala: Wavah, 2011).
Mamdani, Mahmood, *Politics and Class Formation in Uganda* (London: Heinemann Educational, 1976).
Marchetti, Fr Mario, *Too Long in the Dark: The Story of the Two Martyrs of Paimol and their Relevance to Uganda Today* (*Profilo Dei Due Asseriti Martiri Di Paimol Troppo A Lungo Rimasti Nell'Ombra*) (Gulu: Archdiocese of Gulu, 1999).
Martin, Phyllis M. *Catholic Women of Congo-Brazzaville: Mothers and Sisters in Troubled Times* (Bloomington: Indiana University Press, 2009).
Mbiti, John, *African Religions and Philosophy* (Oxford: Heinemann, 1967).
Médard, Henri, *Le royaume du Buganda au XIXe siècle: Mutations politiques et religieuses d'un ancien état d'Afrique de l'Est* (Paris: Karthala, 2007).
Meredith, Martin, *The Fate of Africa: From the Hopes of Freedom to the Heart of Despair* (New York: Public Affairs, 2005).
Morier-Genoud, Eric, *Catholicism and the Making of Politics in Central Mozambique, 1940–1986* (Rochester, NY: University of Rochester Press, 2019).
Mudimbe, V. Y., *The Idea of Africa* (London: James Currey, 1994).
Mudoola, Dan, *Religion, Ethnicity and Politics in Uganda*, 2nd edn (Kampala: Fountain, 1996).
Mutibwa, Phares, *Uganda since Independence: A Story of Unfulfilled Hopes* (Trenton, NJ: Africa World Press, 1992).
Oded, Arye, *Islam in Uganda: Islamization through a Centralized State in Pre-Colonial Africa* (Tel Aviv: Israel Universities Press, 1974).
O'Neil, Robert, *Mission to the Upper Nile* (London: Mission Book Service, 1999).
Orobator, Agbonkhianmeghe E., *Theology Brewed in an African Pot* (Maryknoll, NY: Orbis, 2008).
Parsons, Timothy, *The African Rank-and-File: Social Implications of Colonial Military Service in the King's African Rifles, 1902–1964* (Portsmouth, NH: Heinemann, 1999).

Peterson, Derek R., *Ethnic Patriotism and the East African Revival: A History of Dissent, c. 1935–1972* (Cambridge: Cambridge University Press, 2012).
Pinkman, Kathryn, *A Centenary of Faith: Planting the Seed in Northern Uganda* (Kampala: Comboni Missionaries of the Heart of Jesus, 2010).
Pirouet, M. Louise, *Black Evangelists: The Spread of Christianity in Uganda, 1891–1914* (London: Collings, 1978).
——, *Historical Dictionary of Uganda* (London: The Scarecrow Press, 1995).
Reid, Richard J., *A History of Modern Uganda* (Cambridge: University of Cambridge Press, 2017).
——, *Political Power in Pre-Colonial Buganda: Economy, Society & Welfare in the Nineteenth Century* (Oxford: James Currey, 2002).
Reno, William, *Warfare in Independent Africa* (Cambridge: Cambridge University Press, 2011).
Royce, Mark, *The Political Theology of European Integration: Comparing the Influence of Religious Histories on European Politics* (Basingstoke: Palgrave Macmillian, 2017).
Rubongoya, Joshua B. *Regime Hegemony in Museveni's Uganda: Pax Musevenica* (New York: Palgrave Macmillan, 2007).
Sathyamurthy, T. V., *The Political Development of Uganda: 1900–1986* (Brookfield, VT: Gower, 1986).
Scherz, China, *'Having People, Having Heart': Charity, Sustainable Development, and Problems of Dependence in Central Uganda* (Chicago IL: University of Chicago Press, 2014).
Shorter, Aylward, *Cross and Flag in Africa: The White Fathers during the Colonial Scramble (1892–1914)* (Maryknoll, NY: Orbis, 2006).
Southall, Aidan W. and Peter C. W. Gutkind, *Townsmen in the Making: Kampala and Its Suburbs* (Kampala: Uganda Bookshop for the East African Institute of Social Research, 1956).
Ssekitto, Freddie, *Uganda Martyrs Canonisation: 50 Years After, 1964–2014* (Kisubi: Marianum Press, 2015).
Stephens, Rhiannon, *A History of African Motherhood: The Case of Uganda, 700–1900* (Cambridge: Cambridge University Press, 2013).
Taylor, John V., *The Growth of the Church in Buganda: An Attempt at Understanding* (London: SCM Press, 1958).
Thompson, Gardner, *African Democracy: Its Origins and Development in Uganda, Kenya, and Tanzania* (Kampala: Fountain Publishers, 2015).
——, *Governing Uganda: British Colonial Rule and Its Legacy* (Kampala: Fountain Publishers, 2003).
Tourigny, Yves, *So Abundant a Harvest: The Catholic Church in Uganda, 1879–1979* (London: Darton, Longman and Todd, 1979).
Tripp, Aili M., *Museveni's Uganda: Paradoxes of Power in a Hybrid Regime* (Boulder, CO: Lynne Rienner, 2010).
——, *Women and Politics in Uganda* (Madison: University of Wisconsin Press, 2000).
Tumusiime, James. *Uganda 30 Years: 1962–1992* (Kampala: Fountain Press, 1992).
Tusingire, Frederick, *The Evangelisation of Uganda: Challenges and Strategies* (Kisubi: Marianum, 2003).

Twaddle, Michael, *Kakungulu & the Creation of Uganda, 1868–1928* (London: James Currey, 1993).
Vansina, Jan, *Antecedents to Modern Rwanda: The Nyiginya Kingdom* (Madison: University of Wisconsin Press, 2005).
Vincent, Joan, *Teso in Transformation: The Political Economy of Peasant and Class in Eastern Africa* (Berkeley: University of California Press, 1982).
Waliggo, John Mary, *The Catholic Church in the Buddu Province of Buganda, 1879–1925*, 2nd edn (Kampala: Angel, 2011).
Warner, Carolyn M., *Confessions of an Interest Group: The Catholic Church and Political Parties in Europe* (Princeton, NJ: Princeton University Press, 2000).
Welbourn, Frederick B., *Religion and Politics in Uganda, 1952–1962* (Nairobi: East African Publishing House, 1965).
White, Luise, *Speaking with Vampires: Rumor and History in Colonial Africa* (Berkeley: University of California Press, 2000).
Whitmore, Todd D., *Imitating Christ in Magwi: An Anthropological Theology* (London: T&T Clark, 2019).
Wild-Wood, Emma. *The Mission of Apolo Kivebulaya: Religious Encounter and Social Change in the Great Lakes c. 1865–1935* (Oxford: James Currey, 2020).
Wrigley, Christopher, *Kingship and State: The Buganda Dynasty* (Cambridge: Cambridge University Press, 1996).
Young, Crawford, *The African Colonial State in Comparative Perspective* (New Haven, CT: Yale University Press, 1994).

Articles

Amone, Charles, and Okullu Muura, 'British Colonialism and the Creation of Acholi Ethnic Identity in Uganda, 1894 to 1962', *Journal of Imperial and Commonwealth History*, 42 (2013), 239–57.
Austin, Gareth, and Chibuike Ugochukwu Uche, 'Collusion and Competition in Colonial Economies: Banking in British West Africa', *Business History Review*, 81 (2007), 1–26.
Boureau, Alain, 'L'adage vox populi, vox dei et l'invention de la nation anglaise (VIIIe–XIIe siècle)', *Annales. Histoire, Sciences Sociales*, 47 (1992), 1071–89.
Brennan, James R., 'Lowering the Sultan's Flag: Sovereignty and Decolonization in Coastal Kenya', *Comparative Studies in Society and History*, 50 (2008), 831–61.
Carney, J. J., 'Beyond Tribalism: The Hutu-Tutsi Question & Catholic Rhetoric in Colonial Rwanda', *Journal of Religion in Africa*, 42 (2012), 172–202.
——, 'The Politics of Ecumenism in Uganda, 1962–1986', *Church History* 86 (2017), 765–95.
Coupland, Philip, 'Western Union, "Spiritual Union," and European Integration, 1948–1964', *Journal of British Studies*, 43 (2004), 366–94.
Earle, Jonathon L., 'Dreams and Political Imagination in Colonial Buganda', *The Journal of African History*, 58 (2017), 85–105.
——'Political Activism and Other Life Forms in Colonial Buganda', *History in Africa*, 45 (2018), 373–95.
Edmunds, Martha Mel, 'Gabriel's Altar for the Palace Chapel at Versailles: Sacred Heart

and Royal Court in Eighteenth-Century France', *Journal of the Society of Architectural Historians*, 65 (2006), 550–77.

Ellis, Stephen and Gerrie Ter Haar, 'Religion and Politics: Taking African Epistemologies Seriously', *The Journal of Modern African Studies*, 45 (2007), 385–401.

Emwanu, G., 'The Reception of Alien Rule in Teso: 1896–1927', *Uganda Journal*, 31 (1967), 171–82.

Friedman, John B., 'Medieval Cartography and "Inferno" XXXIV: Lucifer's Three Faces Reconsidered', *Traditio*, 39 (1983), 447–56.

Gee, T. W., 'A Century of Muhammedan Influence in Buganda, 1852–1951', *Uganda Journal*, 22 (1958), 139–50.

Gray, John M., 'Kakungulu in Bukedi', *Uganda Journal*, 27 (1963), 31–59.

——, 'The Sieges of Bukumi, Mubende District, in 1898', *Uganda Journal*, 25 (1961), 65–85.

——, 'The Year of the Three Kings of Buganda', *Uganda Journal*, 14 (1949), 15–52.

Hancock, I. R., 'Patriotism and Neo-Traditionalism in Buganda: The Kabaka Yekka ('The King Alone') Movement, 1961–1962', *The Journal of African History*, 11 (1970), 419–34.

Hastings, Adrian, 'From Mission to Church in Buganda', *Zeitschrift Für Missionswissenschaft Und Religionswissenschaft*, 53 (1969), 206–28.

——, 'Ganda Catholic Spirituality', *Journal of Religion in Africa*, 8 (1976), 81–91.

Hundle, Anneeth Kaur, 'Exceptions to the Expulsion: Violence, Security and Community among Ugandan Asians, 1972–79', *Journal of Eastern African Studies*, 7 (2013), 164–82.

Ibeawuchi Omenka, Nicholas, 'Blaming the Gods: Christian Religious Propaganda in the Nigeria-Biafra War', *Journal of African History*, 51 (2010), pp. 367–89.

Kassimir, Ronald, 'Complex martyrs: symbols of Catholic Church formation and political differentiation in Uganda', *African Affairs,* 90 (1991), 357–82.

Katumba, Ahmed and Fred B. Welbourn, 'Muslim Martyrs of Buganda', *Uganda Journal*, 28 (1964), 151–63.

Kiwanuka, Semakula, 'Kabaka Mwanga and His Political Parties', *Uganda Journal*, 33 (1969), 1–16.

Low, Donald A., 'Uganda Unhinged', *International Affairs,* 49 (1973), 219–28.

Musisi, Nakanyike B., 'Women, "Elite Polygyny," and Buganda State Formation', *Signs*, 16 (1991), 757–86.

Ofuani, Oga A., 'The Traditional and Modern Influences in Okot p'Bitek's Poetry', *African Studies Review*, 28 (1985), 87–99.

Ojaide, Tanure, 'Poetic Viewpoint: Okot p'Bitek and His Personae', *Callaloo*, 27 (1986), 371–83.

Otim, Patrick W., 'Local Intellectuals: Lacito Okech and the Production of Knowledge in Colonial Acholiland', *History in Africa*, 45 (2018), 275–305.

Pallaver, Karin, '"The African Native Has no Pocket": Monetary Practices and Currency Transitions in Early Colonial Uganda', *International Journal of African Historical Studies*, 48 (2015), 471–99.

Peterson, Derek R., 'Violence and Political Advocacy in the Lost Counties, Western Uganda, 1930–64', *The International Journal of African Historical Studies*, 48 (2015), 51–72.

Peterson, Derek R. and Edgar C. Taylor, 'Rethinking the State in Idi Amin's Uganda:

The Politics of Exhortation', *Journal of Eastern African Studies*, 7 (2013), 58–82.

Rigby, Peter, 'Prophets, Diviners, and Prophetism: The Recent History of Kiganda Religion', *Journal of Anthropological Research* 31 (1975), 116–48.

Roberts, A. D., 'The "Lost Counties" of Bunyoro', *Uganda Journal*, 26 (1962), 194–9.

——, 'The Sub-Imperialism of the Baganda', *Journal of African History*, 3 (1962), 435–50.

Rowe, John A., 'Eyewitness Accounts of Buganda History: The Memoirs of Ham Mukasa and His Generation', *Ethnohistory*, 36 (1989), 61–71.

——, 'Myth, Memoir, and Moral Admonition: Luganda Historical Writing, 1893–1969', *Uganda Journal*, 33 (1969), 17–40, 217–19.

——, 'The Baganda Revolutionaries', *Tarikh*, 3 (1970), 34–46.

——, 'The Purge of Christians at Mwanga's Court: A Reassessment of This Episode in Buganda History', *Journal of African History*, 5 (1963), 55–72.

Sathyamurthy, T. V., 'The Social Base of the Uganda Peoples' Congress, 1958–70', *African Affairs*, 74 (1975), 442–60.

Sherman W. Seldon, 'Curing Tales from Teso', *Journal of the Folklore Institute*, 13 (1976), 137–54.

Southall, Aidan, 'General Amin and the Coup: Great Man or Historical Inevitability?' *The Journal of Modern African Studies*, 13 (1975), 85–105.

Summers, Carol, 'All the Kabaka's Wives: Marital Claims in Buganda's 1953–5 Kabaka Crisis', *Journal of African History*, 58 (2017), 107–27.

——, 'Catholic Action and Ugandan Radicalism: Political Activism in Buganda, 1930–1950', *Journal of Religion in Africa*, 39 (2009), 60–90.

——, 'Grandfathers, Grandsons, Morality, and Radical Politics in Late Colonial Buganda', *The International Journal of African Historical Studies*, 38 (2005), 427–47.

——, 'Radical Rudeness: Ugandan Social Critiques in the 1940s', *Journal of Social History*, 39 (2006), 741–70.

Thomas, H. B., 'The Last Days of Bishop Hannington', *Uganda Journal*, 8 (1940), 19–27.

Twaddle, Michael, 'On Ganda Historiography', *History in Africa*, 1 (1974), 85–100.

——, 'The Emergence of Politico-Religious Groupings in Late Nineteenth-Century Buganda', *The Journal of African History*, 29 (1988), 81–92.

——, 'The Muslim Revolution in Buganda', *African Affairs*, 71 (1972), 54–72.

Ward, Kevin, 'The Church of Uganda and the Exile of Kabaka Muteesa II, 1953–55', *Journal of Religion in Africa*, 28 (1998), 411–49.

Webster, J. B., 'Pioneers of Teso', *Tarikh*, 3 (1970), 47–58.

Williams, F. Lukyn, 'Teso Clans', *Uganda Journal*, 4 (1936), 174–6.

Wrigley, C. C., 'The Christian Revolution in Buganda', *Comparative Studies in Society and History*, 2 (1959), 33–48.

Chapters in Edited Volumes

Agonga, Aquinata, 'Soror nostra es: Jesuits, Protestants, and Political Elites in Southern Africa among the Shona and the Ndebele, 1889–1900', in *Encounters between Jesuits and Protestants in Africa*, ed. by Robert A. Maryks and Festo Mkenda (Leiden: Brill, 2017), pp. 132–49.

Branch, Adam, 'Exploring the Roots of LRA Violence: Political Crisis and Ethnic Politics in Acholiland', in *The Lord's Resistance Army: Myth and Reality*, ed. by Tim Allen and Koen Vlassenroot (London: Zed Books, 2010), pp. 25–44.

Carney, J. J., '"The Bishop is Governor Here": Bishop Nicholas Djomo and Catholic Leadership in the Democratic Republic of the Congo', in *Leadership in Post-colonial Africa*, ed. by Baba G. Jallow (New York: Palgrave Macmillan, 2015), pp. 97–122.

Doyle, Shane, 'Bunyoro & the Demography of Slavery Debate: Fertility, Kinship & Assimilation', in *Slavery in the Great Lakes Region of East Africa*, ed. by Henri Médard and Shane Doyle (Kampala: Fountain Publishers, 2007), pp. 231–51.

Earle, Jonathon L., 'Intellectual History and Historiography', in *The Oxford Research Encyclopedia: Guide to Methods, Sources and Historiography in African History*, ed. by Thomas Spear (Oxford: Oxford University Press, 2019).

Fallers, L. A., 'The Modernization of Social Stratification', in *The King's Men: Leadership and Status in Buganda on the Eve of Independence*, ed. by L. A. Fallers (London: Oxford University Press, 1964), pp. 117–57.

Gertzel, Cherry, 'Kingdoms, Districts, and the Unitary State: Uganda, 1945–1962', in *History of East Africa*, ed. by D. A. Low and Alison Smith (Oxford: Clarendon Press, 1976), III, 65–106.

Hanson, Holly E., 'Queen Mothers and Good Government in Buganda: The Loss of Women's Political Power in the Nineteenth Century', in *Women in African Colonial Histories*, ed. by Jean Allman, Susan Geiger, and Nakanyike Musisi (Indiana University Press, 2002), pp. 101–34.

——, 'Stolen People and Autonomous Chiefs in Nineteenth-Century Buganda: The Social Consequences of Non-Free Followers', in *Slavery in the Great Lakes Region of East Africa*, ed. by Henri Médard and Shane Doyle (Kampala: Fountain Publishers, 2007), pp. 161–73.

Hastings, Adrian, 'Catholic History from Vatican I to John Paul II', in *Modern Catholicism: Vatican II and After*, ed. by Adrian Hastings (New York: Oxford University Press, 1990), pp. 1–13.

Heron, G. A. 'Introduction', in *Song of Lawino Song of Ocol* (Long Grove, IL: Waveland Press, Inc., 2013), pp. 1–33.

Karugire, Samwiri R., 'The Arrival of the European Missionaries: The first fifteen or so years', in *A Century of Christianity in Uganda, 1877–1977*, ed. by Tom Tuma and Phares Mutibwa (Nairobi: Uzima, 1978), pp. 1–15.

Lonsdale, John, 'Moral Ethnicity and Political Tribalism', in *Inventions and Boundaries: Historical and Anthropological Approaches to the Study of Ethnicity and Nationalism*, ed. by Preben Kaarsholm and Jan Hultin (Roskilde: International Development Studies, Roskilde University, 1994), pp. 131–50.

Médard, Henri, 'Introduction', in *Slavery in the Great Lakes Region of East Africa*, ed. by Henri Médard and Shane Doyle (Kampala: Fountain Publishers, 2007), pp. 1–37.

Meierkord, Christiane, Bebwa Isingoma, and Saudah Namyalo, 'Towards Assessing the Space of English in Uganda's Linguistic Ecology: Facts and Issues', in *Ugandan English: Its Sociolinguistics, Structure, and Uses in a Globalising Post-Protectorate*, ed. by Christiane Meierkord, Bebwa Isingoma, and Saudah Namyalo (Amsterdam: Johns Benjamins Publishing Company, 2016), pp. 19–50.

Peterson, Derek R. and Emma Hunter, 'Print Culture in Colonial Africa', in *African Print Cultures: Newspapers and Their Publics in the Twentieth Century*, ed. by

Derek R. Peterson, Emma Hunter, and Stephanie Newell (Ann Arbor: University of Michigan Press, 2016), pp. 1–45.

Powesland, P. G., 'History of the Migration in Uganda', in *Economic Development and Tribal Change: A Study of Immigrant Labour in Buganda*, ed. by Audrey I. Richards, 2nd edn (Nairobi: Oxford University Press, 1973), pp. 17–51.

Richards, Audrey I., 'Epilogue', in *The King's Men: Leadership and Status in Buganda on the Eve of Independence*, ed. by Lloyd A. Fallers (London: published on behalf of the East African Institute of Social Research by Oxford University Press, 1964), pp. 357–95.

Sanyal, Sunanda K., '"Being Modern": Identity Debates and Makerere's Art School in the 1960s', in *A Companion to Modern African Art*, ed. by Monica Blackmun Visona and Gittii Salami (Malden, MA: Wiley-Blackwell, 2013), pp. 255–75.

Summers, Carol, 'Force and Colonial Development in Eastern Uganda', in *East Africa in Transition: Communities, Cultures, and Change*, ed. by J. M. Bahemuka and J. L. Brockington (Nairobi: Acton Publishers, 2002), pp. 181–207.

Tinkasiimire, Therese, 'Women's Contributions to Religious Institutions in Uganda (1962–2011)', in *The Women's Movement in Uganda: History, Challenges, and Prospects*, ed. by Aili Mari Tripp and Joy C. Kwesiga (Kampala: Fountain, 2002), pp. 138–45.

Titeca, Kristof, 'The Spiritual Order of the LRA', in *The Lord's Resistance Army: Myth and Reality*, ed. by Tim Allen and Koen Vlassenroot (London: Zed Books, 2010), pp. 59–73.

Tripp, A. M. and Sarah Ntiro, 'Women's Activism in Colonial Uganda', in *The Women's Movement in Uganda: History, Challenges, and Prospects*, ed. by Aili Mari Tripp and Joy C. Kwesiga (Kampala: Fountain, 2002), pp. 25–6, 31–2.

Tuck, Michael W., 'Women's Experiences of Enslavement and Slavery in Late Nineteenth and Early Twentieth-Century Uganda', in *Slavery in the Great Lakes Region of East Africa*, ed. by Henri Médard and Shane Doyle (Kampala: Fountain Publishers, 2007), pp. 174–88.

Twaddle, Michael, 'Was the Democratic Party of Uganda a Purely Confessional Party?', in *Christianity in Independent Africa*, ed. by Edward Fasholé-Luke, Richard Gray, Adrian Hastings and Godwin Tasie (Bloomington: Indiana University Press, 1978), pp. 255–66.

Waliggo, John Mary, 'Archbishop J. Kiwanuka and the Vision of Integral Development', in *The Man of Vision: Archbishop J. Kiwanuka*, ed. by John Mary Waliggo (Kisubi: Marianum, 1991), pp. 33–50.

——, 'The Life and Legacy of Archbishop Joseph Kiwanuka', in *The Man of Vision: Archbishop J. Kiwanuka*, ed. by John Mary Waliggo (Kisubi: Marianum, 1991), pp. 7–32.

——, 'The Role of the Christian Churches in the Democratisation Process in Uganda, 1980–1993', in *The Christian Churches and the Democratisation of Africa*, ed. by Paul Gifford (Leiden: Brill, 1995), pp. 205–24.

Ward, Kevin, 'African Nationalism, Christian Democracy and "Communism": The Rise of Sectarian Confessional Politics in Uganda 1952–1962', in *Changing Relations between Churches in Europe and Africa: The Internationalization of Christianity and Politics in the 20th Century*, ed. by Katherina Kunter and Jens Holger Schjorring (Wiesbaden, Germany: Harrassowitz Verlag, 2008), pp. 73–88.

Unpublished

Alava, Henni, '"There is Confusion." The Politics of Silence, Fear and Hope in Catholic and Protestant Northern Uganda', unpublished PhD thesis, University of Helsinki, 2017.

Fernandez de Aller, Fidel Gonzales, 'La Idea Misionera de Daniel Comboni, Primer Vicario Apostolico del Africa Central, en al Contexto Socio-Eclesial del Siglo XIX', unpublished ThD thesis, Universidad Pontificia de Salamanca, 1979.

Fitchett Climenhaga, Alison, '"I want to be a convinced and influential Catholic": Catholic Action and Church-Society Relations in Uganda, 1930–1990', unpublished conference paper, American Catholic Historical Association annual meeting, New York, January 2020.

Karlström, Mikael, 'The Cultural Kingdom in Uganda: Popular Royalism and the Restoration of the Buganda Kingship, Volume I', unpublished PhD thesis, University of Chicago, 1999.

Kiwanuka, M. S. M., 'The Uganda National Movement and the Trade Boycott of 1959/60: A Study of Politics and Economics in Uganda on the Eve of Independence' (Cambridge CAS: (676.1): Box 320, n.d.).

Laruni, Elizabeth, 'From the Village to Entebbe: The Acholi of Northern Uganda and the Politics of Identity, 1950–1985' (unpublished PhD, University of Exeter, 2014).

Lockard, Kathleen, 'Religion and Political Development in Uganda, 1962–72', unpublished PhD thesis, University of Wisconsin-Madison, 1974.

Magunda, Darius, 'The Role and Impact of the Missionaries of Africa in Planting the Church in Western Uganda 1879–1969', unpublished ThD thesis, Pontifical University Sancta Crucis, Rome, 2006.

Manarin, Tim, 'The Word Became Kigambo: Literacy and Language in Buganda, 1875–1935' (unpublished PhD, University of Indiana, 2008).

Otim, Patrick W., 'Forgotten Voices of the Transition: Precolonial Intellectuals and the Colonial State in Northern Uganda, 1850–1950' (unpublished PhD, University of Wisconsin-Madison, 2016).

Taylor, Edgar, 'Histories of an Event: The Ugandan Asian Expulsion of 1972', unpublished PhD thesis, University of Michigan, 2015.

Waliggo, John Mary, 'The Catholic Church in the Buddu Province of Buganda, 1879–1925', unpublished PhD thesis, University of Cambridge, 1976.

Internet Sources

Allen, John L., 'Beatification of El Salvador's Oscar Romero a Turning Point for Catholicism', May 16, 2005, https://cruxnow.com/church/2015/05/16/beatification-of-el-salvadors-oscar-romero-a-turning-point-for-catholicism, accessed 28 July 2020.

'Benedicto Kiwanuka Foundation', www.youtube.com/channel/UC1vZntKWjNCqVH-B16y4IgWQ, accessed 7 August 2020.

'Feature: The life and times of Cuthbert Obwangor', *Observer*, 22 May 2012, www.observer.ug/features-sp-2084439083/57-feature/18873-feature-the-life-and-times-of-cuthbert-obwangor, accessed 15 June 2018.

'Museveni Mourns Former Minister Obwangor', *URN*, 21 May 2012, https://ugandaradionetwork.com/story/museveni-mourns-former-minister-obwangor, accessed 20 June 2018.

'Pastoral Constitution on the Church in the Modern World, Gaudium et Spes', Pope Paul VI, 7 December 1965, www.vatican.va/archive/hist_councils/ii_vatican_council/documents/vat-ii_const_19651207_gaudium-et-spes_en.html, accessed 20 June 2018).

Index

Achebe, Chinua, 9
Acholi, first use of term, 111
Acholi people, 18; as labourers, 115; loyalties of, 135–7
Acholiland, 18, 20, 109–38; as DP stronghold, 196; ethnicity and religious authority in, 111–14
Action Française, 49
Adenauer, Konrad, 47
African Muslim Association, 69
African nationalism, 21
Agostoni, Tarcisio, 31–2, 50, 55, 56, 192, 197
agriculture, 82, 111, 132, 136
Alava, Henni, 113
All-Africa Leaders Meeting of the Lay Apostolate, 50
'All Asians Must Go' headlines, 190–2
Alur people, 120
Amba people, 73
Amin, Idi *see* Idi Amin Dada
Amnesty International, report on death of Benedicto Kiwanuka, 193
Amone, Charles, 111
Anglican Church, 31, 44, 60, 75, 114, 149–51; arson against, 70
Anglican Church, Native, 4, 6 133, 141–2
Anglo-Egyptian Condominium, 112
Anglo-Egyptian military, expansion of influence of, 82
Ankole, 7, 18, 20, 74, 111–11, 139, 196; monarchism in, 129; party insurrection in, 109–38
Ankole Agreement (1901), 132
Ankole Agreement (1962), 134
anonymous letters, circulation of, 105

anthems *see* songs
anti-Catholicism, 114, 121, 129, 155, 159, 170, 196
anticolonialism, 12, 41, 51–2, 57, 133, 176
Appointments Board, 105
Apter, David, 9, 14
arson, 10, 94; against Anglican churches, 70
Asians: and Europeans, voting rights for, 52; expulsion of, 190; in ministerial positions, 51; traders, boycott of, 51
see also Indian traders
Atkinson, Ron, 61, 111
authenticité, 24

Baamba people, 72, 76
Babiiha, John, 76
Bade, Albert, 14, 96
Baffire, Michael, 105
Bafumbira people, 98, 196
Baganda people, 61, 75, 84, 87, 88, 89, 91, 92, 93, 96, 97, 100, 109, 112, 120, 153, 154, 159, 169, 176; as administrators, 94; as protected subjects, 157
Bagorogoza, Isidoro, 109, 131, 138, 178
Bahima class, 111, 131, 132, 133, 196
Bahinda clan, 111, 132, 196
Bahororo people, 98, 100, 102, 103
Bahutu people, as migrants, 99
see also Hutu people
Bairu class (cultivators), 110–11, 131, 132, 133, 138, 196
Baker, Samuel, 31
Bakiga people, 20, 98, 99, 100, 102, 103, 196
Bakonjo people, 72, 76, 78

Bakonzo Life History Research Society, 73
bakopi rural populations, 53, 60, 160
Balikanda, a writer, 154
Balikuddembe, Joseph Mukasa, execution of, 27
Balubaale gods, 162
Bamba people, 78
Banakazadde Begwanga (Mothers of the Nation), 151
banana campaign, 92
Banoro people, 154
Banyankole people, 99
Banyarwanda people, 99, 104
Banyoro people, 87, 88, 89, 94, 97
Basajjansolo, 153
Basudde, Leonard, 156
Bataka activists, 141, 155
Bataka Union (BU), 141
Bataringaya, Basil K., 111, 129, 131, 135, 138, 178; joins UPC, 137, 181
Batoro people, 72, 78, 102
  see also Toro people
Batutsi people, 98, 102, 103
Bayart, Jean-François, 1
Belgium, 99
Berkeley, E. J. L., 86–7
birthing the nation, 22
bride wealth, 100, 151
  see also dowry
British administration and interests see United Kingdom
British Institute of Commerce and Accounting, 38
British Institute of Engineering and Technology Near East, 38
British National Archives, 17
Brown, Leslie, 47, 106, 181
Buddu, 26, 33, 34, 140, 148, 160, 161, 196; as 'place of slaves', 84, 147; Catholicism of, 32
Budo Junior School, 122
Buganda, 1, 2, 3, 4, 6, 7, 8, 10, 11, 13, 18, 20, 21, 25, 27, 38, 46, 50, 51, 70, 86, 91, 94, 96, 97, 98, 99, 115, 118, 135, 138, 151, 158, 159, 161, 162, 164, 171, 172, 186, 196; as place of poverty, 116; bid for independence, 19; Catholic patronage in, 139–65; interest in secession, 75, 116; political order of, 5; protectorate established, 29; special status of, 169
Buganda Martyrs see Uganda Martyrs
Bugangaizi, 83
Bukedi, 61
Bunyangabu, 71
Bunyoro, 7, 20, 72, 75, 80, 98, 111; agriculture in, 112, Catholic violence and political revolution in, 81–108; kingdom of, 18, reunification project in, 87–8; Southern, Catholic authority in, 82–6
Bunyoro-Kitara empire, 82
Burahya, 71
Busoga, 7, 115
Busongora, 71, 77
Busujju, 160, 161
Butambala, 5
Buyaga, 83
  see also Mubende
Bwamba, 71, 77
Bwambale, E. B., 126
Bwavumpologoma Cooperative Union, 34
Bwete, Erieza, 67

Cabana, Louis J., 41, 42–3
'Canticle of the National Vow', 85–6
capitalism, opposition to, 167
Cardijn, Joseph, 49
Carswell, Grace, 99, 100
Catholic Action, 49–50
Catholic Church, 13, 14, 19, 20, 43, 60, 75, 109, 118, 137, 147–8, 162, 164, 170, 181, 185, 194, 199, 201, 203, 205; criticism of, 110; education accord with government, 180; indigenisation of, 13, 24, 26; viewed as degenerate, 115
Catholic Herald newspaper, 42
'Catholic Marseillaise', 86
Catholic patronage, in Buganda, 139–65

Catholic-Protestant relations, 28, 81, 196
Catholic Studies, 11–14
Catholicism and Catholic politics, 9, 11, 13, 14, 17, 20, 39, 79, 80, 91, 108, 113, 119, 141, 155, 195, 197, 200; historiography of, 205–6; political, 140; transnational nature of, 30
see also Democratic Party, Catholic orientation of; Munno newspaper
Catholics, 1, 4, 5–6, 21, 64, 70, 102, 103, 105, 106, 109, 124, 127, 128, 137, 141, 158, 163; in Acholiland, 110, 113; discrimination against, 74; divisions among, 21, 79–80, 98, 165; elites among, 103; empowerment of, 47, 53; as enslaved and enslaving class, 147; government crackdown on, 198; Kampala demonstration by, 180; in Kigezi, 100; in land allocations, 87; marginalisation of, 19, 45, 47; migration of, 29; in Mubende, 86; petitions of, 84–5; political representation of, 36; schools burned, 171–2
see also chiefs, Catholic; Ganda Catholics
cattle, rearing of, 67, 70, 131
Cavanaugh, William T., 49
celibacy of priesthood, 33, 152–6, 200
Centenary Bank, 34
centralisation of governance, 60, 108, 195–6; supported by DP, 107
ceremonial heads, installation of, 107
chiefs, 10, 47, 62, 84, 133; appointment of, 63; Baganda, assassinated with arrows, 94; become politicians, 94; Catholic, 20, 81, 83, 90, 156, 160 (criticism of, 158; firing of, 180; placed in Protestant schools, 114); control of electoral processes, 175; conversion of, 84; discrimination against Catholics in appointments of, 74; Protestant, 3, 4, 5, 6, 62, 101, 125; provision of goods for, 102
Chile, 48
Christian Democracy movement, 2, 25, 47–8, 138, 199

Christian Democratic Union (CDU) (West Germany), 48
Church Missionary Society (CMS), 4, 26, 27, 30, 68, 113, 114; schools of, 64
church-state relations, 164; decentring of, 14
Chwa II, king, 141
cigarettes, consumption of, in Tesoland, 67
civil service, Africanisation of, 51, 55
Climenhaga, Alison Fitchett, 49
Cody, Lisa Forman, 22
coffee: destruction of trees, 88, 169; prices of (lowering of, 136; protests regarding, 179; raising of, 53)
Cohen, Andrew, 151
colonialism, 12, 61–5, 86, 100, 109, 142, 151
Colvile, Henry, 83, 87
Comboni, Daniel, 31, 113
Combonis see Verona Fathers of the Sacred Heart of Jesus
communal labour, 101; abolition of, 112
communism, 42–3, 47, 54, 121, 126, 155
Congo, 12, 49, 76, 78, 104; smuggling of weapons into, 129
Congress of People Against Imperialism, 41–2
Constitution, 186, 200; historiography of, 9; of 1962, suspension of, 16, 181; of 1967, 8, 185; 'pigeonhole constitution', 182; as political Bible, 68–9; viewed as sacred, 182
Contesting Catholics, choice of title, 11
conversion, 4, 19, 29, 60, 71, 78, 85, 133; of chiefs, 84; of Tutsi elites, 13
converts, execution of, 4
cotton: prices of (lowering of, 136; manipulation of, 144); production of, 67, 70 (forced, 112); taxation of, 62
Coutts, Walter, 175
crops: burning of, 104; slashing of
see also slashing and destruction of crops
crossing oneself, act of, 119
cuius regio, eius religio, 5

damage to property, 94
dance, 101; battle dances, 89; at election rallies, 126
Daudi Chwa II, king, 4
De Gasperi, Alcide, 48
decaying tooth, trope of, 93, 95
decentralisation of political forms, 81
democracy and democratisation, 1, 53, 54, 58, 59, 117, 139, 167, 176, 179, 181, 183, 185, 188, 195, 199; as gospel, 23–80; relation to kingship, 162
see also Christian Democracy
Democratic Party (DP), 1, 2–3, 14, 20, 21, 22, 25, 31, 65, 74, 75, 78, 82, 86, 91, 100, 104, 105, 110, 111, 118, 124, 131, 134, 144, 145, 147, 155, 158, 159, 164, 165, 167, 176, 195, 206; Acholi branch, 109, 135–7; alleged arms shipment from Rwanda, 178; in Ankole, 129–35; awards scholarships, 125–6; banning of, 200; Catholic orientation of, 2; in Catholic scholarship, 205–6; centralising tendencies of, 195–6; and Christian Democracy movements, 57; colours of, 101, 187; complaints regarding communal labour, 101; cosmopolitanism of, 107; criticism of, 119–22; declining delegate attendance, 178; democratisation agenda of, 59; dismantling of, 140; electoral failure of, 8, 20 (in 1962 elections, 129–30, 161; in Tesoland, 70; in West Nile, 128, 131); fades from political scene, 200; fieldwork regarding, 18; 'Forward to Freedom' manifesto, 52, 55, 58, 125; founding of, 19, 45–50; framed as non-sectarian party, 46; gratitude to Idi Amin, 188; historiography of, 14–15; imprisonment of members of, 198; inclusion of Muslims and Protestants, 52, 57; issue of 'Lost Counties', 94; Benedicto Kiwanuka elected secretary-general of, 51; Joseph Kiwanuka's support for, 163; leadership contest within, 135–7; marginalisation of, 168; masculine politics of, 140; as masculine project, 149; meetings of, banned, 186; members expelled from Lukiiko, 169; members join UPC, 181; non-celebration of Independence Day, 187; in Northern Uganda, 124–9; not allowed to hold press conferences, 183; as parliamentary opposition, 169 (in minority, 179); party symbol of, 175; police search HQ of, 187; political context of, 15; position on secession, 77; prevented from holding public meetings, 185; reframed as anticolonial party, 51; retaliates against attackers, 177–8; royalism of, 129–35; runs female candidates, 149; runs Protestant candidates, 53; scholarships, 127; seen as sympathetic to Parmehutu, 102; seen as traitors, 10–11; splits within, 129–35; sun symbol of, 55; supports centralisation of governance, 107; in Tesoland, 19; truth and justice motto of, 11; use of clenched fist salute, 103, 120, 173; victory in 1962 elections, 77; viewed as Catholic party, 6–7, 79, 95, 110, 114, 118, 122, 171; viewed as Dini ya Papa, 52, 196; viewed as party of disruption, 106; viewed as party of suffering, 199; violence and intimidation against, 10, 21, 81, 104, 105–6, 164, 168, 169, 170, 171, 172, 175, 177, 197; weakness of, in south-west Uganda, 108
Doornbos, Martin, 133
dowry: elimination of, 151–2; reduction of, 152
see also bride wealth
Doyle, Shane, 82, 83
drums, royal, 3–4

Earle, Jonathon, 145
East African Federation, 47
East African High Commission, 45
East African Railways and Harbours, 151, 156

Eastern Uganda, colonial administration in, 61–5
Ebitongole chieftaincies, 84
education, 31, 50, 96, 122; grants for, 64; Obote government's policy regarding, 180; primary, 64, 125 (free, 53); secondary, 125; tertiary, 54, 125; of young women, 34
Edward Muteesa II *see* Muteesa II, Edward
egalitarianism, 79
Eishengyero, 133–4
Ekitebe kyaBakaiso (Uganda Martyrs Guild), 49
elections, 51, 118, 125; boycott of, 50, 118, 158; direct, DP commitment to, 54; indirect, 175, 179; Legislative Council (Legco), 51, 170; municipal, 136; of 1955, 45; of 1961, 53, 100, 126, 158, 159, 171, 200 (boycott of, 7, 160–1, 165, 169–77; complaints regarding, 106–7); of 1962, 8, 77, 100, 110, 129, 149, 161, 162, 164, 165, 175, 176, 177, 196, 1962, 126–7; of 1967, postponed, 182, 183, 185; of 1980, 198, 199, 200 *see also* registration of voters
Elizabeth I, Queen, 86
endogamy, 142
Enkola Enkatolike *see* Ekitebe kya-Bakaiso
Ethiopia, 76–7
ethnicity, 71–2, 100, 104; in Acholiland, 111–14; in Toro, 71–2
excommunication, power of, 44
executions, of court pages, 27
extensive obligation, 151

Faller, Lloyd, *The King's Men*, 10,
Faller, Margaret, 99
famine reserves, 100
fieldwork, scope of, 18
finger millet, production of, 112
firearms *see* weapons
Fisher, Geoffrey, 58
forced labour, 63
    see also communal labour

Foreign Office (UK), 89–90
Fort Portal, 73, 74, 77, 78, 102, 104
Forum for Democratic Change, 200
Foster, Elizabeth, 13
Foundation for African Development, 14
France, 26
free speech, right to, 24, 53
freedom of worship, right to, 24, 53
Frei, Eduardo, 48

Gahwerra, Paulo, 90
Gale, H. P., 30–1
Galt, Harry George, assassination of, 132
Ganda Catholics, 2, 19, 25, 32, 33, 38–44, 70, 83, 84, 86, 96, 109, 133, 140, 144, 159; seen as wafaransa, 28
Ganyi chiefdom, 111–12
Gasyonga II, Omugabe, 132, 138
Gayonga, Harry, 87
Gbenye, Christophe, 129
gender egalitarianism, 54
Gifford, Paul, 36
Gingyera-Pincycwa, A. G. G., 10
gold, acquisition of, 78
Gondokoro, 112
Great Britain *see* United Kingdom
Gulu Diocese, 125
Gulu High School, 114
Gulu Primary School, 122

habeas corpus, 192, 193–4
Hancock, I. R., 159
Hancock, W. K. 146
Hancock Commission, 34, 162
Hanlon, Henry, address to Kabaka Mwanga, 30
Hannington, James, 27; killing of, 143
Hanson, Holly, 3–4, 84, 151
hereditary authority, abolition of, 112
heroism and bravery, importance of, 153
Hirth, Jean-Joseph, 30
historiography: of Catholicism, 205–6; of Uganda, 6–11, 108
Hoima, mural in, 90–1
Hunter, Emma, 16
hut tax, 62

Hutu people, 13, 20, 71, 82, 103, 108
  see also Bahutu people

Ibingira, Grace, 133, 194
Idi Amin Dada, 22, 31, 168, 182, 194, 197, 198; coup d'état by, 188; hailed as God's Agent, 169; hosts dinner, 188–9; releases Benedicto Kiwanuka from prison, 21, 188; responsibility for killing of Benedicto Kiwanuka, 188–9; seen as 'Liberator in Democracy', 188
immigration, 104; in south-west Uganda, 99
  see also migrant labour
imojong (old men), 69
Imperial British East India Company (IBEAC), 3, 29
imprisonment, 187, 189; without trial, 183, 185, 186, 192
imurok (s. emuron), witch doctor, 62
indentured servitude, 83
independence, 6, 10, 11, 19, 22, 55, 86, 87, 95, 96, 98, 114, 115, 117, 118, 120, 121, 122, 125, 126, 139, 145, 167, 169, 170–1, 195, 206
Independence Day, 187; not celebrated by DP, 187
Indian landowner, plea to Benedicto Kiwanuka, 190
Indian traders, criticism of, 67, 69
  see also Asians
indigenisation of clergy, 13, 24, 26, 33, 56
indigenous culture, support for, 125
industrialisation, 53
Institute of Commonwealth Studies, 17
intimidation, use of term, 172
Iran, 156
Islam, 26
Iteso people, 61, 62, 120

Jesus Christ, 147, 176, 179, 187; mural depicting, 90
Jeunesse Ouvrière Chrétienne (JOC), 49
John XXIII, Pope, 13

Judas Iscariot, 147

Kabaireho, John, 133–4, 138
Kabaka Yekka party (KY), 7, 8, 10, 21, 89, 95, 110, 111, 123, 128, 133, 134, 138, 140, 156–65, 177, 179, 181, 196; backed by Catholic activists, 159; Catholic membership of, 161, 162–3; Catholics ordered to reject, 163; demonstration by, 91; establishment of, 161; mob attack on DP sympathisers, 171, 172–3, 177; party symbol of, 172; relations with UPC, 103, 123, 124; success in 1962 election, 165, 175; viewed as anti-Catholic party, 159
Kabalega, Omukama, 33, 92
Kafero, E. D., 94
Kaggwa, Apolo, 5, 62, 70, 81, 88, 132, 151
Kahaya II, Omugabe, 132
Kajubi, William S., 52
Kakungulu, Semei, 70, 81
Kalema, king, 3, 28
Kalibbala, Dr, 146
Kampala, description of, 115–16
Kamya, Augustine, 159
Kanaaneh, Rhoda Ann, 22
Karamagi, Prince Stephen, 74
Karugire, Samwiri, 131, 133
Kasozi, A. B. K., 9
Katanga, secession of, 76, 78
Katholieke Volkspartij (Netherlands), 48
Kayibanda, Grégoire, 98, 99, 102
Kayole, Eddie, 92–3, 95
Kennedy, John F., meeting with, 126
Kenya, 22; white settlers in, 87
Kenyan African National Union (KANU), 167
Kenyatta, Jomo, 167, 193
Kibede, Wanume, 193
Kibuuka, god of war, 21, 140, 153–4
Kigezi, 80, 100–1, 102, 104, 105, 129, 135; 1959 census of, 100; Catholic violence and political revolution in, 81–108
Kiggundu, Clement, 192; killing of, 197
Kigozi, S. B., 93

'kill the red ant', 173
kingdoms, 18, 132; abolition of, 8, 108, 117, 186; status of, 177
King's College, Budo, 110, 114, 122
kingship *see* monarchy
Kinobe, Simon Peter, 203
Kintu, Gabriel, 29
Kintu, Mikaeri, 45, 156
Kirenga, E. S., 118
Kirose, Zabuloni, 85
Kisabwe, 178
Kisosonkole, Damali, 142
Kisubi Seminary, 50
Kitaburaza, F. T., 106
Kitagana, Yohana, 133
Kitago, Geoffrey, 105
Kiwanuka and Company Associates, 50
Kiwanuka, Benedicto Kagimu Mugumba, 1, 7, 8, 11, 110, 111, 118, 123, 161, 163, 165, 167, 184, 195, 198, 206; anticolonial activities of, 41; appointed Supreme Court Justice, 22, 189; arrests of, 1, 180, 186 (final, 193, 201; second, 187 (release from, 21)); assassination of, 15, 22, 165, 169, 188–94, 197 (circumstances of, 201); attacks on Semakula Mulumba, 155–6; attends Mass, 200; attends signing of Ankole Agreement, 134; becomes close to Edward Muteesa II, 42; biography of, 19; builds new home, 188; bust of, creation of, 203; buys a gun, 21, 188; buys life insurance, 21, 188, 190; calls for banning of kkanzu dress, 38; canonisation of (petition regarding, 200–1; quest for, 194; unofficial, 203); commentary on 1962 election, 32–3, 129, 175, 179; commitment to direct elections, 54; compared with Grégoire Kayibanda, 103; complaints filed with police, 9; correspondence of, 104–5; critical of Milton Obote, 21; criticised for use of Luganda language, 70; criticised for political weakness, 108; criticism of OAU, 181; criticism of UPC, 78, 185; death of son, 98; death threats against, 177, 188; defeated in election, 122; detention in hospital, 187; in the diaspora, 38–44; difficulties in Buganda, 139–40; early life of, 25–37; education of, 36, 38, 56 (enrols in overseas courses, 38; studies accounting, 38; studies at St Peter's Secondary School, 31; studies law, 19, 39, 41 (completes degree, 50); studies Swahili, 41); elected secretary-general of DP, 51; emotional collapse of, 178–9; employment at High Court, Kampala, 39; enlists in King's African Rifles, 38; enrols at Pius XII Catholic University, 41; framed as persona Christi, 168; Ganda Catholic nationalism of, 38–44; and gospel of democracy, 23–80, 103; has fence placed around home, 21; historiography of, 14–15; and issue of 'Lost Counties', 19–20, 81–2, 91–8, 107; joins DP, 50; late-period speeches of, 186; leadership of, contested, 135–6, 138, 145–6, 160, 178; letter to Idi Amin, 192; lobbies for scholarships, 126; location of, within Christian Democracy, 48, 59; marital negligence of, 148–9 (criticised, 146); marriage of, 39; martyrdom of, 197; meeting with J. F. Kennedy, 126; memorialisation of, 199, 200–1; military service of, 19, 56, 151; named Prime Minister, 55; newspaper archives of, 15, 16; orders Miraculous Medal, 43; perceived revolutionary republicanism of, 109; plans to reform local magistrates, 189; political project of, 14, 18, 22; prays at DP annual conferences, 53; private papers of, 15, 17, 18, 96; proponent of truth, 44; purported communist sympathies of, 42–3; reads *Apologia Pro Vita Sua*, 43–4; rejects election boycott, 158; relationship with Semakula Mulumba, 140; relationship with Toro monarchy, 74; religious convictions of, 25–37;

Kiwanuka, Benedicto Kagimu Mugumba (*continued*)
remembrance of, in Catholic scholarship, 205–6; revolutionary rhetoric of, 52; role in building DP, 2; sacrament of anointing, 193; secretary of Uganda Students Association, 41; seen as anathema, 129–30; seen as associated with Hutu politicians, 108; seen as Catholic republican, 79; split with Idi Amin, 190; statement on independence, 170–1; thanks Idi Amin for release, 188–9; threatens to leave Catholic Church, 43; tours in Acholiland, 136–7; tours in Ankole, 74; tours in Kigezi, 106; tours in Mubende, 95, 97; tours in Tesoland, 70; tours in US and Canada, 146; trope of resistance, 167, 169, 176; view on role of women, 151; viewed as having Indian connections, 190–2; views on case of Stanislaus Mugwanya, 46; views on reasons for failure of DP in West Nile, 128–9; views on Uganda's political history, 6

Kiwanuka, Joseph, 21, 33–6, 41, 42–3, 140, 152, 154, 155, 165, 180, 181, 196; pastoral letter of, 161, 170; political intervention of, 161–2

Kiwanuka, Maurice Kagimu, 15

Kiwanuka, Maxencia née Zalwango, 28, 39, 82, 96, 98, 107, 148, 181, 187, 189, 193; illness of, 146, 148–9

Kiwanuka, Semakula, 3

Kiweewa, king, 3

kkanzu dress, 117; Benedicto Kiwanuka calls for banning of, 38; in party colours, 101; wearing of, 91

Kongolo mission station, 12

Konzo people, 72, 73

Kutoria Arab traders, 111

Kwebiha, Mr, speech by, 90–1

Kyagulanyi, Robert 'Bobi Wine', 195, 200

Kyebambe III, Kasagama, 72, 74

Lady Irene, remarriage of, 141–2

lake, artificial, building of, 3–4

Lancaster House conference (1961), 171, 175

land: allocation of, 87 (disproportionate, 84; grievances regarding, 83); ownership patterns of, 100

land holdings, private, 5; creation of, 141

land reform, 133

Lango, 18; electoral disparity in, 127

languages, 96, 97, 115; Ateso, 65; English, 16, 25, 65; Luganda, 4, 59, 123, 124, 151 (imposition of, 84; used in Benedicto Kiwanuka speech, 70); Luo-Shillok, 112; missionaries' knowledge of, 113; Rukiga, 104; Runyaruanda, 104; Runyoro, 87; Rutoro, enforced usage of, 72; Swahili, 41

Laruni, Elizabeth, 124

Latim, Alexander, 137, 182, 196, 198; criticism of UPC policy, 185

Lavigerie, Charles, 12, 28

Lawrence, J., 67

Lay Apostolate Council, 50

Leadership magazine, 50

Legion of Mary, 43

Leo XIII, Pope, 30

Lincoln, Abraham, Gettysburg Address, 178

livestock, maiming of, 10

Livinhac, Léon, 86

Lobo Mewa magazine, 124–5

Loffman, Reuben, 12

London School of Economics, 17

'Lost Counties', issue of, 7, 19–20, 81–2, 83, 86–91, 91–8, 107, 109, 196; referendum regarding, 181–2

loudspeakers, Benedicto Kiwanuka's use of, 106

Lourdel, Siméon (Mapera), 4, 26, 29, 33

Low, Donald A., 15, 159

Lubowa, Aloysius D., 21, 138, 139, 140, 165, 196; Catholic royalism of, 156–65; critique of Catholicism, 162

Lukiiko, 5, 6, 7, 50, 51, 69, 83, 91, 97, 98, 156–7, 169, 170, 176, 194;

expulsion of members of, 171; local halls burned, 88
Lunyiigo, Samwiri Lwanga, 3, 125
'Luweero Triangle', 198
Luwero conflict, 65
Luwum, Janani, killing of, 197–8

Mackay, Alexander, 4
Maini, Amar, 51
Makerere University, 23, 115, 122, 200; Africana collection, 17
Mao, Norbert, 196
Marianism, 32
Marquis of Salisbury, 86–7
marriage, 49, 146, 151–2; controversies regarding, 142
martyrdom, 3–4, 143, 155, 165, 167–94; of Benedicto Kiwanuka, 192–3, 197, 203
Masaka, Diocese of, establishment of, 33
masculine politics, 155
 see also DP, masculine politics of
Masembe-Kabali, S. K., 159
Matalisi newspaper, 151, 156
matooke, 102, 152
Mau Mau, 22, 67
Mayanja, Abubakar, 103, 104, 163, 164
Mbaguta, Nuwa, 132
Mbazira, a Baganda politician, 148
Mbiti, John, African Religions and Philosophy, 24
Médard, Henri, 29, 83
mercy, trope of, 85–6
Metropolitan College of Law, 39
Mgwany, Matayo, 146
migrant labour, 99; Acholi as, 112
militarisation of public life, 109
Mill Hill Mission, 19, 26, 31, 36, 56, 58, 60, 64, 68, 79, 81; lack of success in Tesoland, 64–5
minimum wage, 55
missionaries, 4, 12, 18, 27, 32, 42, 93, 100, 121, 206; French, 13; Jesuit, 12; Protestant, 62
Missionaries of Africa (White Fathers), 4, 12, 13, 26–8, 29, 30, 31, 36, 43, 50, 56, 68, 73, 85, 133, 145; schools of, 64

Mmengo, 160, 163, 165, 176; Battle of, 182; collective culture of, 156–7; instructions regarding elections, 158
Mobutu, Joseph, 24
Molson Commission, 89
monarchy, 6, 73, 74, 75, 103, 108, 111, 129–35, 138, 194, 196; British, 162; hostility towards, 82; political legitimacy of, 78; Protestant, 90, 91; Toro, challenges to, 81; weakening of, 82
 see also royalism
Morier-Genoud, Eric, 12
Mothers Unions, 149–51
Mozambique, 12
Mpagi, Latimer, 159
Mpanga, Fred, 97
Mubende, 20; declared disturbed area, 89; status of, 87–8
Mubende Banyoro Committee (MBC), 82, 87–8, 91, 96; banning of, 89
Mubiru, Joseph, 197
Mudoola, Dan, 10
Mugabe, Robert, 13
Mugwanya, Stanislaus, 5; banned from parliament, 45–6; elected president-general of DP, 46; expulsion from DP, 51
Mugwanya, Matayo, 45, 51
Mukasa, Hamu, 62, 81; Journey to Bukedi by the Saza Chiefs, 62
Mukura Massacre, 66
Mulindwa, Gilbert, 174; home destroyed, 172–5
Mulira, Enoch E. K., 52
Mulira, Eridadi M. K., 53
Mulumba, Alipo, 145
Mulumba, Semakula (formerly Brother Francis), 21, 43, 138, 139, 140, 141–8, 150, 165; Okuzukusa obuzira bwa Baganda, 153; calls for resignation of Bishop Stuart, 142–4; challenge to leadership of Benedicto Kiwanuka, 145; critical of Benedicto Kiwanuka, 144; offers help to Maxencia Kiwanuka, 148–9; shared history with Benedicto Kiwanuka, 146

Mulwanyi, Peter T. K., 128
Munno newspaper, 10, 144, 154, 170, 192, 197
Muntu, Mugisha, 200
Musajjakawa, Benjamin, death of, 98
Musazi, Ignatius, 46, 67, 144
Museveni, Yoweri, 66, 198, 200
music, 125; musical instruments sent to Muteesa II, 155, 159
Musisi, Mr, an activist, 128–9
Muslims, 5–6, 23, 28, 57, 79, 105, 128, 200
Musoke, J. P., 91
Mutaibwa, Nikodemu Kakoko, 85
Muteesa I, king, 3, 26–7
Muteesa II, Edward, king, 5, 20, 42, 45, 47, 50, 74, 142, 163, 164, 196; arrest and escape of, 8, 146; exile of, 21, 144, 156, 182, 200, refusal to ratify 'Lost Counties' referendum, 181–2; removed from power, 98; return from exile, 34, 154, 157–8
Mutibwa, Phares, 9
Muura, Okullu, 111
Mwanga, king, 3–4, 27, 29, 30, 33, 83, 143; goes into exile, 28; removed from power, 4
Namilyango College, 31, 65
Namirembe Conference, 146, 162
Namugongo, site of Uganda Martyrs' shrine, 180
National Resistance Army (NRA), 198, 199
National Resistance Movement (NRM), 65
Native Anglican Church *see* Anglican Church, Native
Ndawula, a Baganda politician, 148
Newman, John Henry, Apologia Pro Vita Sua, 43–4
Newman Society, 43
Nimule, 112
Nkima clan, 142
Nkrumah, Kwame, 54, 182
Nkubayamahina, J. N., 104

Northern Uganda, political rivalries in, 124–9
Nsibirwa, Martin Luther, killing of, 143–4
Nsubuga, Benedicto, 26
Nsubuga, Emmanuel, 163, 192, 198
Ntandayarwo, U. K., 104
Ntiro, Sarah, 149
Nyangire uprising, 84–5, 88
Nyerere, Julius, 23, 167, 198, 201
Nyoro people, 196

Obonyo, J. H., 126, 130, 136, 137
Obote, Milton, 8, 16, 21–2, 23, 25, 31, 65, 78, 82, 98, 117, 123, 124, 126, 136, 138, 167, 168, 169, 170, 177, 178, 180, 181, 183, 186, 193, 194, 197, 198, 199; attempted assassination of, 21, 65, 187; cabinet putsch against, 181; government of, 177–87; likened to Hitler, 189; meets with DP leaders, 182; 'Move to the Left' project, 68
Obwangor, Cuthbert J., 19, 58, 65–71, 81, 137, 196; egalitarian ethos of, 69; joins UPC, 65; ministerial positions of, 65; writings of, in the national press, 68
Ocheng (Ochieng), Daudi, 20, 110, 114–24, 137–8; education of, 122; serves as advisor to Muteesa II, 122; Yekka Party document, 123
Oda, Gaspare O. B., 71, 180, 182
odium fidei, 201
Ogez, Jean Marie, 106
Okae, J. M., 71
Okelo, Martin, 136
Okeny, Atwoma T., 136
Omugabe Wenka party, 111, 133
Omukuule, the uprooted one, 93
Onama, Felix, 50
one-party state, 23, 167, 168, 178, 180, 183, 186
Onek, Lakana, Kwo-na Ikare Macon, 113
Onma, Felix, 137
Opoti, V. J., letter to Benedicto Kiwanuka, 128

Organisation of African Unity (OAU), 24, 181
Otim, Patrick, 113
Owinyi-Dollo, Alphonse, 203
ownership of property, right of, 24
Oyet, Santo, 113

pagans, 23, 105, 119
pan-Africanism, 24
papal infallibility, 44
Paray-le-Monial, 86
Parti du Mouvement de l'Emancipation Hutu (Parmehutu), 99, 103
patriarchal authority, 148–52
Paul VI, Pope, 24, 180; planned visit to Uganda, 186
p'Bitek, Okot, 20, 110, 114–24, 137–8, 196; education of, 114–15; Lak Tar Miyo Kinyero Wilobo, 115; Song of Ocol, 110; Wer pa Lawino (Song of Lawino), 110, 118–2
Peagram, R. C., 169–77
penance, 34
People Power movement, 200
Peterson, Derek, 16, 72
petitions, of Catholics, 84
Pirouet, Louise, 62, 74, 113
Pius XI, Pope, 49
Pius XII, Pope, 33, 164
Pius XII Catholic University, 41
police: employment as, 113; issue of escorts, 137
political parties, 159; ban on, 199; usefulness of, 156–7
politique du ventre, la, 1
polygamy, 27
post-colonial Uganda, project of, 14–22
Powesland, P. G., 99
press, role of, 16
priestly authorities, contesting of, 152–6
priests: Catholic, 152–6; authority of, 21
prisoners, used as forced labour, 63
Privy Council Commission, 91
Progressive Party, 52, 76
property, inheritance of, 54
Protestant politics, intersection with Catholic politics, 81
Protestant power, 5–6, 46–7, 52, 80, 110, 124–5, 127, 128, 143
Protestant revivalism, 60, 72
Protestantism, 81, 123, 138; in Tesoland, 63–4
Protestants, 2, 4, 21, 23, 26, 57, 64, 74, 79, 84, 90, 102, 103, 105, 106, 110, 113, 128, 133, 137, 138, 156, 159, 160, 196; in Acholiland, 113; in Kigezi, 100; and land allocations, 83, 87
 see also Catholic-Protestant relations; chiefs, Protestant; missionaries, Protestant; monarchy, Protestant
Pulteny, Mr, 87

Queen Mother, visit to Uganda, 51

railways, construction of, 62; proposed line Lira to Gulu, 126
rape, 10, 176; by KY mob, 177
Referendum of 1964, 98
refugees, 121
regalia of Nyoro, 111
regional politics of Uganda, 58
registration of voters, 106–7, 160, 170, 175
Reid, Richard, 20, 83
religious conflict in Uganda: roots of, 3–6; wars of 1890s, 83
reproductive politics, 22
republicanism, 59–80, 109, 110; Catholic, 65–71; in South-western Uganda, 98–107
resistance, discourse of, 21, 167–94; during Obote government, 177–87
 see also Kiwanuka, Benedicto, trope of resistance
Rhodes, Cecil, 12
Rhodesia, 186
Richards, Audrey, 10, 17, 99
right of assembly, 24
right to vote, of women, 149
Rowe, John, 3
royalism, 9–10, 19, 20, 21, 73, 79, 91, 110, 118, 129–35, 138, 156, 158, 168,

royalism (*continued*) 169; Catholic, 156–65; in Buganda, 139–65; in Toro, 71–9
Rubaga Cathedral, burning of, 29
Rubaga Diocesan Archives, 17
Rubanga, term for God, 119
Rugambwa, Laurent, 181
Rugemwa, N. K., 86, 94
Rukidi III, Omukama, 74
Rukurato government of Bunyoro, 89
Rusoke, Cypriano W., 78–9
Rwanda, 20, 22, 49, 71, 82, 98, 102, 178; revolution in, 99
Rwebishengye, Omugabe, 134
Rwenzururu, 77, 78, 196; republicanism and secession in, 19, 58, 59–80, 81, 109, 137
rwot-ship, 111

Sacred Heart tradition, 85
scholarships, awarding of, 125–6; foreign, provision of, 55
schools, Catholic, burning of, 171–2
Schumann, Robert, 47
Scott, R., 88
Sebugulu, Mutaka, 153
sectarianism, 58, 70, 109, 110, 128
secularism, 47
Sermon on the Mount, 55, 197
Shakespeare, William, Henry V, 183
Sir Samuel Baker's School, 114
slashing and destruction of crops, 10, 81, 85, 88, 92, 94, 169, 175
slavery, 112, 83–4, 147–8
socialism, 16, 68
soldiers, employment as, 113
songs, 153, 157; anthems, singing of, 91, 93; of Catholics, 85–6
South-western Uganda, republicanism and revolution in, 98–107
Southall, Aidan, 109
speech, right to free, 24
spiritualism, 153–4
Ssebayigga, Joseph, 163, 180
Ssembeguya, F. C., 71

Ssemogerere, Paul, 14, 59, 69, 77, 104, 129, 137, 181, 182, 183–5, 184, 197, 198–9, 200; arrest of, 186
Ssewannyana, Matia Kigaanira, 21, 140, 153–4, 155
St Joseph's Foreign Missionary Society, 30–1
St Leo's College, Kyegobe, 77
St Peter's School, Nsambya, 31, 38
Stanley, Henry Morton, 26
Stephens, Rhiannon, 22
Stewart, Daniel, Benedicto Kiwanuka hears case of, 192
Streicher, Henri, 27–8, 33
Stuart, Cyril, 142
Summers, Carol, 49, 139, 141

Tanganyika (later Tanzania) African National Union (TANU), 167
tapping of phones by government, 179
taxation, 62, 72, 100, 124; resistance to, 154; unfair assessment of, 183
Tesoland, 18, 20, 195, 196; agriculture in, 112; as Catholic region, 60; DP in, 19; republicanism and secession in, 59–80; UPC in, 58
Thomas, H. B., 88
Tito Winyi IV, king, 90, 91
tornade, la, 13
Toro, 7, 18, 20, 61, 76, 137
Toro people, 120
Tourigny, Yves, 50
trade unions, 67–68
tribalism, 52, 104, 107, 108, 199
Tripp, Aili, 149
truth, value of, 44
truth and justice: discourse of, 1–2, 53, 55, 145, 169, 177, 189, 195, 197, 199, 201, 203; as motto of DP, 11
Tucker, Alfred, 30
Tutsi people, 99
Twaddle, Michael, 3, 61

Uganda, national history of, 6–7
see also historiography
Uganda Agreement (1900), 141, 142

Uganda Argus newspaper, 15–16, 46, 81, 99, 105, 126, 171, 190
Uganda Broadcasting Corporation (UBC), 136
Uganda Council of Women, 151
Uganda Eyogera, 158
Uganda Kwefuga ne Mubende Kwefuga pamphlet, 96
Uganda Martyrs, 4, 21, 22, 27, 169, 170, 194; canonisation of, 180–1; cult of devotion to, 28; shrine to, 180
Uganda National Congress (UNC), 7, 45, 46–7, 76, 156
Uganda National Movement (UNM), 159
Uganda People's Congress (UPC), 2, 8, 16, 20, 23, 25, 59, 60, 61, 65, 68, 76, 77, 79, 81, 95, 100, 102–3, 104–5, 109, 111, 120, 121, 125, 126, 128, 133, 134, 136, 137, 138, 167, 168, 170, 177, 178, 179, 185, 196, 98; authoritarianism of, 169; colours of, 101; criticism of, 186; founding of, 7; in Northern Uganda, 124–9; Protestant membership of, 7; rally disrupted by DP, 106; relations with KY, 103, 123, 124; support for, 104; threats against DP, 105; viewed as Protestant and Muslim party, 79, 196; viewed as religious affiliation, 100; viewed as royalist party, 19, 75, 108
Uganda Post, 45
Uganda Protectorate, 132
Uganda Social Training Centre, 50
Uganda Students Association, 41, 146
Ugandan Cultural Centre, 115
Uhuru, 120, 121, 122
United Kingdom (UK), 8, 26, 31, 38, 44, 55, 56, 61, 72, 73, 91, 112, 133, 141, 143, 145, 155, 175; interests of, 29–30; rebellion against, 33; short-sightedness of policy of, 89–90; view of Benedicto Kiwanuka, 176–7
United States of America (USA), 163; Department of State, records of, 17

University of Cambridge, 74
University of Wales, 110, 114, 122

Vatican Council, Second, 13, 50
Verona Fathers of the Sacred Heart of Jesus (also known as Combonis), 26, 31–2, 36, 113, 119, 121; expulsion of, 185
Villa Maria primary school, 26
violence, 88–9, 95, 101, 104, 112, 153, 168; Catholic, 81–108; against Catholics, 21, 161, against DP *see* Democratic Party, violence and intimidation against; government-led, 9–10; political, 13, 80, 110, 113, 171–2, 183, 199 (proliferation of, 169–77); Rwanda-related, 99; sectarian, 98 (in historiography of Uganda, 6–11); sexual, 142
Virika, 73
 see also Fort Portal
'voice of the people', 185
voter registration *see* registration of voters
voting rights, of women, 54

Waliggo, John Mary, 32, 200
Walugembe, Francis, 159
Wamburi, Samuel, 203
weapons: distribution of, 29; smuggled into Congo, 129; trade in, 27
weddings, 64
Welbourn, Fred, 52, 100, 103, 159, 196
West Nile, 20, 110, 112, 196; make-up of electorate in, 128; sacking of Catholics from government of, 129
White Fathers *see* Missionaries of Africa
witch doctors, 62–3
witchcraft, 119; accusations of, 63
Witchcraft Ordinances (1918), 63
women, 22; Catholic concern for, 50; education of, 34; empowerment of, 54, 140; maternal responsibilities of, 152; political mobilisation of, 148–52; right to vote, 149

Women's Clubs of Uganda, 151
women's movements, 155
Wrigley, Christopher, 84

Young Christian Farmers, 49
Young Christian Students, 49
Young Christian Workers, 49

Zaire, 24
Zake, Luyimbazi, 180
Zalwango, Maxencia *see* Kiwanuka, Maxencia née Zalwango
Zimbabwe, 12
zoning laws for schools, 113

Previously published titles in the series

Violent Conversion: Brazilian Pentecostalism and Urban Women in Mozambique, Linda Van de Kamp (2016)

Beyond Religious Tolerance: Muslim, Christian & Traditionalist Encounters in an African Town, edited by Insa Nolte, Olukoya Ogen and Rebecca Jones (2017)

Faith, Power and Family: Christianity and Social Change in French Cameroon, Charlotte Walker-Said (2018)

Contesting Catholics: Benedicto Kiwanuka and the Birth of Postcolonial Uganda, Jonathon L. Earle and J. J. Carney (2021)

Islamic Scholarship in Africa: New Directions and Global Contexts, edited by Ousmane Oumar Kane (2021)

From Rebels to Rulers: Writing Legitimacy in the Early Sokoto State, Paul Naylor (2021)

Sacred Queer Stories: Ugandan LGBTQ+ Refugee Lives and the Bible, Adriaan Van Klinken and Johanna Stiebert, with Sebyala Brian and Fredrick Hudson (2021)

Labour & Christianity in the Mission: African Workers in Tanganyika and Zanzibar, 1864–1926, Michelle Liebst (2021)

The Genocide against the Tutsi, and the Rwandan Churches: Between Grief and Denial, Philippe Denis (2022)

Competing Catholicisms: The Jesuits, the Vatican & the Making of Postcolonial French Africa, Jean Luc Enyegue, SJ (2022)

Islam in Uganda: The Muslim Minority, Nationalism & Political Power, Joseph Kasule (2022)

Spiritual Contestations: The Violence of Peace in South Sudan, Naomi Ruth Pendle (2023)

www.ingramcontent.com/pod-product-compliance
Lightning Source LLC
Chambersburg PA
CBHW051608230426
43668CB00013B/2023